Estate Planning
for Same-Sex Couples

Second Edition

JOAN M. BURDA

Cover design by Daniel Mazanec/ABA Publishing.

Printed in the United States of America.

16 15 14 13   5 4 3

Library of Congress Cataloging-in-Publication Data
Burda, Joan M., 1952–
    Estate planning for same-sex couples / Joan M. Burda. — 2nd ed.
        p. cm.
    Includes bibliographical references and index.
    ISBN 978-1-61438-323-9
1. Estate planning—United States. 2. Gay couples—Legal status, laws, etc.— United States. I. Title.
    KF750.B87 2012
    346.7305'208664—dc23

                                                                        2012002331

Discounts are available for books ordered in bulk. Special consideration is given to state bars, CLE programs, and other bar-related organizations. Inquire at Book Publishing, ABA Publishing, American Bar Association, 321 North Clark Street, Chicago, Illinois 60654-7598.

www.ShopABA.org

To Spouse A from Spouse B:
I am glad I skipped the Battle of Antietam.

and

To Marty Webb

Contents

Chapter 3

Chapter 4

Chapter 5
Avoiding Probate 77

Chapter 6

Chapter 9
Other Issues and Considerations 165

Chapter 10
Taxes 181

Appendix A
Estate Planning Forms. 199

About the Author

Joan M. Burda is in solo practice in Lakewood, Ohio. She limits her practice to estate planning and working with micropreneurs—very small businesses.

She is also an adjunct Professor of Law at Case Western Reserve University School of Law, where she teaches Sexual Orientation and the Law. For the past nine years, Joan has taught in the Legal Studies Program at Ursuline College. She teaches Civil Procedure, Contracts, and Administrative Law.

Ms. Burda received a Bachelor of Liberal Studies degree from Bowling Green State University. She received her J.D. from Pepperdine University School of Law in Malibu, California.

The Independent Publishers Association selected the first edition of this book for a Benjamin Franklin Award in 2005.

Ms. Burda is active in the American Bar Association and the National LGBT Bar Association. She is a referral lawyer for the National Center for Lesbian Rights and the Lambda Legal Defense and Education Fund.

Ms. Burda speaks to bar associations and private organizations around the country on issues relating to representing LGBT clients. She is a presenter at the annual Lavender Law Conference sponsored by the National LGBT Bar Association and the Family Law Institute that precedes Lavender Law.

She lives in Lakewood with her spouse, Betsy. They were married in Middlebury, Vermont, in September 2010 on their 20th anniversary. That way they did not need to remember another date. Their marriage is recognized in six states and the District of Columbia—even if it is not recognized in Ohio. And, once DOMA is repealed, maybe the federal government will recognize it as well.

Acknowledgments

Writing may be a lonely endeavor, but it does not take place in a vacuum. From start to finish I have been fortunate to have many people involved. Some of the names have changed since the first edition, but many people helped me reach this point.

I appreciate the encouragement from the members of the General Practice, Solo and Small Firm Division Publication Board.

Susan Murray of Langrock, Sperry & Wool, LLP of Middlebury, Vermont; Lisa Ayn Padilla, Estate for Lifemates, New York, New York; Matthew Dubois of Vogel & Dubois of Portland, Maine; Keith D. Elston, Lexington, Kentucky; Ross T. Ewing, Lexington, Kentucky; and Colleen Cleary Ortiz, Pensacola, Florida; Anthony Brown, New York; and Tamara Kolz, Needham, Massachusetts, contributed ideas and forms. It is this kind of collaboration that makes practicing law rewarding.

When I was in law school, Estate, Income, and Gift Tax was a required course. But, it was also the only course you could not flunk—because it was not on the California Bar Exam. I, of course, am licensed in Ohio and it was on that exam. Well, I passed that class. Shortly after, Congress saw fit to change the tax code and all that effort was for naught. However, it did convince me that I would never be a tax lawyer. That being said, I am indebted to Professor Patricia A. Cain, the Inez Mable Distinguished Professor of Law at Santa Clara University School of Law. She has been generous with her time and patient with my questions. I encourage all to check her blog, http://law .scu.edu/blog/samesextax/, on a regular basis for the latest in the tax developments and their effect on LGBT issues.

I am particularly indebted to Melanie Bragg, who read the original manuscript, took the time to make comments and ask questions, and has been an ongoing source of encouragement. Now, she has read this second edition—on her vacation, no less. Once again, her comments, suggestions and questions helped make this book better. She has become a good friend—and my head cheerleader.

Rick Paszkiet is my editor and has been from the beginning. All writers know the value of a good editor. Rick is one who exceeds all expectations. He is resourceful and patient and helps me make the book better. For that I am grateful.

I have a wonderful supportive family. My parents, Jack and Mildred, have been married almost 65 years. They showed me that marriage is a continuing work in progress. My sister, Janet, and brothers, Jack and Bill, are the best. My two nephews, Patrick and Nathan, make me proud to be related to them. My nieces, Shanthi and Sahana, think it is very cool that I wrote a book—nothing like impressing the younger generation.

Dr. Martha A. Webb reminds me that I can do more than I think I can.

And, then, there is Betsy. We have been together for 21 years. In 2010, on our 20th anniversary, we were married at the Swift House Inn in Middlebury, Vermont. It was the same place where we had had our Civil Union ceremony in 2002. Now, she is my spouse—at least in six states and the District of Columbia. Perhaps, one day, Ohio will realize that discrimination is never right and repeal that onerous constitutional amendment, and join the Age of Enlightenment.

Introduction

Much has changed since the first edition of this book was published in 2004. Six states now recognize marriage equality. Recent polls show that an increasing number of Americans support marriage equality. New York, the most recent state to adopt legislation recognizing marriage equality, saw significant financial donations coming from Republican sources.

Yet, most LGBT people live in nonrecognition states, and many of those have state constitutional amendments that prohibit recognition of legal relationships between gay and lesbian couples.

The United States Department of Justice (DoJ) has decided that it will no longer defend the Defense of Marriage Act (DOMA). President Barack Obama, in consultation with legal experts, concluded that DOMA is unconstitutional. The Republican-controlled House of Representatives has retained counsel to continue the fight. DoJ will continue to enforce DOMA, but it will not defend the law in court.

Before the first edition of this book came out, my partner, Betsy, and I entered into a civil union in Vermont. It was not recognized in Ohio, where we live. In 2009, Vermont became the first state to adopt marriage equality through the legislative process. The Vermont House of Representatives voted to override the governor's veto of the measure. So, in September 2010, Betsy and I returned to Middlebury, Vermont, and were married. Our marriage is not recognized in Ohio . . . nor in the other 40 states that have constitutional amendments and/or statues banning recognition.

But! We *are* recognized in the District of Columbia and the six states with marriage recognition: Massachusetts, Vermont, Connecticut, New York, Iowa, and New Hampshire. *And!* Maryland and New Mexico recognize out-of-state marriages between same-sex couples. *Plus!* An additional nine states that permit civil unions or domestic partnerships recognize our legal relationship, albeit not as a marriage.

Section 3 of DOMA is being successfully challenged in the courts. The Internal Revenue Service is beginning to recognize relationships for couples living in recognition states.

The times, they are a-changin'!

The original introduction to this book mentioned that we were waiting for Massachusetts to grant marriage equality. It happened—and life as we know it went on. The Iowa Supreme Court, in a unanimous decision, ruled that the Iowa Constitution prohibited discriminating against lesbians and gay men in marriage. Three of those justices lost their jobs because they stood by their belief in equality under the law. Opponents of marriage equality, funded by out-of-state resources, demonized those justices.

These decisions and legislative actions continue to generate a backlash. Groups like the National Organization for Marriage (NOM) continue the crusade against marriage equality. They seem to believe that if marriage equality is permitted, then heterosexual couples will not marry. Unfortunately, recent news reports state that fewer people are married than at any time in memory. Lesbian and gay men are seeking to be married just when heterosexual couples are avoiding that walk down the aisle.

Religion continues to be the dominant reason for opposing marriage equality. The same type of argument used to support miscegenation statutes,[1] slavery, and opposition to women voting. And, we all know how those turned out.

This second edition covers many of the same topics as the first but also addresses developments in the law that affect estate planning. In this rapidly changing area of law, creativity continues to be an essential part of a lawyer's practice. However, there remain unanswered questions. We do not know what will happen to lesbian and gay (LG) couples who got married in a recognition state but live in a nonrecognition state once DOMA is no longer in force. Everyone expects the United States Supreme Court to have the final word, but that is many years away. Our clients need guidance now—they cannot put their lives on hold pending the outcome of a court case.

Drafting well-considered legal documents for clients gives them peace of mind. The myriad legal issues facing lesbian, gay, bisexual, and transgendered (LGBT) individuals and couples remain volatile. LGBT clients are the only Americans whose legal status and legal rights are dependent on the state in which they live or visit or through which they travel. No other American citizen needs to be concerned about basic rights concerning their children or

---

1. Loving v. Virginia, 388 U.S. 1 (1967)

property in the way that lesbian and gay Americans do. The children of lesbian and gay couples are in limbo, their families are trivialized, and their rights to a safe and secure family are endangered.

Elderly LGBT clients face even greater problems. Their rights on several levels are not based on the law, but on the gratuitous behavior of other people.

Transgender clients find themselves in an ongoing battle against prejudice, misinformation, and ignorance. Even within the LGBT community, transgender issues are often overlooked.

Once again, I intend this book to provide information that will help lawyers represent their clients. Estate planning is more than post-death planning—it is also life planning. It is important for lawyers to rethink how to proceed. Even with all the publicity, many LGBT people remain in the closet. As lawyers, we must look past appearances to be sure we gather all the information needed to help our clients. It is my goal that this book will help you do that.

Lesbians and gay men continue to pay taxes, raise children, cut the grass, and walk the dog. They help their neighbors and volunteer within their communities. They register to vote and go to the polls. The LGBT agenda remains the same as it is for all Americans: equal justice under the law.

Let me know what you think of this book. I have heard from many lawyers about the first edition and have used their suggestions and comments to make improvements for the second edition. I want to know if this book helps you and your clients.

Joan M. Burda
Lakewood, Ohio
jmburda@mac.com

Chapter 1

Developing a Law Practice for Lesbian and Gay Clients

A. A Discrete Client Population

The 2010 Census shows the U.S. population stands at 308,745,538 million.[1] This is a 9.7% increase in 10 years.[2] The Williams Institute published a series of papers interpreting the census data in relation to the LGBT population in the United States.[3] According to the Williams Institute, the census counted 646,464 same-sex couples—514,735 identified as unmarried partners. The balance of 131,729 couples identified as husband/wife.[4]

In 2000, the Census Bureau counted 581,300 same-sex couples. In 1990, when the Census first started counting, there were 145,130 unmarried same-sex partners in the United States. The 1990 census marked the first time a count was taken of unmarried same-sex couples. At the time, no state recognized marriage equality, domestic partnerships, or civil unions. But in truth, no one knows the actual number of people living in the United States who identify as lesbian, gay, bisexual, or transgender (LGBT). Even with the increased visibility of the LGBT community, many of these individuals remain closeted. An April 2011 report[5] from the Williams Institute estimates that 3.5% of adults in the United States identify as lesbian, gay, or bisexual. An estimated 0.3% of adults identify as transgender. That translates into approximately 9 million Americans who identify as LGBT.

With the rapidly changing legal landscape, LGBT individuals and couples require creative legal help to protect their families and their assets. From a legal standpoint, this remains a largely untapped and underserved population.

---

1. www.2010.census.gov/2010census; (last viewed November 2011)
2. www.williamsinstitute.law.ucla.edu; (last viewed November 2011)
3. http://williamsinstitute.law.ucla.edu/category/research/census-lgbt-demographics-studies/; see Census2010Snapshot-US-v2.pdf; (last viewed November 2011)
4. www.census.gov/prod/2003pubs/censr-5.pdf; (last viewed November 2011)
5. Gary J. Gates, *How Many People Are Lesbian, Gay, Bisexual, and Transgender?*, WILLIAMS INST., Apr. 2011, http://williamsinstitute.law.ucla.edu/research/census-lgbt-demographics-studies/how-many-people-are-lesbian-gay-bisexual-and-transgender/.

Many LGBT people do not know how to find a lawyer or how to identify one who will understand and be familiar with the unique legal issues they face. For example, a 59-year old woman living in a rural area of a southern state e-mailed me for help. She had many questions and no idea where to turn. It took me more than a week to locate the legal resources she needs.

Lawyers who want to provide services to this client base need to be proactive in reaching out. Identifying yourself as a lawyer who will provide services to the LGBT community is a good way to expand your practice.

Many LGBT people do not have any legal documents that protect them or their families. Moreover, because of the variables among the states, documents signed in one state may not be enforceable in another. Sometimes it depends on a state's willingness to accept out-of-state documents—or it might be nothing more than anti-gay policies. As lawyers, we need to prepare for these contingencies and teach our clients how to respond.

B. Establishing an LGBT Law Practice

Lawyers in solo practice and in law firms of all sizes see the value in marketing to the LGBT community. This may remain a niche market for some lawyers; for others, it is the primary focus of their practice.

When this book was first published in 2004, Massachusetts was the only state that recognized marriage equality for lesbians and gay men. Since that time, five states—Vermont, New Hampshire, Iowa, New York, and Connecticut—and the District of Columbia have joined them.[6]

Maryland and New Mexico recognize out-of-state marriages between same-sex couples. California also recognizes marriages between same-sex couples that married out of state on or after November 8, 2008, when Proposition 8 passed, as well as the 18,000 couples that married in California between May and November 2008. California recognizes Registered Domestic Partnerships. These relationships enjoy all the rights of marriage—but not the term "marriage."[7]

In 2007, the Rhode Island attorney general issued an opinion that marriages entered into in Massachusetts by lesbian and gay couples would be recognized. That opinion does not have the force of law. Rhode Island enacted a law in June 2011 to establish civil unions; it became effective in July 2011. Whether Rhode Island will recognize marriages entered into in other

---

6. Massachusetts (2004), Iowa (2009), New Hampshire (2009), Vermont (2009), Connecticut (2009), District of Columbia (2010), New York (2011).
7. CAL. FAM. CODE § 308.

marriage equality states is unknown. Those marriages may be given the legal status of civil unions. There is no civil union residency requirement.

Rhode Island included a religious exemption clause in its 2011 civil union law. This means that a same-sex couple in a Rhode Island civil union may be discriminated against in a hospital connected with a religious organization. There is no similar exemption to marriage recognition. While the hospital may discriminate under Rhode Island law, the new federal regulations prohibit such discrimination by hospitals receiving federal funds. Under those regulations it appears that the Rhode Island exemption would be moot.

California, Illinois, Delaware, Hawaii,[8] Oregon, Nevada, New Jersey, and Washington recognize civil unions or domestic partnerships. These legally recognized relationships provide rights that are comparable to those enjoyed by heterosexual married couples. .

Colorado, Maine, Maryland, and Wisconsin provide limited rights to lesbian and gay couples. The range of legal rights varies within those states. For example, Maine offers domestic partnerships, but the rights granted under that law are limited. Maine voters repealed the state's marriage law that applied to lesbian and gay couples. Under Maine law, couples that register a domestic partnership are considered each other's "next of kin." This gives the couple inheritance rights, including those under the intestate succession law. The law also grants the right to make funeral arrangements, be named guardian if one of them becomes incapacitated, and administer each other's estate.

Forty-one states[9] prohibit marriage equality by either state constitutional amendment or state statute—or both. Ohio, for example, takes the "belt and suspenders" approach.

C. Continued Market Growth

This book focuses on preparing an estate plan for LGBT individuals and couples. However, those estate plans require more than just wills or trusts. An increasing number of same-sex couples—22%, as of the last census—are raising children. Whether through adoption or artificial reproductive technology (ART), these couples and their children require an increasing sophistication in their legal documents.

---

8. Delaware and Hawaii will provide civil unions/domestic partnerships on January 1, 2012.
9. Alabama, Alaska, Arizona, Arkansas, California, Colorado, Delaware, Florida, Georgia, Hawaii, Idaho, Illinois, Indiana, Kansas, Kentucky, Louisiana, Maine, Maryland, Michigan, Minnesota, Mississippi, Missouri, Montana, Nebraska, Nevada, North Carolina, North Dakota, Ohio, Oklahoma, Oregon, Pennsylvania, South Carolina, South Dakota, Tennessee, Texas, Utah, Virginia, Washington, West Virginia, Wisconsin, and Wyoming.

Life planning for gay men and lesbians involves more than financial issues. Unlike heterosexual individuals or couples, LGBT couples need to document the very existence of their relationships. Nothing can be taken for granted. Even with the advances made in the courts and state legislatures, lesbian and gay couples require more protection because of their nontraditional relationships.

D. Basic Legal Information

Attorneys who intend to market to the LGBT community need to do their homework. It is not enough to provide the same documents that you draft for heterosexual clients. We need to be familiar with client goals, their birth families, and their plans for travel. We need to provide them with documents that will transcend the idiosyncrasies of individual states. This is not an easy task.

Much of the information you need in this practice area can be obtained through websites maintained by major LGBT organizations. The Lambda Legal Defense and Education Fund (Lambda) and the National Center for Lesbian Rights (NCLR) are leaders in providing spot-on information to help you represent your LGBT clients. These organizations have led the way in major litigation that your clients will benefit from. They are also available to assist local lawyers. In return, you might offer to serve as a volunteer lawyer. You could find yourself on the cutting edge of the law.

E. Preliminary Considerations

Before deciding whether to represent LGBT clients, consider your own comfort level. This is about more than tolerance; it is about acceptance. You will be using your skills and talents to represent clients whom many people find morally objectionable.

Representing LGBT clients could have an adverse effect on your practice. Sometimes people vote with their feet. They will not want you to represent them because you represent LGBT clients. This is a legitimate consideration.

Not long ago I received a call from a man who wanted updated wills for himself and his wife. We had several conversations about what he wanted and how to proceed. Several days after our last conversation, I got a message from him. It seems that he had checked my website and learned that I represent LGBT clients. He had a problem with it. He said, "Well, those people are just something our religion doesn't accept." He told me that he did not think I would want to represent him—a different take on the issue, but the result was the same. This man did not want me for his attorney because I represent lesbians and gay men.

Like that prospective client, you need to decide whether you are comfortable dealing with LGBT clients. Be aware of your own feelings about gay men and lesbians. If the client senses hostility on your part, the client will not be candid with you. Without that candor you cannot do your job properly, and both of you will suffer.

I would rather have a lawyer—or client—tell me up front that she does not want to work with me than hide it and have it come out in other less productive ways. That type of passive aggressiveness does no one any good.

Few LGBT people go through life without experiencing legal discrimination and social ostracism. This is especially true for those who are "openly gay." This can result in a prospective client being reluctant to approach a professional for fear of the consequences.

All lawyers want an open and honest relationship with their clients. That is impossible if the attorney has issues with the client's sexual orientation.

None of us like all of our clients. Many of us can tell stories about "clients from hell" that we wish we had never met. Most of us have developed the ability to ferret out those types of clients and avoid them. This is different. This is more than "like" or "dislike." This is an examination of whether you object to the essence of the person seeking your help. If you do, be honest enough to decline to represent that client.

Estate planning is intensely personal. Our clients trust us with information and confidences that they keep from most other people. Our clients are entitled to trust us and be comfortable with us. Estate planning is more than figuring out what will happen after death. It also involves life planning. We owe our clients our best efforts, our trust, and our attention.

Prejudice does not need to be overt. It can be reflected in a tone of voice, a reluctant handshake, or a refusal to make eye contact. All of us have prejudices that we learn as we grow up. The challenge is recognizing and overcoming them. It ain't easy, but nothing worthwhile ever is.

Clients may ask questions on the following issues:

1. What is your experience working with LGBT clients?
2. What is your experience with sexual orientation or HIV+/AIDS-related issues?

3. Do you have any personal doubts about or issues with equal rights for LGBT clients or clients with HIV or AIDS?
4. Are you familiar with legal arguments used against the interests of LGBT clients?
5. Are you familiar with the current laws that protect or discriminate against LGBT people?

None of these questions are out of place. In fact, you can preempt these questions by including LGBT information in your waiting room or on your website. The latter is preferable since social media is often the first introduction a client has to you.

Keep in mind that not all LGBT clients will be open about their sexual orientation. In family law practices, the reason for a divorce may be the sexual orientation of one of the spouses. Look beyond the obvious. That can save you time and your client money.

F. Expanding Your Practice to Include LGBT Clients

LGBT individuals and couples look for lawyers who understand their needs. Representing LGBT clients means dealing with unique legal issues.

Lawrence v. Texas[10] marked the first time that the United States Supreme Court recognized the right to privacy in same-sex relationships. Unfortunately, *Lawrence* has not become the catalyst that many hoped for. Most federal and state courts refuse to use the decision to expand LGBT rights under existing laws. Many focus on the limiting language and find ways to differentiate the cases before them with *Lawrence*.

Although the legal landscape is changing, many states continue their inequitable treatment of lesbians, gay men, and transgender persons. This includes being excluded from intestate succession statutes, civil marriage contracts, and family law statutes.

Still, there is hope. When this book first came out, Florida prohibited adoption by lesbians and gay men. That was the law in Florida, and state and federal courts upheld it. In *Florida Department of Children and Families v. In re Matter of Adoption of X.X.G. and N.R.G.*[11] the appellate court concluded that there was no rational basis for the Florida statute prohibiting adoptions by lesbians and gay men. The state did not appeal the case to the Florida Supreme Court. This decision gives hope that more rational voices will

---

10. 539 U.S. 558 (2003).
11. Case No. 08-3044 (Fla. Dist. Ct. App., Sept. 22, 2010).

prevail in cases involving discrimination against people because of their sexual orientation.

On the surface, the legal issues appear similar to those faced by unmarried heterosexual couples. The major difference is this: With a couple of "I dos" and two signatures on a piece of paper, that heterosexual couple automatically and immediately gains access to all the legal benefits and protections marriage has to offer. In most states, gay men and lesbians do not enjoy the same option.

G. Necessary Changes in Your Practice

There is no software specifically designed to prepare estate-planning documents for LGBT clients. Document assembly software, like HotDocs, can be used to prepare templates for use in your practice. However, most such programs, including HotDocs, do not work with Macintosh computers. One option is to create forms in Adobe Acrobat. This software allows you to create forms from any electronic format. The exception once again involves Macs—you can create forms only from portable document format (PDF) files.

Available estate planning software addresses married and unmarried persons, with and without children. LGBT couples are treated as "unmarried persons" in the software. This may work in nonrecognition states, but it creates issues when the clients are married and living in a recognition state.

LGBT clients need customized documents because there are few boilerplate clauses. Once you have drafted a few documents for LGBT clients, you may reuse them. This requires you to cut and paste; creating a fill-in form is preferable.

The estate documents used for LGBT clients stand as a unified statement of the client's intent. Interconnecting the documents serves the client's desire to ensure that the estate plan will be honored. It may also discourage legal challenges by family members.

Appendix A contains forms that you may find helpful.

Office Setup

While reorganizing your document assembly, reconsider everything else in the office. A law office is more than the paperwork that is produced. Your office forms, questionnaires, staff attitude, décor, and waiting room publications all become a factor. Reviewing everything allows you to use your office environment as part of your marketing strategy.

A prospective client may ask about your office employment policies, either directly or indirectly. Take the initiative and include "sexual orientation" and "gender identity" in your firm's nondiscrimination policy. Post that policy in a conspicuous place.

I look for that language when I consider doing business with a new company. Granted, there is no federal law prohibiting discrimination based on sexual orientation or gender identity, but that does not let you off the hook. A nondiscrimination policy is good business. Period. And clients will notice.

Most large companies provide benefits to the partners of their LGBT employees because it makes good business sense. Implementing policies that reflect your belief in diversity and nondiscrimination will serve you well when marketing to the LG community. Although most solo and small firms have limited resources, making an effort where possible will be noticed—and it might lead to your firm becoming more successful.

Be sure to review your form letters and standard mailings. Make your form letters, intake sheets, and retainer agreements gender neutral. This can be accomplished by using the non-gender-specific pronoun "you" or simply referring to "the client." It is an inexpensive and subtle way to market your firm.

Staff Considerations

A law office's staff is an essential part of the practice. Anyone considering expanding a practice to include estate and life planning for LGBT clients must include the staff in that process.

Find out how your staff feels about marketing to the LGBT community. Each person is responsible for his or her own attitude toward clients, but negative perceptions are often due to ignorance rather than malice. These discussions are important, and staff opposition is one more factor to consider.

Few things shatter an attorney-client relationship faster than an inhospitable staff. If any staff member is uncomfortable serving gay and lesbian clients, you may have difficulty attracting and retaining clients. The word will get out to avoid you—no matter how persuasive your marketing may be.

However, a welcoming atmosphere can result in long-term client relationships and word-of-mouth marketing that no amount of money can buy.

H. Marketing to the LGBT Community

It takes extra effort to market to the LGBT community. Even with a history of discrimination and violence, many lesbians and gay men are living openly gay lives. However, a significant number of older members of the LGBT community keep their sexual orientation quiet.

This predilection for secrecy makes it more difficult to find the client base. Lawyers representing lesbian and gay clients must also be prepared for the question, "Are you gay?" This question will come from clients as well as members of the legal community. One Cleveland lawyer encountered this question after giving a continuing legal education (CLE) presentation on estate issues affecting same-sex couples. She began receiving calls asking if she is a lesbian. Her colleagues could not understand why she would speak on the subject if she were not gay. She was surprised and a bit disconcerted by this reaction, but it gave her a better understanding of what her clients face daily.

Finding Clients

In 2010, the American Bar Association (ABA) Standing Committee on the Delivery of Legal Services commissioned Harris Interactive to conduct a poll on how people find lawyers. The committee released their report, *Perspectives on Finding Personal Legal Services*, in February 2011.[12]

The majority of respondents, 46%, would ask a family member, colleague, or friend for a referral. An interesting outcome was the virtual dead heat between online searches and printed listings.

Whereas younger people, ages 25 to 34, prefer to ask someone they know for a referral, older folks tend to call a lawyer they know for a referral. But a key statistic involves the 18-to-24-year-olds. While they will ask someone they know for a referral, they are also the group most likely to search the Internet for a lawyer.

The ABA report indicates that people prefer lawyer websites that allow them to ask questions. This is not surprising since many people see the Internet as a source of free information—and legal advice is just another type of information.

Social networking sites, blogs, Facebook, and Twitter were at the bottom of the preferred online models. Whether that will change is unknown. Perhaps as social media sites mature, they will present a more practical model for finding a lawyer. At present, however, word-of-mouth remains the preferred method.

---

12. http://www.in.gov/judiciary/probono/survey-report.pdf.

This preference for personal referrals tracks the pattern within the LGBT community. People looking for a lawyer ask their friends—and these clients tend to stick with that lawyer and then recommend their friends.

Few lawyers market their services directly to the LGBT community, either in gay publications or through LGBT organizations. This may be because of a failure to understand the community or a fear that people will think they are gay. The latter group should continue to steer clear of this market. It will not be a good fit.

Referral Sources

For some professionals, the LGBT community presents an untapped, or at least underserved, market. Financial planners and insurance companies have begun to increase their outreach to prospective lesbian and gay clients, and those professionals look for lawyers who can serve their clients' legal needs.

Collaboration with other professionals falls under the "a rising tide lifts all boats" scenario. This situation does not involve fee sharing, but it does give all parties an opportunity to expand their practices.

Another referral source comes from participating in LGBT organizations such as the National Center for Lesbian Rights (NCLR),[13] NCLR, and Lambda Legal Defense and Education Fund (Lambda). People contact NCLR and Lambda[14] looking for gay-friendly lawyers, so these organizations look for lawyers to whom they can refer paying and pro bono clients.

Planning

As with any marketing proposal, it is important to have a plan, a goal, and a benchmark against which to evaluate the success of the endeavor. In some areas of the country, openly marketing to the LGBT community may be problematic. There may be a price to pay for providing legal services to an unpopular client base. It is something to consider. Sometimes practicing law takes courage of conviction as well as a good business plan. For that reason, drafting a business plan with a comprehensive marketing strategy is one way to investigate the advantages and disadvantages of providing services to the lesbian and gay community.

Estate planning is a promising field for developing a lesbian and gay client base. The first of the Baby Boomers have turned 60, and many have yet to arrange their estate plan. Older lesbians and gay men may have avoided

---

13. http://www.nclrights.org
14. http://www.lambdalegal.org

Suggested Reading

Virtual Law Practice: How to Deliver Legal Services Online, Stephanie L. Kimbro, ABA, 2010

Women Rainmakers' Best Marketing Tips, 3d Ed., Theda C. Snyder, ABA, August 2010

Minding Your Own Business: The Solo and Small Firm Lawyer's Guide to a Profitable Practice, Ann M. Guinn, ABA, May 2010

Marketing Strategy and the Law blog, written by Adrian Dayton; http://www.abajournal.com/blawg/marketing_strategy_and_the_law/

---

making arrangements because they do not know any safe lawyers. And, for many lesbians and gay men, inertia has taken hold and they just never got around to it.

The time is ripe to develop and implement a marketing strategy that can put your name and experience before prospective clients. Prepare to throw out a wide net.

Consider this to-do list for preparing a strategic marketing plan:

- Develop a mission statement to express your core beliefs, the purpose of your practice, and your vision for the law practice.
- Define the scope of services to be offered.
- Identify the targeted audience: lesbians, gay men, or both.
- Identify your referral sources (current clients, word of mouth referrals, etc.).
- Describe what to include in your marketing materials.
- Decide how to market the practice.
- Determine the marketing model.
- Create a website.
- Outline the requirements for staff training.

The Appendix includes additional resources.

Practice Tips

Develop and write down your strategic marketing plan.

Define your target audience.

Determine the relevant benefits you offer.

Identify how they appeal to the target audience.

Incorporate contact strategies in the plan.

Devise a media plan, including direct marketing and detailed advertising copy.

These ideas allow you to determine what you want to accomplish and the steps you need to take to realize your goal.

A marketing plan requires focus: It is more effective when geared toward a targeted audience. Providing legal services to the LGBT community is a niche practice that targets a specific segment of the population. It allows you to get good value by focusing your marketing budget.

Limiting the scope of your marketing effort also allows you to focus on the type of law that most interests you and the structure that best suits your skills, talents, and interests. Develop a reputation in this area, and it can result in referrals from other attorneys.

Include your staff in developing a strategic marketing plan. This is particularly true for solo practitioners and small firms. Staff contributions to the plan can build consensus concerning its focus. A professional, well-trained staff makes the marketing effort more productive, because your staff is the first level of contact with clients. Equip your staff with their own business cards; this adds to their professional appearance and allows clients to contact them directly.

Lesbian and Gay Organizations

The National LGBT Bar Association is a national association of lawyers, judges, and other legal professionals. It is an affiliate of the ABA, sponsors CLE sessions at ABA meetings, and is represented in the ABA's House of Delegates. The LGBT Bar also sponsors Lavender Law, a national conference that includes the Family Law Institute.

The ABA has initiated the Commission on Sexual Orientation and Gender Identity[15] to promote full and equal participation in the ABA, the profession, and the justice system.

Lambda is the premier organization providing legal assistance to members of the LG community. Most of their work revolves around significant legal issues that are groundbreaking in nature. Lambda represented the appellants in the precedent-setting 2003 United States Supreme Court case *Lawrence v. Texas*.[16]

Lambda assists private attorneys who deal with lesbian and gay issues. It seeks out volunteer lawyers to join their attorney referral list and assist in advocacy efforts. Lambda has offices in New York, Los Angeles, Chicago, and Atlanta.

NCLR provides legal assistance to the lesbian community. In 2001, NCLR successfully represented Sharon Smith, the surviving partner of Diane Whipple,

---

15. http://www.americanbar.org/groups/sexual_orientation.html.
16. 539 U.S. 558 (2003).

who was killed by a neighbor's dogs in the hallway outsider her apartment. The court decision gave standing to Smith to bring a wrongful death action.

Like Lambda, NCLR maintains a list of private lawyers to whom prospective clients can be referred. These referrals can be fee generating or pro bono. The key is that lesbians and gay men look to these organizations to locate attorneys who are willing and interested in representing them. They seek attorneys who are familiar with the needs of a gay man or lesbian and who will treat them with respect.

Seminars

Seminars focusing on the legal issues facing LGBT individuals and couples are an effective marketing tool. Estate planning is a natural topic to encourage people to come to the seminar—and it tends to be a nonthreatening issue.

Most generic estate-planning seminars fail to address the needs of same-sex couples. Usually it is because the presenters do not think about it, yet many lesbians and gay men attend these seminars hoping to learn something they can apply to their own situation.

Collaborating with a financial planner or insurance company to present a joint seminar provides an opportunity for an entrepreneurial attorney to expand her client base. Combining estate and financial planning is becoming a popular venture in the LGBT community.

Arrange a seminar at the local LGBT community center. Advertise on the center's website. Provide handouts and include tips on the steps a lesbian or gay couple should take to protect their assets and their families. Point out the pitfalls for not taking any action. For those in a nonrecognition state, explain how state law does not protect the couple if they do nothing. The intestate laws alone are often enough to get someone's attention.

Contact the local gay newspaper and offer to write a column addressing legal issues. Take questions and provide feedback. Most gay newspapers do not have this type of column, and it will be of great interest to their readers.

Do not forget the lesbian and gay senior groups that meet in your area. They may be more difficult to find, but are worth the effort.

In addition, reach out to the transgender organizations in your area. It can be very difficult for a transgender individual to find competent and supportive legal representation.

Technology

Even though the 2011 ABA report indicates that technology is not the best way to find clients, a website is important for any lawyer who wants to expand. The site does not need to be fancy, but it does need to be helpful. Include a link to your contact information on every page. Make the content useful and client friendly.

Think like a client. What makes your firm different? Personalize the site, but provide information about the law, not about how wonderful you are. Emphasize your experience rather than your biography.

Use plain English in clear, concise, and simple declarative sentences. Leave out the "hereinafters," "thereins," and "heretofores." Write in a conversational tone. The site needs to convey information a prospective client can use. It is best not to make them hunt for what they want.

Make the site easy to navigate. Do not clutter it up with buttons and pictures and similar distractions. Forget about fancy fonts and color schemes; it is very difficult to read anything on a black background. Use lots of white space. Include links, and make sure they work.

Some lawyers have developed virtual law practices that allow them to provide legal services through a secure web portal. Stephanie Kimbro, author of *Virtual Law Practice: How to Deliver Legal Services Online*, is considered the most prominent of lawyers practicing in a virtual law office environment.

I. Benefits of a Niche Practice

A niche practice allows a lawyer to concentrate in one area and learn its many nuances. Adding a niche to an existing practice opens up a new client base. Estate planning for gay and lesbian couples is a rapidly changing field of law—what is true one day is superseded the next. Once the word is out that a lawyer provides competent legal services to the LGBT community, the clients will come. The legal issues presented will not be limited to estate planning, but advertising that service is a start.

This practice requires a creative and innovative lawyer because it is often necessary to move quickly. The greatest compliment I received came from a lawyer who was about to close her practice because she was discouraged. She told me that this book gave her a renewed vision of what the practice of law could be. She now has a successful and demanding practice that is devoted to representing LGBT clients. She found a way to turn her skills, talents, and interests into a law practice that gives her great satisfaction. Perhaps you can do the same.

Chapter 2

Legal Issues Affecting Lesbian and Gay Clients

The number of states that provide protection for LGBT residents is growing. However, the majority of states continue to discriminate against LGBT residents and their families. This presents a hurdle for lawyers representing LGBT clients because it is necessary to delve deeper into your clients' lives than might otherwise be done.

Consider these issues:

- Do your clients have a second home in another state?
- Do the clients travel frequently? Do they travel together or individually? Business or pleasure?
- Do they vacation outside their state of residence?
- Do they have family in another state?
- Do the states they travel to have child welfare laws that may create problems?

Documents valid in the state where they were drafted may not hold up in anti-gay locales. Clients need to be made aware of problems. Do not be surprised if your clients do not believe you. For all the press generated by anti-gay incidents, a significant segment of the LGBT community remains clueless about what is needed to protect themselves, their families, and their property.

Since the country is now divided between recognition and nonrecognition states, it is even more important to address travel and residency issues with our clients. Within nonrecognition states you may find individual cities that have more inclusive laws. Those cities may prohibit discrimination based on sexual orientation or gender identity—and those ordinances run counter to the state law or state constitution.

A. General Issues

The ongoing uncertainty concerning legal rights for LGBT persons creates difficulties for our clients. Clients may be unclear about their rights and what is needed to protect themselves, their families, and their assets.

Most lesbian and gay couples are interested in what they need to do to provide for their partners. A growing number of lesbian and gay couples have or plan to have children, which raises additional issues that are not usually present in heterosexual estate planning.

Many clients are estranged from their own parents. They want to know what protections are available to prevent or limit family interference or challenges.

Clients are also concerned about guaranteeing that their partner will make decisions for them if they become incompetent. They want to make sure the legal documents are in place and enforceable.

Simply put, LG clients—both individuals and couples—must do more life and estate planning than typical heterosexual clients.

Some estimates suggest that 80% of LGBT people have not made any estate or life planning arrangements. It is common to hear a client admit to waiting a long time before starting the process.

Identifying health concerns the client may have is important. Under current law, lesbians and gay men are treated as individuals for Medicaid and Medicare purposes, even if they are married or in a long-term relationship. Long-term care insurance can provide a sense of security for LG individuals and couples.

Repealing the Defense of Marriage Act (DOMA) will alleviate many of these concerns, at least for those living in recognition states. The question of whether DOMA's repeal will benefit married lesbian and gay couples who live in nonrecognition states remains an open question.

Attorneys must be cognizant of the open hostility faced by gay men and lesbians. Even the best-drafted legal documents may not protect clients if they face anti-gay bias.

B. LGBT Legal Rights

Most states do not provide legal protection for LGBT people. You may find it helpful to start from the following premise: All legal documents prepared by a same-sex couple are subject to challenge. In most states, the law treats lesbians and gay men differently from their heterosexual counterparts.

Intestate succession laws are an example. The decedent's assets go to the heirs at law according to a state statute. These statutes do not provide for a decedent's same-sex partner. There is no category for "domestic partner," "life-long companion," or similar designation. LG clients who are legally married but living in a nonrecognition state may not know that their marriage is irrelevant under state law.

Never underestimate the ignorance of a client when it comes to legal rights. When working with LG clients, it is important to make sure they understand the limits under which they are operating in the state.

Children present one of the greatest challenges for lesbian and gay couples. In nonrecognition states, only one of them may be considered the child's legal parent. The other party may be a "parent" in name only.

A recent Ohio case presents an excellent example. The Ohio Supreme Court issued a decision on July 12, 2011, in *In re Mullen*.[1] This case involves a typical situation: A lesbian couple decides to have a child. They recruit a friend as the sperm donor and sign a donor agreement. The baby is born, and the two women co-parent the child. The biological .mother repeatedly declares that her partner is a co-parent. Then, the relationship sours. The biological mother moves out and takes the child with her. She refuses to allow her former partner to have any contact with the child. The ex files a lawsuit seeking joint custody and visitation. The trial court, the appellate court, and the Ohio Supreme Court ruled against her.

In many respects, this decision tracks what happens when a stepparent divorces and has no contact, or right to have contact, with the former spouse's children.

The court's decision would have been different had the women executed an explicit joint custody agreement. In the *Mullen* case, the biological mother repeatedly refused to sign such an agreement. Frankly, that should have been a red flag to her partner. Had these women entered into a written joint custody agreement, the court would have honored it. Ohio set that standard in the 2002 case, *In re Bonfield*.[2] In that case, a lesbian couple filed a joint custody agreement with the court. They sought a court order adopting the agreement, and the Ohio Supreme Court approved that move.

Because of this case, lesbian and gay clients who are raising children should be encouraged to file for a court order recognizing their joint custody agreements. The biological or legal parent is giving up specific rights by doing so. For that reason, it is recommended that both parties be represented by counsel. An adversarial process may be better protection for both parents—

---

1. 129 Ohio St. 3e 417, 2011-Ohio-3361.
2. 780 N.E.2d 241 (2002).

and it might lessen the likelihood of a successful challenge later if the parties end their relationship.

C. Same-Sex Couples Are Legal Strangers

In most states, lesbian and gay couples remain legal strangers. There is no familial designation to their relationship. They are a "nontraditional" couple. This must be kept in mind when discussing the client's plans.

When preparing an estate plan for LGBT clients, whether individuals or couples, keep in mind what laws do *not* apply. Here is a partial list of the areas in which same-sex couples may be treated as legal strangers:

- Burial and funeral arrangements
- Claims to the body and personal effects
- Medical decisions regarding diagnosis, treatment, placement, and health care providers
- Mental health decisions
- Organ donation
- Visitation rights in a hospital, nursing home, or prison
- Presumption of guardian or conservator
- Child custody, child support, and visitation
- Joint adoption
- Attorney-client privilege
- Wrongful death
- Support or alimony
- Property division when relationship terminates
- Inheritance
- Estate, income, and gift taxes
- Government benefits such as Social Security and veterans' benefits
- Medicaid and Medicare
- Private and public pensions

Lesbian and gay clients are at a disadvantage in these areas. Their legal documents must take into consideration the fact that, in most states, their legal rights are limited.

For example, Social Security benefits are not available to the client's surviving partner. Neither is the $255 death benefit that Social Security pays to a spouse.

Many private pension plans, and all government retirement plans, restrict survivor benefits to a "surviving spouse." The Employee Retirement and

Income Security Act (ERISA)[3] controls employee benefits, including pensions. Many private companies cite ERISA as the reason they do not provide pension benefits to an employee's same-sex partner or spouse.

The Defense of Marriage Act (DOMA)[4] prohibits recognition of married same-sex couples. Under DOMA, those couples have no right to any federal benefits. Repealing DOMA would have an immediate beneficial effect on married lesbian and gay couples. DOMA's repeal would provide little benefit for couples living in non-recognition states or states that do not recognize marriage equality.

Most state intestacy laws do not cover same-sex couples. Dying intestate usually results in the surviving partner being denied any right to inherit from the decedent's estate. The intestate decedent's heirs at law are legally entitled to claim all of a decedent's assets.

In 2001, the Supreme Court of Washington state held that an inequity results if the state's intestate succession statute is applied against same-sex couples.[5] The court stated, "[e]quitable claims are not dependent on the 'legality' of the relationship between the parties, nor are they limited by the gender or the sexual orientation of the parties."

Since the court issued that decision, Washington's intestate succession statute[6] has changed to include "state registered domestic partners" at the same level of preference as a spouse.

The *Vasquez* case is one example of the lengths a surviving LG partner must go to when faced with an intestate situation and a challenge by the decedent's family.

Some courts are willing to entertain creative resolutions to situations not envisioned by legislatures when drafting intestate succession statutes. This is not a universal willingness. And, rather than depending on the right-brained leaning of a state court judge, have the client sign a will.

D. Government Benefits for Married Couples

In 1997 the General Accounting Office (GAO) prepared a report[7] identifying federal laws that contain benefits, rights, and privileges contingent on marital status. Congress made the request in conjunction with the passage of the

---

3. 29 U.S.C. § 1144.
4. 1 U.S.C. § 7; 28 U.S.C. § 1738C.
5. Vasquez v. Hawthorne, 33 P.3d 735 (Wash. 2001).
6. RCW 11.04.015 (1).
7. Defense of Marriage Act, Pub. L. No. 104-199, 110 Stat. 2419 (enacted Sept. 21, 1996).

Defense of Marriage Act. The GAO identified marital status as a factor in 1,049 federal laws in the United States Code.

The GAO listed 13 categories in which marital status affected rights, benefits, and privileges:

- Social Security and related programs, housing, food stamps
- Veterans' benefits
- Taxation
- Federal civilian and military service benefits
- Employment benefits and related laws
- Immigration, naturalization, and aliens
- Indians
- Trade, commerce, and intellectual property
- Crimes and family violence
- Financial disclosure and conflict of interest
- Loans, guarantees, and payments in agriculture
- Federal natural resources and related laws
- Miscellaneous laws

The GAO stated that their list is representative but not definitive.

Given the extensive nature of these categories, attorneys must be able to create life and estate plans that bridge the deficiencies existent in the law. The GAO list identifies only federal laws—it does not address the problems inherent in state law. State law issues include the following:

- Inheritance
- Adoption
- Dissolution of the relationship
- Custody
- Child support
- Child visitation rights
- Hospital visitation
- Health care

E. Written Agreements

Having a written agreement that delineates a couple's intentions is one of the best ways for them to protect themselves. For the most part, written agreements are most important when the couple terminates their relationship. When tempers run hot and the relationship has soured, a written agreement—made in better times—will help the couple navigate out of a difficult situation.

Use the following list as a starting point. There are no standard agreements or documents in this realm. Each case is unique, so addressing the clients' particular needs, intentions, and wishes is paramount.

- Domestic partnership agreement, aka "Living Together Agreement"
- Health care power of attorney
- Living will
- Durable power of attorney for finances
- Joint custody agreement
- Wills
- Trusts
- Nomination of guardian for an adult
- Nomination of guardian for a minor
- Hospital, nursing home, hospice, or other health care facility visitation authorization
- Authorization for autopsy, disposition of remains, burial arrangements
- HIPAA authorization
- Designation of agent

Examples of these documents are included in Appendix A. Given the lack of legal protection for lesbian and gay couples in nonrecognition states, you may find that contract law is more applicable than family law.

An exception involves documents that address parental rights. Throughout the country the court will always consider the child's best interests when determining issues of child support, custody, and parenting time, as we will see in the next section.

F. Children

Children continue to be an integral part of lesbian and gay families. Many states recognize second-parent adoption, joint adoption, and joint custody agreements for same-sex couples.

However, many states restrict the parental rights of lesbians and gay men. This is particularly true for the nonbiological or non–legally recognized parent.

Denying a child the benefits of two parents, even if both are of the same sex, runs counter to the professed intentions of protecting the child's best

---

Practice Tip

Identify each parent's relationship to the child. Use the word "parent" when describing the parties. Include language showing that the biological or legally recognized parent understands the rights he or she is waiving. If necessary, have that person contact a different lawyer to review all documents before signing.

---

interests. Children who are denied the legal protection of both parents also experience discrimination on other fronts, including being denied financial support, inheritance rights, and Social Security benefits.

Estate documents should include language reflecting the parents' intent to protect the child's best interests. Since this is often a primary judicial consideration, such evidence can help protect the parental rights. Include language that clearly establishes the parents' beliefs concerning the child.

Having the parties retain separate counsel in situations involving their children may seem to be overkill. However, doing so may prevent a future challenge to the agreement based on "But she forced me to do this."

Referring to the agreement as one for "joint custody" rather than "joint parenting" might also be helpful. Some state laws use "parent" in a way that precludes anyone who is not biologically or legally related to the child.

If your state allows second-parent adoption or joint adoption, strongly encourage your clients to file. This is true even if the couple is married and lives in a recognition state and the child is recognized as born of the marriage. If the couple moves to a nonrecognition state, the nonbiological parent may discover that she has no legal rights to the child. A court order gives them protection throughout the country under the Full Faith and Credit Clause of the U.S. Constitution.

Joint representation of lesbian and gay clients is not always a good idea. When children are involved, it is in the clients' interests to have separate counsel. The cost of an attorney hired to review a document is far less than the cost of litigation.

G. Tax Considerations

Many lesbian and gay clients commingle assets without considering the tax consequences. They have joint accounts, add names to real estate, and list

Practice Tip

There is an excellent blog on same-sex tax issues put out by Patricia Cain, Professor of Law, Santa Clara University, College of Law: http://law.scu.edu/blog/samesextax.

each other as beneficiaries for 401(k) and pension accounts. Most never think about what the IRS will do.

The IRS will consider jointly held property to be wholly in the decedent's estate unless the surviving partner can prove half ownership. Unlike heterosexual married couples, lesbian and gay couples need to keep detailed records of their joint financial dealings.

The growth of marriage equality in the United States is calling into question some of the inequities in the tax code. Lesbian and gay clients living in community property states are benefiting from recent IRS decisions.

Commingling funds may trigger gift and income taxes. When the gift tax is triggered, the person making the gift is required to file a gift tax return. The present annual limit for gifts is $13,000. Right now, each person has a $5 million dollar gift lifetime exemption. That amount may change in the next few years, as the IRS has started looking into gift tax issues.

Most people are not tax savvy, and you may find yourself working with clients who have transferred assets and incurred tax liability without knowing it. A recent example involved a woman who wanted to quitclaim her interest in some inherited property to her siblings. When I mentioned the gift tax consequences she replied that the probate attorney told her it was a simple matter. She wanted to transfer the interest because her partner was going to put her name on the house deed. She did not understand the gift tax issues. As far as she was concerned, she was just quitclaiming her interest—she said, "I'm not getting any money."

H. Health Care Considerations

Health care considerations remain an important issue for lesbian and gay couples. Many private companies and some public and government entities provide health insurance for an employee's domestic partner. Some companies restrict these benefits for lesbian and gay employees; others allow unmarried heterosexual couples to sign up.

These benefits are taxable as income to the employee. At the end of the year, the value of the benefits included in the taxable income will be reported

Practice Tip

In situations involving estranged family members, document that fact. Include language that the client has had no contact with her estranged family and specify how much time has passed. Include anecdotal information about any interaction between the client and the family. This may assist the client in arguing that the family has no right to make decisions. An argument can be made that estranged family members are not entitled to make any decisions that contradict those intentions expressed by the client in a signed document.

to the IRS. Clients who are in this situation should take steps to ensure they are withholding enough to pay the taxes.

Some companies, and at least one municipality, are increasing their lesbian and gay employees' salaries to make up for the added tax hit. Of course, a higher salary means higher income taxes, so that is another trade-off that is not experienced by straight married couples.

Companies in recognition states are starting to cancel domestic partnership benefits because their lesbian and gay employees can now marry. This reflects the continued belief that employer-provided health insurance should be based on one's marital status. The growth of the nontraditional family may, one day, result in a reevaluation of this policy.

If a client has a life-threatening medical condition, a special needs trust might be in order. These trusts are discussed in Chapter 4.

Clients may want to discuss their health care decisions with their biological family. When a lesbian names her partner as the person to make health care decisions, the family may take exception. It is better to get this out early rather than have the argument outside a patient's hospital room. Of course, this works only if the client is not estranged from her family. In that case, the estranged family may attempt to circumvent the health care documents being prepared.

Estranged or not, the client should send notice, by certified mail, to the family advising them of the decision made. In this way, the family is on notice that the documents exist, and the U.S. Postal Service receipt is proof of that notice.

The attorney can also arrange to videotape the client signing the documents. Affidavits, signed by individuals familiar with the client's intentions, can also be helpful.

Advance Directives

State law governs advance directives (aka living wills or health care powers of attorney). The instructions given by an individual, and reflected in a written document, can usually be challenged only under strict conditions. These controlling statutes will establish the basis for challenging the directives.

Generally, hospitals will honor the expressed, written instructions of an individual. However, that is not always true. For that reason, it is best to be as explicit as possible when drafting these documents.

A living will permits an individual to express, in writing, his wishes concerning the type of medical care he wants when he is no longer competent. This document establishes clearly and in writing what the person authorizes. It can include a "do not resuscitate" (DNR) order, a withdrawal of hydration and nutrition, and a limitation on the use of life support systems. The more specific the person is concerning his wishes, the less there is left to chance. There can be no argument that the patient did not express any preferences.

A health care power of attorney (HCPA) allows an individual to designate a person as the one responsible for making health care decisions when the grantor is no longer able to do so. The HCPA becomes active when the grantor is in a permanently unconscious state or terminal condition from which there is no hope of recovery. The grantor's physician and another physician make this determination. Neither of these documents is effective unless and until the grantor is no longer able to make his own health care decisions.

Take advantage of the advance directive forms developed by your state. They represent the format agreed to by a variety of organizations and may be most recognizable by health care personnel. While it may look nice to retype the form on your letterhead, the client may be better served by the standard form. Adapt the form as needed to reflect your client's situation.

Clients may want to execute multiple copies of these documents, with an original signature on each document. Using blue ink to sign the documents will eliminate confusion between copies and originals.

Practice Tip

Offer to provide your client with electronic copies of all documents. Traveling with electronic documents is much easier than a pile of paper. Clients may also take advantage of "cloud" computing and store their documents in an online resource like Dropbox (http://www.dropbox .com).

The client should offer a copy of the documents to her family doctor, the person named as the agent for health care decisions, and any hospital or health care facility upon admission. Many hospitals, doctors' offices, and other health care facilities are moving to electronic medical records, and these documents are easily scanned.

Hospital Visitation

Visitation issues have long been a problem for lesbian and gay couples, but things came to a head with a Florida case. Lisa Marie Pond was the catalyst.

Lisa and her life partner, Janice Langbehn, were scheduled to take a cruise with their four children. As they were boarding the ship, Lisa collapsed. She was taken to Jackson Memorial Hospital Ryder Trauma Center in Miami. The admitting clerk, who controlled family access to emergency personnel, refused to provide Janice with access or information. A hospital social worker told Janice she should not expect any information about or access to Lisa because they were in an "anti-gay city and state." He also told her she would not be able to get a court order because it was a holiday weekend.

Even after receiving Lisa's power of attorney authorizing Janice to act on her behalf, the hospital refused to acknowledge the document's legal effect. Lisa was moved to another area of the hospital. A priest escorted Janice into Lisa's room when last rites were given. The visit lasted five minutes.

The lawsuit, *Langbehn, et al. v. Jackson Memorial Hospital, et al.*[8] was filed in United States District Court, Southern District of Florida, Miami Division. The court granted the defendants' motion to dismiss. The court found that the hospital staff's behavior lacked compassion and was "unbecoming of a renowned trauma center like Ryder." However, there was no available relief for the allegations stated in the complaint.

On the issue of visitation, the trial judge held, "But decisions as to visitation must be left to the medical personnel in charge of the patient, without second-guessing by juries and courts."

HHS Regulations on Hospital Visitation

On April 15, 2010, President Obama issued a Memorandum on Hospital Visitation to the secretary of Health and Human Services (HHS).[9] The memorandum required HHS to promulgate rules directing hospitals to address a patient's right to choose visitors. HHS issued the new regulations, *Medicare*

---

8. Case 1:08-cv-21813-AJ (Sept. 29, 2009).

9. Press Release, The White House, Presidential Memorandum—Hospital Visitation (Apr. 15, 2010), http://www.whitehouse.gov/the-press-office/presidential-memorandum-hospital-visitation.

and Medicaid Programs: Changes to the Hospital and Critical Access Hospital Conditions of Participation to Ensure Visitation Rights for All Patients,[10] in November 2010. The regulation became effective in January 2011.

These regulations require all hospitals that accept Medicare or Medicaid funds to comply. Since all hospitals accept these funds, this rule applies across the board—but rules and regulations work only if people know about them. Lawyers need to know and force hospitals to comply. Biased employees cannot be counted on to do the right thing. As seen in the *Langbehn* case, two individuals were primarily responsible for keeping Janice Langbehn and her children from seeing her partner and their mother—and they did it because no one stopped them.

Many hospitals have policies that limit visitation to "immediate family only." Many do not include same-sex partners in that category. The new HHS rule should counter these policies.

The Joint Commission

The Joint Commission (TJC), formerly the Joint Commission on Accreditation of Healthcare Organizations (JCAHO), is an independent organization that accredits over 19,000 U.S. health care programs and organizations. TJC accreditation is recognized as a symbol of quality and commitment to maintain certain performance standards: No reputable health care facility wants to risk losing its TJC accreditation.

In 2011 TJC issued new regulations that apply to hospitals specifically including domestic partners and same-sex domestic partners. The regulations require these medical care facilities to notify the patient of his visitation rights.[11]

The United States Supreme Court ruled in *Cruzan v. Director, Missouri Dept. of Health*[12] that every individual has a constitutional right to direct her own medical care. To that end, it is imperative for the client to provide clear written instruction and make sure that all medical personnel have those instructions.

It is useful to include specific instructions in the health care power of attorney and living will concerning the type of care desired, the type of care that is not to be provided, and other instructions that will set forth the individual's state of mind.

---

10. 42 C.F.R. pts. 482, 485.
11. TJC, Requirements Related to CMS Patient Visitation Rights Conditions of Participation (CoPs) (July 1, 2011), http://www.jointcommission.org/requirements_cms_pt_visitation_rts_cond_of_participation/.
12. 497 U.S. 261 (1990).

Citing the HHS regulations and TJC requirements may also be helpful. If nothing else, it puts the hospital and doctor on notice that the client is aware of her rights. In tandem with the advance directives, a designation of agent form can be used to address visitation, receipt of personal property, disposition of remains, and funeral arrangements. A sample Designation of Agent form is in Appendix A.

Health Insurance Portability and Accessibility Act

One of the many troubling aspects of the *Langbehn* case involves the hospital's cavalier attitude toward the release of medical documents and information. The Health Insurance Portability and Accessibility Act (HIPAA) controls the release of medical records, patient information, and similar issues. Jackson Memorial failed to comply with basic HIPAA requirements.

There is no private cause of action for violating HIPAA. A complaint can be filed within 180 days of the violation with the Department of Health and Human Services.[13]

The HIPPA document should also include explicit language about releasing medical records that complies with the requirements of HIPAA. A sample HIPAA authorization form is included in Appendix A.

Medical expenses can create financial stress for some clients. These clients may need to learn about financial alternatives available to them. A viatical settlement is one way for a seriously ill person to afford health insurance. This involves the sale of the client's life insurance policy before the policy matures. The sale price is discounted from the face or cash value of the policy and is paid in a lump sum. The viatical company then assumes ownership of the policy.

Reverse mortgages may also be an option for clients facing financial difficulties. But clients must carefully investigate a reverse mortgage because the interest rates can be high and the return less than expected.

I. Senior Members of the LGBT Community

According to the U.S. Administration on Aging (AOA), the older population, defined as persons 65 or older, totals 39.6 million people. That represents 12.9% of the U.S. population—or 1 in every 8 Americans. The AoA expects that number to rise to 72.1 million by 2030—19% of the total population.[14]

---

13. U.S. Dep't of Health & Human Servs., Health Information Privacy, http://www.hhs.gov/ocr/privacy/.
14. Dep't of Health & Human Servs., Admin. on Aging, Aging Statistics, http://www.aoa.gov/AoARoot/Aging_Statistics/index.aspx.

The AoA[15] estimates there are between 1.75 and 4 million LGBT seniors who are 60 or older. Those numbers assume that the general LGBT population is between 3 and 8% of the total U.S. population.[16]

The National Gay and Lesbian Task Force groundbreaking report on aging estimates there are 3 million LGBT elders living in the United States.[17] By 2030 that number is expected to double. Most of those seniors are not open about their sexual orientation. In fact, sexual orientation, heterosexual or homosexual, is not an issue that comes up when dealing with seniors or elder care policies.

Consider the widely accepted proposition that old people are asexual and LGBT individuals are only sexual. Since old people do not have sex and LGBT people have sex constantly, there cannot be any old LGBT people. And, if there are no LGBT old people, there is no need for any policies, laws, or other protections. And, because there are no LGBT old people there is no discrimination against them.

Did you follow that reasoning?

The growth in the elder population, however, has caused a change in focus. The needs of LGBT elders are beginning to be recognized and addressed. Unfortunately, the effort is not widespread.

Ageism is common within the LGBT community. Most emphasis within the LGBT community is placed on young people. Some view the current "It Gets Better"[18] campaign as shortsighted because of the problems faced by LGBT elders. Many lesbian, gay, and transgender elders return to the closet as they age out of fear and a need for self-preservation.

Ageism within the LGBT community, internalized homophobia, and homophobia among mainstream elders result in a vulnerable LGBT elder population. "They are unable to speak for themselves and others are unwilling to speak for them."[19]

The primary concerns for many LGBT elders are:

- The lack of a recognized legal status for their chosen family
- Financial insecurity

---

15. *Id.*
16. Dep't of Health & Human Servs., Admin. on Aging, Technical Assistance Resource Center: Promoting Appropriate Long-Term Care Supports For Lgbt Elders (2010), http://www.aoa.gov/AoARoot/Grants/Funding/docs/2010/FINAL_LGBT_Elders_TA_Resource_Ctr.pdf.
17. Jaime M. Grant, Outing Age 2010: Public Policy Issues Affecting Gay, Lesbian, Bisexual, and Transgender (Lgbt) Elders (Nat'l Gay & Lesbian Task Force 2009), http://www.thetaskforce.org/reports_and_research/outing_age_2010.
18. http://www.itgetsbetter.org.
19. Nancy J. Knauer, *LGBT Elder Law: Toward Equity in Aging,* 32 HARV. J.L. & GENDER 1, 4 (2009), *available at* http://www.law.harvard.edu/students/orgs/jlg/vol321/1-58.pdf & http://ssrn.com/abstract=1309182.

- The unavailability of LGBT-positive housing and eldercare
- Isolation

The Baby Boomers are not the only people who are aging in the United States. The LGBT elder population addressed in Knauer's article range in age from 67 to 97. They came of age during a time when homosexuality was criminalized, demonized, and deemed a mental illness. They hid their sexual orientation from their families, friends, co-workers, and often, themselves. This is the pre-Stonewall[20] generation. Their experiences then and now are different. Most of them have never been "out and proud."

The pre-Stonewall generation usually depends on their chosen families rather than their biological or families of origin. Their chosen families are not legally recognized under existing elder care policies. Those policies presume the existence of a support system that is composed of the elder person's family. For LGBT elders, that presumption is often a myth.

LGBT elders face significant problems because their chosen families are not recognized. The law prefers relationships that are defined by blood or marriage. As a result, existing law creates a legal disability for those whose relationships do not fall within those categories.

Marriage equality does not provide any benefit for those LGBT elders whose support system is comprised of friends. Further, nontraditional estate planning must consider this chosen family scenario when preparing documents. Standard drafting procedures may be insufficient to give an LGBT elder's chosen family the legal "next of kin" status. However, LGBT elders must rely on contracts and estate planning documents to secure the rights of their chosen family.

While it is usually not possible to create "next of kin" status through estate planning documents or contracts, some states have laws that allow an individual to designate an heir. Ohio[21] law allows an individual to name any person as a designated heir. If the individual dies intestate, the designated heir falls into the category of "child" in the Ohio descent and distribution statute.[22] The Designation of Heir Statute allows a testator to write someone into the descent and distribution statute. Such a law would benefit a LGBT elder. Unfortunately, Ohio is the exception. Most states do not have such a law.

---

20. The Stonewall riots began June 27, 1969, in Greenwich Village, New York City. NYPD conducted a raid on a gay bar, the Stonewall Inn—only this time the gay men, lesbian, and drag queens did not go quietly into the night. They fought back.
21. Ohio Rev. Code § 2105.15.
22. Ohio Rev. Code § 2105.06.

When medical, legal, and mental health policies fail to accept or ignore the existence of a support system that varies from the norm, the elder person is placed in peril. The policies then presume the LGBT elder has no support system and the government steps in to "protect" the elder. That protection too often results in injury to the elder—injury that cannot be remedied.

Then there are the situations when government employees ignore the legal documents.

Clay Greene and Harold Scull spent 20 years together. They executed all the legal documents necessary to provide for each other: wills, powers of Attorney, and advance directives. After Harold fell in April 2008, Sonoma County, California, government officials separated the men. Within three months the county terminated their lease, auctioned their possessions without legal authority, and moved Clay into assisted living. The county ignored the legal documents. County officials prevented the men from seeing each other. Harold died in August 2008 without seeing his long-time partner.

A year later, Harold's estate and Clay sued Sonoma County. The National Center for Lesbian Rights represented Clay.[23] The complaint included the following allegations: elder abuse, elder financial abuse, breach of fiduciary duty, intentional and negligent infliction of emotional distress, and false imprisonment.

On July 22, 2010, Sonoma County settled the case for $600,000. The county also agreed to require county employees to follow protocols before seizing private property, prevent those employees from involuntarily relocating elders, and prohibiting county employees from backdating information in the guardian database.

Clay lost his home, his pets, his possessions, and his partner. The county got off cheap.

This is an egregious example of the discrimination and mistreatment experienced by LGBT elders. Too often, the mistreatment, abuse, and neglect go unreported or are ignored by those with the power and obligation to protect this vulnerable population.

Within the LGBT community, there is little intergenerational mingling. Youth is preferred. Old is unacceptable. This seems to be truer among gay men than lesbians. This age-based separation means the crisis in LGBT elder care is ignored primarily because it is unknown.

---

23. *See* Nat'l Ctr. for Lesbian Rights, Greene v. County of Sonoma, http://www.nclrights.org/site/ PageServer?pagename=issue_caseDocket_Greene_v_County_of_Sonoma_et_al.

Twelve states prohibit discrimination based on sexual orientation and gender identity.[24] Eight states prohibit discrimination based on sexual orientation.[25]

For LGBT elders living in the other 30 states, there is no protection against discrimination, mistreatment, abuse, or neglect because of sexual orientation or gender identity.

Aging gay couples want to stay together. The question is whether the care facility will recognize their right to do so. Federal law does not prohibit sexual orientation or gender identity discrimination in elder care facilities.

State and federal laws are not addressing this issue. Nursing home litigation is becoming problematic because of efforts to prevent plaintiffs from collecting judgments. Lawyers involved in this area will need to be creative and determined. Fair housing and equal protection claims may be possible. Looking at Medicaid and Medicare regulations may also provide the basis for a viable cause of action. The last thing lesbians or gay men want is to return to the closet in their senior years.

Transgender elders face even greater problems and are even more at risk. Many transgender persons fear for their safety in most situations. Few states have laws that protect against discrimination based on gender identity. Many transgender elders fear what will happen to them when they are no longer able to age in place.

J. Prevalidating Wills

Four states—Ohio,[26] Arkansas, North Dakota, and Alaska—have statutes permitting testators to prevalidate a will. (Delaware[27] allows prevalidation of trusts.) A will validated by the court cannot be contested after the testator dies.

The New York bar has opposed efforts to enact a will prevalidation law in New York. New Jersey is leaning toward allowing predeath will contests where there are allegations of undue influence or testamentary incapacity.

It is unfortunate that lawyers work to defeat these laws. They provide an opportunity for those who might be beneficiaries to raise issues during the testator's lifetime. The statutes also give the testator peace of mind that there will be no contest after she dies.

---

24. California, Colorado, Illinois, Iowa, Maine, Minnesota, New Jersey, New Mexico, Oregon, Rhode Island, Vermont, Washington, and the District of Columbia.
25. Connecticut, Hawaii, Maryland, Massachusetts, Nevada, New Hampshire, New York, and Wisconsin.
26. Ohio Rev. Code §§ 2107.081–.085, http://codes.ohio.gov/orc/2107.
27. *See* Del. Code. tit. 12, http://delcode.delaware.gov/title12/index.shtml.

K. Defense of Marriage Act

DOMA is under attack on several levels. The government continues to enforce the law but will not defend it. The House of Representatives has hired its own attorney to defend the statute. The government's action has created interesting scenarios for LGBT people.

In 2009, the Gay and Lesbian Advocates and Defenders (GLAD) filed *Gill, et al. v. Office of Personnel Management, et al.*[28] in federal district court in Boston, to challenge Section 3 of DOMA, which prohibits the federal government from recognizing same-sex marriages. Next, the Commonwealth of Massachusetts filed a DOMA challenge in *Commonwealth of Massachusetts v. Health and Human Services.*[29] The suit argued that Congress "overstepped its authority, undermined states' efforts to recognize marriages between same-sex couples, and codified an animus towards gay and lesbian people."

On July 8, 2010, the district court issued its decision in both cases and found Section 3 of DOMA unconstitutional. In its *Gill* decision, the court held: "As irrational prejudice plainly *never* constitutes a legitimate government interest, this court must hold that Section 3 of DOMA as applied to Plaintiffs violates the equal protection principles embodied in the Fifth Amendment to the United States Constitution." In the *Commonwealth of Massachusetts* case, the court held that the government encroached on the state's right to recognize same-sex marriage, thereby violating the 10th Amendment.

In February 2011 U.S. Attorney General Eric Holder sent a letter to the first circuit clerk in Boston concerning the DOMA challenges.[30] The attorney general advised the court that the government would no longer defend DOMA. The letter stated, in part, "[T]he Attorney General and President have concluded: that heightened scrutiny is the appropriate standard of review. . . . Section 3 of DOMA may not be constitutionally applied to same-sex couples whose marriages are legally recognized under state law; and that the Department will cease its defense of Section 3." The letter specifically referenced the appeals in the *Gill* and *Commonwealth of Massachusetts* cases.

November 2010 was a busy time for DOMA challenges. GLAD filed a new complaint in U.S. district court in Connecticut in the case of *Pedersen*

---

28. 699 F. Supp. 2d 374 (D.Mass. 2010).
29. 698 F. Supp. 2d 234 (D. Mass. 2010).
30. U.S. Dep't of Justice Letter re: Massachusetts v. HHS et al., No. 10-2204; Hara et al. v. OPM et al., Nos. 10-2207 and 10-2214; Case No. 10-2204, Document: 00116175339, Date Filed 02/24/2011; Entry ID: 5528735.

et al. v. Office of Personnel Management et al.[31] And the American Civil Liberties Union (ACLU), in conjunction with the law firm Paul, Weiss, Rifkind, Wharton & Garrison, filed *Windsor v. United States* in the U.S. District Court for the Southern District of New York.[32] This suit seeks a refund of the estate tax levied on a married lesbian couple. The plaintiffs argue that the levy violates the U.S. Constitution because there is no estate tax on heterosexual married couples.

These are exciting times in the DOMA arena. Republicans in Congress are fighting to retain DOMA. The issue will ultimately end up in the United States Supreme Court unless Congress repeals the statute. Should that happen, there will be a slew of new issues raised. DOMA's reach extends beyond recognition of marriage. Immigration, states' rights, and public benefits are among the issues affected by DOMA.

L. What Happens after DOMA Is Repealed?

What effect will DOMA's repeal—in whole or in part—have on lesbian and gay couples living in nonrecognition states? Will DOMA's repeal apply only to married lesbian and gay couples living in recognition states?

The majority of states do not recognize same-sex relationships and most lesbians and gay men live in nonrecognition states.

Will DOMA's repeal be a nonevent for couples living in nonrecognition states? State law will continue to determine whether a marriage is recognized. Married lesbian and gay couples living in nonrecognition states will not be able to file joint federal tax returns and will not benefit from any federal laws that use marriage as an eligibility base.

Will lesbian and gay couples that married in a recognition state, but live in a nonrecognition state, benefit from DOMA's repeal? Will they be able to file joint federal tax returns? The consensus among the tax lawyers seems to be "No."

What happens to married lesbian and gay couples that move from a recognition to a nonrecognition state? Will the process of moving across state lines erase the rights gained from DOMA's repeal?

Will benefits continue to be restricted based on one's marital status? Will domestic partnerships and civil unions be viewed as synonymous with "marriage" but with a different name?

---

31. No. 310 CV 1750 (VLB) (D. Conn. filed Nov. 9, 2010).
32. 10 Civ. 8435 (S.D.N.Y. filed Nov. 9, 2010).

The current focus is on repealing DOMA and the effect of repeal on married lesbian and gay couples living in recognition states. But what happens next? Is the LGBT community about to embark on a "separate and unequal" standard that is based on one's state of residency?

How will Lambda, NCLR, GLAD, and the other LGBT legal advocates address these questions? What thought is being given to DOMA's repeal on the rights of married lesbian and gay couples living in nonrecognition states.

Will attention shift to finding the LGBT version of *Loving v. Virginia* so all lesbian and gay couples will enjoy the equal rights throughout the country.

Should we pursue a course that limits family recognition to only those LGBT persons who marry? Should marriage be the defining factor?

If the LGBT community limits recognition and family rights only to married couples, is that position contrary to laws banning discrimination based on marital status?

Repealing DOMA is not a panacea. It is merely a partial solution to providing equal rights to LGBT people in the United States.

M. A Sad Tale

Lawyers are not immune to legal issues involving their own relationships. The lure of close family ties can result in bad decisions being made. Consider the case involving Sarah Ellyn Farley and her partner, Jennifer Tobits. Farley died in September 2010, and Tobits is now immersed in a bitter fight with Farley's parents. The anti-gay, conservative St. Thomas More Society is representing the parents. The organization's executive director, Peter Breen, stated that Tobits was trying to "pad her pocketbook."

Farley's parents are fighting for control of her estate and the profit-sharing plan from her law firm. Tobits is opposing them. The day before Farley died, her parents presented her with a beneficiary designation form to sign. Farley signed the designation but Tobits is challenging the validity of that form. She is claiming the parents pressured their daughter into signing the form on her deathbed.

This is an example of how important it is for all lesbian and gay couples to have an inclusive estate plan. Even lawyers sometimes neglect to do it.

Chapter 3

Contracts

Most lesbian and gay couples do not have formal agreements. The need for one does not seem important until the relationship ends—and then it's often too late. The agreements discussed in this chapter allow clients to create a complete life-planning package. Use these documents to create legally binding contracts that reflect the clients' intentions concerning their relationship. They can be helpful in refuting challenges to a surviving partner's rights by estranged family members.

A growing number of states and cities have enacted laws that prohibit discrimination against LGBT persons in employment, housing, credit, and public accommodations. There continues to be opposition to those laws, however, from people who often base their position on religious arguments.

A. Marriage Equality Jurisdictions

Connecticut

District of Columbia

Iowa

Massachusetts

New Hampshire

New York

Vermont

B. Jurisdictions Recognizing Civil Unions or Domestic Partnerships

California

Delaware

(effective January 1, 2012)

District of Columbia

Hawaii

(effective January 1, 2012)

Illinois

(effective June 1, 2011)

Nevada

New Jersey

Oregon

Rhode Island

(effective July 5, 2011)

Washington

C. States Recognizing Limited Rights for Lesbians and Gay Men

Colorado	Maryland
Hawaii	Wisconsin
Maine	

In these jurisdictions, state law controls the rights granted to lesbian and gay couples. Many of these jurisdictions also protect transgender persons through laws that prohibit gender identity discrimination.

Maryland, New Mexico, New York, Rhode Island, and California also recognize same-sex marriages entered into outside the state. This is significant since Maryland and New Mexico are nonrecognition states. There are efforts in New Mexico to pass a constitutional amendment prohibiting recognition of same-sex marriages. This is another example of a "mini-DOMA."

New Jersey and Illinois treat out-of-state same-sex marriages as civil unions.

California is unique because it recognizes some 18,000 same-sex marriages and registered domestic partners. Following passage of Proposition 8 in November 2008, marriage is no longer an option for lesbian and gay couples, but Proposition 8 has no effect on same-sex marriages entered into before that date. Those couples have all the rights and privileges of marriage under California law.[1]

D. Status of Recognition of Same-Sex Relationships in Foreign Jurisdictions

Ten foreign countries have marriage equality laws: The Netherlands (2000), Belgium (2003), Canada (2005), Spain (2005), South Africa (2006), Norway (2009), Sweden (2009), Argentina (2010), Iceland (2010), and Portugal (2010).

The Mexican Supreme Court approved same-sex marriages in Mexico City and ruled that these marriages must be recognized throughout Mexico. Israel recognizes same-sex marriages entered into outside that country. Because of their connection to the Netherlands, the islands of Aruba, Curacao, and St. Maarten also recognize marriage equality.

Some foreign jurisdictions recognize same-sex relationships through court decisions, partnership registration, or official policies. They include

---

1. CAL. FAM. CODE § 308.

Andorra, Australia, Austria, Brazil, Colombia, Costa Rica, Croatia, Czech Republic, Denmark, Ecuador, Finland, France, Germany, Greenland, Hungary, Ireland, Luxembourg, New Zealand, Slovenia, Switzerland, United Kingdom, Uruguay, and Venezuela.

E. The Importance of Contracts and Agreements

The United States legal system provides little protection if a lesbian or gay couple fails to make their choices and intentions known. State laws are based on a traditional family model, and lesbian and gay relationships fall outside that model. Most states prohibit recognition of lesbian and gay relationships through either statute or an amendment to the state constitution. In those states, a formal, written agreement is essential for lesbian and gay couples.

A formal, written agreement can provide lesbian and gay couples with legal protection based on contract law. Under contract law, people can agree to anything—even if the law states that there is not protection otherwise. As long as the agreement does not involve an illegal activity, the contract will be enforced.

The United States Supreme Court decision in *Lawrence v. Texas*[2] declared that sodomy laws are unconstitutional. Sodomy laws were the basis for many determinations that homosexuality was a criminal offense. But even with the *Lawrence* decision, there remains opposition to same-sex relationships. And that opposition continues to cite sodomy statutes and biblical citations as the justification.

Virginia, for example, enacted a law that prohibits two people of the same sex from entering into a contract. The Affirmation of Marriage Act states:

> A civil union, partnership contract or other arrangement between persons of the same sex purporting to bestow the privileges or obligations of marriage is prohibited. Any such civil union, partnership contract or other arrangement entered into by persons of the same sex in another state or jurisdiction shall be void in all respects in Virginia and any contractual rights created thereby shall be void and unenforceable.[3]

Under this statute, a lesbian or gay couple could not enter into a binding contractual agreement between themselves. This statute has not been challenged. While a state has the right, at this time, to restrict who can marry, it is doubtful

2. 539 US 558 (2003).
3. Va Code § 20-45.3.

that such a broad restriction would withstand judicial scrutiny. The second sentence of the statute is problematic because it prevents recognition of "any contractual rights." There is no government interest involved in two people entering into a contract. Using this language, could two same-sex persons who enter into a business agreement be prevented from enforcing that agreement? Could a same-sex couple be prohibited from selling their house? These questions may seem preposterous, but that is what the statute seems to be saying.

Because so many states prohibit recognition of same-sex relationships, it is advisable for all lesbian and gay couples to execute specific written agreements that reflect their understanding of the relationship.

Married same-sex couples will balk at this because they believe their marriages should be recognized. While that is a legitimate belief, the reality is that those marriages are *not* recognized. Until that situation changes, lesbian and gay couples should be encouraged to sign an agreement that addresses their relationship.

F. Domestic Partnership Agreements

Lesbian and gay couples may use domestic partnership or "living together" agreements to describe their relationship. These are similar to prenuptial agreements. A domestic partnership agreement is a good method for a lesbian or gay couple to address their property interests. This agreement will be enforceable under contract law.

Financial inequity between the partners is an excellent justification for recommending a domestic partnership agreement. Likewise, if there is significant commingling of finances, an agreement is also recommended.

Use Plain English

The best agreement is one the parties understand—one that is written in plain, functional, and comprehensive English and that clearly reflects the parties' intent.

Identify the parties as "partners" or "domestic partners," not "lovers." There is no standard lexicon for how lesbian and gay couples describe each other. However, using the word "lovers" can be problematical because it focuses on only one aspect of the relationship.

Include the following details in the agreement:

- Identify the parties.
- Identify the consideration for the contract.

- Describe jointly held property, if any, including how any property purchased in the future will be titled.
- Include a provision for gifts between the parties.
- Describe how real estate will be divided upon sale or termination of the relationship (appraisals, refinancing, and procedures to establish current fair market value).
- Describe any individual real estate owned at the start of the relationship.
- Provide for the dissolution or termination of the relationship.
- Include a separate property schedule for each party.
- Provide for the death of either party during the relationship or during the process of dissolving the relationship.
- Include a full disclosure provision.   .
- Include a confidentiality and privacy provision.
- Indicate any changed financial circumstances and how that affects the parties' financial agreement.
- Provide for mediation and/or nonbinding or binding arbitration.
- Describe personal property brought to the relationship.
- Describe how inherited property or gifts received during the relationship will be treated.
- Include an agreement about payment of individual and household expenses.
- Include a clause requiring counseling before terminating the relationship.
- Describe arrangements for custody, visitation, and support for any pets.
- If there are children, refer to and incorporate the agreement concerning custody, support, and visitation.
- Describe the parties' intentions about their relationship.
- Make a disclosure of all individual and joint assets.
- Make provisions for current and future support.

Properly drafted and executed, this agreement will constitute a binding contract that is enforceable in court. There are examples of these agreements in Appendix A.

In 1981, a California appellate court refused to enforce a written agreement because it explicitly referred to sex in exchange for assets. The court construed the agreement to be one of prostitution.[4]

---

4. Jones v. Estate of Daly, 122 Cal. App. 3d 500 (1981).

Practice Tip

Do not include any language that makes any mention of the parties' sexual relationship. These "meretricious relationships" could cause a court to declare the entire agreement invalid and unenforceable.

The original case addressing this issue is *Marvin v. Marvin*.[5] In that case, the California Supreme Court held that an agreement could not be based on "meretricious sexual services." The court did enforce the contract based on other considerations and thus created "palimony."

Some courts refuse to enforce domestic partnership agreements because the judge decides the parties' relationship is immoral. A Georgia trial court refused to enforce a domestic partnership agreement because of the parties' "illegal and immoral"[6] relationship. Fortunately, the Georgia Supreme Court reversed the decision, because the agreement did not require sexual activity. The lower court decision also would not stand under *Lawrence v. Texas*.

In *Whorton v. Dillingham*, the court struck the reference to sex and enforced the contract.[7] That court saw the reference as a severable clause.

Including a severance clause in the agreement allows a court to sever any clause that violates the law without declaring the entire agreement unenforceable. The best way to avoid the situation is to leave out any language that could be construed to be a meretricious basis for the contract. Use language that specifies other consideration exchanged by the parties.

These agreements can include any provision the parties see as important. Use them to describe the ownership status of individual and jointly owned personal and real or credit card responsibilities. They can also include a list of each person's individual property.

A domestic partnership agreement can have a sobering effect on the couple. Until this point, they may not have considered that they created a legal connection between them. It is not romantic, but it is an essential consideration.

If there is a significant difference between the financial resources or property of the couple, an agreement will help them resolve potential difficulties. When the agreement is signed, the couple is in a good place, but the agree-

---

5. 18 Cal. 3d 660 (1976).
6. Crooke v. Gilden, 414 S.E.2d 645 (Ga. 1992).
7. 202 Cal. App. 3d 447 (1988).

ment will only benefit them when they no are no longer speaking to each other.

Not long ago, I prepared an estate plan for a couple, which included a domestic partnership agreement. Everything was signed, except the domestic partnership agreement. I made every effort to have them sign. The couple had been together for over 25 years, and most of their assets were jointly owned.

Then I received "the call"—Allen left a message telling me that Paul was leaving, and would I represent him. Paul called shortly after with the same announcement and the same request.

Neither understood why I would not represent either of them. Rather than return the phone calls, I sent an e-mail to both of them. I reminded them that I could not represent either of them because of the conflict. I provided both a list of local LGBT attorneys.

Terminating the Relationship

Specifying the process for dissolving the relationship is important. Mediation should be the first avenue for dispute resolution. This is the cheapest way to proceed, as litigation is expensive. The mediator will help the couple resolve their differences, vent their anger, and arrive at a mutually agreeable solution. As the attorney, you are in a good position to explain the advantages of mediation over arbitration and litigation.

Having the couple specify the procedure, and the entity to be used, can save time and aggravation. The American Arbitration Association, for example, will not agree to conduct arbitrations unless they are specifically mentioned in the agreement's arbitration clause.

Contact a local or national mediation organization[8] for suggestions if you do not know any mediators. Make sure the mediator has been trained. This is an unregulated profession, and most states have no rules concerning who may call themselves mediators.

The agreement can provide for litigation, but you may want to include a provision that mediation and/or arbitration be attempted first. The parties can also agree to binding arbitration or, at least, mandatory, nonbonding arbitration before entering litigation.

Collaborative law[9] is another vehicle available to the parties. This concept requires the attorneys representing the parties to agree to work on resolving

---

8. One such organization is the Association of Conflict Resolution, http://www.acrnet.org.
9. For example, see the International Academy of Collaborative Professionals, http://www.collaborative practice.com.

the situation outside of court. The parties agree not to file legal action against each other. If an agreement is not possible, both attorneys must withdraw, and the parties must retain new counsel and start from scratch.

The American Bar Association published *Collaborative Law: Achieving Effective Resolution in Divorce without Litigation* by Pauline Tesler. The book explains the benefits of collaborative law and why its use can benefit attorneys and their clients. This is not a widely used method of resolution, but it is a growing area of practice in the family law.

G. Joint Custody Agreements

An increasing number of lesbian and gay couples are raising children. Most states do not permit second-parent or joint adoptions. This leaves many lesbian and gay parents and their children in a legal limbo.

Many lesbian and gay couples believe that discussing and verbally agreeing to start a family and raising children is enough to establish parental rights. The nonbiological or nonlegal parent performs the same parental tasks, invests time with the child, and develops a parent-child relationship, usually with the consent and encouragement of the "legal" parent.

In some cases, a court may find that the nonbiological or legally recognized parent has become a "de facto parent" or "psychological parent." In those cases, a court may award parental rights that include custody, visitation, and support rights and obligations.

In recognition states,[10] children born during the relationship are, by law, presumed to be of that relationship. Thus, both adults in the relationship are considered the child's parent.

However, in many cases, the person who is neither the child's biological parent nor legally recognized has no rights. In those cases, the child's natural or adoptive parent has sole rights to the care, custody, and control of the child—to the exclusion of all others, except the other natural or adoptive parent.

Usually, this situation does not arise until the adults have terminated their relationship and the child's legally recognized parent restricts or terminates the former partner's access to the child. Then there is a wailing and gnashing of teeth.

---

10. Recognition states are those that recognize same-sex relationships through marriage, civil unions, or domestic partnerships.

A recent Ohio Supreme Court decision[11] highlights this situation. The court ruled that the child's biological parent was under no obligation to allow her former partner access to the child. The court, in a 4–3 decision, stated that the biological mother's actions and verbal statements did not establish a right to joint custody. If the parties had had a written joint custody agreement, the outcome would have been different. In this case, the biological mother repeatedly refused to sign the agreement. That should have raised alarms for her partner.

It is also important to note that these agreements should be classified as joint custody agreements and not joint parenting agreements. Some state laws restrict the term "parent" to biological or adoptive parents. Joint custody is the preferred description.

While many argue that the law should recognize the actions or verbal agreements of legal parents, many courts do not agree. For this reason, lesbian and gay parents must understand that what the law *should* do and what the law *does* do may not be the same. This is unfair, but it is not illegal. And, until the laws change, the people raising these children must take the necessary legal steps to protect their relationships with the children they are raising.

H. Document Challenges

Challenges are often mounted by estranged or disgruntled family members who believe their rights are adversely affected. The estranged family members may disapprove of or refuse to accept the decedent's sexual orientation and his relationship with the surviving partner or spouse.

Often, disgruntled family members challenge any document by denying that the decedent was gay and denying that there was an intimate relationship between the decedent and the surviving partner. These arguments may find a sympathetic ear from a judge who shares the families' distaste for same-sex relationships.

With the rise in same-sex marriages, another issue has come into play. Many gay and lesbian couples that marry have been together for years. The question arises whether the years spent together *before* the marriage count toward a division of assets. In some cases, state court judges are counting those premarital years when calculating the parties' respective interests. This issue most often arises when the relationship ends and a divorce ensues. In

---

11. *In re* Mullen, 2011-Ohio-3361 (July 12, 2011).

situations in which divorce is not an option, the parties may seek a division of assets through a court of general jurisdiction. Without a written agreement, the judge is left without specific information about the parties' intentions throughout their relationship.

Written documents can alleviate this problem by creating a paper trail showing a long-standing desire, by the lesbian and gay parties, to be considered a couple.

When a will is contested, a written agreement also makes it more difficult to allege mental incompetency, duress, undue influence, or fraud.

Samples of the agreements are included in Appendix A.

California Update

In September 2011, the California state legislature passed SB 651, which amends the California Family Code[12] concerning the residency requirement for divorces. Same-sex couples that married in California but now live in a nonrecognition state may obtain a divorce in California if their current state will not allow them to divorce. The divorce must be filed in the county where the couple was married.

The legislation also includes provisions that eliminate many of the differences between marriages and registered domestic partnerships. For example, the bill eliminates the common residence requirement, allows minors to register with parental consent or a court order, and establishes a process for registering a confidential domestic partnership.

The language concerning the divorce jurisdiction is as follows:

S.B. 651, SEC. 4. (amending Family Code Section 2320) (effective Jan. 1, 2012)

Section 2320.

(a) Except as provided in subdivision (b), a judgment of dissolution of marriage may not be entered unless one of the parties to the marriage has been a resident of this state for six months and of the county in which the proceeding is filed for three months next preceding the filing of the petition.

(b) (1) A judgment for dissolution, nullity, or legal separation of a marriage between persons of the same sex may be entered, even if neither

---

12. S.B. 651, § 4, amending Family Code § 2320 (effective Jan. 1, 2012), http://leginfo.ca.gov/pub/11-12/bill/sen/sb_0651-0700/sb_651_bill_20111009_chaptered.html.

spouse is a resident of, or maintains a domicile in, this state at the time the proceedings are filed, if the following apply:

(A) The marriage was entered in California.

(B) Neither party to the marriage resides in a jurisdiction that will dissolve the marriage. If the jurisdiction does not recognize the marriage, there shall be a rebuttable presumption that the jurisdiction will not dissolve the marriage.

(2) For the purposes of this subdivision, the superior court in the county where the marriage was entered shall be the proper court for the proceeding. The dissolution, nullity, or legal separation shall be adjudicated in accordance with California law.

This legislation will help and may be used as a format that other recognition states can adopt.

Chapter 4

Wills and Trusts

Preparing an estate plan can be one of the most emotional events in a client's life. This process requires the client to plan for their eventual death, which is hard for most people.

Some of my clients procrastinate about signing their wills because they are convinced that they will die as soon as the ink dries on the page. My response is always this: "You are going to die anyway, so you might as well sign the damn thing."

There is no upside to not preparing an estate plan. These legal documents, detailing the relationship and the division of assets, are necessary to avoid a post-death disaster. The drafting process can be complex because it requires a creative approach to addressing changing legal issues. An attorney familiar with the legal issues is in the best position to explain the benefits and advantages of a complete estate plan to the client.

Having a will avoids the law of intestate succession—a fancy phrase for dying without a will.

A. Intestate Succession

When there is no will, the decedent's estate is subject to the state law of intestate succession. Intestate succession statutes are designed to distribute estate assets to blood relatives. A will prevents the imposition of the intestate succession statute.

Most state intestate succession laws allow married couples to inherit from each other, even without a will. Under those statutes, a spouse is first in line to inherit. The statutes sometimes provide an inheritance to the children, but the spouse receives a majority share.

As a rule, inheritance laws in recognition states treat lesbian and gay couples that are in marriages, civil unions, or domestic partnerships the same as heterosexual married couples. In nonrecognition states, however, lesbian and gay couples do not enjoy a comparable preference. Nonrecognition state inheritance laws treat lesbian and gay couples as legal strangers.

When there is no will, the results can be devastating to the surviving partner. A Florida example is pertinent. A gay couple was in a committed relationship for years. The couple made the decision to hold the house, property, bank accounts, and other assets in the name of only one partner. That man became ill and died. He had no will.

On the day of the funeral, the decedent's family encouraged the surviving partner to take a walk on the beach. While he was gone the family changed the locks, emptied the contents of the house, and took the dog to an animal shelter in another county.

When the surviving partner returned he was told the house was not his, he could no longer live there, and everything in it belonged to the decedent's family—including his own clothing. The family also refused to tell him where they had taken his dog. He could not even prove ownership of the dog. With the help of a lawyer, the man obtained a court order to return to the house, but it took six months.

This situation could have been avoided if the couple had executed wills or other documents providing for the disposition of the estate. The cost of the estate plan would have been far less than the attorney fees paid for the surviving partner to regain the property.

B. Joint Representation

Many lesbian and gay couples come in to the lawyer's office together. There is an ongoing debate within the LGBT legal community about the advisability of representing both parties in the estate plan process. The ABA Model Rule 1.7 Conflict of Interest: Current Clients addresses this issue. Rule 1.7(b) states:

> (b) Notwithstanding the existence of a concurrent conflict of interest under paragraph (a), a lawyer may represent a client if:
>   (1) the lawyer reasonably believes that the lawyer will be able to provide competent and diligent representation to each affected client;
>   (2) the representation is not prohibited by law;
>   (3) the representation does not involve the assertion of a claim by one client against another client represented by the lawyer in the same litigation or other proceeding before a tribunal; and
>   (4) each affected client gives informed consent, confirmed in writing.

According to the American Bar Association, California is the only state that does not have professional rules that follow the ABA format.[1]

Using a joint representation agreement allows a lawyer to represent a couple in developing their estate plan. This agreement can be used to meet the Model Rule requirements. Having both clients sign the agreement constitutes informed, written consent. Include a clause that allows the attorney to withdraw from representation if a conflict arises. If either party determines that a conflict exists, withdrawal will be necessary. (See Appendix A for a sample Joint Representation Agreement.)

This is the first step in establishing the attorney-client relationship. The clients need to be comfortable with the lawyer. Discussing potential conflicts and how you would respond to them is important. The clients make the decision about whether they will both work with you to develop the estate plan. While there may be no obvious conflicts at the beginning, that may change as you get into the estate plan.

Some lawyers opt to represent only one partner. The other may seek counsel elsewhere. There is no concrete rule in this situation; the lawyer's judgment is the best barometer.

C. Client Will Questionnaires

A good first step is to have a client complete a will questionnaire. (A sample is included in Appendix A.) Have each client complete an individual questionnaire. Since most states do not recognize lesbian and gay relationships, a joint questionnaire is less helpful. We must consider each party in the couple as an individual, since they have no legal connection.

While the questionnaires will give the lawyer a good idea of each client's assets and intentions, it will also serve to help the clients clarify their own intentions. This questionnaire can start the conversation about what the clients want to do.

Basic information is included on the questionnaire. The client can also identify intellectual property she may own—such as e-mail accounts and messages, websites, and copyrighted works—and decide what she wants to do about them.

---

1. *See* ABA, Model Rules of Professional Conduct, http://www.americanbar.org/groups/professional_responsibility/publications/model_rules_of_professional_conduct.html.

Sometimes, clients will own assets that are not readily identifiable. The questionnaire allows the client to list them.

Some lawyers have clients complete a family tree. This is done at the beginning. Having the client complete this task gives the lawyer information that can be used in the future if family members must be notified. It also sets the stage to discuss the client's relationship with family members. Doing so helps the lawyer understand if there are potential problems with the family.

The questionnaire is a good way to start the conversation with clients.

D. Wills

At one time, people said the only sure things were death and taxes. That is no longer true. The only remaining sure thing is death. Preparing a will ensures that the disposition of a person's estate is addressed.

Most people do not like thinking about wills. Many people believe they will die if they execute a will. Irrational? Perhaps, but such thoughts are undeniably part of the process. Further, you will hear excuses such as, "I'm too young," "I don't need a will because I don't have a lot of money or property," and "I cannot afford a lawyer."

The will is an essential step in the estate planning process. A will is the tool that allows a person to provide for the disposition of assets after death. It is the primary method for having some control after death. It is used to take care of assets that are overlooked or that cannot be disposed of outside of probate.

Even when a trust is being prepared, a will is needed. It will provide for assets that are left out of a trust or otherwise not considered. Many clients forget to include all assets in a trust. If there is no will, those assets pass through the intestate succession process.

A will can provide for family and nonfamily members. This is important for lesbian and gay clients to know. In nonrecognition states, most lesbian and gay couples will choose to leave their assets to the surviving partner. Many of the provisions will mirror both wills.

So far no state has enacted a law that restricts a person's right to name beneficiaries. One exception, in most situations, involves a spouse. As a rule, one spouse cannot disinherit the other spouse. A spouse can limit the surviving spouse to the statutory share, but outright disinheritance is not permitted. As with any other legal concept, there are exceptions. It is unlikely that any state would place restrictions on named beneficiaries in a will. That type of state interference would be unpopular and unlikely to be upheld by the courts.

Lesbian and gay clients are best served with a well-constructed will that addresses their relationship and their intentions concerning the disposition of their respective estates.

Most people want to avoid probate—and cost is not the only consideration. If an asset is not subject to probate, there is less likelihood of a contest. Limiting the assets that are covered by the will is beneficial to lesbian and gay clients. Placing assets in a revocable trust is one way to accomplish this; joint title or "transfer on death" provisions are other ways.

E. Jointly Held Assets

Many assets can be held jointly. This takes the asset out of the decedent's probate estate and allows title and possession to pass to the surviving partner.[2] When assets are held in both names, the decedent's heirs or other family members cannot contest title through the probate process.

Real estate is the asset that is most often held jointly. In states that permit joint ownership with right of survivorship, title to the property transfers to the surviving partner upon the decedent's death. There may be a requirement that a survivor's affidavit be filed to finalize the transfer of title.

In addition to real estate, couples may jointly own other assets:

- Bank accounts
- Securities, stocks, and bonds
- Motor vehicles, including boats, motorcycles, etc.
- Mineral rights

Holding assets in both names is not a panacea. And, doing so can raise other issues that many clients do not consider. Unfortunately, most clients place their assets in both names before they consult an attorney.

One downside for jointly held assets is the difficulty in dissolving that joint tenancy. With real estate, neither party can dispose of the property without the other's consent. Many lesbian and gay couples jump into joint ownership of real estate without considering the long-term consequences. In many situations, there is no problem, but that is not always the case.

---

2. For purposes of simplicity, "surviving partner" will be used as a catchall phrase. Since most states do not recognize same-sex relationships, the term "partner" is the most common designation for the parties in a will.

F. Untitled Assets

The assets just described have some type of title associated with them. Couples may also jointly own household furnishings and other household goods, which do not have a formal title. When dealing with these assets, it is best for the couple to save receipts or other evidence showing they are jointly owned. It may be helpful to include language in the will that such property is also jointly owned. Acknowledging that fact may help avoid a contest later.

For any asset that cannot be jointly titled, a written document will be helpful. This is particularly true for valuable assets such as artwork, antiques, and collections. Planning for all contingencies is an important part of developing an estate plan for lesbian and gay couples.

G. Separate Property

It is customary for many lesbian and gay couples to hold all or most of their property separately. For some couples, this makes good financial sense.

The house may be held in the name of one party through a general warranty deed. At the owner's death, the house must pass through probate. At a minimum, a will is needed if the property owner wants her partner to inherit the house.

If no provision is made for the transfer of the real estate, it becomes part of the decedent's estate and is subject to creditors' claims. A successful will challenge may also mean that the house is transferred to the decedent's biological family and not to the surviving partner.

H. Transfer on Death

Some states[3] have laws that permit real estate to transfer on the titled owner's death. This takes place outside of probate. The format is either a "transfer on death" deed or an affidavit. The named beneficiary has no present interest in the property, which means that the owner can change the named beneficiary or revoke the transfer on death deed or affidavit at any time.

The deed or affidavit is notarized and recorded with the appropriate government agency that deals with real estate.[4] There are specific deeds or affidavits designed to accomplish a transfer on death. The language must specifically provide that the transfer has no effect until the death of the grantor.

---

3. Arkansas, Arizona, Colorado, Indiana, Kansas, Minnesota, Missouri, Montana, Nevada, New Mexico, Ohio, Oklahoma, and Wisconsin.
4. Usually the county land records office.

Transfer on death provisions enable a property owner to avoid probate and retain control over the property. Lesbian and gay couples may use this tactic to allow the surviving nonowner partner to obtain title to the house without fearing a will contest. A transfer on death deed or affidavit cannot be contested.

There are also transfer on death statutes for securities and motor vehicles. Most states adopted the Uniform Transfer-on-Death Securities Registration Act (UTDSRA). This allows the owner of securities to name someone to inherit stocks, bonds, or investment accounts without going through probate. It is similar to a payable-on-death account. Doing so will make a huge difference when you are putting together an estate's inventory and transferring assets. Not making a beneficiary designation delays the distribution of assets—and also increases attorney fees.

At present, ten states[5] allow owners to name someone to inherit their motor vehicles. This is another form of a transfer on death law. The protocol varies by state, but most states allow an individual to register the vehicle on a "beneficiary" form. If you practice in one of these states, it is another way to protect property. As with real estate transfer on death forms, the beneficiary has no present legal right to the vehicle.

I. Will Contests

Will contests can be based on fraud, duress, incompetence, or undue influence. The burden of proving any of these factors rests with the contesting party. If that burden cannot be sustained, the contest fails.

Some states, such as Ohio[6] and Arkansas,[7] have laws that allow a person to designate someone as an heir. Under these statutes, the designated heir stands in the same place as a child under the state's intestate succession law. If a will contest is successful, the decedent may be deemed to have died intestate. The designated heir is included in the "child" category of the state's intestate distribution statute. That category follows "spouse" in order of preference. The designated heir would be first in line to inherit from an intestate estate. If the challengers were in a lower class of heirs, they would not inherit. The decedent's wishes would be honored.

---

5. Arizona, California, Connecticut, Indiana, Kansas, Missouri, Nebraska, Nevada, Ohio, and Vermont.
6. OHIO REV. CODE § 2105.15.
7. ARK. STAT. ANN. § 61-901 (repl. 1971) and filed in accordance with ARK. STAT. ANN. § 61-902 (repl. 1971); Ricketts v. Ferrell, 671 S.W. 2d 753 (Ark. 1984).

This is a tool that can be used to prevent a will contest. If a potential challenger knows that there is a designated heir, it would waste time and money to contest the will.

It may also be worthwhile to reconsider the standard language that the current will revokes all earlier wills and codicils. If a will is successfully challenged, it ceases to exist—as do all the provisions in it. The goal should be to reinstate an earlier will if the current one is challenged. If clients retain their earlier, original wills, this may serve as protection from a will contest. If family members learn they must successfully challenge a line of wills, they may be less inclined to start the process at all.

Many lesbian and gay clients are estranged from their families. They may be concerned that family members will show up and contest the will. And, many people believe that wills are easily contested. If available, offering the designation of heir option is another way to alleviate a client's concerns.

J. Statement of Intent

When clients leave biological family members out of their wills, they may want to include written statements explaining their reasoning. Setting forth the testator's reasons for naming her partner and not naming her biological family may alleviate a potential contest. Including a specific clause is evidence of the testator's intent and can be used to refute a will contest.

Another reason for including an express provision involves the possibility of a future action against the testator's attorney. Some states permit unhappy heirs to sue the testator's attorney. Preempting this possibility by including specific language identifying the heirs, or class of heirs, who are not provided for in the will is helpful to the client. This clause can include language such as the following:

> Debra is my life partner. We have been together since September 26, 1990, and are in a committed and loving relationship. In 2002, we entered into a civil union in Middlebury, Vermont. We would have married in a civil ceremony had the law allowed.
>
> During our relationship we have accumulated all our assets. We may not have receipts for everything, but we own everything together. No one else contributed to our assets.
>
> I leave my estate to my life partner, Debra. I do not do this out of any disrespect or lack of love or affection for my family. Rather, I do so because she is the person I love and with whom I have spent my life. We shared our lives together. I expressly intend to benefit her. She has

been a source of great love, comfort, and companionship to me. I believe my family is adequately cared for and does not need any support from me. I ask my family to recognize the commitment that Debra and I share and to accept wishes expressed in this will.

K. Using "Spouse" to Identify the Parties

There is an ongoing discussion in the LGBT legal community about using "spouse" to define the couple in their wills. For married, same-sex couples in recognition states, there is no question that "spouse" can be used. The situation for lesbian and gay couples living in nonrecognition states is less certain.

The common definition of "spouse" refers to "husband and wife." With the introduction of civil unions and domestic partnerships, the word has been used to refer to the members of same-sex couples in either of those recognized relationships. Few states define "spouse" specifically; most state marriage laws refer to "husband" and "wife." Many lesbian and gay couples do not like the historical connotation of "husband" and "wife" and prefer "spouse."

Using the term "spouse" to define the members of a couple in a will does not interfere with the administration of the estate. Testators are not bound by legal definitions when using terms in wills and trusts. The terms may be defined as the testator wants. For example, "Christine Ashton is my spouse. We were married in Middlebury, Vermont, on September 26, 2010. Whenever I use the term spouse I mean only her."

However, using the term "spouse" may create a problem if the couple is legally married but living in a nonrecognition state. The problem arises when the relationship ends and the couple is unable to obtain a divorce or dissolution because the state does not recognize the relationship or the marriage. Most states have residency requirements that must be met in order to obtain a divorce or dissolution.

Including language in the will or trust addressing the issue is the best way to proceed. Sample language is as follows:

Christine Ashton is my spouse. If, at any time, either of us initiates a legal proceeding to terminate our marriage or our relationship, she shall cease to be my spouse. We live in a state that does not recognize our marriage. Therefore, even if a court refuses to grant a divorce or dissolution, the mere filing of a legal action shall be sufficient to end the spousal relationship.

This is another example of why marriage equality creates problems for lesbian and gay couples that are not faced by hetereosexual couples.

L. Mirror Wills

Many wills drafted for lesbian and gay couples make the same provisions for both partners. The primary and secondary beneficiaries will be the same. There may be no children, and the parties may be unknown to each other's biological family. The couple may decide to name friends or charities as their alternate beneficiaries.

M. Children

When a lesbian or gay couple has children, it is important to define the relationship that the nonbiological parent has with the children. In some states, only one parent is considered the child's legal parent.

Most states do not allow second-parent adoption or joint adoptions. Until recently, Florida law explicitly banned adoptions by lesbians and gay men. Recent cases have struck down that law as unconstitutional.

The wills should include language indicating that both testators are raising the children together. Include a clause in the biological or legal parent's will that he acknowledges his partner's parental status and consents to the child's adoption by his partner if that is possible.

If one partner is pregnant when the wills are drafted, the clients will need to update the will after the child's birth. You may include a prospective child in the will. However, given the current state of affairs with lesbians and gay men raising children, it is worth the cost and effort to update the wills after the child's birth. Identifying current and future children requires creativity in the drafting stage. If there was an adoption, be sure to note that fact in the will. Provide the case number.

This may seem like overkill, but the law is changing in this area. Some judges are reluctant to acknowledge the rights of a nonrecognized parent. When there is the possibility of a challenge, it is best to make the effort to protect the child and the parent-child relationship.

Include a provision for a bridge guardian. This will usually be the biological/legal parent's partner. Naming a bridge guardian reflects the testator's intention about who will have custody of the child before a permanent guardian is named. It protects the child and provides additional evidence of the surviving partner's relationship with the child.

The will should also include references to the joint custody agreement signed by the parties. While leaving this out should not be fatal to establishing the surviving partner's status with the child, it would help to include a reference to the agreement.

A lawyer's detailed notes about a client's intentions are an important component of the file.

N. Prevalidating the Will

Another way for lawyers to provide creative legal assistance to their clients is by recommending that they prevalidate their wills. Alaska,[8] Arkansas, Delaware, North Dakota, and Ohio[9] allow a testator to prevalidate a will, but it may be possible to seek prevalidation even if your state does not have a specific statute.

This proceeding allows the testator, during his lifetime, to ask the court to determine the validity of his will. All parties entitled to notice under the intestate succession statute are notified of the hearing and permitted an opportunity to appear and contest the will. A finding by the court that the will is valid precludes any contest after the testator dies. If the testator changes his will, another validation hearing is required.

This process permits the testator to give notice to the family of his intentions. The family is given the opportunity to contest the will, but they must do so with the testator present.

If the court finds that there is evidence of duress, fraud, incompetence, or undue influence, the will presented for validation is declared invalid. The testator can then take the necessary steps to draft a new will. At that time the testator can return to court to seek validation of the new will.

Challenging a will under these circumstances will be difficult. The fact the testator is seeking prevalidation should preclude a finding of fraud, duress, incompetence, or undue influence.

It may be possible to seek prevalidation even if your state does not have a specific statute. A petition to prevalidate a will is a preemptive move on the part of the testator. Will contests take place after death, and prevalidation is a request to move up the contest to a time when the testator can provide evidence of his state of mind.

This is another way for lawyers to provide creative legal assistance to their clients.

8. Alaska Stat. § 13.16.
9. Ohio Rev. Code § 2105.06.

O. Will Clauses

Clients may be reluctant to go to the expense and trouble of designating an heir or prevalidating the will. Others may believe that there is little chance of a will contest. In those cases, offer clients the option to include a clause that explains the reason for certain provisions that family members may object to.

For example, an "in terrorum" clause may be included to provide that anyone contesting the will receives nothing from the estate. You want to include a bequest of such significance that the potential contestant thinks twice before initiating any action. Further, the clause can include a provision that authorizes the executor to pursue attorney fees and costs in any will contest. The clause can also provide that any expense incurred in defense of a will contest is to be deducted from the contestant's testamentary share of the estate.

A will can also include a clause that sets forth the testator's reasons for disposing of her estate in the way she did. This clause can include language such as this:

> Debra Smith is my life partner. We have been together since September 26, 1990, and are in a committed and loving relationship. In 2002, we entered into a civil union in Middlebury, Vermont. We would have married in a civil ceremony had the law allowed.
>
> During our relationship we have accumulated all our assets. We may not have receipts for everything, but we own everything together. No one else contributed to our assets.
>
> I leave my estate to my life partner, Debra. I do not do this out of any disrespect or lack of love or affection for my family. Rather I do so because she is the person I love and with whom I have spent my life. We have shared our lives together. I expressly intend to benefit her. She has been a source of great love, comfort, and companionship to me. I believe my family is adequately cared for and does not need any support from me. I ask my family to recognize the commitment that Debra and I share and to accept the wishes expressed in this will.

Such a clause serves as evidence of the testator's intent. This can be valuable evidence in a will contest proceeding.

Often, families come into the picture after death and argue that the couple was not getting along, the decedent was not gay, or they were just "roommates." Written documentation attesting to the relationship and its length can refute these allegations.

Another important clause is one that excludes anyone from receiving a part of the estate who has had no contact with the testator for a specified period. The clause can designate a period immediately preceding the testator's death. There are many cases where the decedent was estranged from her family, yet upon her death, the family showed up to collect.

There is no guarantee that a court will enforce these clauses, and the clients must be aware of that possibility. However, such documentation does provide written proof that the testator considered the issue when drafting the will. This is another reason why boilerplate language does not work for lesbian and gay clients.

Pets

If applicable, include a clause about your clients' pets. Designate someone to care for the pets after the testator's death.

More states are recognizing the importance of pets in estate planning. Leaving an entire estate to a pet is unlikely to be honored in court. However, it is possible to provide a monetary bequest for the care of pets in a will.

It is important to discuss pets with the client when planning the estate. The issues include whether the person wants the pet euthanized when the surviving partner dies. Some pets are old and not suitable for adoption or placement in a foster home. Some of these clauses will include a provision that the pet be euthanized if a home cannot be found.

Executor

In most situations, the executor will be the testator's partner. However, it may be necessary to discuss whether a professional entity (such as a bank or trust company) would be better suited to administer the estate. This is particularly true with large estates, where the tax consequences can be significant. Of course, if the estate is that large, tax planning is required.

The executor must be willing to follow the dictates of the testator, enforce her wishes, and dispose of the estate according to the terms of her will.

Guardian

As the number of lesbians and gay men raising children grows, guardians will become more important in the estate planning process. The guardian clause needs to include the following information:

- Primary guardian nominee
- Alternative nominee
- Bridge guardian nominee

Practice Tip

Look at the explanation of who will be a child's guardian in light of potential litigation. Establishing the record while the parent is alive may provide the evidence necessary to carry out the decedent's intentions.

The refusal of some states to recognize out-of-state adoptions has been resolved. State laws that sought to prevent recognition of out-of-state adoptions have been successfully challenged in federal court.[10] There is no legal justification to refuse recognition of a court-ordered adoption. The Full Faith and Credit clause of the U.S. Constitution applies in those situations.

Generally, when a parent dies, the surviving biological parent has superior rights to all others unless that parent is deemed unfit. In cases involving lesbian or gay parents, there is usually only one parent legally recognized by the state. Without some type of court order, the nonbiological surviving partner has no legal rights. For this reason, appointing a guardian for a child is important. How to decide who will be the guardian can lead to disputes.

The court will consider the child's best interests when making its placement decision. Without guidance or in spite of guidance, the child may be placed with a member of the decedent's biological family, which could be someone the child does not even know.

Nominating a guardian for the child in a will presents a rebuttable presumption of the deceased parent's preference. This may enhance the surviving partner's claim to be named the child's guardian. Include the parent's reasons for selecting the nominee. Incorporate language explaining why the parent decided to not name family members.

The biological parent may nominate the nonbiological parent, but the court is under no obligation to follow that suggestion. The court may instead appoint a member of the decedent's family, and this can effectively terminate contact between the child and the surviving partner.

Second-parent and joint adoptions are not permitted in all states. Second-parent adoption lends legal validity to the nominated guardian's claim, because courts must respect the decisions of other courts. That is the basis for the Full Faith and Credit Clause of the United States Constitution.

---

10. Finstuen v. Edmondson, 496 F.3d 1139 (10th Cir. 2007).

One issue that may crop up involves the nonadversarial aspect of a joint or second-parent adoption—that is, no one involved contests the adoption. Most adoptions are not adversarial, so someone may raise the lack of an adversary to question the legitimacy of the adoption. This is something that needs to be discussed with the clients if there is any chance someone may challenge the placement.

Drafting a will clause that addresses this possible argument may be advisable. Having the clause and a joint custody agreement will supply additional proof of the parties' intentions.

Consider nominating the surviving partner as guardian for the child's person and estate. A testamentary trust, naming the surviving partner as trustee, may be the tool needed to counter the appointment of another guardian. Retaining control of the child's finances ensures access to the child. Language to that effect should be included in the trust agreement. Remember the movie, *Auntie Mame*? Mame got the kid; the banker controlled the money. So, think of this as the *Auntie Mame* clause.

Ensuring that the surviving partner remains a part of the child's life is in the child's best interests. Children need continuity, and that gives them security.

Bridge Guardian

Another subsection of the guardian clause involves naming someone to serve as the child's interim guardian. If no one is named, the child may be placed in foster care until the courts clarify the issue of who will care for the child. The child might also be placed with a family member who is not the deceased parent's choice and with whom the child has no relationship.

Losing a parent is traumatic enough for a child. A child's best interests are not served by placing her in an unsettled home situation.

In matters involving children, it is difficult to provide for every scenario. It is, therefore, important to investigate all available options, including the status of second-parent adoptions in your jurisdiction. If it is allowed, or if the issue is undetermined, your client may want to pursue such an adoption.

A child is not entitled to any government benefits upon the death of the legally unrecognized parent. There are no survivor benefits for the child even if the decedent was the primary wage earner in the family. The child may also be unable to recoup benefits from the decedent's employer.

For these reasons, second-parent adoption may provide the best protection for children of same-sex couples. This is particularly true in those states that do not recognize families of same-sex couples. Children should be protected, not punished, for the gender of their parents.

Clients must understand their obligation to do whatever is necessary to protect their children and the parent-child relationship. Any legal parent who objects to or balks at taking action should be cause for concern.

P. Trusts

Trusts constitute a separate facet of an estate plan for lesbian and gay clients. In some ways trusts can provide the protection and privacy many clients seek. Trusts can be more difficult for unhappy family members to contest. Trusts are not subject to the vagaries of probate court and may be a better vehicle to protect the parties' intentions.

A trust is a relationship between three parties: the trustor, trustee, and beneficiary. The purpose of a trust is to transfer property owned by the trustor into the trust, where the trustee manages it for the benefit of a beneficiary. The trustor can also be called the grantor, settlor, donor, or creator.

Legal title to property resides in the trustee, but the beneficiary has equitable title to the property. The trustee has a fiduciary duty to the beneficiary. This means that the trustee is personally liable if the trust is mismanaged.

There can be multiple trustors, trustees, and beneficiaries. Generally, though, it is better to have a single trustee. Multiple trustees can create problems in managing the trust.

The trustor can also be a trustee and a beneficiary.

A trustee may be an individual or a legal entity such as a bank. Trustees are responsible for managing the trust assets. This may include investing assets and protecting and preserving those assets. A trustee may be paid for the time spent administering the trust.

The terms of the trust govern its administration. The trust terms must specify the property to be transferred into the trust. The trustor decides when the trust begins, how it is managed, how much power the trustee has, and when the trust ends.

Trusts can be revocable or irrevocable. The latter should be consider ed carefully. Once an irrevocable trust is set up it cannot be changed.

Revocable trusts have no gift, income, or estate tax consequences because the grantor retains control of the assets. The grantor continues to have the power to amend, revoke, or terminate the trust.

Irrevocable trusts, on the other hand, require the grantor to relinquish all rights to alter, amend, revoke, or terminate the trust. The grantor may retain certain administrative rights. Once established, an irrevocable trust cannot be changed.

Trusts are often used for tax or estate planning purposes. Some individuals with large estates may want to divest themselves of property during their lifetime. Section 2035(a) of the Internal Revenue Code (IRC) deals with the transfer of a property interest within three years of death. The IRS considers transfers within that three-year period to have been made in contemplation of death. The transfer is ignored and the value of that property must be included in the decedent's gross estate. This applies only to property that would be included in the decedent's gross estate under the IRC had the interest been retained.

It is important to remind clients that a will is necessary even if a trust is set up. The basic trusts used in estate planning are testamentary trusts, living trusts, and irrevocable life insurance trusts.

Transfer of Assets

Transferring assets into a trust is one area in which many clients fall short. Most lawyers can relate stories about clients who paid thousands of dollars for a living trust but never funded the trust. Without transferring assets into a trust, the grantor ends up with nothing more than an expensive wad of papers.

Attorneys are well suited to advise the client on what property to transfer into the trust and to assist the client in effecting the transfer. Clients also need an annual reminder to transfer recently acquired property into the trust.

Living Trusts

Living trusts are established during the client's lifetime. The primary purpose of a living trust is to avoid probate. One may also be used as a planning tool for unforeseen circumstances such as disability or incompetency.

A living trust does not avoid federal or state estate or inheritance taxes. While a trust is not subject to probate, it is also not protected by the probate court. There is no protection against mismanagement, embezzlement, or other nefarious activities by the trustee. Trusts are conducted in private, without judicial oversight.

Including a "pour-over" provision in the will transfers assets, not included in the living trust, into the trust. For this reason, a will is an integral part of any estate plan that includes a living trust. Otherwise any asset left out of the living trust will become a probate asset and pass under the state's intestate succession statute.

Living trusts can be an appropriate vehicle to protect assets, maintain privacy, and avoid potentially negative family interaction when one of the partners dies.

There are two kinds of living trusts, irrevocable and revocable. In an irrevocable living trust, the grantor relinquishes all authority over the trust. The trust cannot be terminated, nor can its provisions be changed. Once established, it remains in effect under the trust provisions and the trustee's supervision.

In a revocable living trust, the grantor retains control over the administration and enforcement of the trust. A revocable living trust can be amended or revoked by the person creating the trust. The grantor retains all the benefits of property placed into the trust. As with any type of trust, its terms are spelled out in the trust document. This stipulates the duties and powers of the grantor and the trustee. The language also specifies what happens to the trust property during and after the grantor's life.

The beneficiary of a trust cannot contest any action taken by the grantor. The grantor and the trustee must both sign the trust. Often, the grantor is the trustee during his lifetime.

Most people use a living trust to avoid probate because they fear a protracted court battle. Probate is less onerous than in the past. There are also other avenues available to avoid probate that do not require the expense of establishing a living trust. These include payable on death accounts, transfer on death deeds, and joint accounts.

A living trust avoids probate because the grantor transfers all property into the trust. This includes property owned at the time the trust is established and other property accumulated during the grantor's lifetime. Anything not placed into the trust is, potentially, a probate asset.

Trusts can be used to meet the unique needs of a couple that has no statutory legal resource in the estate planning area. A living trust will give the parties privacy since the trust will never become a public record. The trust gives more control because the probate court is not involved. The trustee has considerable power and is not required to answer to anyone other than the grantor and, potentially, the beneficiary.

The downside, of course, is the lack of judicial oversight and legal protection for the beneficiaries. Should the trustee abscond with the trust assets for an island in the Pacific, the beneficiaries may have little recourse.

Having the trustee post a bond may alleviate some concern. But, alas, that is a decision the grantor must make—and the beneficiaries cannot require a bond retroactively. Their only recourse is to seek a court order removing the trustee.

A trust can be set up to begin making distributions to the beneficiary soon after the grantor's death. This differs from probate, where it can take months to distribute assets.

Placing real estate into a trust can provide another advantage, particularly if the real estate is located in different states. In probate, this situation would require an ancillary proceeding for real estate located outside the decedent's residence state. There is no need for an ancillary proceeding when a trust is involved.

A living trust can provide a significant benefit to the grantor if she becomes incompetent during her lifetime. Without a trust it would be necessary to initiate a guardianship proceeding. This can be time-consuming, expensive, and frustrating.

A guardianship proceeding also raises the prospect of a family member being named the guardian rather than the grantor's partner. Depending on how the couple arranged their assets, it is possible for the competent partner to be financially deprived.

Sharon Kowalski[11] is a well-known example of what can happen in a guardianship contest. Her partner, Karen Thompson, ultimately prevailed over Sharon's parents, but it took years of court battles and many thousands of dollars in attorney fees and court costs to reach that point. And, during that time Sharon had virtually no contact with Karen because her parents would not allow it.

Sharon became completely disabled following a 1983 automobile accident. At the time of the accident Sharon shared a home with Karen. Sharon's parents were unaware of her lesbian relationship. The guardianship battle began in 1984 when Karen and Sharon's father cross-petitioned for guardianship. Karen agreed to the father's appointment as guardian. She fully expected to be able to visit and have input on Sharon's medical care decisions. The guardianship order, however, gave full authority over visitation to Mr. Kowalski, and he, with the court's approval, terminated Karen's visitation rights in 1985.

Three years later another court granted Karen's visitation rights. In 1988 Karen again applied to be appointed Sharon's guardian. In spite of substantial evidence supporting her petition, the court appointed a friend of Sharon's family as guardian. Karen appealed to the Minnesota Court of Appeals. That court reversed the case and remanded with instructions to appoint Karen as Sharon's guardian. The case took eight years to resolve.

Creditors can access assets in a revocable living trust, but irrevocable living trusts are different. A bona fide irrevocable living trust precludes creditors

---

11. *In re* Guardianship of Kowalski, 478 N.W.2d 790 (Minn. Ct. App. 1991).

Practice Tip

A discussion of tax ramifications is beyond the scope of this book. One resource is the *Same-Sex Tax Blog*, written by Patricia Cain, Professor of Law at Santa Clara Law School: http://law.scu.edu/blog/samesextax.

---

from attaching any assets because the grantor relinquishes all authority of administration and enforcement of the trust.

The assets placed in a living trust, whether revocable or irrevocable, are included in a decedent's taxable estate. Probate does not control a decedent's taxable estate. Probate controls only the distribution of the estate through a will. Nonprobate assets can remain part of a decedent's estate and, therefore, subject to estate taxes. For example, if the trust assets are valued in excess of $5 million dollars,[12] there will be federal estate tax due on the amount that exceeds that amount.

A living trust should not be seen as the only tax-planning tool. Clients with large estates must consult a tax planner to take advantage of all available tax planning. And lawyers who are not well versed in tax law should ally themselves with a competent tax expert to assist the client.

In addition to federal estate tax, the assets in a living trust may also be subject to state estate taxes. This is also a consideration when drafting the trust documents.

Living trusts provide lesbian and gay clients another avenue to protect their assets and their relationship from inquiry by courts and the public. The trust can hold both shared and individually held property. This makes the setup and administration easier. However, if the couple's primary goal is to avoid probate, there are other ways to accomplish that without resorting to a trust.

Joint Trusts[13]

Joint trusts, where both partners are the co-grantors, co-trustees, and co-beneficiaries, can be problematic. And, as long as DOMA is in force, the marital deduction is not available to married lesbian and gay couples. Any joint trust used for a same-sex couple should be revocable.

A joint trust may trigger gift tax issues because the parties are commingling their property. When the parties need to keep their separate property

---

12. The current federal amount, at least through 2012.
13. Two IRS private letter rulings address joint trusts: P.L.R. 2002-10-051 (Mar. 8, 2002) and P.L.R. 2001-01-021 (Jan. 5, 2001).

segregated to avoid an unintentional gift, there is no reason to have a joint trust. In addition, separate trusts are easier to set up and manage.

Joint trusts are often used as an estate-planning tool in community property states. This may make sense if everything is 100% community property. That means it was never either partner's separate property—not when acquired nor throughout its ownership by the couple.

An alternative for lesbian and gay couples in community property states is to set up separate trusts for their separate property and a third trust for the community property. If the couple has extensive holdings and taxes are an issue, working with an experienced tax-planning lawyer is in the couple's best interest.

Testamentary Trusts

Testamentary trusts are created inside a will. The trust is created either at or shortly after death; it becomes effective upon the testator's death. A will may contain more than one testamentary trust. Testamentary trusts are often used to benefit minors, or in lieu of a living trust. Since no assets are transferred into the trust before death, the assets are part of the decedent's probate estate. Unlike the case with a living trust, the probate court is an integral party to establishing a testamentary trust.

A testamentary trust can be created to address assets accumulated during the testator's life or those that may result from the death itself, as in a wrongful death settlement.

Since the trust is established after the testator's death, that person has no authority over the trustee or the administration of the trust. The beneficiaries' needs tend to drive a testamentary trust more than tax considerations.

Testamentary trusts are an advantage if minor children are involved. The testator can include trust provisions concerning the disposition of the estate assets for the benefit of a minor child. Such a trust can protect the child's assets from any adults who are appointed the child's guardian.

For lesbian and gay couples raising children, a testamentary trust can ensure that the surviving partner maintains a relationship with the child.

The trustee must make an annual report to the probate court about the trust administration, which adds to the administrative and trustee costs. Those costs are deducted from the trust's principal.

The testator may appoint the trustee in the will, but that person is not required to accept the appointment. In that case, unless an alternative is listed in the will, the probate court will appoint a trustee. It may also be difficult for beneficiaries to challenge a trustee's action. Any challenge will be time-consuming and expensive, with no guarantee of success.

Testamentary trusts are often used with small estates. However, state law must be reviewed to ensure that the trust will come into existence. Many states allow a trust to be terminated, and the proceeds distributed, if the principal falls below a certain level.

Spendthrift Trust

A spendthrift trust is created for the benefit of one person. Usually the beneficiary is someone who is unable to manage his finances. The trustee is given full authority to manage the trust for the beneficiary's benefit. Creditors cannot get to the trust principal because the beneficiary does not control the trust.

A spendthrift provision in an irrevocable trust prevents creditors from attaching the beneficiary's interest before the proceeds are paid to the beneficiary. Most irrevocable trusts include a spendthrift provision even if the beneficiary is not known to be a spendthrift. The provision helps protect the trust assets from creditors.

Some creditors may be able to obtain payments. Usually these creditors have provided necessaries to the beneficiary, such as food or shelter. The trust may also be required to pay child support and alimony.

A caveat to this is that a trustor cannot create a spendthrift trust to avoid his own debts. The spendthrift clause in a self-settled trust does not protect the beneficiary from creditors if the beneficiary and trustor are the same.

A spendthrift trust can prohibit the trustee from making direct cash payments to the beneficiary. The trust can authorize the trustee to make payments directly to a provider of services, such as a landlord or utility company.

This type of trust can be as rigid or flexible as the trustor deems appropriate. But do not create a trust that places so many restrictions on the trustee that no one wants to serve in that capacity.

It is also important to determine when and how the trust will be terminated, and what happens to the trust principal when termination occurs.

A spendthrift provision can be included in any trust. It is a restraint on the voluntary or involuntary alienation of a beneficiary's interest in a trust. The clause provides that the beneficiary shall neither transfer nor assign the interest. Likewise, the beneficiary's interest is not subject to creditor's claims. A sample provision may be as follows:

> No beneficiary shall have the right to transfer all or part of his interest either in income or principal unless the Trustee, in its discretion, shall consent in writing. The Trustee shall not be compelled to exercise this discretion. No person, having a claim or demand of any sort against the beneficiary, shall have the right to reach the interest of

any beneficiary by judicial process while the Trustee has possession of any trust assets.

Special Needs Trust

The Omnibus Budget Reconciliation Act of 1993[14] (OBRA '93) authorized special needs trusts. These trusts are also known as supplemental needs trusts or Medicaid payback trusts because they require the trust to pay back an amount equal to what the state spent in providing the beneficiary with medical care. In this statute a special needs trust is defined as:

> A trust containing the assets of an individual under age 65 who is disabled (as described in § 1382c(a)(3) of this title) and which is established for the benefit of such individual by a parent, grandparent, legal guardian of the individual or a court if the state will receive all amounts remaining in the trust upon the death of such individual up to an amount equal to the total medical assistance paid on behalf of the individual under a State plan under this subchapter.

The statute is codified at 42 U.S.C. § 1396p(d).

A special needs trust is used to allow a disabled (physically or mentally) person to benefit from property left to them. These trusts can be either living trusts or testamentary trusts.

A special needs trust should be established if either partner is ill. In the gay community one or both partners may be diagnosed with AIDS or be HIV+. A special needs trust may help in this situation.

Note that a specific class of people must establish the trust. If the partner is named the legal guardian of the other, then a special needs trust can be established. The drafting requirements for this type of trust are stringent and must be carefully followed. However, such a trust can provide additional resources to a disabled surviving partner for items that are not covered by Medicaid.

Many states define the supplemental services that can be covered. This includes in-home nursing care or assistance. Most people want to stay home as long as possible. This type of trust may allow a disabled surviving partner to do just that.

Pet Trusts

Testamentary trusts may also be used to provide for the care and maintenance of a pet after the owner's death. Forty-five states and the District of Columbia

---

14. Pub. L. No. 103-66, 107 Stat. 312 (enacted Aug. 10, 1993); 42 U.S.C. 1396p(d)(4)(a).

have laws permitting trusts for pets. Only Kentucky, Louisiana, Minnesota, Mississippi, and Vermont do not have pet trust laws.

In states that do not permit pet trusts, all is not lost. A client might establish a connection with a state that does have a pet trust law. Some examples of how to do it:

- Name a trustee who lives in a state with a pet trust law.
- The caretaker named in the will may live in a state with a pet trust law.
- The testator may own property in a state with a pet trust law.
- The testator may select a retirement home for the pet in a state that honors pet trusts.

The trusts work for people who are concerned about the care of their pets and do not want to leave the pet and a sum of money to an individual outright. There is no limit on how much can be left for a pet, but the court can reduce the amount designated to fund the trust if the judge finds that amount to be excessive. It is best to leave a reasonable amount or run the risk of a will contest.

Section 408 of the Uniform Trust Act (UTA) of 2000 specifically allows a trust for the care of an animal. The UTA also authorizes a court to appoint someone to enforce the trust.

Section 2-907 of the Uniform Probate Code (UPC) of 1993 includes parallel language. Under the UPC, a trust for the care of a pet or companion animal is valid and can continue until the animal's death. "An individual designated for that purpose in the trust instrument" can enforce this trust. If no one is designated, the court can appoint someone when an application is filed.

Most of the states that have these trusts include similar provisions. For example, the Colorado law provides that a trust can continue until the pet's offspring that were in gestation at the time of the owner's death die. New York and New Jersey, on the other hand, limit the trust length to 21 years.

The pet trust statutes treat these trusts in a manner similar to that for a minor child. The person appointed to enforce the trust is in a position comparable to that of a guardian.

A trustor need only name a class of animals and provide the funds. There is no need to name each animal individually, by name. The client should also name a trustee, caretaker, and enforcer, if different from the trustee, and alternatives to each. It is best to ensure that these people will follow the trustor's instructions and intent.

The trust must also include the provisions or guidelines the trustor wants to establish for the pet's care. This includes annual or monthly expenditure expectations, how to pay expenses, type of food, whether there will be a caretaker's fee, payment of vet fees, and payment of pet health care insurance premiums. These same details may be included in a separate document, but including them in the trust language gives them greater emphasis.

The trustor may want to stipulate how major decisions concerning the pet are to be made. This would include when and if to euthanize the animal. The trust can provide that such decisions are to be made by a panel of designated people.

Another form of trust is to name the caretaker as the beneficiary. Then the caretaker can enforce the trust, demanding payment for services provided. Include a clause to allow the trustee to enforce the trust by withholding payments or replacing the caretaker if proper care is not provided. Alternative caretakers can provide another form of enforcement by demanding proper care for the pet and, if it is not given, to demand that the caretaker be replaced.

This type of trust can last for the life of the caretaker, plus 21 years, or terminate when the pet dies, whichever comes first. Of course, in the event that the pet outlives the caretaker and the 21 years, the trust may provide for what happens in that event.

One problem with a caretaker/beneficiary trust arises when no one named in the trust wants to assume the responsibilities involved. If this situation is a possibility, the trustor may want to name an organization rather than an individual. A number of groups have established homes that provide animals with lifelong care. One example of this is the Bideawee Golden Years Retirement Home[15] in Westhampton, New York.

Being able to discuss pet trusts or other provisions for the care and maintenance of a client's pets is a good service to provide.

Charitable Remainder Trusts

Charitable remainder trusts are one way for wealthy clients to provide for themselves and their partners during their lifetimes and pass on a bequest to a charity. Charitable remainder trusts are authorized by § 664 of the IRC. This is an irrevocable trust and has two main characteristics:

1. It distributes a fixed percentage of assets to a noncharitable beneficiary.

---

15. http://www.bideawee.org.

2. At a specified time, usually when the beneficiary dies, the remaining assets are distributed to charity.

Distributions are usually made on an annual or semiannual basis. Often, but not always, the trustor is the beneficiary. The trustee determines the fair market value of the assets at the time they are contributed and on subsequent valuation dates. The distributions must be at least 5% and no more than 50% of the assets' fair market value. The remainder, which goes to the charity, must be at least 10% of the fair market value of the assets contributed to the charitable remainder trust.

These trusts must meet both IRC and state law requirements for a charitable remainder unitrust. The charity must be an organization recognized by § 170 (c) of the IRC.

Only the named beneficiary or the charity may receive distributions from the trust. Payments are made for the life of the beneficiary or for a fixed time that cannot exceed 20 years.

The donor is entitled to a charitable deduction[16] that is based on the present value of the remainder interest. Section 2055(a) of the IRC also provides a deduction from the donor's gross estate, so the contribution to a charitable remainder trust is not included in the donor's taxable estate.

There are various benefits to this type of trust:

1. They represent an income tax deduction for the trust's creator.
2. The charity benefits from any increase in the property's appreciated value.

If estate taxes are a potential problem, the value of the donated property is removed from the grantor's estate, thus eliminating or lowering the tax liability.

There are two types of charitable remainder trusts: charitable remainder annuity trusts and charitable remainder unitrusts (CRUTs). They are defined in Sections 664(d) and 664(a), respectively, of the IRC. The IRS has also issued sample charitable trust forms[17] that may assist you in developing an appropriate charitable remainder trust for your clients.

Irrevocable Life Insurance Trusts

An irrevocable life insurance trust provides the client with an opportunity to buy an insurance policy but remove it from the taxable estate. This trust is

---

16. Treas. Reg. § 1.664-4(e)(3), (4).
17. Internal Revenue Serv., Rev. Proc. 2007-45, Bulletin No. 2007-29 (July 16, 2007), http://www.irs.gov/irb/2007-29_IRB/ar10.html; Internal Revenue Serv., Rev. Proc. 2007-46, Bulletin No. 2007-29 (July 16, 2007), http://www.irs.gov/irb/2007-29_IRB/ar11.html.

established during the life of the policyholder. The trust is the owner and beneficiary of the insurance policy. Once transferred, the trust has complete control over its administration.

When the insured dies, the trustee invests the proceeds and manages the trust for the beneficiaries' benefit. This means that the trust is not funded until the insured dies. The trust provides liquidity to the insured's estate.

There are requirements for a valid life insurance trust:

1. The trust must be irrevocable.
2. Any retention of rights will invalidate the trust for tax purposes.
3. The policy owner cannot be the trustee.

If the client funds an irrevocable life insurance trust with an existing policy and dies within three years, the trust will be discarded, and the full value of the policy will be included in her gross estate.

Since these trusts are irrevocable, it is important to consider all possibilities before setting one up.

Q. Other Considerations

A client may write a letter of instructions to his executor and survivors. This letter is an informal document that gives specific instructions that cannot be altered. The client can leave the letter with the executor or include it with the will. This letter would include the following information:

- Client's name (including aliases), address, date of birth, place of birth, citizenship status, Social Security number
- Marital status, including partner's name, contact information, date of birth, place of birth, Social Security number, citizenship status
- All children's names, contact information, dates of birth, places of birth
- Information on armed forces service, including date of discharge and location of discharge papers (DD-214)
- Address of employer, with human resource contact information
- Names and contact information for everyone the client wants notified upon death
- Location of key documents, including the will
- Funeral and burial instructions, even if included in the designation of agent form
- Personal matters not included in the will, but helpful to the executor:
  - location of bank accounts and numbers
  - location of insurance policy and policy numbers

- brokerage accounts (type)
- names and contact numbers for broker, banker and insurance agent
- names of beneficiaries on each account or policy
- credit card accounts, including location of all cards, and the three-digit security code on the back
- contact information for credit card companies
- location of deeds
- location of safe deposit box or home safe and how to get into it
- name of all who have access to safe deposit box or home safe
- description of death benefits due
- list of assets (personal and real estate)
- emotional maturity of any children
- description of relationship with biological family members
- Instructions for what to include in the obituary—biographical information including major employers, honors received, education, membership in professional organizations, and notable achievements
- Inscription to be placed on the headstone or grave surface
- Passwords and login information for computers, online banking, and other electronic applications

R. Conclusion

Creating an estate plan for your lesbian and gay clients requires consideration of issues not usually apparent or applicable in heterosexual estates. You are in a position to guide your clients through the process and remind them to consider matters they may not otherwise think about.

Preparing an extensive and comprehensive client will questionnaire is a good way to start the process. The questionnaire serves as the means to prod clients into thinking about the entire process and all their assets. It requires them to consider more than the obvious, which for many clients is simply how to avoid probate.

Chapter 5

Avoiding Probate

Avoiding probate can benefit lesbian and gay clients, because keeping assets out of probate lessens the chances of a will challenge. Creating an estate plan that allows clients to control their assets and keep them out of probate is preferred.

After all, if the only thing the challenger can win is the decedent's jockeys, why bother. People challenge wills because they want the money. Take the money out of the equation, and probate challenges disappear. People also want to avoid probate because they believe it is time-consuming and costly—and it can be if proper planning is not implemented.

Like most people, lesbian and gay clients want an estate plan that will protect their designated beneficiaries, honor their relationships, and prevent challenges from estranged or vindictive family members. Couples want to protect each other and the assets they accumulated together.

There are times when probate may be helpful. The probate court provides supervision, which can be useful to clients who want judicial oversight. For the most part, however, settlement of the estate moves faster if the assets are outside probate.

Probate requires creditors to submit claims against the estate. Those claims must be filed within a specified period. Failure to meet those requirements leaves the procrastinating creditor in the dust. However, if most of the decedent's assets are nonprobate assets, the creditors may file a claim against an estate that either does not exist or consists solely of the decedent's "stuff."

Creditors can file only against the decedent's assets. If the assets are transferred to a beneficiary, there is nothing available to pay debts.

A. Estate Planning Issues Involving Marriage Equality

If a lesbian or gay couple marries, is the surviving spouse liable for the deceased spouse's debts? If the couple lives in a nonrecognition state, does their marital status matter? If the marriage is not recognized by the state, can creditors claim that a marriage exists? Will the courts recognize the marriage for purposes of paying creditors? What happens if the couple married while living in a recognition state? Could a creditor argue that the marriage is valid even though the couple moved to a nonrecognition state?

These questions are cropping up with increasing frequency—and creditors are not the only ones raising these issues. What happens if a will is successfully challenged but the couple was married in a recognition state? Can the probate court in a nonrecognition state ignore the marriage? Is the surviving spouse entitled to a spousal share under the intestacy statutes? Could a court recognize the marriage to allow creditors to recover from the surviving spouse, but refuse recognition for other purposes?

These questions have not been answered. Repeal of DOMA may provide some answers or arguments. But, the 11th Amendment will also come into consideration. How does it affect an individual state's response? Unless the U.S. Supreme Court issues a decision similar to *Loving v. Virginia*[1] about marriage equality, we will not know for sure.

B. Standard Methods of Avoiding Probate

Avoiding probate is not difficult but does require advance planning. Living trusts, joint tenancy with right of survivorship, payable on death accounts, transfer on death provisions, life insurance, pension or retirement fund designations, and inter vivos gifts are ways to avoid probate. Some of these formats are easy to create and administer, while others require more time, effort, and money.

Living Trusts

Living trusts are discussed in Chapter 4. A living trust, also known as an inter vivos trust, can be either revocable or irrevocable.

A revocable living trust gives the grantor complete control over all property transferred to the trust during her lifetime. These trusts provide a flexible format, allowing the grantor to make changes to the trust.

Living trusts are often more expensive to set up than a will. They are usually more expensive to administer both during the grantor's life and after her death. And, the grantor must fund the trust when it is established and remember to title all property accumulated in the future in the trust. Clients often forget that even though the trust exists automatically once they sign the document, there is nothing in it until they fund it.

---

1. 388 U.S. 1 (1967).

Practice Tip

The initial will questionnaire can be an important tool if you intend to assume responsibility for transferring assets. The clients must disclose all assets on the questionnaire.

The engagement agreement should include a provision that you are not responsible for transferring assets that are not disclosed by the client. Include a provision telling the client of his continuing responsibility to let you know about newly acquired assets.

Using an annual reminder letter to trust clients should be sufficient notice that they need to tell you about anything they acquired during the previous year. Use this letter even if you are not responsible for adding assets to the trust, but do not forget to let the client know whether there will be additional fees involved. The letter can make an ongoing offer to help.

It is our responsibility, as the lawyer involved, to show the client how to transfer their assets into the trust. Failure to fund the trust leaves the client with a sheaf of papers and a potential probate nightmare.

Some lawyers assume responsibility for transferring assets into the trust. This increases the cost but does ensure that the trust is funded. It is a service to offer a client and one that can be handled by an attorney's support staff.

An annual written reminder regarding any assets accumulated during the year is a good client service. Your malpractice carrier will also approve.

Joint Tenancy

This is a form of property ownership; its main benefit is the "right of survivorship" provision. When one joint tenant dies, the surviving joint tenant takes sole ownership of the property, outside of probate. That means that title is transferred by "operation of law."

The title transfer is immediate, although some states may require an affidavit of survivorship or similar document. Check with the local probate court for the appropriate form. A sample of the Ohio Survivor Affidavit is included in Appendix A.

This can be the best way to avoid probate if the couple has joint ownership of real estate. Another advantage is that this title is not subject to challenge.

Not all couples will benefit from holding real estate in joint tenancy. This is a discussion to have with your client. Some clients will want to hold title with multiple joint tenants. This situation, while not common, raises additional legal issues the clients may not consider.

The property may become subject to the debts of each individual joint owner. Creditors may file a claim against the share owned by the decedent even after title has transferred.

An individual owner may sell his share to someone else or mortgage his share. That action may destroy the survivorship provisions and make all owners tenants in common.

Joint tenancy works well with two people. Each holds a 50% share of the property. The surviving joint tenant receives the decedent's share and gains full title of the property.

One disadvantage involves taxes. The IRS presumes that the first person to die owned 100% of the property. This is a rebuttable presumption. The survivor must provide documentation showing his contributions to the purchase and upkeep of the home. The couple should maintain written records that reflect their individual contributions to the property.

With the current federal estate tax exemption at $5 million, most clients will not be affected by the presumption. However, state estate taxes may remain an issue.

Tenancy in Common

A tenancy in common is the default form of ownership. Each person named in the deed owns a separate and distinct share of the property. The co-owners may own shares in varying sizes. For example, one person may own a 75% share and the other 25%. A tenancy in common is often used with unmarried owners or those who contribute unequal amounts to the purchase of the property.

Real property transferred through probate is usually titled in this fashion. There is no right of survivorship; each owner has control over her individual share. One owner can mortgage her share and the other owners cannot object.

A tenancy in common may be a viable alternative for lesbian and gay couples that want to purchase a house but are in different financial situations. Each owner could then execute a transfer on death deed or affidavit transferring that person's share to her partner outside of probate. Some states[2] have transfer on death provisions for real estate.

---

2. Arkansas, Arizona, Colorado, Indiana, Kansas, Minnesota, Missouri, Montana, Nevada, New Mexico, Ohio, Oklahoma, and Wisconsin.

Practice Tip

It may help to mention how specific property is titled in the will. This clarifies the status of the property. When the property is sold or transferred, rewrite the will to reflect that change.

Tenancy by the Entireties

Many states[3] allow only married couples to enter into an "estate by the entireties." Some of these states allow tenancy by the entireties only for real estate.[4] This form of ownership protects the property from creditors. Each person is deemed to own 100% of the property. This can be a valuable protection from creditor claims.

Several of the states are marriage equality states, recognize same-sex marriage, or provide legal recognition of and protection for lesbian and gay couples.[5]

A will cannot countermand a recorded deed.

Married couples receive an exemption from property tax reassessment when one owner dies, but this may not be true for lesbian and gay couples. It will depend on state law and whether the couple owns property located in a recognition or nonrecognition state.

A transfer of title from joint tenancy to a surviving partner is a change of ownership for property tax purposes. This transfer may result in a reassessment of property taxes. That is another consideration for a couple to make when deciding to purchase real estate. If one partner is old enough for a homestead exemption or age-based property tax consideration, a reassessment may result in higher property taxes.

Life insurance is a tool that can be used to provide a liquid asset that the surviving partner can use to pay any property tax increase.

Joint Tenancy on Bank Accounts

Joint tenancy is not limited to real estate. People can open bank accounts as joint tenants. Both parties have equal rights in and access to the account. Joint tenancy accounts include checking, saving, certificate of deposit, and other

---

3. Alaska, Arkansas, Delaware, District of Columbia, Florida, Hawaii, Illinois, Indiana, Kentucky, Maryland, Massachusetts, Michigan, Mississippi, Missouri, New Jersey, New York, North Carolina, Oklahoma, Oregon, Pennsylvania, Rhode Island, Tennessee, Vermont, Virginia, Tennessee, and Wyoming.
4. Illinois, Indiana, Kentucky, Michigan, New York, North Carolina, and Oregon.
5. District of Columbia, Hawaii, Illinois, Maryland, Massachusetts, New Jersey, New York, Rhode Island, and Vermont.

common bank accounts. Account owners sign the required bank form as "joint tenants with right of survivorship."

These accounts require only one signature on checks and other withdrawals, as both joint tenants have equal access to the funds. Another format is for the joint tenants to arrange with the bank that two signatures are required for any withdrawal.

Creation of a joint tenancy in a bank account creates an immediate and present interest in both parties to the account assets. However, no gift results from setting up a joint tenancy account.

Gift taxes come into play in another way. If one joint tenant is making all of the deposits, a gift is made whenever the other tenant withdraws money. As long as the total amount, on an annual basis, is $13,000 or less, there is no gift tax liability.

The parties on a joint account need to keep detailed and accurate records concerning deposits and contributions to the account.

In any joint tenancy, whether bank accounts or real estate, the assets will be included in the estate of the first joint tenant to die. If the surviving joint tenant cannot establish, to the satisfaction of the IRS, proof of her contribution, the entire amount will be included in the decedent's taxable estate.

With real estate, this includes any capital improvements. When the surviving owner dies, the full amount of the account will be included in that estate. This can result in double taxation. See Internal Revenue Code (IRC) Section 2040.

Payable on death (POD) accounts, also known as Totten trusts, allow the account holder to name a beneficiary and to transfer the account on death outside of probate. The beneficiary receives all of the money in the account when the holder dies but has no present interest in the account. The bank distributes the property directly to the named beneficiary, and probate is unnecessary.

The bank will provide account owners with information on the procedures for the beneficiary to use to obtain possession of the money. Some bank personnel may believe a court order is required to release the account assets. State law and local court practice will determine the procedure for releasing account assets.

The account holder has full control over the account during her lifetime. The beneficiary has no present interest in and no authority to access the account during the holder's lifetime.

The account holder can name multiple beneficiaries on a POD account. Each beneficiary receives an equal share of the account assets. Alternative beneficiaries cannot be provided for in a POD account. If the account holder is concerned that a named beneficiary will not outlive him, then a POD account may be inappropriate. Or, the account owner will need to change the beneficiary as needed.

When a named beneficiary predeceases the account holder and a new beneficiary is not named, the account proceeds are paid into the decedent's estate. This can create a probate asset.

POD accounts are a good way for a gay or lesbian couple to provide for a partner. Many couples have joint bank accounts. However, some may retain separate accounts for any number of reasons. The POD account gives the client an opportunity to avoid probate and its potential for challenge to the holder's disposition of assets. Family members cannot dispute a POD designation.

The money in a POD account is included in the holder's taxable estate. This type of account carries no tax planning benefit, unless the beneficiary is a charity.

There is no real downside to creating a POD account. Most financial institutions have standard forms used to name the beneficiary. There is no special procedure needed to establish a POD account. Parents often use POD accounts to transfer assets to children.

Government securities, or **T-bills**, can also carry a POD designation. However, on these holdings there can only be only one owner and only one beneficiary.

More than one person can hold **United States Savings Bonds** as joint tenants. The forms for purchasing the bonds, generally Series E, can be found on the Federal Reserve Bank's website (http://www.frb.gov). The site also contains the information and forms necessary for cashing in the bonds.

Savings bonds do not seem to hold the allure they once did, but they are still held by many people. Some people have them from childhood, when they received them as gifts. The client can name a partner as the joint tenant of the savings bond. If there is no designation, the bonds are included in the probate estate.

In 2011, the government announced that all future sales of U.S. savings bonds will be done electronically, and paper certificates will no longer be issued. This will not only save money but will also make it easier to find the bonds.

Clients who have savings bonds should make a record of where the paper bonds are located. Making a list of the individual bonds, serial numbers, amounts, dates of purchase, and beneficiaries will make life much easier for executors, heirs, and the lawyer involved. The value of an individual bond can be learned via the Federal Reserve website. If paper bonds exist, they must be mailed to the Federal Reserve at the specified address. Electronic formats will make cashing in or transfer of the bonds much easier.

Transfer on Death (TOD) securities accounts are another format that can be used to transfer assets outside of probate. Some states refer to these as payable on death designations. Most brokerage firms have the necessary forms.

The client can designate individual stocks or brokerage accounts to be transferred upon death to a named beneficiary. This takes place under the Uniform Transfers-on-Death Securities Regulation Act (UTDSRA).

Not all states permit a transfer on death of securities. In those that do, the securities or brokerage account assets are transferred promptly to the named beneficiary. The UTDSRA must be adopted by the state to be effective. The following states have *not* adopted the UTDSRA:[6] Alaska, Colorado, Louisiana, Michigan, Missouri, New Mexico, North Dakota, and Texas.

Even if the client lives in a state that does not recognize TOD registration, it may be possible to accomplish this if the brokerage's principal office is in a state that does permit registration. This also holds true if the stock issuer is incorporated in a state that allows registration or the transfer agent's office is in such a state.

A living trust may be an appropriate alternative if none of these opportunities present themselves. It may be possible to create the living trust in a state that does recognize the TOD designation for securities.

Another reason a living trust is better than joint tenancy is because the grantor retains complete control over the asset and the beneficiary does not enjoy a present interest. The securities, bonds, and other holdings are transferred to the TOD beneficiary upon the death of the holder. These are not considered probate assets.

C. Transferring Title in Real Estate

Another tax pitfall involved with joint tenancies that is often seen with lesbian and gay clients involves transferring title into both names. The usual scenario is that one partner owns the house when the couple enters the relationship. Eventually, the parties decide they want the house held in both names as joint tenants with rights of survivorship. Without thinking about

---

6. *See* Unif. Law Comm'n, TOD Security Registration Act, Enactment Status Map, http://www.nccusl.org/Act.aspx?title=TOD%20Security%20Registration%20Act.

the consequences, the couple executes a joint and survivorship deed with right of survivorship and records the deed.

According to the IRS, a taxable gift is made when a joint tenancy is created—that is, when the deed is signed. Recording the deed is not required for a completed gift. If both partners did not make an equal contribution to the purchase of the property, the amount over $13,000 is deemed a gift and subject to gift taxes.

Using the above example, the parties merely added the second partner's name to the deed without a contribution. If the property is worth $100,000, the owner gave her partner a gift of $50,000. The gift is the amount that exceeds $13,000. The original owner must report a gift of $37,000 on a gift tax return.

The gift tax need not be paid when the return is filed; however, the assessed tax is deducted from the giftor's lifetime exemption of $5,000,000.[7]

The couple must also consider the possibility of one of them becoming incompetent. If one joint tenant becomes incompetent, it may be difficult or impossible for the other joint tenant to sell, encumber, or otherwise dispose of the property without filing for guardianship. The couple can plan for this possibility by executing a general durable power of attorney (GDPOA) for finances. A sample is in Appendix A.

D. Life Insurance

Life insurance proceeds are not a probate asset. Insurance proceeds are paid directly to the named beneficiary outside of probate. These proceeds are, however, part of the federal taxable estate. Some states also include life insurance proceeds in the taxable estate.

The only way life insurance proceeds are subject to probate jurisdiction is when the estate is the named beneficiary or the named beneficiary is dead. There are very few reasons to name the estate as the beneficiary. An example is in the case of a large estate that has no assets to pay taxes or costs. Then an irrevocable life insurance trust may be something to consider.

Life insurance is included in the decedent's taxable estate if the decedent owned the policy in the three years immediately preceding death. Estate taxes are paid on the net estate, after all appropriate deductions are made. Estate taxes do not distinguish between probate and nonprobate assets.

---

7. $5 million is the current lifetime exemption for gifts through 2012.

The federal estate tax is in flux. A $5 million exemption from estate taxes runs through 2012—after that is anyone's guess.

If the client has life insurance, find out the amount and the beneficiary's name when starting the estate plan process. Some of these policies may be significant, and their existence may affect your advice and planning strategy. If the client has no life insurance, you may suggest a consultation with a financial planner to whether it should be part of their overall estate plan.

The IRS will identify whether the decedent retained significant power over the policy. The agency's purpose is to determine if the policy proceeds are to be included in the decedent's taxable estate. The IRS looks at the "incidents of ownership" to determine who actually owned the policy. "Incidents of ownership" include the right to change or name beneficiaries; borrow against the policy; pledge the cash reserve, if any; surrender, convert, or cancel the policy; and select the payment option for paying premiums. All of these reflect ownership rights. To avoid the "incidents of ownership," a policy owner can transfer a policy to someone else. That person becomes the policy owner and is responsible for paying the premiums and controlling the policy. Usually, this is the policy beneficiary.

Life insurance that is transferred within three years of death falls into the "contemplation of death" category. The transferor cannot retain any "incidents of ownership." If the decedent retained these powers, the IRS will disallow the transfer and include the proceeds in the taxable estate.

Assigning Life Insurance Policies

Lesbian and gay clients may want to take out an insurance policy on each other. In order to take out an insurance policy on another person, however, the purchaser must have an "insurable interest" in the insured. Lesbian and gay clients may establish an insurable interest in their partner by showing they hold joint property or are in business together.

If an insurable interest cannot be established, a party can take out a policy and assign it to her partner once it is issued. The partner then becomes the policy owner and is responsible for paying all premiums. The insured has no control over the policy. Assigning a policy takes the insurance out of the insured's taxable estate.

The clients must inform the insurance company of the assignment, because that is the only way the insurance company will recognize the transfer. There is no assignment without following the required procedures. The insurance company has the necessary forms.

The insured can name anyone as the beneficiary, and that designation cannot be challenged. It is another way that a gay or lesbian client can provide for a partner without going through probate.

A transfer of a life insurance policy constitutes a gift to the transferee. The gift tax is based on the cash value of the policy. There are two types of life insurance: term life insurance and whole life insurance.

Term life insurance provides pure insurance. It pays a specified sum on the death of the insured. If the insured is alive at the end of the term, the policy expires. It may be renewed, but the premiums will usually be higher. Term insurance has no cash value. Transferring a term life insurance policy will not trigger a gift tax situation.

Whole life insurance, also known as universal life or cash value insurance, is permanent insurance. These policies are designed to provide permanent life insurance for the insured's entire life. This type of policy features a level premium and the opportunity to accumulate equity in the policy.

Transferring a whole life policy will trigger a gift tax situation. When the insured transfers a cash value policy to another, often the beneficiary, the current cash value of the policy will determine whether a gift tax return is required. The current annual exemption is $13,000. If the cash value is less than the exemption amount, no gift tax is involved. If it is over that amount, the insured must file a gift tax return. The gift tax will be due when the insured dies.

IRS regulations determine ownership of a policy. The "three-year rule" applies to transfers: Policies transferred within three years of the insured's death are subject to federal estate tax. This rule applies to transfers to an individual or an irrevocable life insurance trust (ILIT).

The IRS will also look for incidents of ownership. When a policy is transferred, the insured must forfeit all control over the policy. He cannot pay the premiums, change the beneficiary, borrow against the policy, surrender or cancel the policy, or select any beneficiary payment options. Retaining any of these rights will negate the transfer.

The insured may give the new owner an annual maximum gift of $13,000 to pay the premiums.

The transfer is an irrevocable event—once it is done, the insured cannot cancel the transfer. So, if a lesbian or gay couple assigns their respective policies to each other and then break up, there is no way to undo the transfer. This must prompt a serious discussion.

If the couple ends the relationship and either one stops making the premium payments, the policy will be canceled. The insured may no longer be able to get insurance, which could create a serious situation. This is one reason to consider an ILIT.

It is important for the client to understand the present value or worth of the policy when contemplating a transfer. IRS rules[8] are the primary source of information on valuing insurance. The regulations use the "replacement cost" (the premium) of the policy to establish the gift tax value.

Most insurance companies are able to provide an estimate of the gift tax value of a policy. This should be done before making the actual gift. Once made, the gift is irrevocable and cannot be rescinded. Insurance companies can provide the form required by the IRS to be included with the gift tax return.

Calculating the gift tax value of a life insurance policy can be simple or complicated. When there are any doubts, resolve them before the policy is transferred.

Transferring ownership of life insurance policies is a tactic that lesbian and gay clients need to know about. These clients want to take advantage of as many possibilities as are available to protect their assets and provide for each other.

E. Irrevocable Life Insurance Trusts

The irrevocable life insurance trust is another method of transferring policy ownership. Once transferred, the trust owns the policy and has complete control over its administration.

An ILIT can be funded or unfunded. A funded ILIT results when the trust owns the policy. The grantor also transfers income-producing assets that the trustee uses to pay some or all of the premiums. If the trust is an intentional defective grantor trust (IDGT), it will have no income tax liability on earned income. The grantor will be responsible for the income tax. Drafted properly, an IDGT allows a person to lower her taxable estate.

An unfunded ILIT holds only the life insurance policy. The grantor makes annual gifts to the trust, and the trustee uses those funds to pay the premiums.

The trust must be irrevocable and not subject to amendment. Any retention of rights will invalidate the trust for tax purposes.

---

8. Gift Tax Regulation § 25.2512-6(a).

The owner of the policy cannot be the trustee. The three-year rule applies to these trusts. If the insured dies within the three-year period, the proceeds are included in the decedent's taxable estate.

F. Transfer on Death Vehicle Certificates

Some states[9] allow owners to name a beneficiary to inherit their vehicle. The forms are usually available at the Department of Motor Vehicles.

Naming a beneficiary takes the vehicle out of the decedent's probate estate. If the clients own classic motor vehicles or very expensive ones, naming a beneficiary is a good way to exclude the asset from the probate estate. This designation does not take the vehicle out of the decedent's taxable estate.

These are statutory creations, and the statute will define what is meant by "vehicle." The definition can include automobiles, motorcycles, and boats.

G. Transfer on Death Deed/Affidavit

A transfer on death deed or affidavit permits a homeowner to name a beneficiary to receive title to the real estate after the owner's death. The property is transferred to the beneficiary outside of probate. This is similar to a survivorship deed. However, the homeowner does not relinquish any present ownership rights. The property is included in the estate of tax purposes.

Transfer on death provisions relating to real estate are more fully discussed in Chapter 4.

It is important to remember that neither a transfer on death deed or vehicle registration creates a current interest in the property for the named beneficiary. There is no gift tax, because the gift is not complete. The owner of the property can change the beneficiary at any time. The beneficiary has no legal right to object or interfere with any change.

This is a viable alternative for lesbian and gay couples who are contemplating adding their partner's name to their real estate or other property.

---

9. Arizona, California, Connecticut, Indiana, Kansas, Missouri, Nebraska, Nevada, Ohio, and Vermont.

Chapter 6

Children

As the "gayby" boom continues to thrive with lesbian and gay couples, legal issues abound. Various national organizations[1] estimate that lesbian and gay parents are raising 6 to 14 million children. According to the Williams Institute, more than one in three lesbians and one in six gay men are parents.[2]

An estimated 65,500 adopted children and 14,000 foster children live with lesbian or gay parents. That adds up to lots of kids, lots of lesbian and gay parents, and some unique and challenging legal issues. And, with more lesbian and gay couples in legally recognized relationships, the legal issues parents and children face become more important.

Children being raised by same-sex parents may be the product of adoption, artificial insemination, surrogate birth, or biological parenthood. In most cases only one party is recognized as the legal parent. The other parent is a legal stranger to the child.

When children are involved, or if clients plan to have children, including family issues in the estate plan is essential—and these issues involve more than a will or trust.

A. Nontraditional Families

The phrase "nuclear family" has traditionally referred to a married heterosexual couple raising children. This, for many people, still constitutes the only "family" that can be recognized.

The U.S. Census Bureau indicates that 70% of children live in a traditional family scheme. Most live with their married parents; others live with their unmarried biological parents. The 2000 Census[3] figures show that

---

1. Family Law Section, American Bar Association; Lambda Legal Defense Fund.
2. Gary J. Gates, M.V. Lee Badgett, Jennifer Ehrle Macomber & Kate Chambers, *Adoption and Foster Care by Gay and Lesbian Parents in the United States*, WILLIAMS INST., Mar. 2007, http://escholarship.org/uc/item/2v4528cx.
3. Sam Roberts, *Most Children Still Live in Two-Parent Homes, Census Bureau Reports*, N.Y. TIMES, Feb. 21, 2008, http://www.nytimes.com/2008/02/21/us/21census.html.

24.1% of children live in a traditional, nuclear family with married parents. That is down from 40.3% in 1970.[4]

Today, however, the term "nuclear family" is giving way to a greater reality. More children are living in nontraditional families then ever before. Unfortunately, the law in most states is not keeping up with these changes in familial makeup. This is most apparent for children living with lesbian or gay parents.

Children with same-sex parents often face a situation in which only one of the people they consider a parent is legally recognized as one. This is bad enough when the couple is together and raising the children. It can become a nightmare scenario if the couple ends their relationship and the non-legally recognized parent tries to maintain contact with the child.

Children living in families with only one legally protected parental relationship face myriad issues. These include:

- No right to inherit from the nonrecognized parent
- No right to receive Social Security benefits on that parent's account
- No right to be added to the health insurance benefits of that parent
- No right to other insurance benefits from that parent's employer
- No right to have the nonrecognized parent consent to needed emergency medical treatment or visit the child in the hospital.

Children tend to develop relationships with the adults in their lives without regard for the legal niceties. The parents and their lawyers, however, must concern themselves with how the law views the family and what protection, if any, is provided.

While the legal landscape is changing and lawyers are making creative arguments, there remains a great deal of work to do.

B. Questions to Ask

One of the first questions to ask a client is, "Who are the parents?" The answer could surprise you. In this day of in vitro fertilization and surrogacy, there may be four possible parents involved, and not just the two people sitting before you.

---

4. Brian Williams, Stacey C. Sawyer & Carl M. Wahlstrom, Marriages, Families & Intimate Relationships (Pearson 2005).

Sometimes a gay man will enter a legal marriage with a lesbian in order to start a family. The parties then continue their relationships with their same-sex partners while raising the children of the "marriage" together.

Another scenario may involve a gay male couple hiring a surrogate mother to have their child. The surrogate mother may be a lesbian who intends to remain a part of the child's life. Alter the sex and you can have a lesbian couple entering into an agreement with a gay male to father their children. The man may be the father of children birthed by both women.

Or the lesbian couple may swap eggs that are then fertilized by the same male donor. There is a genetic connection between all of them.

Yet another possibility: A male friend agrees to be the father. Initially, he agrees to forfeit all parental rights to the child, until his son is born. He always wanted a son, so now he wants to be involved.

It is important to know the players. It is essential to understand the subtle nuances that exist in this family unit. Your clients may not meet any definition of "family" you ever considered. But we are still talking about families, and your client will want to know how to protect them.

If the couple fails to, or is unable to, formalize their relationship and parental responsibilities, the results may be traumatic for all concerned.

In July 2011, the Ohio Supreme Court issued a decision[5] that created a tsunami effect in the state. Kelly Mullen and Michelle Hobbs were in a committed relationship. In 2003, Mullen decided she wanted to have a baby. Hobbs contacted a friend, Scott Liming, and asked him to be the sperm donor, and he agreed.

According to the decision, Mullen and Hobbs signed a purported donor-recipient agreement on insemination. This document, prepared by a lawyer, provided that Liming would be listed as the child's father but would have no other parental rights or responsibilities.

Mullen gave birth on July 27, 2005. The women created a ceremonial birth certificate listing them both. Liming formally acknowledged paternity. After the child's birth, Liming moved back to Ohio and began visiting his daughter even though he had waived all such rights in the agreement.

Mullen and Hobbs began having problems, and Mullen moved out, with the child, in October 2007. Two months later Hobbs filed a court action for visitation with the child. The juvenile court magistrate agreed with Hobbs and issued an order for visitation. The juvenile court judge, ruling on objections

---

5. *In re* Mullen, 2011-Ohio-3361 (July 12, 2011).

filed by both women, rejected the magistrate's decision. Hobbs appealed and lost. The Ohio Supreme Court accepted the case and upheld the lower court decisions.

According to the Ohio Supreme Court, in a 4–3 decision, Hobbs had no rights. The court held:

> Because the holdings of the juvenile and appellate courts are supported by the evidence and are not clearly against the manifest weight of the evidence, we must affirm them. . . . [We] decline to disturb the juvenile court's decision. We hold that competent, credible, and reliable evidence supports the juvenile court's conclusion that Mullen did not create an agreement to permanently relinquish sole legal custody of her child in favor of shared legal custody with Hobbs. Consequently, the juvenile court may not reach the questions of whether Hobbs is a suitable person to be a custodian of the child or whether shared legal custody is in the child's best interests. [citations omitted]

It is interesting to note that the court decided that Mullen never "permanently" intended to share custody with her former partner. Mullen executed a will appointing Hobbs as the child's guardian. She executed other documents giving Hobbs authority for medical care for the child. However, Mullen did not indicate that any of the documents were irrevocable. Without that stipulation, as far as the court was concerned, she had the right to change her mind—and Hobbs could do nothing about it.

It is also important to note that Hobbs repeatedly refused to execute a joint custody agreement with Mullen. Had she done so, Hobbs would have had enforceable rights under *In re Bonfield*.[6]

In *Bonfield*, the Ohio Supreme Court granted a juvenile court jurisdiction to consider a joint custody arrangement for a lesbian couple. Ohio law does not recognize a same-sex partner as a parent. However, the court stated that the parties could enter into such an agreement and have it adopted by a court.

Bonfield is unusual because the initial decision stated that second-parent adoptions were not permitted in Ohio. The court took the unusual step of rescinding the original decision and issued a revised opinion that deleted any reference to second-parent adoption. This action has been interpreted as leaving open the question of second-parent adoptions in Ohio. *Mullen* also does not mention second-parent adoption.

---

6. 97 Ohio St. 3d 387, 2002-Ohio-6660, 780 N.E.2d 241.

Mullen is a sad decision on many levels, but it provides a teachable moment: Lawyers can use this case to encourage their lesbian and gay parents to execute joint custody agreements. There is no upside to not having such an agreement.

And, if the biological or adoptive parent balks at signing such an agreement, the other partner will have a clear understanding of the ramifications.

Another lesson to be learned from this case is the value of unknown donors. As long as the donor is known, there is always the chance that the person will come back later seeking parental rights. So far, there is only one case—from Canada—that recognizes three parents for a child.[7] No U.S. court has done so, and it is unlikely that such an outcome will occur in the foreseeable future.

Oh, and, Mullen's legal woes are not yet over. Liming is currently seeking custody and visitation with the child. Mullen is arguing that he waived those rights with the donor-recipient agreement on insemination. However, he *is* the child's father and Mullen *did* encourage visitation. Liming and Mullen will be linked together for a long time to come.

C. Parents Misbehaving

One thing the *Mullen* case has in common with heterosexual custody cases is the example of bad behavior by parents. In this respect, lesbian and gay parents act just as poorly as heterosexual parents when the relationship ends: "When there is nothing left to fight about, we still have the kids."

Mullen is neither the first nor the last example of how adults use their children against their former mates. There are more cases involving lesbians fighting over children than gay men fighting over children. There is no empirical evidence explaining why, but the answer may simply be because more lesbians have kids than gay men.

When lesbians and gay men end their relationships and children are involved, one side usually raises the anti-gay arguments that have been raised for years. Lesbian and gay lawyers or LGBT-friendly lawyers are known to raise some of those very arguments.

Clients are entitled to more than knee-jerk reactions from their lawyers. All lawyers have had idiotic clients, but that is no excuse to initiate a course of action that benefits no one. The courts are filled with idiotic clients and their lawyers. We have all seen cases that dangled for years in the system

---

7. A.A. v. B.B., 2007 Ont. Ct. App. 2 [38] (20070102).

Practice Tip

While lawyers must be assertive in their representation, it does no one any good to raise the arguments that we fight against on a daily basis. This is a difficult but conquerable conundrum for lawyers.

Lawyers have a variety of tools available to help their clients. Mediation is preferable to litigation or arbitration, especially in family law situations. Use alternative dispute resolution in these situations. Learn about collaborative law and pursue a different philosophy. The outcome will benefit all concerned—including the children.

---

because the clients were intent on destroying each other and the lawyers did not want to interfere.

D. Protect the Children

The basic protection for a child's well-being is often defined as follows:

- Right to inherit; intestacy rights
- Right to be guardian, conservator, or executor of the parent's estate
- Right to have the parent make medical decisions
- Right to be covered under the parent's health insurance plan
- Right to have the family unit protected under the Family and Medical Leave Act
- Right to sue for wrongful death
- Right to receive Social Security benefits as a dependent child
- Right to maintain a relationship with the parent
- Right to receive financial support during the child's minority

Every child is entitled to the emotional security inherent in the legal recognition of family relationships. Parents and lawyers have a duty to ensure that those children are protected.

E. Estate Planning Issues

Important estate planning questions include the following:

- How to provide for children when only one parent is legally recognized
- How to protect the parenting rights of the nonrecognized parent

- How to ensure that the surviving partner will be named as the children's guardian if there is no adoption
- How to provide for the children when the state does not recognize them as a family

Lawyers need to know how to counsel clients who want to protect their children. If they live in a state where they cannot legally marry, the parenting questions become complex and convoluted. The Human Rights Campaign[8] is one of many good sources of information on the status of same-sex relationship recognition.

Guardian

An essential clause in any will involving minor or disabled children concerns guardianship. There is no excuse or reason to not name a guardian—the probate court will name a guardian if the parent does not.

Lesbian and gay partners generally name one another as the child's guardian. In states where second-parent adoption is not permitted, this will be the primary way for the surviving partner to continue his parent-child relationship.

If the couple has a joint or second-parent adoption order, their individual wills must clearly reflect that fact. Either include a reference to the case number and the issuing court or incorporate the court order into the will.

If there was no second-parent adoption, the legal parent may want to include a will provision indicating his consent to having his surviving partner adopt the child. Include language explaining why this consent is given. This establishes a paper trail reflecting the parent's intentions.

Naming an alternative guardian will govern a situation if the primary nominee is unable or unwilling to accept the appointment.

The guardian nomination guides the court in the matter, but unfortunately, there is no guarantee that the court will accept that guidance.

The testator may nominate a guardian of the person and estate. This may be the same person or different people. The guardian of the estate controls the child's finances. If there is a concern that the parent's surviving partner will not be named or that a relative will contest the appointment, the best defense is a trust. The trust can name the surviving partner as trustee. That authorizes the surviving partner to maintain contact with the child. In fact, the trust can specify regular interaction between the trustee and the child.

---

8. http://www.hrc.org.

The nonlegal parent has the option of naming a guardian in her will. However, since she has no legal rights, the nomination has no effect. If the child's legally recognized parent survives, that person has paramount rights.

As you can see, these complicated issues require clear and creative planning.

Bridge Guardian

In addition to naming a guardian for the child's person and estate, the will should include a clause naming a bridge guardian or "standby guardian."

A bridge guardian cares for a child after the parent's death or incapacity and before a court appoints the custodial guardian. This allows the parent to provide continuity in the child's life. It also allows a lesbian or gay couple to establish their intention concerning the child. It will give further evidence of the parent's intention that the surviving partner continue as the child's custodian.

If a bridge guardian is not named, a court may order the child removed from the home pending the appointment of the custodial guardian. The child may be placed in foster care or with relatives of the deceased parent. The child may not know these relatives if her parent was estranged from the family.

Children dealing with the death of a parent should not also be subjected to inter-adult combativeness. Continuity is very important to children. Since the parent's partner is a legal stranger to the child, there is no automatic right to custody of the child. Naming the partner as the bridge guardian may prevent additional trauma for the child.

Specifying a bridge guardian will also provide the authorities with an alternative to placing the child in foster care. If the child is not placed in foster care, she may be placed with a relative who is a stranger to the child or one the deceased parent dislikes. The goal is to protect the child and provide for the child's best interests. That should be specified in the clause naming the bridge guardian.

Illinois and New York permit the appointment of a bridge guardian and will grant immediate custody of the child to that person. This is a temporary order that continues until the court can address the child's future. However, the appointment can remain in effect until the will is probated.

If the deceased parent's partner is named as the child's guardian in a will, the bridge guardian stipulation follows the decedent's expressed interest.

Testamentary Provisions

Couples with minor children need an estate plan to provide for those children. While same-sex couples are no different from other parents, there is one exception. In most cases involving same-sex couples, only one member of the couple is considered the "legal parent." Without a second parent or joint adoption, there is no guarantee that the surviving partner will be granted any access to the children.

Both parties can provide for their children in a will. Naming the child in the will means that the bequest will be paid out after the testator dies without considering the child's age. If the child is a minor, the child's guardian will administer the funds. When the child turns 18, the guardianship ends and the child receives the bequest.

In order to forestall a challenge, the legal parent may want to give the surviving partner total control over the child's estate. A challenger learning that she may get the child but not the child's money may have second thoughts.

Remember the 1958 movie, *Auntie Mame?* starring Rosalind Russell? Mame's brother died and named her the guardian of his son. She got the nephew, Patrick. But her brother named the Knickerbocker Bank as the child's trustee. Mame got the kid . . . and Mr. Babcock, the banker. So, think of this as the "Auntie Mame" clause.

A testamentary trust will alleviate some concerns. The decedent's assets flow into the trust after death; there is no transfer of assets during the testator's lifetime.

The testator controls the disposition of assets to the child. A trust names the trustee who is responsible for administering the trust. The trust will also set the time when the trust terminates. That gives the testator the option of continuing the trust until the child reaches a more mature age. Rather than paying out the assets at 18, the trust may continue until the child turns 25 or 30 or later.

An irrevocable life insurance trust may be a viable alternative if the client anticipates a will contest. Even if the will is successfully challenged, the child's trust fund will remain inviolate. This type of trust may be used in conjunction with other estate planning techniques, including a living trust or testamentary trust.

F. Joint or Shared Custody Agreements

The purpose of joint custody agreements is to establish a written record of the parties' intentions concerning their children. While these agreements are private in nature and, usually, not sanctioned by a court, they do provide a record that the parties can refer to should a dispute arise.

Joint custody agreements can serve the purpose of providing the nonbiological parent with specific rights and responsibilities toward a child. Specifying rights provides support for the nonbiological parent if the parties break up and an attempt is made to prevent the child from continuing a relationship with that person.

The parties may agree to share custody and parental rights that are not provided for in state law. However, the legal parent has the right to waive any constitutional rights and share parental rights with a nonparent.

A joint custody agreement must clearly state the couple's intention to continue joint custody even if their relationship ends. The agreement should include provisions dealing with all aspects of the child's life during minority, such as custody, visitation, support, and college tuition.

Important Considerations

Some considerations need to be addressed. First, there is no guarantee that a court will recognize or uphold the agreement. Whenever possible, the parties should petition a court to accept the agreement. That turns it into a court order. This is the next best method to adoption.

Second, there are inherent conflicts between the parties to this agreement. One partner is the child's biological or adoptive parent. The other has no legal standing in relation to the child. The former is relinquishing specific parental rights that are superior to all others. The latter is accepting responsibilities and obligations that do not exist in law.

Third, there may be a donor or surrogate involved with creating the child. That person may also be a party to the agreement. The donor or surrogacy agreement should be incorporated into the joint custody agreement.

Because of the inherent conflicts, it is best for both parties to be represented by an attorney. At the very least, one of the parties must be encouraged to consult with a lawyer who can review the agreement.

The bare minimum is for the parties to acknowledge that they were encouraged to consult with a lawyer and elected not to do so. Redundancy in language on this issue is recommended.

As a practical matter, most couples that seek a joint custody agreement will see no need for separate counsel. That leaves the lawyer with the chore of documenting the file and confirming the advice in writing to both parties. A separate letter to each may be appropriate. Reiterate the significance of the agreement, the couple's actions, and the effect it will have on their individual legal liability concerning the child.

Watch Your Language

State law will determine whether the word "parent" may be used in the agreement. Some states limit the definition of parents to those with biological or adoptive ties. Using the word "parent" may create a problem for the client if there is a challenge to the agreement.

Most clients understand once the legal issues are explained. They may share custody, but in reality they are jointly parenting the children.

While a joint custody agreement cannot prevent an acrimonious split, it will make the parties think about the children's best interests during a time when the relationship is going well.

A joint custody agreement should serve the following purposes:

- Define the relationship between the parties.
- Define the parties' understanding of the relationship between the nonrecognized parent and the child.
- Provide an acknowledgment by the biological/adoptive parent that she understands her constitutional rights to the full care, custody, and control of the child and voluntarily waives those rights.
- Include a provision that any dispute will be resolved through mediation rather than litigation.
- Include a provision that neither party shall dispute the agreement or its effectiveness and that either can seek enforcement in court.
- Include a clause granting power to the nonlegal parent to approve medical treatment for the child. This avoids delays in an emergency when the child requires care and medical personnel balk because "you're not the mother."
- Including co-parenting clauses to provide for the child's care.
- Include a provision that reflects the parties' decision concerning custody, visitation, and support.

Practice Tip

Rather than taking an unwarranted risk, use "joint custody agreement" in lieu of "joint parenting agreement."

Practice Tip

Precise drafting is important. The more definite the language used, the more likely the court will sanction the agreement.

Practice Tip

Write the joint custody agreement in plain English. This is not the time to be obtuse. Clear, concise language is in order. Make sure the client understands all the words being used. Use names, not designation. It personalizes the document.

If the agreement is challenged, every effort will be made to have the agreement deemed unenforceable because of the words used. Err on the side of caution. The parties are agreeing to joint custody of the children. That will include custody, visitation, and support.

A joint custody agreement may be used to assist the court in reaching a decision on custody. While there is no guarantee that these agreements will be recognized by the court, they can be used to prove the parties' intentions concerning the children.

Anticipating that one parent may use the existing laws to avoid responsibilities under the agreement will help during the drafting stage. Remember that either party can use a legal argument to challenge the agreement.

The nonrecognized partner may have second thoughts about parenting when the relationship ends. Children are expensive. There is no legal obligation for anyone other than the biological or adoptive parent to support the child.

Agreeing to be legally responsible for a child's support is a voluntary action. The agreement language should be clear about what rights a party is waiving and what obligations a party is accepting. This gives rise to the existence of the "consideration" that is required in any contract.

Viewing the joint custody agreement as a contract between the parties will help in drafting the language.

In the beginning, there were few guidelines to follow, but that is changing. The courts are issuing decisions that can be used to further hone these agreements. No one should be afraid to adopt language from other sources. This is an agreement being entered into by two adults.

Clients are often reluctant to retain separate counsel to review the joint custody agreement. They are in sync and cannot foresee future problems. When clients refuse the suggestion to have the agreement independently reviewed, include a provision in the agreement concerning addressing the issue. Have both clients initial the clause. No one can force a client to follow sound advice.

A joint custody agreement is included in Appendix A.

Practice Tip

While there may be many occasions for joint representation, it is better to recommend that each party have his own lawyer, or at least have a separate lawyer review the agreement.

G. Second-Parent Adoption

Second-parent adoption provides legally recognized parental status to both partners in a same-sex couple that is raising children. This form of adoption permits the second parent to adopt without the first parent relinquishing any legal or parental rights. This results in the child having two legal parents. It also grants both parents the same legal rights concerning the children as those enjoyed by other parents. Because adoptions result from a court proceeding, the Full Faith and Credit clause of the United States Constitution comes into play. This means the adoption must be recognized in every state.

Second-parent adoptions usually occur when one partner is the biological parent or has already adopted a child.

Second-parent adoptions are not possible when the child is from a previous heterosexual relationship and the other biological parent retains parental rights. This type of adoption also does not work when the sperm or egg donor has not waived his or her parental rights. In that case the donor is the child's legal parent. This would also be true in a surrogacy case where the surrogate mother has not relinquished her parental rights.

The child benefits most from second-parent adoptions in these areas:

- The custody rights of the second parent are guaranteed if the other parent dies or becomes incapacitated.
- The child enjoys additional financial security because he will be eligible for Social Security survivor benefits if the second parent dies.
- The child is the recognized heir of both parents.
- The child is eligible for health benefits from both parents.
- The child can seek support from the second parent if the couple separates.

The following states recognize second-parent adoptions either by statute or through published court decision: California, Colorado, Connecticut, District of Columbia, Illinois, Indiana, Iowa, Maine, Massachusetts, Nevada, New Hampshire, New Jersey, New York, Oregon, Pennsylvania, Rhode Island, Vermont, and Washington. Hawaii and Delaware will begin recognizing civil unions in January 2012. That will allow lesbian and gay couples to have joint adoptions by using the state stepparent adoption procedures.[9]

In August 2002, the Pennsylvania Supreme Court ruled that second-parent adoptions are permitted under the state's adoption law. The court held, in a unanimous decision, "There is no language in the Adoption Act precluding two unmarried same-sex partners . . . from adopting a child who had no legal parents. It is, therefore, absurd to prohibit their adoption merely because their children were the biological or adopted children of one of the partners prior to the filing of the adoption petition."[10]

Some state court judges are granting second-parent adoptions. The decisions were issued in Alabama, Alaska, Delaware, Louisiana, Maryland, Michigan, Minnesota, Nevada, New Mexico, Texas, and West Virginia.

Florida used to have the most onerous state law that expressly prohibited lesbians and gays from adopting children. In 2010, the 3rd District Court of Appeal[11] affirmed the trial court and declared the statute unconstitutional under the Florida Constitution. The case was not appealed to the Florida Supreme Court.

Not all states permit second-parent adoption. Kentucky, Mississippi, Nebraska, Utah, and Wisconsin either prohibit or limit adoption by LGBT individuals or couples. Arkansas law prohibited lesbians and gay men from adopting or fostering children by a law passed in 2009 via a voter initiative, Arkansas Initiative Act 1. However, the Arkansas Supreme Court declared that law unconstitutional.[12]

The situation in Ohio is less clear. A 1998 case, *In re Doe*,[13] held that Ohio does not permit second-parent adoptions. However, a later Ohio Supreme Court case, *In re Bonfield*,[14] has thrown the issue into muddy waters. Initially, the decision included language that Ohio law did not permit second-parent adoption. The appellants requested a reconsideration of the decision. The Supreme Court rescinded the decision and reissued it without the language about second-parent adoption. Since then, no one knows whether the court would allow second-parent adoption.

---

9. Nat'l Ctr. for Lesbian Rights, Adoption by Lesbian, Gay, and Bisexual Parents: An Overview of Current Law (2011), http://www.nclrights.org/site/DocServer/adptn0204.pdf?docID=1221.
10. *In re* Adoption of R.B.F. and R.C.F. & *In re* Adoption of C.C.G. and Z.C.G., No J-100-2002, 2002, WL 1906000 (Pa. Aug. 20, 2002).
11. Fla. Dep't of Children & Families v. Adoption of X.X.G and N.R.G., 45 So. 3d 79 (Fla. Ct. App. 2010).
12. Ark. Dep't of Human Servs. v. Cole, 2011 Ark. 145 (Ark. Apr. 7, 2011).
13. *In re* Adoption of Doe, 719 N.E.2d 1071 (Ohio Ct. App. 1998).
14. 780 N.E.2d 241.

At present, there are no cases pending in Ohio on the issue. Many sources indicate that second-parent adoption is not permitted in Ohio. But, since the *Bonfield* decision, that is not necessarily accurate. The question remains open, and the right case and facts are needed to resolve the matter.

In December 2010, the North Carolina Supreme Court issued a decision[15] in *Boseman v. Jarrell* that sent waves of dismay through the LGBT community. This dealt with a lesbian couple that had obtained a second-parent adoption. The court ruled that second-parent adoption is not available in North Carolina. The court also ruled that any such adoptions that had been granted were void. The nonbiological mother, Julia Boseman, is an openly gay member of the North Carolina General Assembly.

The court ruled that the state's adoption statute does not allow adoptions when the legal parent retains parental rights unless the parent is married to the petitioner. North Carolina does not recognize marriage equality. The court also held that the county judge who granted the adoption did not have subject matter jurisdiction to do so.

The decision declared that all second-parent adoptions granted in North Carolina are void. The effect on the children involved in those adoptions is unknown.

While the court declared the adoption void ab initio, it also found that Boseman had consistently acted as the child's parent and could petition for custody. Further, the court found that Jarrell had acted inconsistently with her paramount parental status. The court stated:

> The record . . . indicates that defendant [Jarrell] intentionally and voluntarily created a family unit in which plaintiff [Boseman] was intended to act—and acted—as a parent. The parties jointly decided to bring a child into their relationship, worked together to conceive a child, chose the child's first name together, and gave the child a [hyphenated] last name. The parties also publicly held themselves out as the child's parents at a baptismal ceremony and to their respective families. The record also contains ample evidence that defendant allowed plaintiff and the minor child to develop a parental relationship [and] created no expectation that this family unit was only temporary. Most notably, defendant consented to the proceeding before the adoption court relating to her child. As defendant envisioned, the

---

15. Boseman v. Jarrell, 365 N.C. 577 (416PA08-2) (Dec. 20, 2010).

adoption would have resulted in her child having "two legal parents, myself and [plaintiff]."

This provides some consolation for North Carolina parents in a similar situation. However, custody is only one aspect of parenting. The children will have no rights to Social Security survivor benefits, and the nonbiological parent can walk away from any support obligations if joint custody is not sought. There is no indication the biological parent can force the other partner to assume parental duties after the relationship ends.

Another issue that arises because of this decision deals with lesbian and gay parents who obtained a second-parent adoption in North Carolina but no longer live there. Their adoptions are also void. If they live in a state that does not permit second-parent adoptions, they need to reassess their parental situation. The Full Faith and Credit clause will not protect them because of the North Carolina decision.

One caveat: The *Boseman* decision does *not* affect the rights of lesbians and gay men who want to adopt as individuals.

Colorado and Connecticut courts came to similar conclusions when interpreting their state statutes. The legislatures in those states responded by amending their adoption laws to permit second-parent adoptions. The same result is unlikely in North Carolina.

H. Should Adoptions Be Adversarial?

Adoptions are conducted in a court. The adoption decree is a court order entitled to be recognized throughout the country. The Full Faith and Credit clause applies to these court orders. Yet some within the LGBT legal community wonder whether these orders are enough.

Should counsel represent both parties? Would that lend greater credibility to the court orders? Would such a "contested" proceeding protect the parties if they move to a state that does not permit second-parent adoptions?

None of these questions have been answered; but they have been raised. When a heterosexual couple adopts a child, the court order is final and unassailable. Can the same be true of adoptions involving lesbian and gay couples?

The common response is that a court order must be honored. But, what would happen if one party challenges the adoption at some future date? Could the challenger argue there was no consent because the same lawyer represented both parties? Do lawyers representing these couples incur any liability? An argument against challenging the adoption is the biological parent consented at the time and failed to appeal the court's decision within the statutory period.

Again, the questions are raised with no answers. The family issues surrounding lesbian and gay parents are neither simple nor common. Because the majority of states do not recognize same-sex relationships, it behooves lawyers and their clients to consider worst-case scenarios.

I. Does the North Carolina Decision Portend Future Problems?

The *Boseman* case raises an issue about the validity of a second-parent adoption granted by a judge without explicit statutory authority. A general rule of law is that a validly entered adoption decree is valid unless set aside by an appellate court.

Adoption is a statutory creation. The adoption statute must be strictly construed, so the North Carolina decision raises an interesting issue. It is well established that subject matter jurisdiction cannot be waived. If the statute does not give a court authority, then it has none, and any judgment issued is void.

If a judge grants a second-parent adoption when the state law is silent or unclear on the issue, can the judgment be attacked later? Can it be attacked by anyone other than the parties to the adoption? Does the issue of standing arise? Can one state refuse to recognize an adoption when it was granted in another state whose law does not permit second-parent adoptions? If a court decision is void where entered, is it entitled to protection under the Full Faith and Credit clause?

This may be a topic for a law review article, but the questions need to be considered by lawyers seeking to help their clients. There are judges granting second-parent adoptions in states where the law is silent or unclear. No one, other than the children and the parents, are parties to that judicial process. However, what happens if things go south between the parties or others who take an interest?

For example, could the biological grandparents file an action to set aside the adoption if the biological parent dies? What are their rights? One question prompts another . . . and another . . . and another.

Nevertheless, lesbian and gay couples that want to raise children are to be encouraged to seek an adoption order—and to include language concerning the parties' intention to have a second-parent adoption in the joint custody agreement. Including that information will support the contention, by either party, of their intent concerning adoption.

J. Adoption Tax Credit

Section 36 (c) of the Internal Revenue Code (IRC) authorizes a one-time adoption credit of $12,000 for qualified adoption expenses. The credit phases out for those with an adjusted gross income (AGI) over $183,180. It is unavailable for people with an AGI over $222,180.

There is also a federal child tax credit for dependents 16 years old or younger of $1,000.00. This credit phases out for AGI over $75,000.

Normally, a parent cannot claim the credit for adopting a spouse's child. DOMA prohibits the IRS from recognizing same-sex couples as "spouses." However, domestic partners are not spouses. Congress wrote the law to extend the credit to all but stepparent adoptions.[16]

The IRS has denied the adoption credit to some same-sex couples. One reason is because the birth mother has not terminated her parental rights. The other reason is because the second parent is the birth mother's domestic partner.

In October 2011, the IRS notified a lesbian couple that it reconsidered the denial of the tax credit and would issue a full refund. It appears the IRS will no longer challenge the credit to lesbian and gay couples in second parent adoptions.

A client who is denied the adoption credit has 30 days to appeal the IRS ruling. The appeal should demand that the IRS provide the legal authority upon which the decision is based.

Section 36(c) does not require termination of parental rights. It also does not mention domestic partnership or joint responsibility for supporting the child. These tend to be the reasons given for the denial.

Notice 97-9 allows an unmarried couple that adopts the same child to combine the qualified adoption expenses and then allocate the adoption credit between them.[17] However, a second-parent adoption is not a joint adoption. The couple may want to give the credit to the one with the higher income. But, if one is subject to the phaseout, allocate the credit to the other. The credit can be carried forward for five years if the tax liability is less than the credit amount. Multiple adoptions are eligible for multiple credits and carried forward on a first in, first out (FIFO) basis.

The appeal should demand that the IRS provide the legal authority upon which the decision is based.

---

16. *See* Santa Clara Law, The Adoption Credit for Second Parent Adoptions (Aug. 3, 2011), http://law.scu .edu/blog/samesextax/the-adoption-credit-for-second-parent-adoptions.cfm.
17. I.R.C. § 23(i); I.R.S. Notice 97-9.

An article, *Tax Treatment of Adoption Expenses*, in the April 2010 issue of Journal of Accountancy, provides a good discussion of this issue.[18]

K. Artificial Reproductive Technology

Lesbian and gay couples may use several methods to start a family. Adoption is one. Artificial reproductive technology (ART) and surrogacy are two others. These methods present their own set of problems. There is no national policy concerning ART, and the state laws are wide-ranging.

ART includes artificial insemination, egg donation, sperm donation, embryo donation, and in vitro fertilization (IVF), including intracytoplasmic sperm injection (ICSI)[19] and embryo transfer.

ART can result in fragmented parentage. For example, there may be five different "parents": sperm donor, egg donor, surrogate/gestational host, and two non–biologically related individuals who will raise the child. As a result, ART contracts are essential to avoid problems after the birth. Further, these contracts must be completed *before* pregnancy.

The fragmented parentage of the child may cause legal issues that challenge the intended parents' rights. The surrogate, gestational host, egg donor, embryo donor, and sperm donor may all claim parental rights. Use the ART contract and the joint custody agreement to address and resolve these issues.

Artificial reproductive technology has exceeded the laws in place in most states. Those laws were passed at a time when ART was the stuff of science fiction.

Attorneys whose practice is concentrated in reproductive law are at the forefront in the ever-changing landscape of this area. Reproductive attorneys must make a continuing effort to stay on top of new case law and legislation that affect client rights.

Known Donors

There are risks involved in using known donors. The reasons for using a known donor may be obvious, but the prospective parents may not consider the risks. For example, a lesbian couple using a known sperm donor may discover that the donor wants to exercise his parental rights concerning the child.

---

18. http://www.journalofaccountancy.com/Issues/2010/Apr/20092398.htm.
19. Intracytoplasmic sperm injection is an in vitro fertilization procedure in which a single sperm is injected directly into a single egg.

Some egg donors, like sperm donors, are anonymous because there is no direct interaction between the intended parents and the donors. Sometimes using an unknown donor can simplify matters by reducing the number of known persons involved in the process.

Some courts may not honor an agreement in which the donor relinquishes his parental rights. Generally, a parent's duty to financially support a child cannot be waived. The duty is owed to the child, not to the other parent. Children have a right to be financially supported by their parents.

In most donor agreements the donor agrees to waive all parental rights. The donee agrees to hold the donor harmless from all obligations, including support. This is the most common way in which lesbian couples start families.

Gay men require the services of an egg donor or surrogate. One of the men provides the sperm used to fertilize the egg. These agreements are similar to those used by lesbian couples. One significant difference involves surrogacy.

If the surrogate uses her own eggs, she is the child's biological mother. However, even if an egg donor is used and the fertilized egg is implanted in the surrogate, maternity issues remain. The surrogate may refuse to release the child to the gay couple. She can seek full custody from a court unless she relinquishes all parental rights. That may result in a more traditional custody battle involving the mother and the father.

The father's gay partner will have not only have no legal rights to the child, he will have no ability to obtain any.

L. Donor Agreements

Donor and surrogacy agreements must be carefully drafted. It is important for a lawyer to represent each party. The parties to these agreements will include some or all of the following:

- Sperm or egg donor
- Prospective biological mother or father
- Partner of the prospective mother or father
- Spouse of the donor or surrogate

A separate contract between the intended parents and an egg donor is advisable. This contract must include a waiver of all parental rights on the part of the donor. This contract will be necessary only if a known egg donor is used.

Incorporating the donor contracts into the joint custody agreements is a good way to ensure continuity. It is less helpful to write one agreement that covers all aspects of the ART process. This complicates the legal drafting, but the effort pays off in developing a comprehensive plan for all concerned.

Egg donation consists of the removal of the donor's eggs, fertilization by the intended father's sperm, and transfer to the intended recipient mother or to a surrogate. Sperm donation is similar. It involves the use of a donor's sperm to fertilize the egg of either the intended mother or an egg donor. It is possible for a couple to use both a sperm and egg donor and a gestational host.

M. Egg and Sperm Donor Contracts

A donor contract is needed when a known donor is used. No contract is required for unknown donors because those eggs or sperm donations come from a registry.

The following is a nonexhaustive list of possible contract provisions for egg and sperm donor contracts:

- Explicit relinquishment of all parental rights by donor
- Voluntary and informed legal and medical consent
- Financial responsibility of the intended parents for all expenses
- Compensation, if any, due the donor
- Full legal custody and parental rights for intended parents
- Required testing of everyone (including donor's partner/spouse, if any) involved for STD, including HIV and AIDS
- Medical examination of the donor to determine if suitable
- Financial responsibility for the use, storage, and disposal of excess embryos
- Specification of the responsibilities, privacy, or confidentiality concerns of all parties
- Specification of the laws that will govern the contract and its terms
- Provision reflecting the intentions of the parties
- Agreement by the donor to assist the intended parents in obtaining any court orders needed to establish their parental rights and responsibilities
- Agreement by the donor not to file any legal action against the intended parents with the intent of gaining custody or parental rights with the child

- Agreement by the donor not to attempt to establish a parent-child relationship (may not apply where a gay male couple and lesbian couple agree to co-parent children)

N. Surrogacy

The majority of states have no laws directly related to surrogacy. Some states criminalize paid surrogacy contracts; others declare all surrogacy contracts void and unenforceable. Surrogacy is expensive, with costs exceeding $100,000, including health insurance and medical expenses. Some state laws require health insurance policies to include surrogacy expenses. Of those, some specifically exclude single people, lesbians, gay men, and transgender individuals. As a result, DIY surrogacy does not bode well for anyone involved—especially the child.

Arkansas, California, Illinois, Massachusetts, New Jersey, and Washington permit surrogacy. The type of surrogacy contract permitted in the six states varies. Illinois allows only gestational surrogacy; New Jersey and Washington only permit uncompensated surrogacy agreements.

Eleven states[20] prohibit surrogacy agreements. The law in the remaining states is either mixed or unclear.[21]

There are four different approaches for determining maternity in gestational surrogacy arrangements: (1) intent-based theory (California, Nevada, New York), (2) genetic contribution theory (Ohio), (3) gestational mother preference theory (Arizona, North Dakota,), and (4) the "best interest of the child" theory (Michigan, Utah).[22]

Surrogacy remains an unsettled area of law. There is no national surrogacy policy, although California has adopted a progressive view of surrogacy cases, including cases involving lesbian and gay couples.

A traditional surrogacy involves a woman using her own egg, and she is, therefore, the biological mother. This arrangement is fraught with danger. While cheaper up front, if the surrogate changes her mind later, it becomes much more expensive. Many lawyers will not touch a traditional surrogacy arrangement.

---

20. District of Columbia, Florida, Michigan, Nebraska, Nevada, New York, North Dakota, Texas, Utah, and Virginia.
21. *See* Human Rights Campaign, Surrogacy Laws and Legal Considerations, http://www.hrc.org/issues/parenting/surrogacy/surrogacy_laws.asp.
22. Amy M. Larkey, *Redefining Motherhood: Determining Legal Maternity in Gestational Surrogacy Arrangements*, 51 Drake L. Rev. 605, 622 (2003); *see also* Malina Coleman, *Gestation, Intent, and the Seed: Defining Motherhood in the Era of Assisted Human Reproduction*, 17 Cardozo L. Rev. 497, 505–29 (1996).

A gestational surrogacy, on the other hand, involves a surrogate who has no biological connection to the child. This involves an egg and sperm donor.

Article 8 of the Uniform Parentage Act (UPA) specifically addresses surrogacy agreements, but most states have not adopted it. Article 8 treats a surrogacy agreement as one that should be approved by a court through an adoption-like process. The court could verify the qualifications for the surrogate and the intended parents. The UPA also provides that any surrogacy contract not approved by a judge is unenforceable. Under the UPA, if the prospective parents renege on an unapproved surrogacy agreement, they may be liable for child support.

In 2008, the ABA adopted a model act[23] addressing reproductive technologies, including surrogacy. This model proposes two alternatives to handling surrogacy agreements. One requires preapproval by a judge for any agreement where neither prospective parent has a genetic tie to the child. The other introduces an administrative procedure. This would be used in cases where at least one of the prospective parents has a genetic tie to the child. All parties are required to submit to specific requirements, including a mental health evaluation, health insurance coverage, and legal consultation.

One case worth noting is *K.M. v. E.G.*[24] The couple terminated their long-term lesbian relationship in 2003. During the relationship, E.G. gave birth to twins. K.M. donated her eggs for the IVF procedure, and E.G. served as the gestational host. The couple used an anonymous sperm donor. The twins were five years old when their mothers separated.

K.M. signed the standard egg donor document relinquishing all parental rights to any children born. However, the couple agreed to have children together. The custody battle began after the relationship soured.

E.G. argued that K.M. had no legal rights concerning the children. The California Supreme Court disagreed. The court decided that the standard language in the egg donor contract did not apply to K.M. She and E.G. were co-parents. This landmark decision came down the same day as two other cases involving lesbian parents, *Kristine Renee H. v. Lisa Ann R.* and *Elisa B. v. Superior Court.*[25]

---

23. ABA Model Act Governing Assisted Reproductive Technology (Feb. 2008), http://www.americanbar .org/content/dam/aba/publishing/family_law_quarterly/family_flq_artmodelact.authcheckdam.pdf.
24. 37 Cal. 4th 130, 117 P.3d 673 (2005).
25. Kristine Renee H. v. Lisa Ann R., 37 Cal. 4th 156 (2005); Elisa Maria B. v. Superior Court, 37 Cal. 4th 108, 117 P.3d 660 (2005).

In *Kristine H.* the California couple used artificial reproductive technology to beget their child. California[26] law allows intended parents to seek a determination of maternity before the child is born. Kristine and Lisa obtained such an order that declared them both the child's mothers.

When the couple separated a few years later, Kristine challenged Lisa's rights and prevented her from seeing their child. The California Supreme Court ruled that Kristine was barred from challenging the court order she sought before the child's birth.

Unfortunately, we continue to see parents challenging orders they sought and consented to after the relationship ends. California holds the parents to their earlier actions; North Carolina does not.

Elisa B. presents a different situation. Elisa and her partner, Emily, had twins. Emily gave birth to the children. One of the children, diagnosed with Down syndrome, requires constant care.

After the couple separated, Elisa stopped visiting and ended financial support for the children. Elisa claimed she had no legal responsibility for the children because she was not their biological mother. The California Supreme Court disagreed. The court held that Elisa is a co-parent and obligated to pay child support.

This decision is especially important because the court ruled that same-sex couples that use artificial reproductive technology are both legal parents. The court stated that the parties' gender, sexual orientation, or marital status does not matter when determining legal parentage.

These cases are examples of how courts are establishing equity in parenting and family law for same-sex couples and their children.

Gay male couples most often use surrogacy. These couples may want to consider contracting with an egg donor rather than using the surrogate's eggs. That makes the surrogate a gestational host with no biological connection to the child.

If the surrogate initiates a custody challenge, the egg donor and the biological father may trump her standing. A clear and precise surrogacy agreement will also help refute the surrogate's position.

This argument does present a potential problem for lesbian couples. In some cases, one partner will donate her eggs to her partner, who serves as the gestational host. Many egg donor agreements require the donor to relinquish all parental rights. Should the couple split, the birth mother tends to use that

---

26. Colorado, Connecticut, Florida, Illinois, Maryland, Nevada, Pennsylvania, Virginia, and Wisconsin also allow prebirth determinations.

as a weapon to deny parenting status to the donor. Couples anticipating egg donation need to read the agreement and cross out the language requiring the donor to give up her rights.

The couple can also sign an agreement addressing this issue. A well-written agreement between the parties will alleviate concerns. The couple needs legal advice before starting the process.

The adoption credit that is available under the Internal Revenue Code does not cover surrogacy costs.

O. Surrogacy Contracts

The variation in state law concerning surrogacy contracts presents additional challenges to couples pursuing this form of ART. Clients and lawyers must consider the following:

- The jurisdictional law relative to the state where the surrogate lives
- The state where the children will be born
- The state where the family will live
- The state law that will govern the contract

The essential parties to these contracts include the intended parents, the surrogate, her spouse, and the egg donor (and her spouse), if one is used.

The contract must specify the intended parents' legal rights and terminate the surrogate's parental rights. The contract should specify who would be the legal parents. Each party to the agreement must have separate counsel. This may include separate counsel for the surrogate and her spouse.

There are specific provisions to include. The following list is offered as guidance for the initial draft. It does not exhaust the possible clauses:

- Financial issues: surrogate compensation, attorney fees, use of trust account
- Medical and psychological screening within designated parameters
- Who pays for health or life insurance and contingencies if the insurance lapses
- Termination of the surrogate's parental rights and those of her husband
- Addressing multiple births, including whether selective reduction will apply
- Agreement concerning aborting the pregnancy if medically necessary
- Incorporation of the egg or sperm donor contract if one exists

- The parties' intentions regarding parental rights, obligations, and responsibilities[27]
- Specification that intended parents are financially responsibility for the child, even if the child is born/becomes disabled
- Legal and medical consent forms, including HIPAA language, signed by all parties
- Testing by all parties, including surrogate's spouse, for STDs, including HIV and AIDS
- Confirmation that the surrogate is physically able to conceive and carry the child to term
- Agreement by the surrogate to refrain from sexual relations during specified periods
- Attachment of all applicable laws from all states involved
- Description of the specific responsibilities of all parties, during and after the pregnancy
- Agreement by the surrogate not to establish a parent-child relationship and not to interfere with the parental rights of the intended parents
- Provision for individual and group therapy for the surrogate and her spouse
- Designatation of the law that applies to contract enforcement
- Mediation or arbitration of disputes, which court has jurisdiction, liability for costs and attorney fees

P. Federal Laws Affecting Children

The federal statutes that govern custody and visitation are the Parental Kidnapping Prevention Act (PKPA)[28] and the Uniform Child Custody Jurisdiction Enforcement Act (UCCJEA). The National Conference of Commissioners on Uniform State Laws drafted the UCCJEA to correct discrepancies between the old Uniform Child Custody Jurisdiction Act (UCCJA) and PKPA. The two are now compatible in relation to the child custody orders and their enforcement. As of June 1, 2006, 43 states adopted the UCCJEA.[29]

---

27. Johnson v. Calvert, 5 Cal. 4th 84, 19 Cal. Rptr. 2d 494, 851 P.2d 776 (1993).
28. Parental Kidnapping Prevention Act, 28 U.S.C. § 1738A.
29. See appendix B for a complete list of state statutory citations. Indiana, Louisiana, Massachusetts, Missouri, South Carolina, Vermont, and Puerto Rico have not adopted the UCCJEA.

Q. Categories of "Parent"

A "psychological" parent, also known as a "de facto" parent, is someone who developed a parent-child relationship but has no biological, adoptive, or legal relationship.

Many lesbians and gay men have developed this type of relationship with their partner's children. Some of those children are from earlier relationships or marriages. Some of the children have other biological, adoptive, or legal parents as well. However, in many lesbian and gay couples, the adult who developed this relationship with the child is the only other parent the child knows.

There is no common-law history of "psychological" or "de facto" parents. Most states do not include these categories in their definition of "parent." Some courts acknowledge the existence of adults who qualify as "psychological" or "de facto" parents. Many lesbian and gay adults seeking to continue their parent-child relationship argue that they qualify as "psychological" or "de facto" parents, but not all courts agree.

Two leading cases, involving lesbian couples and their children, provide excellent resources on the history of the concept and the conflict among the states.

In re Parentage of L.B.[30] is a 2005 case decided by the Washington Supreme Court. The court defined "de facto parent"[31] and "psychological parent."[32] The court decided that Carvin, the nonbiological mother, qualified as a "de facto parent" for visitation purposes.

The Washington court adopted the concept of psychological parenting under its authority to fill gaps in existing statutes. As is common, societal changes proceed faster than statutory updates.

The other case is *Jones v. Barlow*,[33] decided by the Utah Supreme Court in 2007. Unlike the Washington case, the *Barlow* court refused to adopt the "psychological parent" doctrine. The court rejected the doctrine because it would create a standard that would be difficult to administer, and the question was

---

30. *See In re* Parentage of L.B., 122 P.3d 161, 174–75 & 175 n.23 (Wash. 2005); Petition for a Writ of Certiorari at 11–24, Britain v. Carvin, 547 U.S. 1143 (2006) (No. 05-974), http://www.telladf.org/UserDocs/BritainvCarvinPetition.pdf (discussing the conflict among the states and describing the holdings of the states on both sides of the issue).
31. "de facto parent": one who functions as a child's actual parent.
32. "psychological parent": one who has a "parent-like relationship" that is based on daily interaction, companionship, and shared experiences of the child and adult.
33. 154 P.3d 808, 815–19 (Utah 2007).

one for the legislature. The Utah court held to the principle that parental rights were paramount absent a showing of unfitness.

Most states adhere to the position that a parent must be shown to be unfit before a court will interfere with parental rights. The main problem lies in the restricted definition of "parent."

Some courts are beginning to consider the child's best interest in relation to the "psychological parent," independent of what the biological parent may want. This can include a nonbiological parent who is living with the child. It is a creative argument made in the child's best interest.

Courts are considering the child's rights to parenting time, independent of what the biological parent may want.

One example occurred in a New York family court.[34] The court permitted a foster mother to visit with a former foster child over the biological father's objections. The court allowed the visitation because the child had a First Amendment right and due process interest in visitation regardless of the parent's opposition.

The court decided that the child had a fundamental right to maintain contact with the person with whom he had developed a parent-like relationship. In this case, the foster mother achieved "psychological parent" status. The child's best interest was met by continuing contact even though the parent objected.

Liberty interests are protected by the due process clauses of both the federal and state constitutions. The child's best interest is supposed to be the primary concern. Having the court appoint an attorney to represent the child may be required to ensure protection of the child's interests.

Most courts will appoint a guardian ad litem (GAL) for the child. However, many GALs are less concerned with the child's legal rights than with the accepted standard. The GAL must be more assertive in advocating for the child than they usually do. Often the GAL will decide which parent is "better" and argue for that person rather than deciding what is best for the child.

R. Life Planning Issues

Authorization for Medical Care of a Minor

The biological parent should execute an authorization for medical care of a minor. This allows the parent to name her partner as the person allowed to consent to the child's medical treatment.

---

34. Webster v. Ryan, 729 N.Y.2d 315 (N.Y. Fam. Ct. June 21, 2001).

A general durable power of attorney may also include such a provision, but it is generally better to have a separate, clearly written document. The partner needs to keep a copy or the original readily available. Copies should also be given to the child's school and doctor.

Travel

Traveling domestically or internationally presents unique challenges for lesbian and gay families.

In one situation, a lesbian couple found themselves being interrogated by personnel from a U.S. airline when they attempted to travel to Mexico on vacation. Airline personnel demanded to see documentation from the children's father allowing the women to remove the children from the United States. This was a public confrontation in full view and hearing of the children.

The airline's employees could not understand how two women could have two children if there was no father involved. The women explained that the children were conceived through in vitro fertilization. The airline personnel told them there was a possibility they would not be allowed into Mexico on the outgoing flight or back into the United States on their return. These women, and their children, were United States citizens.

These situations result from ignorance, and clients need to be aware of the potential problems.

Carrying legal documents that establish parental rights is one solution. A notarized statement that the children were conceived by artificial insemination may seem unnecessary, unless your clients run into ignorant airline employees.

Gay male couples may be subject to even greater scrutiny because of a general suspicion about men traveling alone with children. This may be particularly true if there is no familial resemblance.

Schools

Lesbian and gay couples must also deal with school authorities. Handling things on the first day of registration is best. Explaining the nature of the family to school officials will alleviate future problems.

The legal parent should execute a formal, written statement authorizing the school to consider his partner as having the same standing as the parent. The authorization should specify that the parent's partner is an emergency contact on an equal footing with the parent.

The parent should give the school a copy of all court orders that affect the children, and learn the identity of the people who are responsible for ensuring that the instructions are followed. It is important to get their names and contact information, including cell phone numbers, just in case. And, clients must be assertive and not afraid to call.

Taking the time to draft these statements will help the couple to plan for all contingencies. Include parent-teacher conferences, signing report cards, and attendance at school functions in the authorization. Use a catchall phrase such as "and any other situations, incidents, functions, or similar possibilities where a parent is needed by school officials." Review it with the school principal to determine if something should be added or clarified. This will help the child, the school, and the parents.

Attorneys should put contact information on all documents in case questions are raised. Sometimes having a lawyer's name on a document can help.

S. Conclusion

Raising children is always a challenge. The variations in state laws make it even more challenging for lesbian and gay couples.

Whenever possible, lesbians and gay men who are raising children must remember there are no shortcuts. If second-parent or joint adoption is available, the couple must pursue it. The other option is to file a petition in court to have the joint custody agreement formalized into a court order.

Court orders will bring the Full Faith and Credit clause into play. That will help the clients whether at home or abroad.

Chapter 7

Essential Estate Planning Documents

Lesbian and gay clients cannot be satisfied with just a will and a trust. Several other documents make up a complete estate plan:

- Living will
- Health care power of attorney
- HIPAA authorization
- Designation of agent
- General durable power of attorney (GDPOA)
- Business powers of attorney

A. Living Will and Health Care Power of Attorney

Living wills and health care powers of attorney (aka advanced directives) are essential for same-sex couples. Without them medical providers and medical institutions will look to blood relatives for health care guidance. The patient's partner will not be consulted and may, in fact, be prevented from visiting or participating in health care decisions.

A living will (LW) provides the patient's instructions concerning health care. The patient uses this document to specify the type of treatment plans he wants—or to prohibit the use of certain treatments.

No one is limited to the preprinted language. The signor may add additional instructions to the standard form. This makes the document a very powerful tool for the person signing it.

Signing a LW means that the individual continues to control her health and medical care even if she can no longer communicate with her doctors or other health care providers. The LW also lets the family know what the individual does and does not want. This means that the family can carry out the decisions the patient made and set down in writing.

The LW is used only if the individual becomes incapacitated and is unable to give informed consent or refuse treatment. As long as the patient is competent and able to communicate, she remains in control.

The health care power of attorney (HCPOA), also known as a health care proxy, is the companion document to the living will. It is similar to a General Durable Power of Attorney, but it is specifically designed for use in health care situations. It allows an individual to name a person to carry out the instructions listed in the living will.

HCPOAs come into play only when the principal (the person signing the HCPOA) is incapacitated. The agent named in the HCPOA only has authority to carry out the principal's wishes. The agent has no independent authority to make treatment decisions that are contrary to the principal's living will. For this reason, it is important for the principal to name someone who will carry out his wishes. That may mean someone other than the principal's partner or spouse if that person is unable or unwilling to carry out the principal's wishes.

Many LWs and HCPOAs include "do not resuscitate" (DNR) instructions. Some state forms include this authority as a standard provision. However, if there is no standard language, the individual executing the documents may include a DNR provision as a special instruction. The HCPOA agent has the authority to include a DNR order on the patient's chart if the LW provides for one.

Some advance directives also include provisions concerning the withholding or withdrawal of nutrition and hydration. In Ohio, the declarant must initial these clauses for them to be effective. The client should discuss any questions about withdrawing or withholding nutrition and hydration with her doctor.

Some clients may want to execute multiple original documents of the HCPOA and LW. This reduces the possibility of someone challenging the legitimacy of a copy.

At one time, signing in blue ink was a good idea because it was easy to identify the original. The advent of color laser copiers compromises this effort. However, notarizing the original, with an original embossed seal, is recommended. The raised seal cannot be duplicated on a copier.

Attorneys should use the forms prepared by the state. Hospitals and health care providers recognize the "official" documents. They may include seals from the state bar association and state medical association. Using pre-printed documents, rather than one on your letterhead, may give a level of comfort to health care providers because of their familiarity with the form. This does not prevent the client from adding specific instructions.

B. Tell the Family

Whenever possible, the clients should discuss their plans with their families and document those discussions. A written confirmation of the discussion memorializes the conversation and may preempt future challenges.

If the client is estranged from his family, a letter sent by certified mail, return receipt requested, might be useful.

This may be particularly difficult for clients who are not "out" to their families. And, such clients may refuse to tell their families. In those situations, the clients must understand, and the attorney must clearly document the file, about the potential problems facing the surviving partner.

There is case law in several states that occurred because the family of origin learned of the decedent's sexual orientation only after death. Litigation ensued because the family refused to recognize the surviving partner's rights or accept that the decedent was gay.

Will challenges may occur citing undue influence or lack of capacity as the grounds to overturn the will. The law presumes that the testator will leave his estate to his family. Naming a legal stranger, also known as the surviving partner, runs contrary to that presumption.

Clients who are closeted where their families are concerned tend to believe their families will be "fine" with it. Many clients also claim the family has no problem with the partner because "they have seen us together for years." And, heterosexual relatives are not the only ones who may object. In *In re Estate of Kenneth Ranftle*,[1] the decedent's gay brothers challenged their late brother's will. He and his partner were married in Canada. The brothers challenged that marriage and lost. His straight brother supported the will and Mr. Ranftle's surviving spouse.

C. Health Insurance Portability and Accountability Act

The Health Insurance Portability and Accountability Act (HIPAA) of 1996[2] limits the release of health care information by health care providers. The law is designed to protect the patient's privacy.

The Office of Civil Rights enforces the HIPAA privacy rule. It falls under the purview of the Department of Health and Human Services (HHS).

---

1. 1 A.D.3d 566, 917 N.Y.S.2d 195, 2011 WL 650739, 2011 N.W. Slip Op. 01407 (Feb. 24, 2011).
2. Pub. L. No. 104-191, 110 Stat. 1936 (enacted Aug. 21, 1996).

The Patient Safety Rule protects identifiable information. Violations constitute a federal offense, but there is private cause of action. You may not file a lawsuit for a HIPAA violation. HIPAA violations are filed with the HHS Office of Civil Rights.[3]

Clients need to execute a HIPAA authorization that designates who is authorized to speak with their doctors and has access to medical records and information.

Including HIPAA authorization language, with the names of the authorized persons, is also advisable in the living will and HCPOA. A simple way to do so is to attach the authorization and include it by reference.

The HIPAA authorization language should expressly authorize the health care provider to release all medical information to the designated person. Explicit language will go far in ensuring the designated agent's access to information.

Including language in a preexisting form may be insufficient to meet HIPAA requirements. A sample HIPAA authorization form is included in Appendix A.

The HIPAA rules are no longer new. However, as seen in the *Langbehn v. Jackson Memorial Hospital* case (discussed in Chapter 2), it does not stop hospital personnel from ignoring the law's provisions.

Note the violations of HIPAA that occurred in the *Langbehn* case. Hospital personnel conferred with people and released medical records to people who were not authorized—and they refused to do the same for the one person who did have signed, legal authority to receive the information.

As if you needed convincing . . .

In February 2007, Janice Langbehn, her partner, Lisa Marie Pond, and their three minor children, Danielle, Katie, and David traveled to Miami, Florida to board a cruise ship. They never left port.

Thirty-nine year old Lisa suffered an aneurysm and collapsed aboard the ship. She was taken to Ryder Trauma Center at Jackson Memorial Hospital. Janice arrived with the children shortly after Lisa was admitted. Janice informed the admitting clerk that she was Lisa's life partner and could provide any necessary medical information. She also told the clerk that she was Lisa's health care attorney in fact.

---

3. U.S. Dep't of Health & Human Servs., How to File a Complaint, http://www.hhs.gov/ocr/privacy/hipaa/complaints/index.html.

The hospital admitting clerk controlled all access to patients. She rejected Janice's offer, refused to provide her with any information about Lisa's condition, and refused to allow Janice and the children to see Lisa.

A hospital social worker told Janice she should not expect to receive any information because they were in an "anti-gay city and state." He also told Janice she would be unable to get a court order requiring the hospital to grant access because it was a holiday weekend.

Hospital personnel received a faxed copy of the power of attorney naming Janice as Lisa's guardian and health care attorney in fact. They placed the document in Lisa's file but did not inform Janice.

Several hours after Lisa was admitted, Janice was allowed to see her for five minutes. During the time Janice was prevented from seeing Lisa, other families and children were admitted to the restricted area. Lisa was placed in restraints for her own protection because no family member was present to provide care and supervision.

Lisa was transferred to the neurosurgery intensive care unit without Janice's knowledge. The clerk did not tell her about the transfer.

Lisa's sister arrived almost eight hours after admission and was recognized as a relative and informed of the transfer. At this time, Janice and the children were able to visit with Lisa. Lisa was in a coma when she died at Jackson Memorial Hospital. Janice and their children were never allowed access to Lisa while she was conscious.

Janice filed suit in U.S. District Court.[4] The Court granted the Defendants' Motion to Dismiss. The court held that the defendants were insensitive and caused needless distress BUT, they were not liable for any damages. Janice did not appeal the decision.

Also, note the violations of HIPAA that occurred in this case. Hospital personnel conferred with people and released medical records to people who were not authorized. And, they refused to do the same with the one person who did have signed, legal authority to receive the information.

D. Presidential Memorandum on Hospital Visitation

As discussed in Chapter 2, on April 15, 2010, President Obama issued a Presidential Memorandum on Hospital, Visitation[5] to the secretary of Health and Human Services (HSS). The memorandum instructed the secretary to draft

---

4. Langbehn v. Jackson Memorial Hospital, Case No. 08-21813*CIV-Jordan (September 28, 2009)
5. Press Release, The White House, Presidential Memorandum—Hospital Visitation (Apr. 15, 2010), http://www.whitehouse.gov/the-press-office/presidential-memorandum-hospital-visitation.

rules that would prevent a recurrence of the Miami debacle. The pertinent section of the memorandum is as follows:

My Administration can expand on these important steps to ensure that patients can receive compassionate care and equal treatment during their hospital stays. By this memorandum, I request that you take the following steps:

1. Initiate appropriate rulemaking, pursuant to your authority under 42 U.S.C. 1395x and other relevant provisions of law, to ensure that hospitals that participate in Medicare or Medicaid respect the rights of patients to designate visitors. It should be made clear that designated visitors, including individuals designated by legally valid advance directives (such as durable powers of attorney and health care proxies), should enjoy visitation privileges that are no more restrictive than those that immediate family members enjoy. You should also provide that participating hospitals may not deny visitation privileges on the basis of race, color, national origin, religion, sex, sexual orientation, gender identity, or disability. The rulemaking should take into account the need for hospitals to restrict visitation in medically appropriate circumstances as well as the clinical decisions that medical professionals make about a patient's care or treatment.

2. Ensure that all hospitals participating in Medicare or Medicaid are in full compliance with regulations, codified at 42 CFR 482.13 and 42 CFR 489.102(a), promulgated to guarantee that all patients' advance directives, such as durable powers of attorney and health care proxies, are respected, and that patients' representatives otherwise have the right to make informed decisions regarding patients' care. Additionally, I request that you issue new guidelines, pursuant to your authority under 42 U.S.C. 1395cc and other relevant provisions of law, and provide technical assistance on how hospitals participating in Medicare or Medicaid can best comply with the regulations and take any additional appropriate measures to fully enforce the regulations.

3. Provide additional recommendations to me, within 180 days of the date of this memorandum, on actions the Department of Health and Human Services can take to address hospital visitation, medical decision making, or other health care issues that affect LGBT patients and their families.

In January 2011, the Department of Health and Human Services published the final Rule.[6] This Rule is designed to prevent the situation Janice Langbehn endured. Failure to comply with the Rule could result in a provider being terminated from the Medicare program.

These rules do not affect medical decision making when the patient is unconscious or unable to make decisions. State law applies in those situations. The rules also do not include a "conscience clause" allowing hospital personnel to ignore the rule if it violates their values. No one can refuse to permit a patient's same-sex partner to make medical decisions simply because the doctor or nurse does not like gay people.

The rules also try to educate medical personnel about including medical care for a gay or lesbian couple's children. There is information in the rule about "de facto" and "equitable" parenthood.

A patient may orally designate someone a "support person" who has the right to visit and make decisions for the patient. Documentation can be required only if the patient is unconscious or incapacitated. The documentation is more than an advance directive. It could also be evidence of a shared residence, business ownership, financial interdependence, or existence of a legal relationship recognized in another state.

This rule does NOT provide a private cause of action against a hospital or critical access hospital. Complaints may be filed with the state agency responsible for overseeing compliance. However, that does not resolve the immediate problem if a lesbian or gay man is denied access to his or her partner because a hospital employee is a bigot.

The Rule is a start, but it is not the final word on the subject. Until hospitals and their employees are held financially responsible for their action, it is possible that another incident will occur. It is only a matter of time before a hospital that is affiliated with a specific religion denies access because to do so violates their religion.

Perhaps next time a judge will hold the hospital and its employees liable for their actions rather than merely telling them they were insensitive. The fact that no heterosexual couple would be treated this way should be enough to establish liability. Unfortunately, the federal judge in this case saw it only as an unfortunate situation . . . some harm but no foul.

The *Langbehn* case should be the main argument to use with clients who waffle on whether they need these documents. The new Rule gives some

---

6. Medicare and Medicaid Programs: Changes to the Hospital and Critical Access Hospital Conditions of Participation to Ensure Visitation Rights for All Patients, 42 C.F.R. pts. 482, 485.

additional power to the living will and health care power of attorney, but without the documents, the Rule will have no effect.

E. Hospital Visitation Policies

Hospital policies that once limited visitation to "immediate family only" would run counter to the new Rule. A rare hospital included same-sex partners in that category.

The Joint Commission (TJC) was formerly the Joint Commission on Accreditation of Healthcare Organizations (JCAHO). TJC publishes the national hospital accreditation standards. TJC defines "family" as, "The person(s) who plays a significant role in the individual's [patient's] life. This may include a person(s) not legally related to the individual."[7]

In July 2011, TJC issued its Hospital Accreditation Program (HAP) Visitation Rights Rule under the Hospital Accreditation Standards. These rights include the following language: "Visitation rights include the right to receive the visitors designated by the patient, including, but not limited to, a spouse, a domestic partner (including a same-sex domestic partner), another family member, or a friend. Also included is the right to withdraw or deny such consent at any time."[8]

Remember that **all** hospital and critical access hospitals must have TJC accreditation to operate. If they fail to comply with TJC rules, they may lose their accreditation. Operating outside of TJC raises myriad problems for the provider. Keep this information handy as it may provide the basis for a viable cause of action against a recalcitrant hospital.

The more information that you have on these issues, the better equipped you will be to protect your clients.

F. Traveling

Americans are travelers. Vacations, relocations, Sunday drives. Lesbian and gay couples and individuals should carry their legal documents with them. In the realm of health care, there is no presumption in their favor. What may be allowed in their home state may not exist in the one they visit.

---

7. Requirements Related to CMS Patient Visitation Rights Conditions of Participaton (CoPs); http://www.jointcommission.org/joint_commission_online_january_12_2011/
8. Requirements Related to CMS Patient Visitation Rights Conditions of Participation (CoPs); http://www.jointcommission.org/requirements_cms_pt_visitation_rts_cond_of_participation/

Modern technology allows people to avoid having to carry sheaves of paper with them. Scanning documents onto a thumb drive may be the answer. Using "cloud-based" depositories such as Dropbox[9] or Mozy[10] is another option. Both of the latter provide sufficient free storage space to accommodate these documents. Further, both have applications that allow access to the stored documents from a smartphone. Storing documents in the cloud means they are accessible anytime and anyplace and from any computer.

G. Designation of Agent

The designation of agent form may be considered a catchall that includes the following authorizations:

- Hospital visitation, including authority to decide who does and does not visit
- Funeral arrangements
- HIPAA authorization
- Receipt of personal property
- Disposition of remains and autopsy authorization

This is part of the paper trail establishing the client's intent.

A sample designation of agent form is included in Appendix A.

H. Funeral Arrangements

It's interesting that the last thing over which anyone has control is often the one thing everyone neglects. Funeral arrangements require serious thought if the clients want to ensure that their wishes are honored.

At a time of great personal tragedy, it is amazing how some people will go out of their way to make someone else miserable. Funerals fall into this category.

By making arrangements in advance, and being very specific about the funeral, it may be possible to avoid the trauma so many lesbian and gay surviving partners have experienced.

Many state laws authorize only the decedent's next of kin to make funeral arrangements. This includes overriding the decedent's own arrangements, such as a prepaid funeral contract. This can create a problem if the family

---

9. http://www.dropbox.com.
10. http://www.mozy.com.

wins the race to the funeral home and signs the contract. The estate is presumed to be responsible for the cost of the funeral. The estate may be required to pay for a funeral from which the surviving partner is excluded.

One suggestion to deter interference with the decedent's funeral arrangements is to include a clause in the will restricting payment to only those expenses that are specified by the decedent. The testator can include an instruction prohibiting the executor from paying any bills associated with a funeral deviating from her expressed wishes.

Will it work? That is one of those great unknowns.

The family may argue that they have the right to make funeral arrangements. They may also argue that they are under no obligation to honor the decedent's funeral arrangements. And, they are probably right. But do they have the right to expect the estate to pay the bill?

Again, one of those unknowns.

Another facet of the argument is under contract law. The contract is between the funeral home and the person signing the contract, but the funeral home can file a claim against the estate. Putting the funeral provider on notice of the decedent's expressed wishes and the executor's intent to oppose any claim may cause the provider to rethink its position.

Do not put funeral instructions in a will. The funeral usually takes place before the will is read. It is better for the testator to include the funeral instructions in a separate document.

Include language limiting the estate's liability for expenses that exceed the testator's wishes or deviate from her instructions. Include the same language in the will.

Restrict the executor's authority to pay any funeral bill that does not conform to the testator's wishes.

And, if the testator anticipates a problem with her family, arrange the funeral in advance and pay for it in full. Having funeral instructions that reference a paid contract will buttress the executor's position that the estate not be liable for the expenses of an alternate funeral. Funerals can be expensive, and it is unlikely that the family will want to incur a significant expense if they know it will come out of their own pockets.

Do not forget that the executor has a fiduciary duty to the heirs to manage the estate in a reasonable manner. Paying for a funeral that does not conform to the decedent's wishes may constitute a breach of that fiduciary duty.

The prepaid funeral option is also important because the funeral home may not listen to someone who is the named but not yet appointed executor.

Research your state law concerning funerals. Questions to ask include these:

- Who has the right to control the funeral?
- What is the burden of proof?
- Are there limits on liability?
- Who has standing to sue?

The Federal Trade Commission (FTC) Funeral Rule[11] governs providers who sell both goods and services.

The Funeral Rule requires that all guidelines be met when the prepaid contract is discussed, the purchase is made, and the funeral is held. The Rule does not cover the actual language of the prepaid funeral contract.

The Rule does not apply to prepaid contracts that existed before 1984. If any changes are made to a pre-1984 contract, the Rule will apply to the modifications.

The FTC Funeral Rule does not cover the actual prepaid funeral contract. The FTC recommends that purchasers consider the following:

- What has been purchased—goods, services or both?
- Where are the funds being held?
- Who gets the interest on the prepaid funds?
- What happens if the funeral home goes out of business or is bought out or merged?
- What is the specific cancellation or revision policy?
- What is the refund policy?
- Can the contract be transferred to another funeral home?
- What is the cost of transferring the contract?
- What are the ongoing or upfront administrative or other fees?

Because federal law does not cover prepaid funerals, learn what state law has to say. Is the funeral industry governed in your state?

It should come as no surprise that the FTC does not advocate for purchasing preneed funeral contracts. The FTC has a consumer guide for funerals that may help make a decision.[12]

When making funeral arrangements, do not forget about the cemetery. Catholic cemeteries will not allow a lesbian or gay couple to mention

---

11. 16 C.F.R. pt. 453.
12. Fed. Trade Comm'n, Funerals: A Consumer Guide, http://www.ftc.gov/bcp/edu/pubs/consumer/products/pro19.shtm.

anything on the headstone about the relationship. Choosing a religious cemetery may exacerbate the pain of losing a loved one if that cemetery places religious dogma ahead of compassion.

I. Guardian Nomination

Nominate a guardian or conservator in either the GDPOA or the HCPOA. Putting this in writing is another step in establishing a paper trail and expressing intent.

Each partner can name the other as guardian. If either becomes disabled or incompetent, having a written record of the prospective ward's preference may be helpful. Often the court will appoint a family member, and that may present problems for the partners. Sharon Kowalski's partner spent almost 10 years fighting for the right to care for her. Sharon's parents refused to acknowledge their daughter's relationship.

Specifying a nominee and why that person is being named will be evidence of the person's intentions. Including the designation in the GDPOA may facilitate the appointment if the principal becomes incompetent. Research state law to determine who must be notified when a guardianship is filed.

The document provides evidence of the principal's intent concerning a guardian appointment. A sample form is included in Appendix A.

J. General Durable Power of Attorney

A General Durable Power of Attorney (GDPOA) is a very powerful document. When it is signed, the appointed attorney-in-fact essentially becomes the principal's clone. The "durable" part of the GDPOA means that it continues in full force and effect even after the principal becomes incompetent.

The person signing the GDPOA is known as the "principal." The person appointed in the document is the "agent" or "attorney-in-fact."

There are valid reasons for having a GDPOA. Clients can use these agreements to ensure that their bank accounts, property, and other assets are properly managed if they are absent or become unable to do so personally.

The GDPOA can also preclude the need for a guardianship. Because the power becomes effective immediately upon signing, the agent has the legal authority to manage the principal's affairs even after incompetency.

The GDPOA is only effective during the life of the grantor. It can be rescinded at any time, preferably in writing.

Some states permit these documents to be recorded. If it is, any rescission must also be recorded and original copies recovered. Recording is not recommended because it becomes more difficult to ensure that the original is no longer being used. While copies can be used in lieu of an original, this is not recommended. Having too many copies floating around makes it difficult to maintain control.

Lesbian and gay couples often execute mutual GDPOAs. In these situations, it is advisable to recommend, in the strongest terms possible, that the parties also execute a Domestic Partnership Agreement.

Clients must be aware of the power inherent in these documents. Most people do not understand what a power of attorney means from either a legal or practical standpoint.

Long-term lesbian and gay couples act as one unit. A GDPOA allows them to continue in that vein should one become incapacitated or incompetent. It also provides another piece of evidence in proving their relationship and intentions.

You may also use language to create a springing general durable power of attorney (SGDPOA). Those come into effect only if a specific condition is met. These powers of attorney generally require that the principal's doctor write a letter that the principal is no longer mentally competent. This can be tricky because many doctors may balk at writing such a letter. The SGPOA can include language to overcome those concerns. Another problem is that a court may decide that a guardianship is better and name someone other than the principal's partner.

A third type of power of attorney is a limited power of attorney (LPOA). This is often used when a couple is selling real estate and one has already moved to the new location. The LPOA allows the agent to execute the paperwork needed to close the sale.

Clients should consider including language authorizing gifts and care for their pets. This includes allowing the principal's partner or spouse to make gifts to themselves. Such a clause is especially important in situations where the principal was the primary income provider. It is best to not rely on form powers of attorney. This is one area where clients will benefit from powers of attorney that reflect their wishes and intentions.

Samples of a GDPOA and SGDPOA are included in Appendix A.

K. Business Powers of Attorney

Many lesbians and gay men own a business. Drafting a business power of attorney for these clients provides them with a business planning tool.

Clients who have extensive business dealings or partnerships need to ensure that decisions are made when needed. Clients who have a revocable living trust may consider using the trustee as their business attorney-in-fact.

Generally, it may not be advisable to have the person named in the health care power of attorney serve as the attorney-in-fact under the business power of attorney.

The client's documents should also include a business succession plan and a buy-sell agreement. Anticipating what happens to the business after death is good business practice—and one that is often overlooked.

L. Government Accounts

Federal employees under the Federal Employees Retirement System (FERS) are entitled to participate in the Thrift Savings Plan (TSP). At present, employees are able to contribute a maximum of 15% of their pretax income to the plan. The government provides a maximum match to 5%. A federal employee can designate her same-sex partner as the beneficiary of the TSP account.

Same-sex domestic partners of federal employees are now eligible to receive a survivor annuity under the federal employee retirement program. The proposed rule, *Presumption of Insurable Interest in Same-Sex Domestic Partners,* appeared in the Federal Register on March 3, 2011. The deadline for comments was April 4, 2011.

According to the Office of Personnel Management (OPM), the term "same-sex domestic partner" means a person in a domestic partnership with an employee or annuitant of the same sex. The term "domestic partnership" is defined as a committed relationship between two adults of the same sex, in which the partners:

- Are each other's sole domestic partner and intend to remain so indefinitely
- Maintain a common residence, and intend to continue to do so or would maintain a common residence but for an assignment abroad or other employment-related, financial, or similar obstacle
- Are at least 18 years of age and mentally competent to consent to contract
- Share responsibility for a significant measure of each other's financial obligations
- Are not married or joined in a civil union to anyone else
- Are not the domestic partner of anyone else
- Are not related in a way that, if they were of opposite sex, would prohibit legal marriage in the U.S. jurisdiction in which the domestic partnership was formed

- Are willing to certify, if required by OPM, that they understand that willful falsification of any documentation required to establish that an individual is in a domestic partnership may lead to disciplinary action and the recovery of the cost of benefits received related to such falsification, as well as constitute a criminal violation under 18 U.S.C. 1001.

This is a major development for federal employees. Until now, a retired federal employee's retirement annuity stopped when the retiree died.

As long as the Defense of Marriage Act (DOMA) remains in effect, lesbian and gay couples are unable to claim Social Security survivor benefits on the decedent's account. Moreover, the nonbiological children of the decedent are ineligible for surviving child benefits.

If DOMA is repealed or if the federal courts declare Section 3 of DOMA unconstitutional, married lesbian and gay couples will be covered by federal benefits, including Social Security. Once that happens, the remaining question will revolve around lesbian and gay couples that married in one state but live in a nonrecognition state. Their rights to federal benefits have not yet been resolved.

The other issue will be military retired pay. As of September 2011, lesbian and gay men are able to serve openly in the United States military. As long as DOMA is in effect, lesbian and gay military personnel who are married will not be entitled to the same benefits as hetereosexual married couples. This will raise another challenge to DOMA based on equal protection.

M. Conclusion

Lesbian and gay clients face many issues in making their estate plans. Sometimes the challenges seem overwhelming. This is where the tortoise takes over. It involves a slow and steady discussion with the clients to identify their goals and determine what they want.

Estate planning for lesbian and gay couples does not include a cookie-cutter approach. It requires thought and creativity.

Lawyers representing lesbian and gay clients have an opportunity to consider possibilities in light of recent legal developments—developments that are not limited to any individual state.

The essential documents may change with time, and some of the documents a client needs might not exist. That just means it is up to the clients and their attorney to figure out what it is and the best way to achieve the goal.

Chapter 8

Silver Threads Inside the Rainbow: Lesbian, Gay, and Transgender Seniors

Ageism isolates seniors in mainstream society. Ageism within the LGBT community is rampant. Current elder-care policies in the United States do not consider the unique situation faced by LGBT elders. And, the Baby Boomers are not the only or even the primary concern. It is the pre-Boomer generations; those born from 1914 through 1944 who are are at even greater risk. LGBT elders between the ages of 67 and 97 are the true invisible segment of the American elder population.

Lesbian and gay elders are aging in silence and anonymity. No one is taking the lead in resolving this growing problem. A 2004 report, *Aging in Equity*,[1] provides a good overview of the issues facing lesbian, gay, and transgender elders.

The type of legal issues affecting older Americans is growing. These include the following:

- Medicare and Medicaid
- Public benefits;
- Social Security
- Advance directives
- Financial and physical abuse
- Discrimination based on age, gender, and sexual orientation
- Long-term care availability
- Rise in nursing home litigation
- Taxes

Healthy aging is usually seen as having access to appropriate housing, quality health care, and supportive public and private services.

The pre-Stonewall LGBT elders came of age in a different era. Most kept their personal lives under wraps and even now are reluctant to go public. I

---

1. Funders For Lesbian & Gay Issues, Aging In Equity: Lgbt Elders In America (2004), http://www .lgbtfunders.org/files/AgingInEquity.pdf.

know a gay couple that recently celebrated 55 years together, yet they still refer to each other as "friends."

Even those in long-term relationships may not identify themselves as lesbian or gay. In those cases, it may be difficult to perform a needs assessment. Elderly LGBT persons may not view being gay the same as younger generations.

Even when lesbian and gay seniors feel safe enough to be "out," they often find it necessary to return to the closet when in need of services from the heterosexual senior community and its service providers.

A 1994 New York survey found that lesbian and gay elders were unwelcome at 46% of senior centers. That percentage increased to 50% in a 1999 New York survey. There is no indication the situation has improved.

Many senior services are concentrated in those centers. If lesbian, gay, and transgender seniors are not welcome in those venues, their ability to obtain services is adversely impacted. LGBT elders who think they would not be accepted in a senior center are unlikely to patronize it.

The 2011 Healthcare Equality Index[2] reports that almost 90% of participating health care facilities include "sexual orientation" in their Patient Bill of Rights. Since the new Department of Health and Human Services (HHS) regulations governing hospitals that accept Medicare and Medicaid require that "sexual orientation" be included, that number should grow to 100%.

While the policies may be in place, there is no guarantee the employees working in the field will honor them. As a practical matter, many lesbian, gay, and transgender elders do not disclose their sexual orientation to their health care providers or social workers. They fear mistreatment, abuse or being denied services.

For transgender elders the situation is even bleaker. Only 60% of the participating hospitals include "gender identity" in their Patient Bill of Rights.

A. Let's Run the Numbers

The U.S. Administration on Aging (AoA) classifies 12.9% of the American public as being over 65. The AoA estimates that number will rise to 19% by

---

2. Published by the Human Rights Campaign, http://www.hrc.org/hei2011/.

2020.[3] Of that number, the AoA estimates LGBT persons comprise 3 to 8% of the total U.S. population.[4]

The National Gay and Lesbian Taskforce estimates that there are 3 million LGBT elders in the United States.[5] That number is expected to double by 2030.

In 1950, 8% of the U.S. population was over 65. By the 2000 Census that number jumped to 35 million people or 12% of the population.[6] The 2010 Census reported a U.S. population of nearly 309 million, a 9.7% increase over the 2000 Census. Almost 50 million Americans are 62 or older. By 2030 it is estimated that 70 million people, or 26.4% of the population, will be over 65, which is a 21% increase since 2000.[7]

B. Unique Issues Facing LGBT Elders[8]

Many LGBT elders are single, living alone, and socially isolated. They are often estranged from their biological families, usually because they are gay, lesbian, or transgender. Most do not have children. Remember, they grew up in an age where homosexuality was criminalized and deemed a mental illness. There was no such thing as "out and proud."

LGBT elders are less likely to use senior services for fear of being discriminated against or mistreated. Many prefer to age in place rather than enter a senior living facility, which places them at greater risk for mistreatment and further isolation.

As with many people in the senior community, poverty is also a major problem facing LGBT elders with limited financial resources.

The standard elder care protocol assumes the existence of a familial based, multigenerational support system. The government, and most elder care service providers, believe an older person's family will step up and assist

---

3. Dep't of Health & Human Servs., Admin. on Aging, Aging Statistics, http://www.aoa.gov/AoARoot/Aging_Statistics/index.aspx.

4. DEP'T OF HEALTH & HUMAN SERVS., ADMIN. ON AGING, TECHNICAL ASSISTANCE RESOURCE CENTER: PROMOTING APPROPRIATE LONG-TERM CARE SUPPORTS FOR LGBT ELDERS (2010), http://www.aoa.gov/AoARoot/Grants/Funding/docs/2010/FINAL_LGBT_Elders_TA_Resource_Ctr.pdf.

5. JAIME M. GRANT, OUTING AGE 2010: PUBLIC POLICY ISSUES AFFECTING GAY, LESBIAN, BISEXUAL, AND TRANSGENDER (LGBT) ELDERS (Nat'l Gay & Lesbian Task Force 2009), http://www.thetaskforce.org/reports_and_research/outing_age_2010.

6. U.S. DEP'T OF HEALTH & HUMAN SERVS., ADMIN. ON AGING, A PROFILE OF OLDER AMERICANS: 2000 (2001).

7. U.S. Census Bureau, 2010 Census Data, http://2010.census.gov/2010census/data/.

8. Nancy J. Knauer, *Gay and Lesbian Elders: Estate Planning and End-of-Life Decision Making*, 12 FLA. COASTAL L. REV. 164 (Fall 2010); Anthony M. Brown, *Estate Planning for Same-Sex Couples: Practicalities, Precautions, Perils, and Proposals*, 12 FLA. COASTAL L. REV. 217 (Fall 2010); Nancy J. Knauer, *LGBT Elder Law: Toward Equity in Aging*, 32:1 HARV. J.L. & GENDER 1 (Winter 2009); Aimee Bouchard & Kim Zadworny, *Growing Old Together: Estate Planning Concerns for the Aging Same-Sex Couple*, 30 W. NEW ENG. L. REV. 713 (2008).

in providing care and support. This system is based on a fallacy. Many elders do not have a family to provide the support. Either the family does not live close enough to provide assistance or the family is unwilling to do so.

Many LGBT elders, especially those in the pre-Stonewall generation, are estranged from their birth families, or they have outlived their birth families. Instead, they have developed a "family of choice." This family is every bit as important as the family of origin, and is often the only family the LGBT elder has available.

Unfortunately, this family of choice is often of the same generation as the LGBT elder. This places significant limitations on long-term care because everyone in the family is also aging. Mutual dependency can continue up to a point. After that, all family members require services either from private or public sources.

The other drawback for the LGBT elder's family of choice is that it is not legally recognized. Society recognizes families to which one is related by blood or marriage. Lesbian, gay, and transgender persons may not have family members that qualify. The family of choice almost certainly will not be legally related to the person needing support. Planning for the recognition of those family members is an essential part of any estate plan for a lesbian, gay, or transgender elder. The LGBT elder, in most states, will not be able to designate her family of choice as "next of kin."

Ohio is one state in which an individual is allowed to designate an heir at law.[9] Under the state intestacy statute,[10] the designated heir will stand in the same position as "children."

This legal conundrum facing LGBT elders' family of choice is only one of the issues they face. LGBT elders also face financial insecurity and anti-gay bias and discrimination by service providers, health care professionals, and venues established to serve the needs of an elderly community. It is important for any lawyer who represents LGBT elders to understand the nuances of being gay and old in American society.

Transgender elders will face many different challenges and have needs that require assistance outside of the usual services. Most states do not include gender identity protection in their anti-discrimination laws.

The usual protocol for developing an estate plan does not work with LGBT elders. Almost every potential beneficiary or fiduciary is a legal stranger. Those LGBT elders who live in recognition states may be able to benefit from

---

9. OHIO REV. CODE 2105.15.
10. OHIO REV. CODE 2105.06.

gay-friendly or gay-neutral laws. The majority, however, live in nonrecognition states where there are no laws to protect them. And, even those living in recognition states may choose not to take advantage of the available protections.

Many LGBT elders are alone. Those in relationships may have a partner who has diminished capacity.

The goal of any estate plan is to ensure that the client's wishes and goals are met and her property is transferred to her intended beneficiaries.

C. Estate Planning for LGBT Elders

The growing number of LGBT elders means they will need retirement, life, and estate planning services that are geared to their unique circumstances. Their concerns about aging include not having a safe place to live, outliving their money, worrying about who will care for them, and discrimination in health care.

Social Security survivor benefits are not yet available to spouses or partners of lesbians and gay men. That will change when DOMA is repealed for those lesbian, gay, and transgender couples that are legally married and living in recognition states. The overall effect of DOMA's repeal on those living in nonrecognition states is unknown. But, for now, clients must be aware of the limitations that law places on them.

There will also be a growing number of lesbian and gay veterans among the seniors. Many of the lesbians and gay men who are currently serving, and survived the "Don't Ask, Don't Tell" purge, will put in their 20 years of service and retire. They are entitled to military retired pay, VA health care, and other veteran's benefits.

Recent rule changes allow lawyers to represent people filing VA claims. Those lawyers will be needed to help people navigate the VA morass and repel any anti-gay attitudes by staff and patients at VA hospitals.

Contrary to popular belief, all lesbians and gay men are not wealthy. And, transgender elders have never been viewed as wealthy. These components of the aging population will require access to, and place a greater burden on, public services.

Medicaid is the largest single payor of direct medical services for Persons with AIDS (PWAs) and children with AIDS. The Department of Health and Human Services estimates that 50% of PWAs and 90% of children with AIDS receive medical services through Medicaid. Yet, states are cutting the Medicaid roles to balance their budgets. These cuts will affect those seniors who are living with AIDS or are HIV+.

In 2007, Harris Interactive conducted a poll for Martindale-Hubbard and found that most people (55%) do not have a will. Fifty-two percent of white Americans have wills. However, only 26% of Hispanics and 32% of African-Americans have wills.

In 2008, Findlaw conducted a telephone survey of 1,000 people and identified 58% of Americans without a will. That number drops as a person ages—people over 50 are more likely to have a will.

While having a will is always important, that is never more apparent than when working with LGBT elders. Intestacy laws do not favor lesbian, gay, or transgender elders. Those laws are designed to ensure a result the state believes the decedent would want to achieve. The state believes the natural beneficiary is a decedent's family—no matter how distant or estranged.

Avoiding probate may be the best way to achieve the client's goals. A living trust, also known as inter vivos trusts, allows individuals to transfer assets into a trust. A trustee is named and that person controls the assets during the settlor's lifetime. The person who creates the trust can also serve as the Trustee. Naming an alternate trustee provides for a smooth continuation of the trust especially if the settlor becomes incapacitated.

Another way to avoid probate is to have property transfer automatically when the titleholder dies. This is usually accomplished through a transfer on death process. Joint tenancy, with right of survivorship, is another way to transfer title to real estate.

D. Decision Making Authority

LGBT elders often rely on their chosen families for assistance. Executing general durable powers of attorney and advance directives allow individuals to designate who will administer their affairs when they are no longer able to do so.

Advance directives include living wills and health care powers of attorney. These documents provide a tool for clients to indicate their choices concerning medical care and end-of-life decisions. All states have advance directive laws and, as a rule, recognize and honor those directives executed in other states.[11]

Advance directives can be better than a durable power of attorney because the client's wishes and instructions remain valid even if the named decision maker is unable to serve. Anyone appointed to carry out the client's medical

---

11. For the exception, see Lambda Legal, Langbehn v. Jackson Memorial Hospital, http://www.lamb dalegal.org/in-court/cases/langbehn-v-jackson-memorial.html (discussing Langbehn v. Jackson Mem'l Hosp., 661 F. Supp. 2d 1326 (S.D. Fla. 2009)).

and end-of-life instructions will have no authority to ignore or alter those instructions.

Using the durable power of attorney format, a client may nominate a prospective guardian. That guardian could assume responsibility for the client in she becomes disabled or legally incompetent.

Failing to take these steps means the court would appoint the next of kin to assume responsibility. If the client is estranged from her family, it could mean complete separation from her support system of choice.

Naming alternative attorneys-in-fact is a wise move for LGBT elders because their initial choice may be someone from the same age group. Naming backups will ensure that the people providing fiduciary support are the ones the client wants. If alternates are not named, the law requires the court to appoint a guardian. That person might be a stranger.

There is little intergenerational interaction within the LGBT community. This is unfortunate because lesbian, gay, and transgender elders would benefit from having younger people available to serve in a support role.

Funeral arrangements involve an area in which LGBT elders are particularly vulnerable. It is never a good idea to include funeral instructions in a will. Clients need to address these issues in a separate document. The Designation of Agent form, included in Appendix A, provides a format that can be used.

Most states give priority to next of kin to make funeral arrangements and claim the decedent's remains and property. Some nonrecognition states, like Ohio,[12] allow an individual to name the person responsible for making the arrangements and claiming the remains. It is important to discuss these arrangements with clients and have them write down their wishes. Leaving the details up to others is often a bad idea.

The Rhode Island legislature amended its law to allow domestic partners to claim remains.[13] Ohio's law does not limit the right to same-sex partners. In that respect it is a better solution because not everyone is in a relationship. Like Ohio, Washington has a personal preference law.[14]

There are a variety of options in other states. Some allow a funeral-planning agent, a combination format or incorporate the designation in the advance directives.[15] Regardless of the format, or whether an individual state has addressed the issue, clients must be encouraged to make these designations

---

12. OHIO REV. CODE § 2108.70.
13. R.I. GEN. LAWS § 5-33.2-24 (2009); R.I. GEN. LAWS § 5-33.3-4 (2009).
14. WASH. REV. CODE § 68.50.160 (2010).
15. N.H. REV. STATE. ANN. § 290:17 (2010); OKLA. STAT. TIT. 21, § 1151 (2010); VT. STAT. ANN. TIT. 18, § 9700 (2010); ALA. CODE § 34-13-11 (2010).

an integral part of their estate plan. A written document will carry weight if there is challenge by the next of kin.

Another tool that may be used is to reference the written instructions in the will and limit the executor's authority to pay for anything that exceeds or fails to follow those instructions. Notifying the funeral director about the restrictions before the funeral may help achieve the decedent's goals. People are often reluctant to insist on something when they find out the money will come out of their pocket.

E. Drafting Considerations

There are certain unstated assumptions that come into play when drafting estate plan documents. Most states give favored-nation status to the next of kin. This preference can be used to challenge even the most carefully drafted document.

There are countless examples of cases where the decedent's family contests a will or burial instructions because their relative could not have been gay. The surviving partner was nothing more than a roommate or good friend.

Incredulous families refuse to accept that their loved one—often someone they have not seen in years—could have meant to leave their estate to a stranger. Obviously, the only way that could happen was due to incompetency or undue influence.

In some situations, the government becomes involved and refuses to accept the legitimacy of a relationship between people of the same gender. Remember what Sonoma County government employees did to Clay and Harold?[16]

A decedent's family may challenge a will if they have a potential financial interest in the estate. LGBT elders who leave their estate to friends and not family have created a document with a non-normative testamentary disposition.

Establishing a person's testamentary capacity requires evidence that the testator

- understood what he was doing;
- how much property he had at the time; and
- the way in which the property would be distributed after his death.

If the testator was elderly at the time he signed the will, his testamentary capacity may be challenged. For this reason, it may be wise to take steps to go

---

16. See "Senior Members of the LGBT Community" in chapter 2.

beyond the usual protocol to establish and clarify the testator's competency and capacity. This may include obtaining a physician's not or videotaping the proceedings. This is also an occasion where pre-validating the will may be advisable. If the family intends to contest the will, let them do so while the testator is sitting in court—-with her lawyer.

It may also be wise to investigate and document the testator's relationship with her family. And, do not limit the investigation to parents and siblings. Pursue it further and look at cousins, nieces, and nephews. How long has it been since any of them had contact with the testator? This evidence can then be presented should a contest take place.

Some family members will use the fact that the testator left her estate to a stranger as prima facie evidence of incompetency. Unfortunately, some courts view a nontraditional disposition as raising a question about the testator's capacity.

When capacity does not work, the family may raise the issue of undue influence. Leaving one's estate to a "friend," "roommate," or even a nonmarital romantic partner is outside the norm and, therefore, suspect.

Undue influence is an especially potent argument when the testator and her partner were not out to the family. A secret or confidential relationship may raise the issue of undue influence and cause the will to be set aside. If the court considers undue influence possible, the burden of proof will shift to the surviving partner to prove there was none.

File documentation is essential. A more extensive client questionnaire may be preferred. Investigating the client's relationship with her family and her partner will provide evidence that substantiates the client's intentions.

If nothing else, raising these possibilities will encourage the client to remove as much property as possible from the probate estate.

F. Older Americans Act

The Older Americans Act,[17] originally enacted in 1965, and reauthorized in 2000, provides services for Americans over 60. The reauthorization extends the Act's programs through FY 2011.

The Administration on Aging (AoA) is the primary vehicle for organizing, coordinating and providing community-based services for older Americans and their families.

---

17. Pub. L. No. 106-501 (Nov. 13, 2000).

A variety of services are provided under the Act, including home-delivered meals, health screenings and counseling, abuse protection, volunteer guardians, and legal services. In addition, eligible seniors may be able to get help with minor home repairs, yard work, housekeeping and respite care.

The reauthorized Act includes a new program, the National Family Caregiver Support Program (NFCSP). This program is designed to help family caregivers of older adults who are ill or who have disabilities. Two-thirds of non-institutionalized persons rely on family and friends for assistance with daily living activities. One quarter supplement family care with services from paid providers.

The NFCSP provides grants to state agencies on aging to work with Area Agencies on Aging, service, and community organizations that provide support services:

- Information to caregivers about available services
- Assistance in gaining access to services
- Counseling, support groups, and caregiver training
- Respite care
- Supplemental services to complement the care being given.

The Act also maintains the original objectives that serve to preserve the rights and dignity of older Americans. There are provisions for low-income minorities and an added focus on older individuals living in rural areas.

This Act can be a source of assistance for lesbian and gay elders who remain in the community. Clients, who need assistance, or their caregivers, should contact their local Area Agency on Aging for more information. They can also contact the AoA at http://www.aoa.gov.

The Eldercare Locator is a national toll-free phone service (800-677-1116) designed to help find appropriate community resources. In 2001 the Federal Office on Aging recognized that the Older Americans Act was not serving lesbian and gay elders in the United States. However, Congress has not considered legislation to remedy the situation.

The National Council on Aging, a nonprofit group in Washington, D.C., set up the Benefits CheckUp website (http://www.benefitscheckup.org) in June 2001. Lawyers can consult the website to determine a client's eligibility for federal and state benefits.

G. Discrimination

The Employee Retirement Income Security Act (ERISA) controls pension plans. Federal law requires pension plans to protect spouses. There is no similar requirement to protect a same-sex partner because domestic partners are not synonymous with "spouse." And, private employers use DOMA to deny lesbian and gay employees the opportunity to name their spouse—even in recognition states.

This discrimination came home to the partner of a Tampa police officer after her partner was killed in the line of duty.

On July 6, 2001, Tampa police officer Lois Marrero was shot and killed in the line of duty. She was due to retire in 15 months. Officer Marrero left behind her partner of eleven years, Tampa police officer Mickie Mashburn.

Unlike the officer's heterosexual counterparts, Officer Mashburn was not entitled to receive any part of Marrero's pension. Florida's pension law provides that only spouses and children are eligible to receive survivor benefits. Mashburn also could not receive a refund of the $50,000 paid into the pension fund by Marrero. And, since Marrero died intestate, her parents inherited her estate. Marrero's family claimed there was no relationship between Marrero and Mashburn.

Mashburn did receive $25,000 from the Florida crime victims' compensation fund. Florida's Attorney General, Bob Butterworth, approved that payment. The eight-member city pension board rejected Mashburn's application and awarded the $50,000 refund of pension premiums to Marrero's mother. The Tampa City Council is reviewing the pension policy. The police and firefighter unions are supporting Mashburn. The National Center for Lesbian Rights represented Mashburn in challenging the pension board's decision.

There is no federal legislation banning discrimination based on sexual orientation in employment, housing or public accommodations. Absent state law restrictions, nursing homes and assisted living facilities are free to discriminate against lesbian and gay elders in their admission policies.

Even when services and benefits are available many lesbian and gay seniors are unaware of either their existence or the eligibility requirements. This is where good lawyers come into play.

H. Housing

Housing is one of the most important concerns facing lesbian and gay seniors. The Fair Housing Act[18] prohibits discrimination in housing. Nursing homes, assisted living facilities, and independent retirement communities constitute housing that is covered by the statute. However, these facilities regularly deny entry to elderly lesbians and gay men because of their sexual

---

18. 42 U.S.C. §§ 3601 *et seq.*

orientation. And transgender seniors are even more likely to experience exclusion and discrimination.

Those retirement communities that exist in states with discrimination statutes that include sexual orientation and gender identity must admit lesbian, gay, and transgender elders.There is a growing industry that is building gay-friendly retirement communities.[19] New ones are planned in other states, including North Carolina. Unfortunately, most of these developments are not affordable.[20]

Over the past few years, the U.S. Department of Housing and Urban Development (HUD) has implemented rules to provide LGBT persons with protection from housing discrimination. The Fair Housing Act prohibits discrimination in rentals, sales, and lending.[21] The protected classes are race, color, national origin, religion, gender, disability, and familial status.

In October 2009, HUD announced that its housing programs would be open to all without regard to sexual orientation or gender identity.[22]

In July 2010,[23] HUD announced that it would retain jurisdiction over complaints filed by LGBT individuals or families.

On January 24, 2011, HUD published its proposed rules concerning equal access to housing for LGBT persons in the Federal Register.[24]

And, in October 2011, HUD announced a study of housing discrimination against members of the LGBT community.[25]

The gay-friendly developments make their nondiscrimination policy clear. When a retirement community's policies do not explicitly include sexual orientation and gender identity in its nondiscrimination clause, it is not farfetched to assume that the facility discriminates or is ignoring the situation.

Not all lesbian and gay seniors want to live in a development marketed to the LGBT community but they may not be welcomed in any other community. Those who want to live in a welcoming, gay-friendly community

---

19. Gay & Lesbian Ass'n of Retired Persons., http://www.gaylesbianretiring.org.

20. *See, e.g.,* Jan Cullinane, *Gay and Lesbian Retirement Communities,* LETLIFEIN.COM, http://www.letlifein .com/articles/gay-and-lesbian-retirement-communities/.

21. 42 U.S.C. §§ 3601–3619; penalties for violations: 42 U.S.C. § 3631.

22. Press Release, U.S. Dep't of Hous. & Urban Dev., Obama Administration to Ensure Inclusion of the LGBT Community in HUD Programs (Oct. 21, 2009), http://portal.hud.gov/hudportal/HUD?src=/press/ press_releases_media_advisories/2009/HUDNo.09-206.

23. Press Release, U.S. Dep't of Hous. & Urban Dev., HUD Issues Guidance on LGBT Housing Discrimination Complaints (July 1, 2010), http://portal.hud.gov/hudportal/HUD?src=/press/press_releases_media_ advisories/2010/HUDNo.10-139.

24. 76 Fed. Reg. 4194 (Jan. 24, 2011), *available at* http://portal.hud.gov/hudportal/documents/huddoc? id=LGBTPR.pdf.

25. U.S. Dep't of Hous. & Urban Dev., LGBT Discrimination Study, http://portal.hud.gov/hudportal/ HUD?src=/LGBT_Discrimination_Study.

may find their options limited by geography and financial resources. LGBT elders want safe, affordable senior housing in which they can live without fear of mistreatment, abuse, or of being ostracized. Some are willing to fight for that right.

Joy Lewis and Sheila Ortiz-Taylor were denied admission to the Florida-based Westminster Oaks Retirement Community. Westminster Oaks denied their application because it violated their policy against allowing unmarried, unrelated couples from living together.

Some Florida counties and local governments have enacted legislation that prohibits housing discrimination because of sexual orientation. Westminster Oaks is located in one of those areas and its policy violated local law. The same law includes prohibitions against discrimination based on gender and marital status.

The National Center for Lesbian Rights represented the women and the parties reached a confidential settlement.[26] Now, Joy and Sheila are becoming active members of the Westminster Oaks community.

Another Florida case, in Boca Raton, involved an apartment complex that refused to rent an apartment to a gay couple. This action violated a county law that protects same-sex couples from housing discrimination. The apartment complex, Colonial Apartments, settled the matter during mediation and agreed to pay $25,000 to each of the men and to the Lambda Legal Defense and Education Fund.[27]

Long-Term Care Facilities

In 2011 the National Senior Law Center released a report, *LGBT Older Adults in Long-Term Care Facilities: Stories from the Field*.[28]

The survey respondents reported problems and issues as follows:

- 22% believed they could be open with the staff about their sexual orientation.
- 89% believed they would experience discrimination from the staff.
- 43% reported mistreatment.
- 93% reported restrictions placed on visitors.
- 24% were denied medical care.

---

26. Nat'l Ctr. for Lesbian Rights, Joy Lewis and Sheila Ortiz-Taylor v. Westminster Oaks Retirement Community, http://www.nclrights.org/site/PageServer?pagename=issue_caseDocket_lewis.
27. Press Release, Lambda Legal, Lambda Legal Declares Victory in Housing Discrimination Case on Behalf of Two Gay Men in Florida (Sept. 30, 2003), http://www.lambdalegal.org/news/pr/fl_20030930_lambda-declares-victory-housing-discrimination-case.html.
28. http://www.lgbtlongtermcare.org/.

Most of the research on discrimination against gay and lesbian elders in long-term care facilities, home health care or retirement communities is anecdotal. There have been cases involving long-time couples who are prevented from sharing a "couple's room" or associating with each other in a facility.

Some nursing home residents have been prohibited from visiting with their non-resident partner. Many lesbians and gay men learn it is safer to return to the closet when entering a nursing home.

The elderly, as a class, are often overlooked. The LGBT community is not addressing the unique needs of lesbian and gay seniors in or out of long-term care facilities. The discriminatory treatment experienced by lesbian and gay long-term care facility residents may become a source of future litigation.

Home health care companies are another source of abuse and discriminatory activities. One report told of an abusive home health care aide who threatened to "out" the elderly patient if he complained about her actions.

Many elderly gay men and lesbians are not as "public" as their younger counterparts about their sexual orientation. They grew up in an age that is quite different from today. They lived in an era of anti-gay statutes that were aggressively enforced.

These seniors are very private about their relationships. And, this habit of being secretive can lead to mistreatment.

Independent Living and Assisted Living Facilities

For some lesbians and gay men, an independent living or assisted living facility may seem to be a viable alternative to nursing home care. However, neither the state nor federal governments regulate assisted living facilities.

These are private pay facilities, and residents do not qualify for Medicaid. The facilities provide some assistance to residents—usually for an additional fee. This assistance may include help with medication, bathing and other daily routines.

Nursing Home Care

Statistics from the AoA show that at least 40% of people turning 65 will stay in a nursing home at least once in their lifetime. Some 50% of those entering a nursing home will stay 6 months or less, 20% will stay a year or more, and 10% will stay 3 years or longer. Most of those over 65 are women. Given these figures, it is likely you will have clients who are in need of nursing home care at some point in their lives.

There are two types of nursing home care: skilled nursing and custodial care. Most people live in a custodial care facility.

According to Consumer Reports 36% of assisted living residents enter a nursing home because their needs cannot be accommodated. Another 2% enter a nursing home because they run out of money.

An unknown percentage of those older persons entering nursing homes will be lesbians and gay men.

The federal Nursing Home Reform Act[29] was attached to the Omnibus Budget Reconciliation Act of 1987. It included amendments to the Civil Rights of Institutionalized Persons Act of 1980. The statute provides certain rights to nursing home residents.

As of 2010, residents have the right to dignity, privacy and freedom from discrimination. Other rights include the following:

- Freedom from restraint
- Right to be informed of medical care and treatment
- Rights of complaint and protection against transfer and unfair discharge
- Right to be admitted without a third-party guaranty as a condition of admission
- Freedom from abuse
- Right to reasonable accommodation
- Right to participate in planning care and treatment and any changes in care and treatment
- Right to refuse treatment
- Right of family and ombudsman to immediately access resident and have reasonable access to facility
- Right to privacy, confidentiality, and visitors
- Right to appeal hearings
- Right to necessary care and services for highest practicable well-being
- Right to have adequate number of personnel
- Various rights respecting the residents' financial matters and need for proper notice and information.

---

29. 42 U.S.C. §§ 1396r, 1395i-3; 42 C.F.R. 483.

State laws that prohibit discrimination based on sexual orientation or gender identity could be used to help lesbian, gay and transgender residents injured in nursing homes.

Since there is no legal sanction against sexual orientation discrimination at the federal level and in many states, it is important to determine if the nursing home accepts lesbian and gay residents.

Some questions for clients to ask: Does the facility treat a same-sex couple the same as a married couple? Are same-sex couples allowed to reside in couple's rooms?

These are important questions to ask *before* entering a nursing home or assisted living facility. Too often an openly lesbian or gay couple or individual will be forced back into the closet in order to be treated well in a nursing home.

Privacy

A person's right to privacy in the facility is a concern for many lesbians and gay men. While many lesbian and gay individuals and couples are open about their relationships, a large number remain closeted.

Maintaining one's privacy may be important to a client. Establishing the privacy policy before moving is an important step.

Outing an elderly lesbian or gay man can be devastating. This is particularly true if the threatened outing is used for nefarious purposes or to prevent the resident from complaining about her treatment.

Mistreatment and Abuse

Even when the resident is open about her sexuality, she may be subjected to discriminatory conduct by the staff. In one instance, the nursing home staff refused to bathe an elderly, female nursing home resident because they did not want to touch "the lesbian."

In many nursing home facilities sexuality is often a problem for the staff. No one wants to think of these "old folks" being sexually active. Many consider gay sex to be deviant behavior.

Each state's Agency on Aging must create an Office of Long-Term Care Ombudsman. This office provides help and information to elderly persons, their families and friends. The office is also charged with visiting nursing homes, receiving and investigating complaints and providing information on LTC facilities. The ombudsman office is also a good source of current information on local nursing homes.

The state Department of Health is responsible for issuing regulations governing nursing home operations. There is also a federal mandate requiring nursing homes to ensure that each resident is able to maintain, as much as possible, the quality of life at the level enjoyed before entering the facility.

I. Health Care Issues

Concern about the availability and affordability of health care remains a concern for everyone. Lesbians and gay men experience additional issues even when they can afford health insurance and care is available.

Many lesbians and gay men do not seek medical care because of their experience with homophobic doctors.

A patient must feel comfortable her doctor. A person's sexual orientation is an integral part of a person. If a patient cannot tell the doctor that she is a lesbian the quality of care will suffer.

For example, women of childbearing age are always asked about the type of birth control used. Lesbians use the only kind that is 100% effective—they do not have sex with men.

Even though the "gayby" boom is in full swing there are still many lesbians who, in response to the question "Are you pregnant?" will answer, "Not unless you've seen a star in the East!"

Aside from the obvious possibilities about reduced medical care, lesbians and gay men experience stress arising from homophobia, the fear of being outed and the fear of being the victim of violence inspired by hate. This situation is even greater when the person is elderly and less able to withstand the assault on senses and person.

Elderly lesbians and gay men are very concerned about the availability of health insurance. Most of these elders are not entitled to supplemental coverage from their partners. An increasing number of corporations and companies of all sizes are offering health insurance and other benefits to same-sex couples. It is something for lawyers representing lesbian and gay elder clients to investigate.

Because of these concerns it is important for lawyers to ensure that their clients are provided with all the legal documents necessary to protect them in a health care facility, including hospitals, nursing homes, assisted living facilities, and home health care situations. It is also important to determine that the client is being treated with respect and that her needs are being met.

J. Social Security

The Old Age, Survivors, and Disability Insurance (OASDI) program[30] is specific concerning eligibility for survivor benefits. No Social Security benefits are available to the surviving partner of a same-sex couple, even if the couple is legally married. This includes retirement benefits, disability benefits and Supplemental Security Income (SSI). Clients must be made aware that a domestic partnership agreement or marriage certificate does not confer any federal benefits on a surviving partner.

However, the Social Security statute includes a definition of "family status" that your clients may fall under in very specific circumstances. 42 U.S.C. § 416(h)(1)(A) of the statute reads as follows:

(h) Determination of family status

(1)(A)(i) An applicant is the wife, husband, widow, or widower of a fully or currently insured individual for purposes of this subchapter if the courts of the State in which such insured individual is domiciled at the time such applicant files an application, or, if such insured individual is dead, the courts of the State in which he was domiciled at the time of death, or, if such insured is or was not so domiciled in any State, the courts of the District of Columbia, would find that such applicant and such insured individual were validly married at the time such applicant files such application or, if such insured individual is dead, at the time he died.

(ii) If such courts do not find that such applicant and such insured individual were validly married at such time, such applicant shall, nevertheless be deemed to be the wife, husband, widow, or widower, as the case may be, of such insured individual if such applicant would, under the laws applied by such courts in determining the devolution of intestate personal property, have the same status with respect to the taking of such property as a wife, husband, widow, or widower of such insured individual.

The key language is in subsection (1)(A)(ii). If an applicant and the insured individual were entitled to the insured's intestate property under state law, and the state law considers the partners to be a "spouse," then the applicant may be eligible to apply for benefits.

---

30. 42 U.S.C. §§ 401 *et seq.*

This federal statute relies on the law of the insured's domicile to determine family status. Since state law controls, a state that grants intestate inheritance rights to lesbian and gay couples, would appear to also make those couples eligible for OADSI benefits under title 42.

DOMA, however, conflicts with this federal law. And, to date, there has been no litigation on this particular issue.

The recognition states treat married same-sex couples the same as married heterosexual couples. Many of the states that provide legal recognition to same-sex couples, through Domestic Partnerships or Civil Unions, also grant them intestate succession rights.

This is an untested theory. There is no case law on the issue, and there appears to be no law review articles on the subject. However, once DOMA falls, this will happen—at least in the recognition states.

K. Medicaid and Medicare

Medicare and Medicaid are often misunderstood. Here is the primary difference: Medicare is a federally funded program that provides health insurance and prescription drug coverage for the elderly. Medicaid is a joint federal and state program that is partially funded by the federal government. It is operated by the individual states that set the eligibility rules. Medicaid is limited to poor people. Many people use Medicaid to pay for nursing home care after they exhaust their private resources.

Medicaid

Medicaid (Title XIX of the Social Security Act) is a federally funded, state-run program that provides medical assistance to low-income and low-resource individuals and families. The federal government establishes general guidelines, but the individual states set the specific program requirements.

There are five broad categories of groups covered by Medicaid:

- Children
- Pregnant women
- Adults in families with dependent children
- Individuals with disabilities
- Individuals age 65 and over

The states are responsible for establishing eligibility standards, type, amount, scope and duration of services, rates of payment for services, and the administration of the program. State rules vary; eligibility in one state does not guarantee eligibility in another. The states can also determine, to some extent, which services will be provided. One of the complications about Medicaid is that the rules can, and often do, change every year.

In addition to the federally funded Medicaid program, most states also have "State-only" programs to assist poor persons who do not qualify for Medicaid.

Lesbians and gay men who are age 65 and over are potentially eligible for Medicaid assistance. Lesbians and gay men under age 65 are eligible but only if they fall within one of the other categories listed above.

To qualify for Medicaid the client must spend down assets to a minimal amount. The current amount ranges between $1,500 and $2000. That represents the total amount of assets an individual Medicaid recipient can possess to qualify.

An individual's monthly Social Security check will be turned over to the senior housing facility, although the resident will be allowed to keep a small amount ($25 to $50) for incidentals.

The resident must dispose of all other assets. Any property sold for less than 80% of its fair market value may be viewed as an improper transfer. This determination can result in the applicant being deemed Medicaid ineligible for a specific period.

Under current law, there is a five-year look-back period. Any transfer of assets made during the five years immediately preceding the application is deemed invalid. The applicant will be ineligible for Medicaid until the value of the transferred assets is spent down.

For example, assume that the monthly cost of the facility is $5,000. If the client transferred $25,000 to his partner three years before applying for Medicaid, he would be ineligible for benefits for five months ($5,000 X 5 = $25,000).

In situations involving same-sex couples, documentation concerning joint accounts will be even more important. It is likely that states will demand proof of actual joint ownership and contribution when making Medicaid eligibility determinations.

Many clients will not have extensive documentation about individual contributions to assets, but the documentation may decide whether the applicant qualifies for Medicaid.

Clients should be encouraged to consider purchasing long-term care insurance. Many states have adopted a partnership program that coordinates

Medicaid payments with long-term care insurance. Nursing home residents who pay for three years of care before applying for Medicaid will be able to avoid state liens on their property.

In June 2011, the Department of Health and Human Services issued new guidance[31] to states concerning liens, transfer of assets and estate recovery. The HHS guidance allows states to use discretion when deciding whether to recognize a domestic partnership. A copy of the letter is included in Appendix A.

Generally a lesbian or gay couple, even if legally married, will not be viewed as a married couple for Medicaid eligibility purposes. They will be viewed as individuals when determining eligibility. There will be no "community spouse" allowance. The couple will be deemed "single."

Consider an example of what can happen in a Medicaid situation involving a lesbian or gay couple.

Amy and Susan have been together for 42 years. They were married in 2010 in Vermont. Amy is 72 and Susan is 68. Susan had a heart attack several years ago. She is suffering from progressive dementia. Amy is no longer able to care for her at home and the couple decides that Susan needs full-time nursing home care.

Their primary asset is their house, valued at $150,000. They have joint bank accounts. Amy receives Social Security and an annuity. Social Security is Susan's only retirement income.

Susan applies for Medicaid. Under Medicaid rules she is considered "single" for eligibility purposes.

She will be required to spend down her assets until she has no more than $1,500 left. Her monthly Social Security check will be used to pay for her care. She will be allowed to keep approximately $25 each month for personal expenses.

Amy explains that most of the money in the joint checking account comes from her annuity payment. The worker attributes all of the money in those accounts to Susan.

The worker informs Amy that $75,000 of the house value belongs to Susan. That amount must be spent for nursing home care before Susan is eligible for Medicaid. The only way to do that is to sell the house.

Amy and Susan sell the home they have lived in for 35 years. Susan moves into the nursing home, Amy into a small apartment in a senior

---

31. *See* Chris Johnson, *Exclusive: Obama Extends Protections to Gay Couples Under Medicaid*, WASH. BLADE, June 10, 2011, http://www.washingtonblade.com/2011/06/10/exclusive-obama-extends-protections-to-gay-couples-under-medicaid/.

high-rise building. Since Amy can no longer drive, it is difficult for her to visit Susan. And, when she does visit, a staff member stays in the room with them to "protect the resident".

Married couples can qualify for a community spouse payment. They are also eligible to keep their home even if titled in the name of the resident spouse. Similar consideration is not given to a same-sex couple. The spouse is also entitled to a portion of his wife's Social Security check. States allow the community spouse to keep enough money to maintain her standard of living.

The June 2011 letter from HHS clarifies that states have discretion to recognize same-sex relationships. Unfortunately, it is too early to tell whether this change will benefit lesbian and gay couples. Many states are cutting back on Medicaid benefits. It seems unlikely that they will take advantage of the new guidance.

It is likely that recognition states will treat married lesbian and gay couples the same as heterosexual married couples. Lesbian and gay couples living in nonrecognition states should not expect the same treatment, even if they were legally married in a recognition state.

Medicaid is a complicated program and it helps to consult with someone well versed in its intricacies. The state's long-term care ombudsman office can be helpful in deciphering the Medicaid rules. Each state is required to establish an Ombudsman office under the requirements of the Older Americans Act.

When DOMA is repealed, the situation may change. However, since Medicaid is a federal/state hybrid program state law will continue to define "spouse".

Medicare

Medicare is a social insurance program to provide health insurance for the elderly and the permanently disabled under age 65. Elderly lesbians and gay men are eligible to apply for Medicare once they reach 65. An individual may be eligible before 65 if he has a disability. Medicaid recipients may also be eligible for Medicare.

The four parts to Medicare are as follows:

Part A covers inpatient care and brief convalescent stays in a skilled nursing facility.

Part B covers what Part A does not and includes physician and nursing services and outpatient services. Part B also covers durable medical equipment.

Part C is the Medicare Advantage plan. It allows people to receive their Medicare coverage through a private insurer.

Part D is the infamous prescription drug plan, with the donut hole. It is not a very good plan and can be very expensive for seniors who have many medications. Congress specifically denied Medicare the authority to negotiate lower drug prices. Old people have less pull than deep-pocket pharmaceutical companies.

Medicare will pay for skilled nursing care only and only for a limited time. Medicare does not pay for custodial nursing home care. This can be a confusing topic to explain to a client.

In a nutshell, medical conditions that require the services of a registered nurse for medical care such as IVs and post-surgical care, usually qualify as skilled nursing care. Some nursing homes have skilled care wings on the property.

Custodial care means the resident requires assistance with daily activities such as dressing, eating and bathing. This type of care does not qualify for Medicare.

Home and Community-based Services

Most seniors prefer to remain in their homes and "age in place." This requires home health care services. State government agencies are finally beginning to realize that home-based services are less expensive and more cost-effective than nursing homes.

The Social Security Act includes authorization for waivers and demonstration programs for specific purposes. This includes home and community-based services.[32] Section 1915(c) provides waivers for long-term care services in community settings. Such programs allow states to stretch their Medicaid dollars and provide in-home services to people who qualify for Medicaid.

These services include health care from visiting nurses and home health aides who assist the senior with the activities of daily living. Those include washing, dressing, and eating. Meals can also be prepared for the senior.

LGBT elders are among those who can benefit from these home-based services. Most of the programs being offered are demonstration or pilot projects. However, as the success rate rises and the cost-effectiveness of such programs becomes apparent, more states will offer them.

---

32. U.S. Dep't of Health & Human Servs., Ctrs. for Medicare & Medicaid Servs., Overview, https://www.cms.gov/MedicaidStWaivProgDemoPGI/01_Overview.asp.

The Centers for Medicare and Medicaid Services (CMS), operated by the U.S. Department of Health and Human Services is a resource for learning about the demonstration and pilot projects available in the states.[33]

Since many LGBT elders are fearful of entering senior housing facilities, these home-based programs offer a viable alternative.

L. Insurance Concerns

It is important for lesbian and gay seniors to consider their insurance needs. This includes long-term care insurance, disability insurance and life insurance.

The long-term care insurance should include coverage for at home and nursing home care. A client may be more comfortable knowing he can remain in his home with proper care and avoid the potential pitfalls of being gay in a heterosexual nursing home.

Life insurance can relieve the couple's concern about the ability of the surviving partner to remain in the home.

Disability insurance can provide a welcome cushion in the event one partner becomes ill and is no longer able to work. The most cost-effective policies are available through professional groups or organizations. A policy that waives premiums at a certain point is also beneficial to the couple.

Disability insurance should also be specific to the insured's profession. If the client is unable to continue in his profession, then the insurance kicks in. This is a better policy than one that requires the claimant to prove he cannot do any job.

Health insurance continues to be a concern for most people. Most employers do not provide health insurance for domestic partners.

Preexisting conditions can prevent people from qualifying for affordable health insurance. The Health Insurance Portability and Accountability Act (HIPAA) prohibits excluding someone for a pre-existing condition if that person was insured during the 60 days immediately before applying. This is important to know because insurance companies will deny coverage because of a pre-existing condition even though the applicant meets the coverage requirements.

Life insurance can benefit the surviving partner by providing a quick source of cash to offset estate or probate expenses.

---

33. U.S. Dep't of Health & Human Servs., Ctrs. for Medicare & Medicaid Servs., Waivers and Demonstrations Through Map of States, https://www.cms.gov/MedicaidStWaivProgDemoPGI/08_WavMap.asp.

The IRS presumes that the first person to die owned all the jointly held property. Until that presumption is rebutted, the estate will be liable for any taxes due. With the demise of the federal estate tax (estates under $5 million), this should become less of a concern. However, for wealthy clients, life insurance should be part of the estate plan.

Transferring property from joint ownership to a sole owner can cause a reassessment of property taxes. The surviving partner may be unable to pay the increased taxes and that places the house at risk. Life insurance can alleviate this concern and provide sufficient funds to pay the property tax increase.

M. Transgender Elders

Most lawyers have limited experience addressing the legal issues affecting transgender individuals. A detailed discussion of transgender issues is beyond the scope of this book. However, transgender clients face significant issues. For elderly transgender clients, the problems are multiplied beyond comprehension.

Most states do not prohibit discrimination based on gender identity. The federal government does not prohibit gender identity discrimination. When offered the opportunity to do so, most legislatures refuse to include gender identity in their non-discrimination laws. Lawyers may assume that nursing homes and other senior facilities will not protect the rights of transgender elders.

Consider this possibility.

Mack is a 68-year-old transgender person. Mack is biologically female and has never undergone sex reassignment surgery, but considers himself male and lives his life as a man. When Mack suffered an incapacitating stroke, his adult sister was appointed his legal guardian. The sister placed Mack in a nursing home. She also insisted on dressing him in frilly female nightgowns and referring to him by a female name and female pronouns. When Mack recovered enough to make his wishes about clothing and pronouns known to the facility staff, the staff concluded that he was "confused." Mack became increasingly withdrawn and depressed. He no longer speaks or interacts with other residents.[34]

---

34. Shannon Minter, *Legal and Public Policy Issues for Transgender Elders*, Nat'l Ctr. For Lesbian Rights (2003), http://www.nclrights.org/site/DocServer/transelder.pdf?docID=1121.

Transgender elders, as a group, maintain anonymity in the LGBT community that is unsupportable. The community's elderly population as a whole is ignored. Transgender elders are in worse circumstances. Tending to their legal, social and medical needs require a conscious effort. To do less will ensure that they remain anonymous.

N. Pensions and Death Benefits

Pension benefits are nonprobate assets. The beneficiary designation is not subject to contest by a decedent's family. However, many plans restrict who can be named as a beneficiary. Some plans require that a beneficiary be only a spouse, legally recognized dependent, or close family member. These plans would not allow the employee to name a domestic partner or other person not related by blood.

If a beneficiary is not named, the pension benefit lapses. That may create a severe financial setback for the decedent's surviving partner. These policies also prevent LGBT elders from naming a member of their chosen family as a beneficiary.

Clients need to provide current beneficiary designation forms when planning their estate. Checking with the plans to make sure the beneficiary designation is current and as stipulated by the client is essential.

Life insurance beneficiaries must also be checked. Some insurance companies will not permit the insured to name a beneficiary who is not a blood relative or a legally recognized spouse. In some cases, the company will change the designation to the insured's estate—often without telling the insured. There may also be situations when a company's employee makes the change because of their personal homophobic bias. For this reason, having a current copy of the designation will give the client peace of mind. Regularly checking that the designation continues to reflect the insured's intentions is also important.

A current case, *Gill v. Office of Personnel Management*[35] is challenging DOMA because the law precludes recognition of Massachusetts same-sex marriage. The Obama Administration is no longer defending this case. The U.S. House of Representatives has undertaken the defense of DOMA.

---

36. 699 F. Supp. 2d 374 (D. Mass. 2010).

O. Integrated Estate Plan

A LGBT elder's mental capacity and competency can be challenged during their lives. Claiming to be involved in a romantic and sexual relationship with another person may cause some to question the elder's competency. Remember, too many people believe the elderly are asexual creatures.

Family members who want to control an elderly person's finances may use the relationship as a reason to assume guardianship. If the family is successful in obtaining guardianship, the lesbian, gay, or transgender elder may be warehoused someplace away from their real support system.

Homophobic bias by the family and elder care professionals may combine to remove the LGBT elder from her support system and isolate her in an unwelcoming facility. The elder's sexual orientation may be used as enough reason to question her competency and provide proof that she suffers from diminished capacity.

An integrated estate plan involves not only testamentary documents but also a plan for what happens during the person's life. How will he pay for health care, housing, and regular expenses? Who will provide ongoing emotional and social support?

If your client is entering a senior retirement facility, is it safe? Does the facility have policies and training in place to protect seniors? Is it gay-friendly?

Think of the toll being closeted will take on the client. Is the level of fear such that it is adversely affecting the client's quality of life in the facility?

P. Conclusion

Lesbian, gay, and transgender elders are facing a world over which they may have little control.Housing, social isolation, medical care, and financial security remain great concerns for the lesbian, gay, and transgender elders.

Having a lawyer who understands what is needed for proper estate planning can give LGBT elders piece of mind.

Most lesbian, gay, and transgender elders want to remain in their homes. But many will require additional assistance as they age. Many LGBT persons do not have an extended family unit. And, their chosen families are not legally recognized. That places them at great risk of isolation and loneliness.

Lawyers assisting LGBT elders must realize their job does not end at the signing. Clients who enter senior housing facilities should be contacted regularly to check on their status. Be aware of changes in the client's demeanor and her surroundings. And, do not be afraid to ask questions.

This is area of law is untested and evolving. Litigation may be necessary to ensure fair and equitable treatment for lesbian, gay and transgender elders. For elder law lawyers this as an underserved population that can fill a practice niche . . . or provide a practice focus.

Chapter 9

Other Issues
and Considerations

Estate planning involves more than writing a will or trust. Providing a complete package of services will help clients identify the areas in which they need more help. Lesbian and gay clients may be faced with challenges not seen with straight clients. This chapter addresses some of the issues to consider when advising lesbian and gay individuals and couples.

A. Debts, Credit Reports, and Credit Cards

Debts, credit reports, and credit cards are necessary components of a client's estate plan. Understanding assets and liabilities will help in preparing a comprehensive plan that will address issues during the client's life and after her death.

Credit

There are no laws that prohibit discrimination based on sexual orientation, so creditors can deny credit to lesbian and gay applicants. State or local laws may prohibit discrimination, but federal law does not. The Equal Credit Opportunity Act (ECOA) does not include sexual orientation as a prohibited basis for denying credit. And, there are no court decisions that extend coverage of the ECOA to sexual orientation.

One exception involves housing. In January 2011, the Department of Housing and Urban Development (HUD) proposed new regulations[1] for its core housing programs. The rules would prohibit a lender from using actual or perceived sexual orientation and gender identity when determining a borrower's eligibility for a Federal Housing Administration (FHA) mortgage.

---

1. Press Release, U.S. Dep't of Hous. & Urban Dev., HUD Proposes New Rule to Ensure Equal Access to Housing Regardless of Sexual Orientation or Gender Identity (Jan. 20, 2011), http://portal.hud.gov/hudportal/HUD?src=/press/press_releases_media_advisories/2011/HUDNo.11-006.

Under the new HUD rule, sexual orientation and gender identity, whether actual or perceived, could not be used to deny an FHA-insured mortgage.

The proposed rule, Equal Access to Housing in HUD Programs Regardless of Sexual Orientation or Gender Identity,[2] would amend 24 CFR Parts 5, 200, 203, 236, 570, 574, and 982.

Credit Reports

In 2003, Congress passed the Fair and Accurate Credit Transactions Act (FACTA).[3] This enacted amendments to the Fair Credit Reporting Act (FCRA)[4] and expands consumer credit rights.

There are different provisions in FACTA, and their effective dates vary. Practitioners must research the client's credit issues to determine whether any of the new amendments apply.

The free credit report is one of the best changes. Consumers now have the right to obtain a free copy of their credit report from each of the four major credit-reporting agencies each year. The Federal Trade Commission (FTC) issued the Final Rule on Free Annual Credit Reports in June 2004.[5]

Consumers must request their free credit report directly from the FTC.[6] They may request an electronic copy or have one mailed to them. The important thing for clients to remember is that these reports are free. The FTC does not sell credit scores. There are commercials that talk about getting a free credit report, but the FTC does not sponsor these commercials. Many companies claiming to offer free credit reports do so only if the consumer buys other products.

Since consumers can get a free copy of their report each year, it is recommended that they stagger their requests over the course of the year. If a consumer is the victim of fraud or identity theft or is denied credit, he may also request a free copy of his report.

Credit-Reporting Agencies

There are four credit-reporting agencies (CRAs): Experian, Equifax, TransUnion, and Innovis. These companies collect credit and debt information on individuals.

---

2. Docket No. FR 5359-P-01; 76 Fed. Reg. 4194 (Jan. 24, 2011).
3. Pub. L. No. 108-159.
4. 15 U.S.C.A. §§ 1681 et seq.
5. 16 C.F.R. pts. 610, 698 (June 4, 2004).
6. Fed. Trade Comm'n, Free Annual Credit Reports, http://www.ftc.gov/bcp/edu/microsites/freereports/index.shtml.

Clients may not need to get a credit report from each credit-reporting agency. Sometimes it is sufficient to get a copy from the company that is nearest to where the client lives. For example, TransUnion, located in Pittsburgh, is the primary CRA for the northeast.

Contacting a CRA directly, rather than going through the FTC, results in a fee being charged for the credit report. Those reports may include a credit score. Not all credit scores are created equal, and not all creditors use the score the CRAs sell.

The Fair Isaac Corporation (FICO) creates the most widely used credit score. However, the FICO score sold to consumers may not be the same score used by creditors.

Credit scores are big business. They are also confusing and convoluted. Consumers should ask any creditor or lender what credit score they are using and what is it based on. That score will determine whether a consumer gets a loan and at what interest rate.

Experian charges $14.95 for an individual credit report and score and $39.95 for reports and scores from all three CRAs.

Equifax charges $39.95 for the complete report. It also has other packages available for purchase.

TransUnion fees start at $9.95 and go up from there. They also offer a "free credit report," but be sure to read the fine print.

Innovis is headquartered in Columbus, Ohio. It began life as ACB Services, evolved into Consumers Credit Associates, and was renamed Innovis, Inc. in 1997. Innovis charges various fees depending on which state the consumer lives in.

The CRAs are required to provide a free credit report in any of the following situations:

- The consumer is unemployed and intends to apply for employment within the next 60 days.
- The consumer is receiving public assistance.
- The consumer believes that the credit file includes inaccurate information because of fraud.
- The consumer received a notice of a denial of credit, insurance, or employment within the past 60 days.

The consumer also has the right to place a freeze on her credit report. This will prevent anyone, including the consumer, from obtaining credit unless the freeze is lifted. Some states allow residents to start and stop freezes without charge; others levy a minimal fee to start or stop a credit freeze. Check the individual state websites for information about these fees.

Credit freezes are a good idea if a client has been the victim of identity theft or has had other credit report problems. If a client intends to seek credit, he must remember to unfreeze the account before applying. Failure to do so will delay the credit application.

Credit-Reporting Agencies
TransUnion Corporation
Consumer Disclosure Center
P.O. Box 1000
Chester, PA 19022
800-888-4213
http://www.transunion.com

Equifax
ATTN: Consumer Department
P.O. Box 740241
Atlanta, GA 30374-0241
800-685-1111
http://www.equifax.com

Experian
Consumer Assistance
P. O. Box 2104
Allen, TX 75013
888-397-3742
http://www.experian.com

Innovis, Inc.
Attn: Customer Assistance
P.O. Box 1689
Pittsburgh, PA 15230-1689
http://www.innovis.com
800-540-2505

Information needed to get a credit report from a CRA:
1. Name
2. Current address
3. Social Security number
4. Date of birth

If the credit report contains inaccurate information, the consumer may file a request for the CRA to investigate the matter. When making a request to investigate, the consumer should include as many details as possible about why the information is inaccurate.

Paying off an old debt does not mean that it comes off a credit report. Most items will remain on the credit report for seven years from the date of the last activity. Paying off a debt after the seven-year period will reactivate it on the credit report.

CRAs are notorious for including inaccurate information or information belonging to someone else. The consumer has the responsibility for checking the reports and ensuring that they are accurate.

The credit-reporting agency is required by the FCRA to correct the report and remove false or outdated information. It is important to correct the report, because inaccurate information will wreak havoc on an individual's ability to obtain credit. It can also adversely affect a person's employment status.

If, after an investigation, the item remains disputed, your client has the right to include a statement about the situation and explain her position. This involves submitting a 100-word statement to the CRA. The statement is included in the report.

Cleaning up a credit report is something many lesbians and gay men must do, especially if there has been a recent breakup. A client will want to make sure nothing from his former partner shows up on the credit report.

All too often a client complains about a former partner ruining her credit. Unfortunately, most clients had authorized the former partner to use a credit card or co-signed a loan. The client will get a sobering education into credit and debt management.

Joint Credit Accounts

Many lesbian and gay couples have joint bank accounts, credit cards, and mortgages. This is not always a good idea. Clients need to be educated about the pitfalls of joint credit.

If clients are jointly liable for debts, they should review their individual credit reports *before* signing any credit agreement. Both parties need to know what the other's credit report looks like. And, each should request their credit reports annually.

Many couples start adding each other to credit cards or co-sign for loans without considering the consequences.

A joint debt is the responsibility of both parties. The creditor does not care who pays the bill. If the couple terminates the relationship, they must decide how they will handle the joint debts. A domestic partnership agreement can address those issues.

An important fact to remember is that the creditor is not a party to the domestic partnership agreement. Any agreement the couple enters into will bind them but not their creditors. Creditors are not bound by private agreements between the debtors.

Regardless of what agreement the parties make, the creditor has the legal right to seek payment from either of them.

The only way to bind a creditor is to make that creditor a party to the agreement, whether private or under a court order. If the couple goes to court, bring the creditors into the action as necessary parties. Any resulting court order will be binding on them as well as on the original debtors.

B. Social Security Benefits

The Social Security Act does not recognize same-sex relationships, although this will change for many married lesbian and gay couples that live in recognition states when DOMA is repealed.

Each member of a same-sex couple is entitled only to her individual Social Security account. There is no eligibility for "spousal" benefits or survivor benefits.

The nonbiological children of one partner are not entitled to receive any benefits upon the death of that partner even if she was their primary or sole support.

This is another reason why second-parent and joint adoptions are so important. Whenever possible, clients who are able to have a second-parent or joint adoption should be encouraged to follow through.

Same-sex couples do not benefit from the federal guarantee of payments to a surviving spouse, former spouse, unmarried children, or children disabled before age 22. It is unlikely (although possible) that the government will make eligibility for federal benefits retroactive once DOMA is repealed. That means that lesbians and gay men whose partners died before the repeal will remain ineligible for surviving spouse payments or survivor benefits.

However, it will be interesting to see if a same-sex couple that divorced will be able to claim benefits on their former spouse's account. The law requires the marriage to have lasted for at least 10 years. Some lesbian and gay couples who married abroad may qualify. It is unlikely a court would include the years a couple was together before the law allowed them to marry.

Individual gay or lesbian clients may have other dependents who could be eligible for benefits. These include grandchildren, great-grandchildren, and dependent parents.

There is no entitlement to the $255 death payment for the surviving spouse or children.

Life insurance remains the best option for clients. Each partner will need to purchase her own policy unless they can establish an "insurable interest" in the other. If the clients own a house together, that is sufficient to establish the interest. Otherwise, they may assign their individual policy to each other after the purchase. Then the partner becomes responsible for paying the premiums. Spouses, business partners, and joint homeowners have insurable interests that can be protected.

Medicare is another area that is limited to an individual. Same-sex couples do not qualify for any joint benefits under Medicare. See the discussion of Medicare in Chapter 8.

C. Pensions and Retirement Plans

Many different pension and retirement plans are available today. The types, allowable contribution limits, and rules change often enough to require a lawyer to take action to keep current.

The issue of retirement benefits can be difficult for lesbian and gay couples. Many plans expressly provide that only surviving spouses or children are eligible for survivor benefits.

Lesbian and gay couples need to review the company's plan and look for any restrictions on naming beneficiaries. They should consider taking advantage of individual retirement accounts (IRAs) or similar types of retirement vehicles. They may also consider retirement plans as a vehicle for charitable bequests. This option can result in tax savings.

Traditional and Roth IRAs are available as a means to save for retirement. The proceeds from these plans go to the named beneficiary, outside of probate. It is important to ensure that your clients have named the beneficiary on these plans. Failure to do so places account funds into the decedent's probate estate. There are no laws that preclude same-sex partners from naming each other as the beneficiary.

The same is true for 401(k) and 403(b) plans. The employee may designate a beneficiary to receive the proceeds at death.

A restriction applies to married employees. The surviving spouse must be named as the beneficiary unless the spouse waives that right. For married lesbian and gay couples, this means that they may be required to name their spouses. However, since a federal law, ERISA, governs pensions, there is a question about whether the rule applies to same-sex married couples.

Naming a beneficiary for these accounts is of primary importance. Failure to do so may result in the asset being deposited into the decedent's probate estate. That, in turn, may be reason enough for the decedent's family to challenge the will. And, depriving the surviving partner of these resources may mean the difference between poverty and financial stability.

Do not take the client's word that the beneficiary designation is current and accurate. Get the paperwork and review it together. Make it part of the estate plan file.

Federal Employees

The federal government offers a Thrift Savings Plan (TSP) for employees covered under the Federal Employees Retirement System (FERS). This system replaced the Civil Service Retirement System (CSRS) that covered federal employees since 1987.

The TSP program is comparable to a 401(k) plan. An employee can contribute a maximum of 15% of gross earnings, and the government contributes a maximum of 5%. The employee can name the beneficiary. The federal government now allows lesbian and gay federal employees to register their domestic partners and provide an annuity for them. This is the same formula that covers married federal employees.

The number of active federal employees who are enrolled in CSRS is dwindling. Under CSRS, employees do not pay Social Security taxes. Employees receive an annuity upon retirement. If the retiree is also eligible for Social Security payments, there is a dollar-for-dollar reduction from the annuity.

There is no provision for nonspouses to receive a portion of the retiree's CSRS benefits. The retiree may elect to reduce the annuity in order to provide for a surviving spouse annuity. However, this does not apply to same-sex couples. Once a retiree selects the retirement option, it cannot be changed.

Employees enrolled in the CSRS program can also contribute to the TSP plan, but their contributions are limited and there is no government contribution. The employee can name his partner as the beneficiary of the TSP proceeds.

Clients who are federal employees may be better off taking the full amount of the CSRS annuity and investing it. The retiree's partner will not be able to file a claim for survivor benefits unless and until Congress changes the law.

Federal employees enrolled in the FERS program can now name a same-sex partner as a surviving annuitant. They must complete the domestic partnership registration paperwork. This is handled through their agency's human resources office. They can also name their partner as the beneficiary of the TSP account.

The TSP account can be rolled over into an IRA in the same manner as a 401(k) when the federal employee leaves government service.

Pensions

The Employee Retirement Income Security Act (ERISA) controls company pensions. If your client is eligible to participate in an employer's pension plan, be sure to get a copy of the summary plan description, a summary annual report, and information on survivor/beneficiary coverage.

Some plans offer a lump-sum payment on retirement. For same-sex couples, this may be the best way to control retirement funds. By removing them from the employer's control, the retiree can then name anyone she wishes as beneficiary. Once the rollover is complete, the retiree or former employee has complete control over the funds. This is beneficial to same-sex couples because any restrictive rules applied by the former employer no longer apply.

Defined benefit plans, where a retiree receives a specific sum every month, are becoming rare. Most companies have changed to a defined contribution plan such as a 401(k). This places fewer burdens on the company and more responsibility on the employee.

D. Military Retired Pay

Military retired pay is an entitlement program and not a retirement plan or a pension plan. Military personnel can retire after 20 years of active duty. Military reservists are eligible to retire after compiling a sufficient number of points and reaching the age of 62. Service members completing 20 years of active duty have no minimum age requirement.

Some in Congress have raised the possibility of changing the military retirement system to create a minimum age before a retiree is eligible to receive benefits. While unlikely to be adopted, lawyers who work with military personnel should keep watch on this effort.

There is no entitlement to military retired pay until the service member completes 20 years of active duty or accumulates the required number of points for reserve duty and retires. Until the servicemember retires, there is no benefit.

There is no accrued value or vested interest while the member is serving. Also, while military retired pay is subject to division in a divorce or dissolution, only spouses are eligible to apply for a portion of a member's military retired pay. The Uniformed Services Former Spouse's Protection Act[7] (USFSPA) governs the division of military retired pay.

At this time, the civilian spouse in a same-sex couple has no right to military retired pay. This may change once DOMA is repealed. However, Congress must take specific action to amend federal law, including the USFSPA, to accomplish the change. That statute created the authority to divide military retired pay. It is a controversial statute for military personnel, who hate giving up their retirement pay to a former spouse.

Active duty military personnel are able to participate in the TSP program. This is in addition to any military retirement benefits the service member may be eligible for upon retirement. Though similar to a 401(k) plan, there is no government match for funds deposited in this account. Service members who serve less than 20 years on active duty or fail to achieve the required number of reserve service points may roll over the TSP funds when they leave military service. This may be a viable option for same-sex married couples until either DOMA is repealed or there is equity for them in military benefits.

With the repeal of "Don't Ask, Don't Tell," in September 2011, lesbian and gay men are able to serve openly, but DOMA will deny them the right to provide for their spouses. Their spouses will not be permitted to share in any benefits provided to married military personnel. Contributions to the TSP program are even more important for lesbian and gay servicemembers.

This situation will likely change when DOMA is repealed. It will be difficult to continue denying equal benefits to lesbian and gay servicemembers.

E. Veterans' Benefits

A veteran has no ability to provide for a same-sex partner from veteran's benefits. And, unless the law is changed, a veteran's same-sex spouse is not entitled to any benefits.

---

7. 10 U.S.C. §§ 1408 *et seq.*

A veteran of the United States military may be entitled to benefits for service-connected disabilities. Any servicemember who received an honorable discharge is entitled to benefits through the Department of Veterans Affairs (VA).[8] The VA website contains a plethora of information for veterans.

In an earlier time, homosexuality was grounds for an undesirable or dishonorable discharge from military service. The military then changed its regulations to give a lesbian or gay servicemember a general discharge, with a notation that it was for "homosexuality." That evolved into an honorable discharge but kept the code for homosexuality. The code would haunt the veteran forever.

Under "Don't Ask, Don't Tell" (DADT), lesbian and gay servicemembers received honorable discharges without a notation.

The earlier discharges may still crop up. A veteran may petition to have their discharge upgraded.[9] This is a time-consuming process with no guarantee of success. However, without an honorable discharge, the veteran can be denied VA benefits, including medical care.

The administrative appeal process following the denial of VA benefits is long and convoluted. Fortunately, federal law now allows veterans to be represented by a lawyer. Earlier laws prohibited lawyers from representing veterans in the appeal process. As a result, many appeals languished without resolution because there was no one forcing action.

F. Foreign Marriages, Religious Marriages, Civil Unions, and Domestic Partnerships

When the first edition of this book came out, Vermont was the only state that recognized civil unions. Vermont is now one of six marriage equality states,[10] and nine other jurisdictions recognize civil unions and domestic partnerships.[11]

Ten foreign countries recognize same-sex marriage.[12] Mexico City recognizes same-sex marriage, and the Mexican high court ruled that those marriages are valid throughout the country. Under DOMA, neither the U.S.

---

8. http://www.va.gov.
9. The application for review of discharge from the Armed Forces is available at http://www.dtic.mil/whs/directives/infomgt/forms/eforms/dd0293.pdf.
10. Connecticut, District of Columbia, Iowa, Massachusetts, New Hampshire, New York, and Vermont.
11. California, Delaware, Hawaii, Illinois, Nevada, New Jersey, Oregon, Rhode Island, and Washington.
12. Argentina, Belgium, Canada, Iceland, Netherlands, Norway, Portugal, South Africa, Spain, and Sweden.

government nor any state is required to recognize those foreign marriages. Once DOMA is repealed, the federal government will recognize those marriages. If DOMA is repealed in its entirety, there will be no federal law giving the states cover to refuse recognition.

There is a growing movement in several religious denominations to recognize marriage equality in the United States. It is still in the talking stage, but advances are being made—and that raises some interesting questions.

There has traditionally been a religious argument against same-sex marriages. Most state laws give members of the clergy authority to preside over marriages. The clergyperson must sign the state-issued marriage license in order for the marriage to be legally recognized. There is no state requirement that a legally sanctioned marriage be conducted in a church.

Is the minister an agent of the state? Can a clergy member refuse to officiate over a lesbian couple's marriage? New York's recently passed marriage law carved out religious exemptions. No church is required to recognize or permit a same-sex marriage in the church.

Should a clergy member sign a license—or refuse to sign it? Can a marriage, sanctioned by a church, be refused legal recognition? What about a church sanctioned marriage where the [heterosexual] couple did not obtain a marriage license?

What happens when a church, through its teachings, recognizes same-sex marriages? Do we enter into a discussion about whose church teachings are acceptable? If the U.S. Constitution is amended to recognize only heterosexual marriages, is there an inherent conflict between that amendment, the First Amendment, and the Fourteenth Amendment? These are unanswered questions.

The courts have ruled on religious teachings in the past and found some that violated secular laws. For example, the use of peyote in Native American rites and polygamy as practiced by the Mormons.

Lawsuits are sometimes filed because a county clerk will not issue a marriage license. Is a marriage license mandatory to establish a valid marriage? At least two New York judges have ruled that it is not.

In 2000, a New York trial court[13] found that a valid marriage existed even though the state never issued a license. The couple exchanged promises during a religious service. More than 100 guests attended the ceremony. This involved a Hindu prayer ceremony and was sufficient to make the couple

---

13. Persad v. Balram, 187 Misc. 2d 711 (Sup. Ct. Queens Cnty. 2001).

husband and wife. Later the husband began philandering and the wife sued for divorce. The husband claimed there was no marriage.

The court held, "[T]here is an old cliché that goes, 'if it walks like a duck and quacks like a duck and looks like a duck, it's a duck.' This familiar maxim appears perfectly suited to the case at bar, as it conforms with the intent underlying the statutory construction enacted by the Legislature. Essentially, the Domestic Relations law establishes that where parties participate in a solemn marriage ceremony officiated by a clergyman or magistrate wherein they exchange vows, they are married in the eyes of the law."

In 2002, a second New York judge arrived at the same conclusion.[14]

G. Business Succession

Part of the estate planning process requires you to determine whether the parties are in business together. You must determine the type of business and what form it takes, as well as whether the client is in a business relationship with anyone else and what form that arrangement takes. Are there written agreements?

The primary areas of concern in business estate planning are providing for the operation of the business after death, identifying estate tax concerns, and avoiding probate with the business.

Does the client have a buy-sell agreement concerning the business? Are family members involved? Is it a family-owned and -operated business that restricts the disposition of any one person's interest on death? Is there a "right of first refusal" agreement between co-owners? What happens if the other owners do not buy out the decedent's interest?

Advise the client to obtain a business valuation by an objective outside appraiser. This helps refute the IRS valuation.

Business succession planning is another part of this process. Review the client's organizational documents and make sure they coordinate with the client's estate plan.

Successful planning is dependent on a number of factors: the relationship between the current and future owners, cash sources, and how the parties deal with each other on an emotional, personal level. It is important to identify and resolve latent, unresolved problem areas that may mushroom in the future.

---

14. Ramyard v. Ali, No. 21297/2002 (Sup. Ct. Queens Cnty. 2002).

H. Long-Term Care Insurance

Long-term care (LTC) insurance is a valuable planning tool for lesbian and gay clients. These policies can cover home health care, nursing home care, physical therapy, and sometimes even more, depending on the policy. The insurance protects the insured against unplanned costs.

Long-term care insurance is best purchased when the insured is young and in good health. Find a flexible plan that provides for different care options. Clients need to consider whether the policy provides for inflation indexing of the benefits provided. Premiums vary and are based on duration and type of coverage selected.

Some companies, such as Ameriprise and New York Life, offer joint policies for same-sex couples that can be very cost-effective when compared to individual policies.

Lesbian and gay federal employees may sign up their partners for LTC through the federal government group plan.

Many younger lesbian and gay clients may question the need for LTC insurance. Take this opportunity to discuss the potential costs involved in caring for someone with a catastrophic illness or injury.

Long-term care insurance can offset the restricted coverage under Medicaid. Lesbian and gay couples are considered individuals when determining Medicaid eligibility and can have no more that $1,500 to $2,000 in assets to qualify.

Generally, premiums remain constant during the life of the coverage. It is a small price to pay for peace of mind.

I. Disability Insurance

Lesbian and gay individuals and couples need to take responsibility for protecting themselves and their families. Many lesbians and gay men will be solely responsible for supporting themselves during their lifetime.

Disability insurance is a necessary topic for discussion during the estate planning process. The disability plan should provide for payments if the insured is unable to perform their current job. They do not want an "any job" type policy. That policy will deny coverage if there is a job they could do, even if they are unqualified for it.

Group plans offered by employers or professional organizations are usually best. Individual plans can be cost-prohibitive. Still, disability insurance is essential because there is no guarantee there will be any other source of income.

If the insured pays the premiums directly, any payments received are non-taxable. Payments received from an employer paid plan are taxable to the recipient.

J. Conclusion

The issues raised in this chapter are designed to get you thinking about possibilities. There are other concerns that an individual client may raise that are not covered here. Do not consider this chapter exhaustive.

Lawyers assisting lesbian and gay clients in these challenging times must be creative. The issues are complex and seem to change daily. There are more questions than answers, and nothing is simple. Lawyers and clients must work together to recognize the potential problems and pitfalls and find viable solutions.

This is an exciting area of practice and it requires patience, tenacity, creativity, and open-mindedness to serve the clients' needs.

Chapter 10

Taxes

[IRS CIRCULAR 230 NOTICE: This material is intended for educational purposes only. It is not intended as tax advice. While this chapter concerns tax matters, it is not intended to be used and cannot be used by a taxpayer to avoid penalties that may be imposed by law.]

Estate taxes on the federal and state level are in flux. Ohio[1] recently abolished the estate tax while Hawaii reinstated its tax on estates over $3.5 million. Other states are lowering or raising the threshold for when the estate tax kicks in. The federal estate tax applies to estates over $5 million, but that is only through 2012.

Taxes are becoming more complicated[2] for lesbian and gay couples because of the different approaches to relationship recognition. Six states[3] and the District of Columbia have marriage equality. Maryland and New Mexico recognize out-of-state same-sex marriages even though those states do not allow those marriages.

California recognizes 18,000 married same-sex couples but no longer permits lesbians and gay men to marry in the state. California continues to have registered domestic partnerships. In addition, California recognizes out-of-state same-sex marriages.

The Defense of Marriage Act (DOMA) prohibits recognition of same-sex marriage on a federal level. DOMA is being challenged in federal courts around the country. A federal court in Massachusetts has ruled Section 3 of DOMA to be unconstitutional, and the Obama Administration has decided it will no longer defend DOMA in court. No one knows when or how this situation will resolve itself.

---

1. Effective in 2013.
2. *See, e.g.,* Liz White, *Analysis: State, Federal Differences Complicate Same-Sex Couple Filings,* BNASOFTWARE, Aug. 19, 2011, http://www.bnasoftware.com/News/Tax_News/Articles/ANALYSIS_State_Federal_Differences_Complicate_Same-Sex_Couple_Filings.asp.
3. Connecticut, Iowa, Massachusetts, New Hampshire, New York, and Vermont.

The marriage recognition states will allow married same-sex couples to file joint state tax returns. These couples must file as unmarried individuals at the federal level. Once DOMA is repealed—at least section 3—these couples will be able to file joint federal tax returns. They will enjoy the benefit of the unlimited marital deduction through which they can pass their estates.

In nonrecognition states, lesbian and gay couples must file as single taxpayers. They cannot file a joint federal tax return. Even those couples that married in a recognition state must file as individuals.

Under existing law, married lesbian and gay couples are denied the benefits of the marital deduction. That can place them at a huge disadvantage concerning their real estate and other assets.

There is a current case[4] pending in U.S. District Court in Manhattan that challenges DOMA and raises the marital deduction issue. Edie Windsor is suing for a refund of the estate tax she was required to pay after her partner died. Their marriage was not recognized and she was denied the marital deduction. The ACLU is representing her.

A. Real Estate

Real estate can present some of the thorniest issues for estate planners working with lesbian and gay couples. Many couples want to own real estate together. They also want to avoid probate.

Joint Tenants with Right of Survivorship

When a couple buys real estate together, they usually hold title as joint tenants with rights of survivorship (JTWROS). Title to the property passes to the surviving partner outside of probate. In many cases, the parties contributed equal amounts to the down payment and monthly mortgage payments. When this is the case, there are few drawbacks.

The couple should execute a side agreement that clarifies their intentions concerning ownership. The agreement should include the following:

- Specify the parties' intention to hold the property as joint owners.
- Detail the specific contributions made by the parties to the purchase.
- State that the parties will divide any sales proceeds according to their individual contributions.

---

4. Windsor v. United States, 10-CIV-8435 (S.D.N.Y.).

This side agreement can also be part of a domestic partnership agreement. The primary reason is to have written documentation of the parties' intentions concerning the real estate. None of this information should be included in the deed.

A joint tenancy can be severed if either party sells their interest in the property. When that happens, title reverts to a tenancy in common.

Property that is held in joint tenancy with rights of survivorship presents a major estate tax issue for lesbian and gay couples.

The IRS includes 100% of the property's value in the estate of the first owner to die.[5] This is a rebuttable presumption that can be overcome if the surviving joint owner can provide evidence of her contribution to the acquisition of the property.

Unfortunately, the IRS does not specify what constitutes sufficient documentation. Each party must establish that they made equal contributions to the mortgage payments. Showing that both parties had sufficient individual assets to make the payments should be sufficient to rebut the presumption.

Nonspousal joint tenancies are high on the list of IRS audits. Couples may want to attach a copy of the documentation reflecting equal contributions to the estate tax return. Without such evidence of the contribution made by the surviving partner, the entire value of the property will be included in the surviving partner's estate when she dies. The property is being taxed twice.

Heterosexual married couples do not face this double taxation penalty. The IRS presumes that husband and wife holding jointly titled property own equal shares. When DOMA is repealed, married lesbian and gay couples, living in recognition states, should be granted the same consideration.

Section 2040 is a special rule that requires including the full value of the property in the estate. There is no fractional share discount as might be available had the property been held as a tenancy in common.

The surviving partner's original contribution must also have come from her assets. The contribution cannot have originated via a gift from her partner.

Tenancy in Common

Using this form of title, the partners each own an undivided share in the real estate. Tenancy in common (TIC) is used when the owners have unequal

---

5. IRC § 2040.

shares in the property. The interest, or share, is in proportion to each owner's individual contribution to the purchase price.

A TIC title does not trigger gift tax liability because both parties hold an interest in proportion to their contribution. Neither is giving anything of value to the other.

Sometimes a couple will want to share ownership in a home already owned by one partner. There may be a taxable gain if the owner transfers an undivided interest in the real estate to his partner. If the interest is sold for fair market value, there is no taxable gift.

However, if the property is the parties' primary residence, and qualifies under § 121 of the Internal Revenue Code (IRC), up to $250,000 in gain can be excluded. If the transferred interest is less than that amount, the balance is available to the first owner when the property is ultimately sold. The other partner, however, will still have the full $250,000 exclusion available.

Holding title as TIC means that each owner's interest becomes part of their probate estate when they die. If a lesbian or gay couple owns property as TIC, they need to take steps to avoid having the property included in their probate estate. If they do nothing, there is the possibility that the surviving partner may end up owning the property with strangers or estranged family members.

A forced sale of a property happens through the partition process. When owners cannot agree on what to do with real estate, one or more of the owners can force the issue by filing a partition action. The court will order the property appraised and sold with the proceeds divided among the owners according to their respective shares.

Tenancy by the Entirety

Tenancy by the entirety (TE) is a type of deed that is available in Hawaii, Illinois, Massachusetts, Oregon, and Vermont, and only for real estate. Usually, this common-law form of joint ownership is limited to spouses. Hawaii, Illinois, and Oregon also permit registered partners to use this form of ownership. Since Massachusetts and Vermont are marriage equality states, married lesbian and gay couples can use this form of ownership on the same basis as heterosexual married couples.

The primary benefit of holding title as tenants by the entirety is that there is no unilateral severance. Each spouse owns 100% of the property. This protects the real estate from creditors. If one spouse has an individual debt, creditors cannot divide the real estate because the other spouse owns it in full.

Creditors do not like tenancy by the entirety and have succeeded in having it repealed in some states. While the effort gave creditors access to more assets, replacing the TE with JWROS ownership also allowed same-sex couples to hold property jointly and avoid probate.

There are potential problems calculating the gift tax because there is no unilateral severance in TE property. This is a main difference from property held in JTWROS, because that is divided into equal, undivided interests between the owners. Since the unlimited marital deduction came into existence, there is no law or IRC section that addresses TE held by married same-sex owners. The IRS has never acknowledged that such a thing could exist. Again, DOMA is involved here. Treasury Regulations § 25.2518-2(c)(4) may be helpful.

The situation is not any clearer when addressing possible estate tax issues because IRC § 2040 addresses "tenants by the entirety by the decedent and spouse." As long as DOMA is in effect, it may be possible to argue that 2040 does not apply. If it does apply, the property will be treated the same as JTWROS.

Real Estate Transfers

Property held as JTWROS do not need to take any other action to ensure that the property transfers to the survivor outside of probate. Some states may require a survivor affidavit to transfer title to the surviving owner.

Those who have a TIC deed must take some action. In states[6] that allow transfer on death deeds, each party can name the partner as the beneficiary after the owner dies. Those deeds allow title to transfer outside of probate.

These deeds are revocable, and no present interest transfers to the beneficiary. They are a good way to pass on real estate without having to include the property in the probate estate. If the couple ends their relationship, the property owner can revoke the transfer on death deed[7] with impunity.

A transfer on death deed, testamentary disposition, or living trust are alternatives for couples who want to have real estate pass from one partner to the other. Only one of them owns the property. There is no transfer of a present interest in the property. If the couple decides later to refinance the mortgage or buy another home, they are able to do so without a gift tax trigger.

---

6. Arizona, Arkansas, Colorado, Kansas, Minnesota, Missouri, Montana, Nevada, New Mexico, Ohio, Oklahoma, and Wisconsin.
7. Ohio uses a transfer on death affidavit.

And, if the relationship ends, the couple has avoided a problem with jointly owned real estate.

When a couple wants to transfer an interest in real estate between them, an appraisal is the first step. That establishes the property's fair market value. Transferring an interest in property can be done in stages. Limiting the value of the transfer to $13,000 can help avoid gift taxes.

Transfer the first two shares, each totaling $13,000, in December of one year and January of the next. That allows the current owner to transfer $26,000 in interest without triggering a gift tax situation.

Mortgages

When property is jointly held and both partners are on the mortgage, either can take the full deduction or they can split the deduction. A domestic partnership agreement would help by having the couple list their individual rights and responsibilities.

A mortgage issue that is often overlooked comes into play when lesbian and gay couples transfers interest in real estate to each other. A standard mortgage clause provides that any dilution of the security interest allows the mortgagee to call the note. This is the "due on sale" clause. When triggered, the mortgage lender has the right to call in the entire note, usually within 30 days.

When a couple decides to add someone as an owner of the property, without the mortgagee's consent, the "due on sale" clause can be invoked. One way to avoid the problem is to contact the mortgagee and get written consent to do so. The other way is to refinance the mortgage and include the new owner.

Adding names to real estate is a common act by lesbian and gay couples. They believe it is a simple process but do not consider the potential ramifications. Unfortunately, many clients take this action before they consult a lawyer.

B. Individual Retirement Accounts

New rules apply to inherited Individual Retirement Accounts (IRAs). This will benefit lesbian and gay couples that name their partner as the beneficiary.

In times past, inheriting an IRA meant that the beneficiary was required to begin withdrawals by December 31 of the year following the inheritance. That is no longer necessarily true.

Distributions from the account are not subject to the 10% penalty. A required minimum distribution is required to balance the account over the beneficiary's remaining life expectancy.

The rules for inherited IRAs can be tricky. But, with careful planning clients will be able to achieve the most benefits for their beneficiaries. Here are some rules to follow:

1. Complete the beneficiary form and do not name the estate as the beneficiary. If the IRA owner fails to name a beneficiary, anyone who inherits the IRA proceeds will not be able to stretch out distributions over their lifetime.
2. Inherited IRAs can never be combined with other assets. They must remain separate.
3. The Inherited IRA is not taxable if it was in the decedent's name.
4. The 10% early withdrawal penalty is not applicable.
5. Make any transfers "trustee to trustee." Do not have the client withdraw the proceeds personally, or else those withdrawals will be taxable.

C. State Estate Taxes

The landscape on state estate taxes is rapidly changing. Some states, like Ohio, repealed their estate tax.[8] Others, like Hawaii, reinstated the estate tax. Connecticut lowered its threshold for the estate tax to $2,000,000. Alabama, Alaska, and Colorado are tied to the federal/state death tax credit.

Essentially, this is an evolving area of law. Lesbian and gay couples that live outside a recognition state are treated as individuals and gain no benefit from laws that protect married couples.

D. Tax Returns

The tax return issue is complicated. The complexities became apparent when Massachusetts became the first recognition state and allowed lesbian and gay couples to marry. These couples could file joint state tax returns as a married couple. However, they were required to file federal returns separately. DOMA applies, and their marriage is not recognized. The couple would need to prepare multiple tax returns:

---

8. Effective in 2013.

1. Individual federal 1040 for both.
2. Joint federal 1040, as married.
3. Joint state tax return, as married.
4. Individual state tax returns for both.

Now married same-sex couples in the other marriage recognition jurisdictions are facing the same chore.

Multiple returns are required because the states and the federal government use comparable numbers when calculating one's tax liability. So, even though DOMA prohibits married lesbian and gay couples from filing a joint federal 1040, they must prepare one in order to properly prepare their state return.

Some people wonder whether they should attach a statement to their federal 1040 indicating they are married. There is a concern that they are committing perjury by marking "single" on their tax return. And, others object to checking "single" when they are legally married.

When DOMA is repealed, it will be prospective in nature. If the law is declared unconstitutional, then it may be retroactive. The latter means that people could file amended tax returns for the three-year period.

Children, and the adults who claim them as dependents, create more angst for lesbian and gay couples. Often it makes sense for the partner with the higher income to claim the deduction. The decision about who will claim the kids needs to be discussed with someone familiar with taxes. This is not a job for TurboTax.

E. Community Property States

Lesbian and gay couples living in a community property state face some unique issues. In a nutshell, community property laws specify that income or property accumulated during a marriage belong equally to both spouses. There are, of course, exceptions.

There are ten community property states:[9] Alaska, Arizona, California, Idaho, Louisiana, Nevada, New Mexico, Texas, Washington, and Wisconsin. Of those, only California and Nevada have specific laws recognizing same-sex relationships. Puerto Rico also has community property laws.

New Mexico's former attorney general issued an opinion that New Mexico would recognize lesbian and gay couples that married in a recognition

---

9. Colorado is a "marital property" state and treats marital assets as jointly owned by both spouses.

state. The current New Mexico governor wants a mini-DOMA state constitutional amendment.

California recognizes registered domestic partners (RDPs) for purposes of its community property law. California extended full community property rights to RDPs in 2007. The 18,000 California couples that married during that brief honeymoon period also have full community property rights on the same basis as heterosexual married couples.

Nevada's legislature passed a domestic partnership law that became effective October 1, 2009. The law is patterned after the one in California. It provides most of the marriage rights to domestic partners. The state's community property laws apply to domestic partnerships.

Washington adopted legislation that established state-registered domestic partnerships (SRDPs). It is the equivalent of marriage under state law. SRDPs are entitled to the benefits of the state's community property laws.

In California, Nevada, and Washington, RDPs can hold property as community property on the same basis as heterosexual married couples. California and Nevada also allow community property to be held with survivorship rights.

Property owned by Washington couples as JTWROS is presumed to be community property, while retaining the survivorship provision.[10] The couple needs to classify the property as community property for the IRS to treat it as such.[11]

In May 2010, the IRS issued a memorandum[12] stating that the U.S. Supreme Court case *Poe v. Seaborn*[13] applies to community property income of California RDPs. Under this ruling, if a lesbian or gay couple creates community property, there is no gift tax. This is true even if the property is created with the earnings of only one partner.

Since there are no gift taxes on creation of community property, only half of the property should be included in the decedent's estate.

The *Seaborn* decision held that California's community property laws applied to federal income tax returns. IRS Publication 555 deals with community property and federal tax implications.

An ongoing tax issue involves the tax return from RDPs and married California same-sex couples. There is no way to report the split community

---

10. WASH. REV. CODE ANN. § 64.28.040.
11. Rev. Rul. 87-98, 1987-2 C.B. 206.
12. Chief Counsel Advice Memorandum, CCA 201021050, 2010 WL 214782; based on I.R.S. P.L.R. 2010-21-048, 2010 WL 2147822.
13. 282 U.S. 101 (1979).

property income on the standard IRS forms. Until the situation is resolved, RDPs should consult a tax preparer who understands the myriad problems. Couples who are not careful may find themselves the subject of an audit.

Lawyers in community property states, or those with clients who own community property, need to be familiar with the many rules concerning creating and changing community property status. For example, if a couple owns a community property asset and divides that property equally between them, there is no taxable gift. However, if the couple owns a house as community property and transfers it into the separate property of only one owner, there is a taxable gift of 50% of the value.[14]

The IRS has published a Q&A for Registered Domestic Partners in Community Property States and Same-Sex Spouses in California.[15]

F. Other Tax Issues

In most states, and under federal law, the tax laws treat same-sex couples as legal strangers. There are virtually no tax benefits. The level of commitment or whether the couple married or entered into a civil union or domestic partnership in a recognition state is irrelevant.

There are many questions how the repeal of DOMA will affect lesbian and gay couples. Will lesbian and gay couples who married in a recognition state but live in a nonrecognition state be able to take advantage of federal benefits for married couples? What about the couples who were living in a recognition state when they married and then moved to a nonrecognition state? Do they lose benefits under federal law because of their current state of residence? Does state or federal law apply to determine who receives federal benefits?

Another question: States like Nevada and Washington have domestic partnerships for same-sex couples that are comparable to marriage in everything but name. Will the nitpicking begin and revolve around the wording used to describe the relationship? Or will the legislative intent control?

What about the legally married same-sex couple that hires a nanny?[16] The higher income spouse, Jamie, claims the kids as dependents. The other spouse, Anna, is also a legal parent and could claim them. Jamie gets an employer identification number (EIN) for the household/employer/payroll taxes. But what happens later if Anna decides to claim one of the kids? Does

---

14. Rev. Rul. 75-551, 1975-2 C.B. 378 (implies unequal divisions would be taxable).
15. http://www.irs.gov/newsroom/article/0,,id=245869,00.html.
16. Thanks to Professor Patricia Cain for these scenarios.

she also get an EIN, and does the couple prorate the nanny tax and associated dependent-care credit?

Later, Anna wants to consolidate her student loans. Perhaps she wants to enter a loan forgiveness program. She needs to provide tax returns, but since she has not been claiming the children, her deductions are lower and income is higher. Will the loan program accept the joint state tax return as a true reflection of her income and tax liability? Most likely, it will not because it is a federal program and DOMA applies. But, does the program use state law to define "spouse"? If so, will DOMA still apply?

These scenarios exist today. They will continue to exist until the law reflects reality.

Gifts

The definition of "gift" is different for income and gift tax purposes. The transferor's motive is key for income tax purposes. The gift tax rule provides that the transfer is a "gift" unless the transferor received "adequate consideration in money or money's worth."

Every person has the right to make unlimited annual gifts up to $13,000 to anyone. These annual gifts do not carry a tax liability to either the giver or recipient.

Gifts that exceed $13,000 must be reported on the federal gift tax return before April 15 of the year following the gift. The amount over $13,000 is deducted from the lifetime exemption. The current exemption is $5 million.

As long as the gifts stay below the $13,000 annual limit, there is no need to file a gift tax return.

Married lesbian and gay couples are not entitled to the marital deduction for gift tax purposes.

Transferring ownership of income-producing assets to the lower income partner may also provide tax relief to the recipient. It is important, however, to consider any gift tax consequences of such a transfer. Clients need to execute a written agreement and talk to their lawyer *before* making the transfer.

Lately, the IRS has been reviewing transfers to determine whether a gift tax return was required and whether it was filed. While there is no tax due, the return must be filed, and the amount is charged against the individual's lifetime exemption.

What is considered a gift? If one partner earns significantly more than the other, and contributes more to household expenses, are those contributions a gift? If Amy pays for the groceries, is half the amount a gift to her partner?

If there is no state law requiring one to support one's partner, it may all count as a gift.

Dependents and Head of Household

Clients should consider "head of household" status, dependents, deductions, and distribution when calculating tax liability. If one partner is providing financial support for the other, it may be possible to file a single return and name the partner as a "dependent."

There are requirements to qualify in this regard:

- The dependent must be an unmarried person.
- The dependent must be a United States citizen.
- The dependent must have gross income under $2,900.
- The support provided must be at least 50% of the total annual support.
- The person must live in the filer's home for a full year.
- The relationship must not violate local law. (This requirement is open to debate since there is no guidance from the IRS as to its meaning.)

Most lesbian and gay couples will not qualify under the "dependent" rule. Likewise, absent a court order requiring support, nonbiological children may not qualify as a "dependent" for the nonlegal parent.

Filing as a head of household is also an option, especially when children are present or if the client provides over 50% of her partner's support. There are three requirements for filing as head of household:[17]

1. You are unmarried or were "considered unmarried" on the last day of the year.
2. You paid more than half the cost of keeping up a home for the year.
3. A "qualifying person" lived with you in the home for more than half the year (except for temporary absences, such as school). However, if the "qualifying person" is your dependent parent, he does not have to live with you.

To be a member of the household, a person must either live with the taxpayer all year as a member of the household or be one of the listed relatives.

---

17. IRS Publ'n 501 (2010), Exemptions, Standard Deduction and Filing.

It may be worthwhile for clients to discuss whether either qualifies as a head of household. The IRS may object to this classification, so clients need to maintain careful documentation to defend the classification.

When one partner is supporting the other, it may constitute a taxable gift if the total support amount exceeds $13,000. The exception is if the support qualifies as educational or medical payments under IRC §2503(e).

For couples living in recognition states, the support should not be treated as taxable gifts unless state law imposes a support obligation on the parties.

Direct Payments

Educational and medical payments can be made by one partner on behalf of the other and claimed as a deduction. There is no restriction on the mount of medical and educational payment, but they must be made directly to the health care provider or the educational institution.

Partnerships

Lesbian and gay couples who own and manage property together or who co-own a business may find some tax advantages in forming a partnership. This includes forming a limited liability company (LLC).

Transferring assets into the LLC/partnership creates a new ownership entity and removes the assets from the transferor's estate. Assets are valued in a different way through a partnership or LLC. There is no market for a 50% share of a partnership. The value of the partnership is significantly less than the value of the assets in the partnership.

One caveat: There must be a business purpose underlying the partnership's creation. That is the only way to obtain gift and estate tax benefits.

Family limited partnerships (FLPs) and family limited liability enterprises (FLLEs) are popular, but those seeking tax benefits have also abused them. The IRS is likely to audit any FLPs and FLLEs that are created shortly before death.

The IRS has successfully challenged these types of entities, and that erases any estate tax savings. Since all that happens after death, couples are advised to avoid them and stick with other types of entities.

G. The Party's Over

Let's face it. Nothing lasts forever. Lesbian and gay couples are not immune from breaking up. The question is how to deal with the fallout.

Divorce

Divorce is one of the trickiest parts of ending a same-sex marriage. If the couple lives in a nonrecognition state, their marriage will be invalid, under state law, and they will not be able to avail themselves of court protection. They may be able to file an action in a court of general jurisdiction to divide their property. But, the marriage itself will remain intact unless one of them establishes residency in a recognition state and files for divorce. Most same-sex couples do not consider this when entering into a marriage.

California's legislature has passed SB 651 that addresses this issue for same-sex couples who were married in California. If that couple now lives in a state that will not grant a divorce, either spouse may file in California without first establishing residency. California's governor signed the bill into law.

A lesbian or gay couple that ends their relationship may incur tax liability when dividing their assets.[18] Under DOMA, married lesbian and gay couples are not considered "spouses" when dividing property.

Internal Revenue Code § 1041 states that transfers by spouses, either during the marriage or as part of a divorce, are not taxable. This section does not apply to RDPs or married same-sex couples because of DOMA.

One work-around on the issue is arguing that same-sex partners are more like married couples than unrelated persons. If the parties are dividing jointly owned property, an argument can be made that it is a tax-free division because both parties are owners. It may be easier to make these arguments for lesbian and gay couples living in community property states or recognition states.

Support

Alimony is usually included in the recipient's income and deductible by the payee. IRC §§71 and 215 cover alimony payments. And, under DOMA, these sections do not apply to lesbian and gay couples.

A nonbiological/nonadoptive/non–legally recognized parent has no legal obligation to pay child support. Many shared custody agreements include provisions for the legally recognized parent to retain custody and the other to pay support. A person may obligate herself to pay support through a contract.

---

18. United States v. Davis, 370 U.S. 65 (1962).

However, support payments that are not required under state law are taxable gifts. If the support paid exceeds $13,000, the payor will need to file a gift tax return for the excess.[19]

When drafting the Shared Custody Agreement it is important to address this matter as well who gets the dependent tax deduction for the child.

Sharing income between partners should not be seen as gifts from one to the other. Those payments are not estate-depleting transfers. And, that is not what Congress intended the gift tax to cover.

Court-ordered support should also not be a taxable gift. There are no rules that classify such payments as nontaxable gifts. However, the transfers are made to satisfy a legal support obligation and should not be considered taxable gifts.[20]

Support consists of food, clothing, shelter, and other things beyond basic necessities.

H. Estate and Gift Taxes

There is no marital deduction available for same-sex couples. Wealthy couples may want to use a form of bypass trust to limit their tax liability. The standard forms cannot be used for lesbian and gay couples. Moreover, limiting funding makes no sense without the marital deduction. Putting everything in a credit shelter trust may be a better move.

A bypass trust will work if the goal is to avoid estate taxes on the death of the second partner.

However, since the tax landscape may change when DOMA is repealed, contingent planning is advisable. One suggestion is to use normal funding clauses in a bypass trust and place everything else in a bypass trust that would qualify as a qualified terminable interest property (QTIP) trust.

A QTIP is a trust used by married couples to postpone estate taxes. It allows a surviving spouse to use the trust property tax-free. The taxes are deferred until the surviving spouse dies and the beneficiaries receive the trust property. No one else can have an interest in the trust during the surviving spouse's lifetime.

Hedging on the repeal of DOMA, include a provision that if a QTIP election is not made, the assets pass to the credit shelter trust. Naming a trust

---

19. Rev. Rul. 54-343, 1954-2 C.B. 318; REV. RUL. 82-98, 1982-1 C.B. 141.
20. Rev. Rul. 1968-379, 1968-2 C.B. 414.

protector with the power to rewrite trust provisions to qualify for the marital deduction is one option.

The couple could have a discretionary bypass trust and authorize the trust protector to divide the trust into a discretionary bypass trust and a marital deduction trust. The trust protector can be authorized to amend the trust terms applying to the marital deduction trust so it complies with the IRC requirements.

Same-sex couples may need to track assets acquired from a spouse in different ways for federal and state taxes. When those assets are sold, there will be a dual gain/loss calculation—again, one federal and the other state.

I. Life Insurance

Life insurance is a good way to meet potential tax liabilities. One tactic is to research whether a first-to-die policy will reduce the overall premium expenses.

Life insurance policies owned at death are part of the decedent's taxable estate. Policies that cover both partners should be transferred into an irrevocable life insurance trust. Neither partner should own their individual policies. Each partner may create an irrevocable life insurance trust. Their estates can borrow money from the trust to pay estate taxes.

In community property states, the partners need to pay premiums on individual policies from their separate property. Otherwise, the policy may be considered community property. Also, group policies will likely be considered community property, with only half going into the decedent's estate.

Many people have life insurance through their employer. It may be possible for ownership of that policy to be transferred to someone else. If the company owns the policy—because they pay the premiums—the insured is not the owner. The company's human resources department may be able to help figure it out. Even though it is a group plan, it may be possible to transfer ownership.

The couple will need to decide who will be the trust protector. Another issue is to determine the trust protector's liability.

J. Conclusion

Nothing in this chapter should replace consulting with an experienced tax lawyer. Look for information on taxes affecting same-sex couples, check out tax blogs,[21] and read white papers on the subject. Recognize your own limitations when it comes to taxes and admit it to the client. Do not hesitate to refer the individual to a lawyer who has more experience in tax planning. There is nothing wrong with admitting that something is outside your comfort zone. Moreover, it helps avoid malpractice.

The information contained in this chapter is not exhaustive. It deals with the basics but is, by no means, the entire discussion. This is an effort to point out possible issues to discuss with clients.

DOMA remains the greatest impediment for fair tax treatment of lesbian and gay couples, married or not. Until it is repealed, there will not be tax equity. And, until all same-sex relationships are legally recognized, DOMA's repeal will merely be the start of the conversation.

---

21. For example, see Santa Clara Law's same-sex tax blog at http://law.scu.edu/blog/samesextax.

Appendix A

Estate Planning Forms

ESTATE PLANNING FORM I

CONFLICT LETTER

Elise Marie Shepherd
Attorney at Law
5 Portman Place
Lakewood, Ohio 44107-5816
Phone: 216-555-5555
E-mail: EMS@elisemshepherd.com

April 18, 2011

Christine L. Grandring
Mellicent A. Resounter
142 Reveley Ave.
Cleveland, OH 44111

Dear Ms. Grandring and Ms. Resounter,

You have asked that I represent you in preparing your estate plan. I am happy to do so. However, representing both of you may present a conflict of interest between you. For example, confidential information about either of you may be disclosed to each other during this process. Other conflicts may also arise.

Representing both of you means that your individual confidential information may be released to each other. I am using this letter as notice to you of that potential conflict of interest. You each have the right to be represented by independent counsel. By signing this letter, you acknowledge that right and the potential conflict of interest and you waive both.

You are expressly consenting to have me represent both of you in preparing your estate plans. Each of you waives any objection to that representation. And, each of you consents to the disclosure of confidential information to the other.

In preparation for the initial interview I am enclosing a questionnaire. I ask that you each complete an individual questionnaire. I will use the information to prepare your estate plan documents. We will review the questionnaires at the time of the interview. Please note anything you want to discuss when we meet.

I know your privacy is important. I understand you trust me to protect the confidentiality and security of that information. The information I collect from you is used only to provide the legal services you request. All of your information is held in strict confidence and will not be released to anyone without your written consent.

Sincerely,

Elise Marie Shepherd
Attorney at Law

Letter of Conflict, pg. 2

I acknowledge receipt of this letter. I understand that I am entitled to separate counsel representing me. I consent to Elise M. Shepherd representing both of us. I waive any conflict of interest arising from that representation. And, I consent to the disclosure of confidential information about myself to my partner.

_____   _____
Christine L. Grandring   Mellicent A. Resounter

Date: _____   Date: _____

ESTATE PLANNING FORM 2

ESTATE PLANNING ENGAGEMENT AGREEMENT

I am looking forward to working with you on an estate plan that will express and carry out your wishes. The purpose of this letter is to confirm your employment of me as your attorney and to explain the nature and terms of my representation.

A.   FEE AGREEMENT

My professional fee for estate planning services is _____. This fee includes the preparation and signing of the following documents:

- ❏   Will
- ❏   General Durable Power of Attorney
- ❏   Living Will
- ❏   Health Care Power of Attorney
- ❏   HIPAA Authorization
- ❏   Designation of Agent
- ❏   Deed
- ❏   Shared Custody Agreement
- ❏   Domestic Partnership Agreement
- ❏   Living Trust
- ❏   Testamentary Trust
- ❏   _____

You are responsible for any additional expenses, such as real estate recording fees.

There may be additional attorney fees if you request services other than what is specified in this Agreement. [This includes the preparation of trusts, parenting agreements, and domestic partnership agreements.] We will discuss whether additional fees are required before any services are provided. [The full fee is payable when the documents are completed.] [The fee is payable as follows: _____.] Additional professional fees: _____.

B.   CONFIDENTIALITY

As your lawyer, I am obligated to keep all information about your estates confidential. I cannot divulge any information to other persons without your consent. This rule is designed to encourage you to tell me everything I need to know to perform the services you request.

This rule does not prevent you from involving other advisors and family members in planning your estates. Their input can be helpful and may reduce the amount of time I need to prepare your estate plans.

You must understand that there is no confidentiality between the two of you. If one of you tells me something that might affect the other's planning, I am obligated to relay that information to the other. I cannot agree to withhold any information from either of you.

C.   JOINT REPRESENTATION

You have asked that I represent both of you in preparing your estate plan. Joint representation raises the possibility that a conflict of interest may arise between you. By agreeing to have me represent you both, you waive any conflict of interest that may arise.

You each have the right to consult with an independent lawyer. There are times when joint representation may be inappropriate. One partner may have different objectives or may be more comfortable consulting with a lawyer separately.

I will rely on you to inform me about any conflicts that exist between you. I will exercise my professional judgment concerning potential conflicts that may arise while planning your estates. If any conflict cannot be resolved, I will no longer be able to represent either of you. You will need to hire individual lawyers.

By signing this Engagement Agreement you waive any existing conflict of interest, consent to my representing both of you, and acknowledge your individual right to have separate counsel. You also consent to the disclosure of confidential information to each other.

_____   Date: _____
Elise M. Shepherd, Attorney at Law

I agree to and accept the terms included in this Estate Planning Engagement letter. I acknowledge receipt of this letter. I understand that I am entitled to separate counsel representing me. I consent to Elise M. Shepherd representing both of us. I waive any conflict of interest arising from that representation. And, I consent to the disclosure of confidential information about myself to my partner.

_____   Date: _____

_____   Date: _____

ESTATE PLANNING FORM 3

GENERAL INVOICE

ELISE M. SHEPHERD
Attorney at Law

5 Portman Place
Lakewood, Ohio 44107-5816

Phone: 216.555.5555
Email: EMS@elisemshepherd.com

March 9, 2011

INVOICE

TO:

For Professional Services:

Appointments:
Initial: 1.5 hours
Signing: 1.5 hours

Preparation of documents: 3.5 hours

Wills (2)
Designations of Agent (2)
Health Care Powers of Attorney (2)
Living Wills (2)
Durable Powers of Attorney for Finances (2)
Transfer on Death Deed
Joint and Survivorship Deed

TOTAL FEE: $_____

Please remit full payment within 30 days of invoice date.

THANK YOU.

Elise M. Shepherd
Attorney at Law

ESTATE PLANNING FORM 4

CLIENT ESTATE PLAN CHECKLIST

Use this checklist to locate important documents and information. Update on a regular basis. Keep the checklist and the listed documents in a safe place. Review your estate plan with your Executor. Make sure your Executor knows where you keep the documents. That saves time later.

A.   PERSONAL INFORMATION

Name: _____   Date of birth: _____

Address: _____

Social Security #: _____   Driver's license #: _____

A. Do you own a house? ❑ Yes ❑ No
Is any other name on the deed? ❑ Yes ❑ No   Whose? _____
Did you buy it together? ❑ Yes ❑ No   When? _____
Is there a mortgage? ❑ Yes ❑ No   Are both names on the mortgage? ❑ Yes   ❑ No
Mortgage Co.: _____
Account No.: _____   Balance: _____

B.   IMPORTANT DOCUMENTS

1. Will

Date signed: _____ Where is it? _____

Executor name and contact info: _____
_____

Alternative executor name and contact info: _____
_____

2. Trust

Date signed: _____ Where is it? _____

Trustee name and contact info: _____
_____

Alternative trustee name and contact info: _____
_____

3. Durable Power of Attorney for Finances

Date signed: _____   Where is it? _____

Attorney in fact name and contact info: _____
_____

Alternative care attorney in fact name and contact info: _____
_____

4. Living Will

Date signed: _____   Where is it? _____

5. Health Care Power of Attorney

Date signed: _____   Where is it? _____

Health care attorney in fact name and contact info: _____
_____

Alternative health care attorney in fact name and contact info: _____
_____

C.   INSURANCE

6. Health Insurance

Carrier name and contact info: _____
_____

Policy #: _____

7. Disability Insurance

Carrier name and contact info: _____
_____

Policy #: _____

8. Long-Term Care Insurance

Carrier name and contact info: _____
_____

Policy #: _____

9. Life Insurance

Carrier name and contact info: _____

_____

Policy #: _____

Beneficiary name and contact info: _____

_____

Insurance agent name and contact info: _____

_____

10. Car Insurance

Carrier name and contact info: _____

_____

Policy #: _____

Insurance agent name and contact info: _____

_____

D.   RETIREMENT/PENSION/ANNUITIES

11. Retirement/Employee Benefits

Company name and contact info: _____

_____

Account type/benefit amount: _____ Account #: _____

Beneficiary name and contact info: _____

_____

12. Pension

Company name and contact info: _____

_____

Account type/benefit amount: _____ Account #: _____

Beneficiary name and contact info: _____

_____

13. Annuity

Company name and contact info: _____
_____

Account type/benefit amount: _____ Account #: _____

Beneficiary name and contact info: _____
_____

E.   ASSETS

MAKE A COMPLETE LIST OF ALL YOUR ASSETS AND ATTACH IT. INCLUDE THE NAME, ADDRESS, AND PHONE NUMBER OF THE COMPANIES.

 ➢ **Bank accounts**: account numbers, address, and hone number of bank/S&L/etc. Check to see that all individual accounts are payable on death.

 ➢ **Brokerage accounts**: adviser's name, address, e-mail and phone; account numbers; transfer on death instructions for beneficiaries. List the names of the beneficiaries and whether you executed a transfer on death form.

 ➢ **U.S. Savings bonds**: value, issue date; if the bonds have stopped earning interest, you may want to cash them in; check the U.S. Treasury website for information. Where are the actual bonds?

 ➢ **Stocks/Bonds**: Where are the actual certificates? Make a list of the name, address, and phone number of the companies in which you own stock. **DO NOT FORGET TO NAME A BENEFICIARY OR MAKE THESE TRANSFER ON DEATH.**

 ➢ **Deeds** to real property. Make sure all deeds have been recorded. Look for recorder's stamp.

 ➢ **Valuable personal property** owned, individual and joint; copies of appraisals (antiques, jewelry, firearms, horses, pedigree animals).

 ➢ **Business Agreements:** partnership papers, corporate filings, and other business-related paperwork.

 ➢ **Intellectual Property:** websites, e-mail addresses, copyrights, patents, etc.

F.   LIABILITIES

MAKE A COMPLETE LIST OF ALL YOUR LIABILITIES. INCLUDE THE NAME, ADDRESS, AND PHONE NUMBER OF YOUR CREDITORS.

 ➢ **Credit cards**: account number, phone number to cancel; issuer's address; note the expiration date and the three-digit security code on the back. This information is needed for online banking purposes. The security code is only on the card—neither the bank nor the credit card issuer has that information.

➢ **Loans**: type of loan, account number, lender's name, address, e-mail, and phone number.

➢ **Tax Returns**: Where are copies located? contact info for tax preparer (address, phone number).

G.   OTHER INFORMATION

14. **Letters of instructions** (funeral and burial; insurance papers; location of safe deposit box; names, addresses, phone numbers of anyone you want contacted; business instructions; who gets specific items).

15. **Doctors**/health care professionals, address and telephone number, e-mail.

16. You can designate an **emergency contact person** on the Ohio BMV website: http://www.bmv.ohio.gov; look for "Next of Kin Emergency Contact Enrollment Online"; click on that and enter the information.

17. You may also sign up for the **Ohio Organ Donor Registry** from the BMV website. There is a link on the right side of the page.

16 & 17 ARE STATE SPECIFIC--CHECK TO SEE IF YOUR STATE HAS A SIMILAR PROGRAM.

18. If you have stock certificates, list the certificate numbers, the number of shares owned, the price you paid for them, and when you bought them. This information will help your Executor value these assets after your death. Also, specify where the stock certificates are located. If you own stock directly, rather than through a broker, you need the certificates to sell or transfer the stock.

19. **Transfer on Death documents**: You may transfer ownership of stocks, bonds, and similar holdings through a transfer on death designation. Talk to your broker or financial planner about getting those forms. **DON'T FORGET TO EXECUTE THE DOCUMENTS**.

20. If you signed a Trust, **DON'T FORGET TO TRANSFER THE PROPERTY INTO THE TRUST. If you do not transfer the property it is NOT part of the trust. That property may need to be included in a probate action.** Let me know if you need help or if you have questions.

21. If you are an organ donor, it's helpful to list basic information. Your family will be asked medical/social questions and the information you give here will help them. The questions are similar to those you answer when giving blood. EX. Provide information about drug use, tattoos, smoking/alcohol, and sexual activity in addition to medical history. Additional information is available from http://www.lifebanc.org.

22. If you use online banking, be sure your Executor has the logon information you use to access that account. Without it, NO ONE will be able to access your online banking information. An alternative is to contact your bank and arrange authorization for your Executor, or another person, to access your online account.

23. Make a list of your passwords and what they go to. Everyone says to never write down a password. However, if you use passwords and something happens to you, your heirs/Executor will not be able to access your computer, accounts, etc. without the password.

24. To prepare for probate, it is important to create a list of immediate family members who must be notified when your will is admitted to probate. This includes children, parents, siblings, aunts, uncles, and cousins. Include the individual's name, address, phone number, and email address. If anyone has died, note the date and place of death.

Please let me know if you have any questions or concerns.

Insert Attorney contact information

ESTATE PLANNING FORM 5

CONFIDENTIAL WILL QUESTIONNAIRE

PERSONAL AND FAMILY INFORMATION

1. **Your legal name**: _____

E-mail: _____
Phone: (H): _____ (W): _____ (C): _____
Date of birth: _____ Social Security #: _____
Place of Birth: _____
Citizenship: [ ] U.S.   [ ] Other: _____ Immigration Status: _____

2. **Partner's legal name**: _____

E-mail: _____
Phone: (W): _____ (C): _____
Date of birth: _____ Social Security #: _____
Place of Birth: _____
Citizenship: [ ] U.S.   [ ] Other: _____ Immigration Status: _____

3. Home address: _____
   Home County: _____

4. Do you currently have a will?   ❑ Yes ❑ No   (Please have it available)

5. Have you been married   ❑ Yes ❑ No   Marriage ended in [ ] death [ ] divorce

6. Do you have a domestic partnership agreement?   ❑ Yes ❑ No (have a copy available)
   Do you want one?   ❑ Yes ❑ No

7. Do you own any digital assets/intellectual property (e-mail, blogs, social network profiles, web pages, domain names, etc.)?   ❑ Yes ❑ No

8. Do you own any firearms?   ❑ Yes ❑ No

9. **Children**
      Do you have any children?   ❑ Yes ❑ No

      (a)   Please list all of your children, including date of birth and state of residence.

      _____
      _____
      _____

(b)   Do you have a special needs or handicapped child?   ❑ Yes   ❑ No
(c)   Do you plan to have children?   ❑ Yes   ❑ No
(d)   Do you have a parenting agreement?   ❑ Yes   ❑ No   (have a copy available)
(e)   Do you have a donor agreement?   ❑ Yes   ❑ No   (have a copy available)

10. EXECUTOR

Name/City/State: _____

Relationship: _____

Phone Number: _____

ALTERNATIVE EXECUTOR

Name/City/State: _____

Relationship: _____

Phone Number: _____

11. WILL CONTEST

You may leave your estate to anyone you choose. Will your family members contest your will?

    ❑ Yes   ❑ No

12. EXPLANATION OF INTENT CLAUSE

You explain and document your intentions about the disposition of your estate.   ❑ Yes   ❑ No

13. SPECIFIC BEQUESTS

Do you wish to make specific bequests in your will?   ❑ Yes   ❑ No

1. _____
2. _____
3. _____
4. _____

14. PETS

Do you have any pets?   ❑ Yes   ❑ No   Whom do you want to care for your pets?

_____

_____

15. BENEFICIARIES OF YOUR ESTATE

Primary Beneficiaries

Beneficiary: _____

Relationship: _____ Amount: _____

Beneficiary: _____
Relationship: _____ Amount: _____

Beneficiary: _____
Relationship: _____ Amount: _____

Alternative Beneficiaries

Beneficiary: _____
Relationship: _____ Amount: _____

Beneficiary: _____
Relationship: _____ Amount: _____

Beneficiary: _____
Relationship: _____ Amount: _____

16. GUARDIAN OF MINOR CHILDREN

FIRST CHOICE:

Guardian: _____
Relationship: _____
Address and Phone Number: _____

ALTERNATIVE CHOICE:

Guardian: _____
Relationship: _____
Address and Phone Number: _____

17.   TRUSTS

Do you want a trust?   ❑ Yes ❑ No

Whom do you wish to serve as your trustee? (For a living trust, you are the current trustee and a successor trustee is named upon your death.)

Trustee: _____
Relationship: _____
Address and Phone Number: _____

Successor Trustee: _____
Relationship: _____
Address and Phone Number: _____

18.   **ASSETS**

A.   **Real Estate** (primary residence, vacant land, rental property, vacation home).

Do you own real estate jointly?   ❑ Yes ❑ No (have your deeds available)

Address: _____
Owner(s) listed on deed: _____
[ ] Paid for   [ ] Outstanding Mortgage   Approximate Value: _____

Did you add your partner's name to the deed after you bought the property?   ❑ Yes ❑ No
Do you own other real estate?   ❑ Yes ❑ No

Address: _____
Owner(s) listed on deed: _____
[ ] Paid for   [ ] Outstanding Mortgage   Approximate Value: _____

B.   **Bank Accounts:**   ❑ Checking   ❑ Savings   ❑ Other _____
Are the accounts: ❑ Joint ❑ Individual   ❑ Both

Name(s) on account: _____

C.   **Vehicles:**

Make/Model/Year: _____
Approximate Value: _____

Make/Model/Year: _____
Approximate Value: _____

D.   **Life Insurance:**

Life insurance passes to the named beneficiaries.

Policy Value: _____
Beneficiary: _____
Who pays the premiums?   ❑ You ❑ _____

Policy Value: _____
Beneficiary: _____
Who pays the premiums?   ❑ You ❑ _____

Insurance agent name: _____
Address: _____
Phone #: _____
Email: _____

E. **Retirement Accounts/Pension Plans**
    ❏ Yes ❏ No ❏ Both

Approximate value of all retirement accounts: _____

Type of Account: _____   Beneficiary: _____

Type of Account: _____   Beneficiary: _____

F. **Investments**

Type of Holdings: [ ] Stocks   [ ] Bonds [ ] Mutual Funds   [ ] 401k
Do you have the stock certificates?   ❏ Yes ❏ No

Approximate total value of holdings: _____

Beneficiary named for each type of holding: ❏ Yes ❏ No

Do you have a financial planner or broker?   ❏ Yes ❏ No

G. **Other Assets** with Approximate Value (collections, antiques, art, etc.)
_____

H.   Do you have a family-owned business (or a sole proprietorship)? _____

If you want the business to continue after your retirement/death, whom do you want to take over?
_____.

19. **POWER OF ATTORNEY/ADVANCE DIRECTIVES/HIPAA**

A. **Financial Durable Power of Attorney**

Do you wish to have a financial durable power of attorney?   ❏ Yes ❏ No

Primary Agent: _____
Relationship: _____
Address and Phone Number: _____

Successor Agent: _____
Relationship: _____
Address and Phone Number: _____

B.   **Living Will**

     ❏ Yes ❏ No

Health Care Power of Attorney
     ❏ Yes ❏ No

Primary Agent: _____
Relationship: _____
Address and Phone Number:_____

Alternate Agent: _____
Relationship: _____
Address and Phone Number:_____

C.   **HIPAA Authorization**

Names of those you authorize to talk to your doctors/other health care providers:
_____
_____

20.   **ESTATE TAXES**

Federal estate taxes: 2011 and 2012 levied on estates over $5 million.

Ohio Estate Tax levied on estates, after allowable exemptions/deductions, over $338,333.

Do you believe Estate Taxes may be an issue for you?   ❏ Yes ❏ No

21.   **VALUE OF YOUR ESTATE**

Include all property you own.

Approximate value of your estate: $ _____

Approximate value of your partner's estate: $ _____

ESTATE PLANNING FORM 6

WILL WITH CHILDREN AND TESTAMENTARY TRUST

LAST WILL AND TESTAMENT

OF

I, _____, of _____, _____, declare this my Last Will and Testament and I revoke all of my previous wills and codicils.

Section 1. Identification of Family

1.01   My partner's name is _____. All references in this Will to my partner, whether or not specifically named, shall mean only her. I intend that she be considered my next-of-kin.

1.02   My partner and I were ([married] [entered into a Civil Union] [are Registered Domestic Partners]. [Describe where and when the ceremony took place] For residents of non-recognition states, acknowledge that state law does not recognize the relationship but the testator is including the information in case that situation changes.)

1.03   My partner and I are raising our child, _____, together.

Section 2. Nomination of Executor

2.01   I nominate my partner, _____, to serve as my Executor. If she is unable or unwilling at any time to serve as my Executor, I nominate _____, to serve as my Alternate Executor.

2.02   I direct that my Executor, and any successor, be permitted to serve without bond in any jurisdiction.

Section 3. Explanation of Intent

3.01   I leave my entire estate my partner _____, because s/he is my life partner. We have shared our lives together in a committed relationship and have accumulated our estates together. I do not make this bequest or provision in this Last Will and Testament because of any disrespect or lack of love and affection for my family.

Section 4. Will Contest

4.01   I expect my family to honor my wishes concerning the disposition of my estate. I understand they may not agree with my decision. And, if anyone chooses to contest any provision of this document, I intend that all contesting parties be denied any part of my estate. I name my partner, _____, as my heir-at-law. I have designated some of my family as alternate beneficiaries. Aside from those named in this Will, I specifically disinherit all members of my biological family for reasons personal to me.

Section 5. Disposition of Tangible Personal Property

5.01   I give, devise and bequeath my tangible personal property to my partner, _____. My Executor has sole discretion to sell any of the property that is not suitable for distribution, and the proceeds shall become a part of my residuary estate. If the devisee named in this section does not survive me, I direct that the designated property be disposed of or distributed with the residue of my estate.

Section 6. Residuary Devise

6.01   The balance of my residuary estate shall consist of all property or money that I own when I die and that is not otherwise provided for in this Will. This includes all insurance proceeds or other death benefits payable to my estate, less the valid claims asserted against my estate and all expenses incurred in administering my estate, including expenses of administering nonprobate assets. This excludes any property over which I may have a power of appointment.

6.02   I give, devise and bequeath the balance of my residuary estate to my partner, _____, if she survives me.

6.03   If my partner predeceases or fails to survive me I give, devise and bequeath the balance of my residuary estate to _____. My child's estate shall be placed in the Residuary Trust established under Section 10 of this Will.

6.04   If my partner and my child predecease or fail to survive me, I direct that my estate be given to _____.

6.05   If I have any pets at the time of my death and my partner does not survive me, I appoint _____, to assume full care, custody and control of my pets.

Section 7. Simultaneous Death/Common Accident

7.01   If my partner, _____, and I should die simultaneously, or in a common accident, or under circumstances that the order of our deaths cannot be definitely established, it shall be presumed that I survived and my estate shall be disposed of in accordance with this presumption.

ALTERNATE LANGUAGE:

Section 7. Simultaneous Death/Common Accident

7.01   If my death and that of my partner (spouse) are caused by a simultaneous death event, defined as a single event or series of related events causing the death of both parties within a (30) day period, then our jointly held property shall be sold and divided equally. Each half shall be divided among the secondary beneficiaries listed in our individual Wills.

Section 8. Appointment of Guardian

8.01   I name my partner, _____, as Guardian of our child, _____. We are raising our child together. We executed a Shared Custody

Agreement in _____ after our child's birth. It is my intention and wish that _____ be the parent responsible for our child.

At the time I am executing this Will, the law concerning second-parent adoption is unsettled I Ohio. It is my wish and intention that _____ adopts our child, _____, as soon as possible. I want this provision to establish that I consent to _____ adopting our child. I am fully aware of my legal and constitutional rights as the biological mother of _____. I waive those rights in order to provide for our child. It is in _____'s best interests to have both of her parents legally recognized.

8.02   If _____ is unable to serve as our child's Guardian, I name _____, as Guardian of her person. I ask that she also be named the interim Guardian until the Probate Court is able to appoint her has _____'s permanent Guardian.

8.03   If _____ is not appointed Guardian of our child's person, I direct that she be named Guardian of _____'s estate. She is best able to provide financial advice for our child.

8.04   Under no circumstances shall _____ be prohibited or prevented from having contact with our child, _____. It is not in our child's best interest to be deprived of the love and affection of her parents.

Section 9. Powers of Executor

9.01   My Executor, and any successor, shall have all of the powers granted to Executors and fiduciaries under the Ohio probate code and other applicable Ohio laws, including the power to execute any joint or individual tax return on my behalf or on behalf of my estate.

9.02   My Executor shall be entitled to reasonable compensation for services actually performed and to reimbursement of expenses properly incurred.

9.03   (A) My Executor shall have, in addition to any other powers, the power to invest, reinvest, sell, mortgage, lease or otherwise transfer or dispose of any part or all of my estate, without the necessity of obtaining prior or subsequent court approval;

(B) To make repairs or improvements to my property as may be deemed necessary to preserve or enhance the value of my estate.

(C) To borrow funds for use in estate administration if there are insufficient liquid assets in my estate;

(D) To employ persons, including attorneys, investment advisors or other agents for assistance or advice, or not to employ such persons, as my Executor deems appropriate.

(E) To compromise and settle any claims against or in favor of my estate on such terms and conditions as my Executor deems best.

(F) To make determinations about the allocation of receipts and the apportionment of expenditures between income and principal. My Executor shall not be required to follow any provision of law regarding such determinations, including Chapter 1340 of the Ohio Revised Code.

9.04   My Executor may make distributions either in cash or in kind. Distributions in kind may be made at the discretion of my Executor. My Executor may make any distributions under this Will either (1) directly to the beneficiary, (2) in any form allowed by applicable state law for gifts or transfers to minors or persons under disability, (3) to the beneficiary's guardian, conservator, or caregiver for the benefit of the beneficiary, or (4) by direct payment of the beneficiary's expenses.

Section 10. The Residuary Trust

I create The Residuary Trust for the benefit of my children. At present my partner and I are raising our child, _____, a minor child. I intend that this Trust include any children that I may have or parent with my partner, _____.

This Trust is to be funded from my estate assets and all property owned by me at my death that is not otherwise distributed according to this Will or other legal document.

Trustee Appointment

10.01   I nominate and appoint my partner, _____, to serve as Trustee of this Residuary Trust.

10.02   If she is unable or unwilling to serve as Trustee, I nominate and appoint, _____, to serve as Alternate Trustee of the Residuary Trust.

10.03   If both of these persons are, at any time, unable or unwilling to serve as Trustee, my Executor shall appoint a person or entity to serve as Trustee of this Residuary Trust.

Designation of Trust

10.04   If my life partner, _____, fails to survive me and I am survived by my children, I direct that the balance of my residuary estate be distributed to the Trustee as provided in Section 6 of this Will. The property shall be held in the Residuary Trust and administered and distributed as provided in this section.

10.05   The Trustee, in her sole and absolute discretion, shall pay over to or apply for the benefit of my children so much of the net income as shall be necessary to provide for the children's health, education, maintenance, care, support and comfort. It is my intention to grant complete flexibility and discretion to the Trustee so that, to the extent reasonably practical in her judgment, my younger child shall be provided with the same advantages that may have been provided for my older child.

10.06   I also intend that the Trustee may, but shall not be required to, make such expenditures from the income or principal of The Residuary Trust as he shall determine to be appropriate for the food, lodging and personal conveniences of my children. This shall include a reasonable amount of spending money and a proportionate share of the maintenance, food and other expenses incurred in the home where my children may reside. Any allowances made shall be within the sole and absolute discretion of the Trustee.

10.07   The Trustee has the discretion to use Trust assets or income, including principal, to address any financial need experienced by my children. This includes any need arising from an accident, illness or other disability or from educational expenses or circumstances of an unusual nature. The Trustee may pay for such need. Any such determination shall be binding upon all interested persons.

10.08   Any net income not distributed under this Section shall be accumulated and added to the Trust principal.

Residuary Trust Termination

10.09   The Residuary Trust shall terminate on my youngest child's 25th birthday. All property belonging to the Residuary Trust, including any accumulated income, shall be divided equally among my children. The Trustee shall make equal payments without regard to the amount paid to either of the children before the termination date.

10.10   **Predeceased Child**. If one of my children shall die before the Trust terminates, the surviving children shall receive the full amount remaining in the Trust.

Administrative Provisions

10.11   My children, once they are over the age of 21, may remove the Trustee that I have appointed. They must agree on and simultaneously appoint a successor Trustee. They may also appoint a successor Trustee any time any Trustee fails to qualify or ceases to act. However, no successor Trustee shall be a person who is not a direct or indirect beneficiary of this Will or Trust.

10.12   Any removal and appointment made under paragraph 10.11 shall be in writing. It shall be effective when an executed copy is delivered to the active Trustee, together with a written acceptance of the Trust by the newly appointed Trustee.

10.13   In addition to and not in limitation of all powers, authorities and discretions granted to any Trustee by common law, statute or under any rule of court, I expressly authorize and empower the Trustee in the her sole and absolute discretion:

        (a) to invest and reinvest in and retain, whether originally a part of my estate or subsequently acquired, such stocks, bonds or other property, real or personal, including options on securities and money market funds, as the Trustee may consider advisable or proper, from time to time, without application to or the approval of any court and without being restricted as to the character of any investment by any statute or rule of law or court governing investments by fiduciaries;

        (b) to sell, lease, without regard to the possible termination of the Trust, improve, partition, mortgage, exchange or otherwise deal with any and all property at any time forming a part of any Trust as the Trustee may deem appropriate;

(c) to hold investments in the name of a nominee and to vote in person or by proxy with respect to any shares of stock or other securities held by the Trustee or a nominee for any purpose and to take any other action that the Trustee may deem necessary or proper in connection with those holdings;

(d) to make divisions or distributions of the assets of any Trust in money or in kind, or partly in money and partly in kind, and to allocate to any such Trust property different in kind from that allocated to any other Trust or beneficiary.

Except as otherwise specifically provided here, the judgment and any determination of the Trustee in connection with this section, including any decision to make a non-pro rata distribution and any decision regarding the values assigned to various assets, shall be binding and conclusive upon all interested persons;

(e) to retain any property, whether or not income-producing, that I may own at the time of my death until such time as the Trustee may deem it desirable to dispose of them;

(f) to borrow money for any purpose connected with the protection, preservation or improvement of any Trust and in connection with it to create one or more mortgages on or pledges of any part or all of the property included in such Trust whenever the same shall be deemed appropriate by the Trustee;

(g) to pay, compromise, modify, renew, adjust, submit to arbitration, release or otherwise deal with any claims or demands of any Trust against others or of others against such Trust as the Trustee shall deem advisable, and to make any payments in connection with them;

(h) to execute, acknowledge and deliver any and all written instruments that the Trustee may deem advisable to carry out any of the foregoing powers, including the power to indicate any division or distribution of any Trust by deeds or other writings or instruments recorded among the public records of any jurisdiction where any such property may be located.

No party to any such instrument in writing signed by the Trustee shall be bound to see to the application by the Trustee of any money or other property paid and delivered pursuant to the terms of such instrument.

10.14 The Trustee shall be excused from filing any account with any court. However, the Trustee shall render an annual, or more frequent, account and may, at any other time, including at the time of the death, resignation or removal of any Trustee, render an intermediate account of the Trustee's administration to the then current income beneficiaries and vested remaindermen.

The written approval of such accounting by all the beneficiaries and remaindermen who are then adults shall bind all persons then having or acquiring or claiming any interest in any Trust.

It shall be a complete discharge to my Trustee with respect to all matters set forth in the account as fully and to the same extent as though the account had been judicially settled in an action or proceeding in which all persons having, acquiring or claiming any interest were made parties and were duly represented.

10.15 The Trustee shall at all times serve without bond.

10.16   Substitute or successor Trustees shall have all the rights, powers, discretions, duties and responsibilities, as well as the limitations, granted to or imposed upon the named Trustee. Such Trustees shall not be liable for the acts of their predecessors if, by the exercise of reasonable diligence, they do not discover such acts upon becoming acting Trustees.

10.17   This Residuary Trust shall not be administered under the direction or jurisdiction of any court.

Distribution of Principal and Income

10.18   Except to the extent that it is explicitly provided to the contrary in this section, the Trustee shall distribute all amounts of income and principal distributable to any beneficiary, directly to such beneficiary. The Trustee shall not distribute any Trust amounts to any other person or entity. This includes any person or entity claiming by a beneficiary's authority or otherwise. No beneficiary may anticipate any distributions. However, any deposit to the credit of a beneficiary's account in a bank or Trust company designated by such beneficiary in writing shall be deemed the equivalent of a distribution to that beneficiary. The Trustee, in her sole and absolute discretion, may make payments directly to any educational institution, health care provider, health care facility that is providing current services to either of my children.

10.19_   The Trustee shall also have the power to make distributions of any income or principal for a beneficiary as follows:
      (i)   to such beneficiary;
      (ii) to the individual who is, in the judgment of the Trustee, in proper charge of such beneficiary, regardless of whether there is a court order to that effect;
      (iii) in the case of a minor, to a custodian named by the Trustee to be held under the OHIO Uniform Transfers to Minors Act; or
      (iv) by distributing or applying any part or total payment for a beneficiary's benefit or on a beneficiary's behalf.

Distribution may be made without any necessity to account to, qualify in or seek the approval of any court. Any such distributions, made in good faith, shall be deemed proper and shall be a complete release of the Trustee.

10.20   In conferring discretion upon the Trustee in this Will, it is my intention to create "discretionary Trusts" as that term is interpreted under applicable law, so that my Trustee shall have sole and absolute discretion about making or failing to make distribution to or on behalf of either of my children.

To that end no creditors, including any state or federal agencies who may furnish services, payments or benefits to a beneficiary under this Residuary Trust, shall have any right to any of the income or principal of any Trust created.

Section 11. Construction and Definitions

The following rules and definitions shall apply in the construction of this instrument and in the administration of my estate:

11.01   Any reference to my "Executor" in whatever form refers to the person, persons, or institution then acting as the personal representative of my estate.

11.02   If any devisee or other beneficiary under this will dies within 30 days after my death or under such circumstances where there is insufficient evidence in the judgment of my Executor to determine whether such person has died within 30 days after my death, the devisee or beneficiary shall be deemed to have failed to survive me.

11.03   Ohio law shall govern all questions concerning the validity and construction of this Last Will and Testament.

11.04   The term "estate and death taxes" shall mean all estate, inheritance, transfer, succession, or other taxes or duties payable because of my death, including interest and penalties.

Section 12. Payment of Taxes and Expenses

12.01   I direct my Executor to pay the expenses of administering my estate, the expenses created by reason of my death. This includes all estate and death taxes payable with respect to property includable in my gross estate or taxable by reason of my death, whether or not such property is part of my probate estate and whether or not such taxes are payable by my estate or by the recipient of any such property. Such taxes and expenses should be paid out of my residuary estate without apportionment.

BEFORE THESE WITNESSES, I sign my name to this instrument on _____ at Cleveland, Ohio.

_____,
                      Testator

STATEMENT OF WITNESSES

Each witness declares, under penalty of perjury and Ohio law, that the following is true and correct. I am over the age of eighteen years and competent to be a witness to the Will of _____. The Testator signed this Last Will and Testament on _____ in our presence. At the Testator's request and in the Testator's presence, and the presence of each other, we now subscribe our names as witnesses.

We declare that the Testator willingly signed and executed this Last Will and Testament, as a free and voluntary act for the purposes expressed. We also declare that each witness, in the presence and hearing of the Testator, signed this Last Will and Testament as witness and to the best of our knowledge the Testator was at the time 18 or more years of age, of sound mind and under no constraint or undue influence.

_____   _____
Witness Signature   Witness Signature

_____   _____
Print Witness Name   Print Witness Name

_____   _____

_____   _____
Witness Address   Witness Address

ESTATE PLANNING FORM 7

WILL WITH CHILDREN, NO TRUST

LAST WILL AND TESTAMENT

OF

I, _____, declare this my Last Will and Testament and I revoke all of my previous wills and codicils.

Section 1. Identification of Family

1.01   My partner's name is _____. All references in this Will to my partner, whether or not specifically named, shall mean only her. I intend that she be considered my next-of-kin.

1.02   My partner and I are raising our child, _____, together.

[An additional clause may be inserted if the couple is married, in a Civil Union or a Domestic Partnership. Acknowledging that formality, even if in a non-recognition state, may be appropriate for the testator.]

Section 2. Nomination of Executor

2.01   I nominate my partner, _____, to serve as my Executor. If she is unable or unwilling at any time to serve as my Executor, I nominate _____, to serve as my Alternate Executor.

2.02   I direct that my Executor, and any successor, be permitted to serve without bond in any jurisdiction.

Section 3. Explanation of Intent

3.01   I leave my entire estate my partner, _____, because she is my life partner. We have shared our lives together in a committed relationship and have accumulated our estates together. I do not make this bequest or provision in this Last Will and Testament because of any disrespect or lack of love and affection for my family.

Section 4. Will Contest

4.01   I expect my family to honor my wishes concerning the disposition of my estate. I understand they may not agree with my decision. And, if anyone chooses to contest any provision of this document, I intend that all contesting parties be denied any part of my estate. I name my partner, _____, as my heir-at-law. I have designated some of my family as alternate beneficiaries. Aside from those named in this Will, I specifically disinherit all members of my biological family for reasons personal to me.

Section 5. Disposition of Tangible Personal Property

5.01   I give, devise and bequeath my tangible personal property to my partner, _____.
My Executor has sole discretion to sell any of the property that is not suitable for distribution, and
the proceeds shall become a part of my residuary estate. If the devisee named in this section does
not survive me, I direct that the designated property be disposed of or distributed with the residue
of my estate.

Section 6. Residuary Devise

6.01   The balance of my residuary estate shall consist of all property or money that I own when
I die and that is not otherwise provided for in this Will. This includes all insurance proceeds or
other death benefits payable to my estate, less the valid claims asserted against my estate and all
expenses incurred in administering my estate, including expenses of administering nonprobate
assets. This excludes any property over which I may have a power of appointment.

6.02   I give, devise and bequeath the balance of my residuary estate to my partner,
_____, if she survives me.

6.03   If my partner predeceases or fails to survive me I give, devise and bequeath the balance
of my residuary estate to my child, _____.

6.04   If I have any pets at the time of my death and my partner does not survive me, I appoint
_____, to assume full care, custody and control of my pets.

Section 7. Simultaneous Death/Common Accident

7.01   If my partner, _____, and I should die simultaneously, or in a common accident,
or under circumstances that the order of our deaths cannot be definitely established, it shall be
presumed that I survived and my estate shall be disposed of in accordance with this presumption.

ALTERNATE LANGUAGE

Section 7. Simultaneous Death/Common Accident

7.01   If my death and that of my partner (spouse) are caused by a simultaneous death event,
defined as a single event or series of related events causing the death of both parties within a (30)
day period, then our jointly held property shall be sold and divided equally. Each half shall be
divided among the secondary beneficiaries listed in our individual Wills.

Section 8. Appointment of Guardian

8.01   I name my partner, _____, as Guardian of our child, _____ and her
person and estate. We are raising our child together. We executed a Shared Custody Agreement
in 2011 after our child's birth. It is my intention and wish that _____ be the parent
responsible for our child.

At the time I am executing this Will, the law concerning second-parent adoption is unsettled I Ohio. It is my wish and intention that _____ adopts our child, _____, as soon as possible. I want this provision to establish that I consent to _____ adopting our child. I am fully aware of my legal and constitutional rights as the biological mother of_____. I waive those rights in order to provide for our child. It is in _____ best interests to have both of her parents legally recognized.

8.02   If _____is unable to serve as our child's Guardian, I name my sister-in-law, _____, as Guardian of her person and estate. I ask that she also be named the interim Guardian until the Probate Court is able to appoint her has _____ permanent Guardian.

8.03   If _____is not appointed Guardian of our child's person, I direct that she be named Guardian of _____ estate. She is best able to provide financial advice for our child.

8.04   Under no circumstances shall _____be prohibited or prevented from having contact with our child, _____. It is not in our child's best interest to be deprived of the love and affection of her parents.

Section 9. Powers of Executor

9.01   My Executor, and any successor, shall have all of the powers granted to Executors and fiduciaries under the Ohio probate code and other applicable Ohio laws, including the power to execute any joint or individual tax return on my behalf or on behalf of my estate.

9.02   My Executor shall be entitled to reasonable compensation for services actually performed and to reimbursement of expenses properly incurred.

9.03   (A) My Executor shall have, in addition to any other powers, the power to invest, reinvest, sell, mortgage, lease or otherwise transfer or dispose of any part or all of my estate, without the necessity of obtaining prior or subsequent court approval;

(B) To make repairs or improvements to my property as may be deemed necessary to preserve or enhance the value of my estate.

(C) To borrow funds for use in estate administration if there are insufficient liquid assets in my estate;

(D) To employ persons, including attorneys, investment advisors or other agents for assistance or advice, or not to employ such persons, as my Executor deems appropriate.

(E) To compromise and settle any claims against or in favor of my estate on such terms and conditions as my Executor deems best.

(F) To make determinations about the allocation of receipts and the apportionment of expenditures between income and principal. My Executor shall not be required to follow any provision of law regarding such determinations, including Chapter 1340 of the Ohio Revised Code.

9.04   My Executor may make distributions either in cash or in kind. Distributions in kind may be made at the discretion of my Executor. My Executor may make any distributions under this Will either (1) directly to the beneficiary, (2) in any form allowed by applicable state law for gifts or transfers to minors or persons under disability, (3) to the beneficiary's guardian, conservator, or caregiver for the benefit of the beneficiary, or (4) by direct payment of the beneficiary's expenses.

Section 10. Construction and Definitions

The following rules and definitions shall apply in the construction of this instrument and in the administration of my estate:

10.01   Any reference to my "Executor" in whatever form refers to the person, persons, or institution then acting as the personal representative of my estate.

10.02   If any devisee or other beneficiary under this will dies within 30 days after my death or under such circumstances where there is insufficient evidence in the judgment of my Executor to determine whether such person has died within 30 days after my death, the devisee or beneficiary shall be deemed to have failed to survive me.

10.03   Ohio law shall govern all questions concerning the validity and construction of this Last Will and Testament.

10.04   The term "estate and death taxes" shall mean all estate, inheritance, transfer, succession, or other taxes or duties payable because of my death, including interest and penalties.

Section 11. Payment of Taxes and Expenses

11.01   I direct my Executor to pay the expenses of administering my estate, the expenses created by reason of my death. This includes all estate and death taxes payable with respect to property includable in my gross estate or taxable by reason of my death, whether or not such property is part of my probate estate and whether or not such taxes are payable by my estate or by the recipient of any such property. Such taxes and expenses should be paid out of my residuary estate without apportionment.

BEFORE THESE WITNESSES, I sign my name to this instrument on _____, 2011 at _____.

                                 _____,
                                                Testator

STATEMENT OF WITNESSES

Each witness declares, under penalty of perjury and Ohio law, that the following is true and correct. I am over the age of eighteen years and competent to be a witness to the Will of _____. The Testator signed this Last Will and Testament on _____, 2011 in our presence. At the Testator's request and in the Testator's presence, and the presence of each other, we now subscribe our names as witnesses.

We declare that the Testator willingly signed and executed this Last Will and Testament, as a free and voluntary act for the purposes expressed. We also declare that each witness, in the presence and hearing of the Testator, signed this Last Will and Testament as witness and to the best of our knowledge the Testator was at the time 18 or more years of age, of sound mind and under no constraint or undue influence.

_____   _____
Witness Signature   Witness Signature

_____   _____
Print Witness Name   Print Witness Name

_____   _____
Witness Address   Witness Address

ESTATE PLANNING FORM 8

WILL WITH NO CHILDREN

LAST WILL AND TESTAMENT

OF

I, _____, declare my Last Will and Testament and I revoke all of my previous Wills and codicils.

Section 1. Identification of Family

1.01   My partner's name is _____. All references in this Will to my partner, whether or not specifically named, shall mean only her. I intend that she be considered my next-of-kin.

1.02   I have no children.

1.03   My partner and I were ([married] [entered into a Civil Union] [are Registered Domestic Partners]. [Describe where and when the ceremony took place] For residents of non-recognition states, acknowledge that state law does not recognize the relationship but the testator is including the information in case that situation changes.)

Section 2. Nomination of Executor

2.01   I nominate my partner, _____, to serve as my Executor. If she is unable or unwilling at any time to serve as my Executor, I nominate _____, to serve as my Alternate Executor.

2.02   If she is unable or unwilling at any time to serve as my Executor, I nominate _____, to serve as my Alternate Executor.

2.03   I direct that my Executor, and any successor, be permitted to serve without bond in any jurisdiction.

Section 3. Explanation of Intent

3.01   I leave my entire estate to my partner, _____, because she is my life partner. We have shared our lives together in a committed relationship and have accumulated our estates together. I do not make this bequest or provision in this Last Will and Testament because of any disrespect or lack of love and affection for my family.

Section 4. Will Contest

4.01   I expect my family to honor my wishes concerning the disposition of my estate. I understand they may not agree with my decision. And, if anyone chooses to contest any provision of this document, I intend that all contesting parties be denied any part of my estate. I name my partner_____, as my heir-at-law. I have designated some of my family as alternate beneficiaries. Aside from those named in this Will, I specifically disinherit all members of my biological family for reasons personal to me.

Section 5. Disposition of Tangible Personal Property

5.01   I give, devise and bequeath my tangible personal property to my partner, _____. My Executor has sole discretion to sell any of the property that is not suitable for distribution, and the proceeds shall become a part of my residuary estate. If the devisee named in this section does not survive me, I direct that the designated property be disposed of or distributed with the residue of my estate.

Section 6. Residuary Devise

6.01   The balance of my residuary estate shall consist of all property or money that I own when I die and that is not otherwise provided for in this Will. This includes all insurance proceeds or other death benefits payable to my estate, less the valid claims asserted against my estate and all expenses incurred in administering my estate, including expenses of administering nonprobate assets. This excludes any property over which I may have a power of appointment.

6.02   I give, devise and bequeath the balance of my residuary estate to my partner, _____, if she survives me.

6.03   If my partner predeceases or fails to survive me I give, devise and bequeath the balance of my residuary estate to _____.

6.04   If my partner and mother predecease or fail to survive me, I give the balance of my residuary estate to _____, equally or to the survivor of them.

6.05   If I have any pets at the time of my death and my partner, _____, does not survive me, I appoint _____, to assume full care, custody and control of my pets.

Section 7. Simultaneous Death/Common Accident

7.01   If my partner, _____, and I should die simultaneously, or in a common accident, or under circumstances that the order of our deaths cannot be definitely established, it shall be presumed that I survived and my estate shall be disposed of in accordance with this presumption.

Section 7. Simultaneous Death/Common Accident

7.01   If my death and that of my partner (spouse) are caused by a simultaneous death event, defined as a single event or series of related events causing the death of both parties within a (30) day period, then our jointly held property shall be sold and divided equally. Each half shall be divided among the secondary beneficiaries listed in our individual Wills.

Section 8. Powers of Executor

8.01   My Executor, and any successor, shall have all of the powers granted to Executors and fiduciaries under the Ohio probate code and other applicable Ohio laws, including the power to execute any joint or individual tax return on my behalf or on behalf of my estate.

8.02 My Executor shall be entitled to reasonable compensation for services actually performed and to reimbursement of expenses properly incurred.

8.03 (A) My Executor shall have, in addition to any other powers, the power to invest, reinvest, sell, mortgage, lease or otherwise transfer or dispose of any part or all of my estate, without the necessity of obtaining prior or subsequent court approval;

(B) To make repairs or improvements to my property as may be deemed necessary to preserve or enhance the value of my estate.

(C) To borrow funds for use in estate administration if there are insufficient liquid assets in my estate;

(D) To employ persons, including attorneys, investment advisors or other agents for assistance or advice, or not to employ such persons, as my Executor deems appropriate.

(E) To compromise and settle any claims against or in favor of my estate on such terms and conditions as my Executor deems best.

(F) To make determinations about the allocation of receipts and the apportionment of expenditures between income and principal. My Executor shall not be required to follow any provision of law regarding such determinations, including Chapter 1340 of the Ohio Revised Code.

8.04 My Executor may make distributions either in cash or in kind. Distributions in kind may be made at the discretion of my Executor. My Executor may make any distributions under this Will either (1) directly to the beneficiary, (2) in any form allowed by applicable state law for gifts or transfers to minors or persons under disability, (3) to the beneficiary's guardian, conservator, or caregiver for the benefit of the beneficiary, or (4) by direct payment of the beneficiary's expenses.

Section 9. Construction and Definitions

The following rules and definitions shall apply in the construction of this instrument and in the administration of my estate:

9.01 Any reference to my "Executor" in whatever form refers to the person, persons, or institution then acting as the personal representative of my estate.

9.02 If any devisee or other beneficiary under this will dies within 30 days after my death or under such circumstances where there is insufficient evidence in the judgment of my Executor to determine whether such person has died within 30 days after my death, the devisee or beneficiary shall be deemed to have failed to survive me.

9.03 Ohio law shall govern all questions concerning the validity and construction of this Last Will and Testament.

9.04 The term "estate and death taxes" shall mean all estate, inheritance, transfer, succession, or other taxes or duties payable because of my death, including interest and penalties thereon.

Section 10. Payment of Taxes and Expenses

10.01   I direct my Executor to pay the expenses of administering my estate, the expenses created because of my death. This includes all estate and death taxes payable with respect to property includable in my gross estate or taxable by reason of my death, whether or not such property is part of my probate estate and whether or not such taxes are payable by my estate or by the recipient of any such property. Such taxes and expenses should be paid out of my residuary estate without apportionment.

BEFORE THESE WITNESSES, I sign my name to this instrument on _____, 2011 at _____.

_____
Testator

STATEMENT OF WITNESSES

Each witness declares, under penalty of perjury and Ohio law, that the following is true and correct. I am over the age of eighteen years and competent to be a witness to the Will of _____. The Testator signed this Last Will and Testament on _____, 20___ in our presence. At the Testator's request and in the Testator's presence, and the presence of each other, we now subscribe our names as witnesses.

We declare that the Testator willingly signed and executed this Last Will and Testament, as a free and voluntary act for the purposes expressed. We also declare that each witness, in the presence and hearing of the Testator, signed this Last Will and Testament as witness and to the best of our knowledge the Testator was at the time 18 or more years of age, of sound mind and under no constraint or undue influence.

_____   _____
Witness Signature   Witness Signature

_____   _____
Print Witness Name   Print Witness Name

_____   _____
Witness Address   Witness Address

ESTATE PLANNING FORM 9

DESIGNATION OF AGENT, WITH HIPAA AUTHORITY

DESIGNATION OF AGENT

I, _____, designate my partner, _____, as my agent empowered with the following authority.

A. VISITATION AUTHORITY: If I am admitted to a medical facility of any type, a nursing home, hospice or similar health care, skilled nursing or custodial facility, my agent, _____, shall be designated as "family" as that term is defined by the Joint Commission on Accreditation of Healthcare Organizations.

My agent shall have priority in being admitted to visit me in such facility. This authority supersedes any policy existing in any health care, medical, nursing home, hospice or similar facility. See 42 CFR Parts 482 and 485.

My agent is the person to be consulted by medical or health care personnel concerning my care and treatment. This conforms to the Health Care Power of Attorney I executed. My agent shall also have the authority to decide who will be permitted to visit me while in the facility and during any recovery at home.

This authorization supersedes any preference given to parties related to me by blood or by law. These instructions shall remain in full force and effect unless I freely give contrary written instructions to competent medical personnel on the premises involved. My subsequent disability or incapacity shall not affect these instructions.

B. RECEIPT OF PERSONAL PROPERTY: My agent shall have the right to receive all items of personal property that may be recovered from me by any health care, medical, nursing home, hospice or similar facility, police agency or any other person or public/private entity at the time of my illness, disability or death. This specifically includes cash or other liquid assets.

C. DISPOSITION OF REMAINS/AUTOPSY and AUTHORIZATION for FUNERAL ARRANGEMENTS: My agent shall have the authority to authorize an autopsy if it is deemed necessary or is required by law.

My agent has the authority to make all decisions necessary for my obituary notice and funeral arrangements. This includes any mortician's role, burial services, interment or cremation, selection of a casket or urn, selection, care and tending of a gravesite and selection of a gravestone including any inscription. [This authority is granted under O.R.C. 2108.70--**some state laws allow an individual to name whomever he wants to make funeral arrangements; others give priority to the decedent's biological family.**] My agent also has the authority to select other persons to carry out my wishes.

D. ADDITIONAL AUTHORITY:

My agent shall have access to all medical records and information pertaining to me and concerning treatments, procedures, treatment plans, etc. This includes the right to disclose this information to other people. I explicitly authorize any medical or health care provider to release information requested by my agent to him/her and consider my agent an authorized person to receive such information under the Health Information Portability and Accessibility Act (HIPAA)

This Authorization applies to any health information protected by the federal Health Insurance Portability and Accountability Act of 1996 (HIPAA), and the regulations implementing it (45 C.F.R. §§ 160-164). It is intended to comply with all specific requirements of those regulations (45 C.F.R. §164.508(c)), and with the relevant privacy provisions of OHIO law.

My agent has the authority to admit or discharge me from any hospital, nursing home, residential care, assisted living or similar facility or service entity. My agent also has the authority to hire and fire medical, social service and other support personnel. My agent is primarily responsible for my medical and health care.

I have executed a Living Will, Health Care Power of Attorney, HIPAA Authorization and General Durable Power of Attorney.

My health care providers are obligated to recognize and accept these documents under federal law: 42 U.S.C. 1395x, 42 U.S.C. 1395cc, 42 CFR 482.13, 42 CFR 489.102(a) and the Presidential Memorandum concerning the rights of hospital patients issued April 15, 2010.

Third parties may rely upon a photocopy of this signed document to the same extent as if the copy were the original.

_____
Principal

State of
County of

_____ , the Principal named above personally appeared before me and acknowledged freely and voluntarily signing this document.

In Testimony Whereof, I have set my hand and official seal at _____ ,
_____ , on _____ 20___ .

_____
Notary Public

ESTATE PLANNING FORM 10

HIPAA AUTHORIZATION

Name: _____

Date of Birth: _____

Social Security No. (last 4 digits):   xxx-xx-_____

This Authorization applies to any health information protected by the federal Health Insurance Portability and Accountability Act of 1996 (HIPAA), and the regulations implementing it (45 C.F.R. §§ 160-164). I intend it to comply with all requirements of those regulations (45 C.F.R. § 164.508(c)), and with the relevant privacy provisions of _____ law. I authorize and direct all "covered entities" under HIPAA, and those entities' "business associates" as follows:

(1)   **Information to be disclosed:** All of my protected health information and medical records regarding any past, present or future medical or mental health condition, and including all information relating the diagnosis and treatment of sexually transmitted disease, mental illness and drug or alcohol abuse.

(2)   **Persons authorized to request disclosure under HIPAA:** _____
_____

The purpose of disclosure to these persons is to allow them to monitor and evaluate my health, my health care, my financial circumstances and obligations and to take any necessary action to ensure my general well being. This authority is limited to those times when I am unable to care for myself or when I am unable to converse with any health care provider.

Expiration. This Authorization shall continue until my death, unless I revoke it in writing. I may revoke or amend this Authorization in writing at any time.

Information Redisclosure. I understand that information disclosed under this Authorization may be re-disclosed and may no longer be protected by HIPAA or other privacy laws.

No liability for disclosure. No "covered entity", "business associate" or health care profession, acting in good faith under this Authorization, shall be subject to any liability to my family, heirs, successors, assigns or others acting in my name.

_____
Grantor

State of _____

County of _____

_____, the Grantor, appeared before me on _____, 2011, and signed this instrument as a free and voluntary act and deed. I subscribe my name and affix my Notary Seal.

_____
Notary

A COPY OF THIS DOCUMENT IS AS VALID AS THE ORIGINAL

ESTATE PLANNING FORM 11

GENERAL DURABLE POWER OF ATTORNEY

This document provides your designated attorney-in-fact with broad powers to act on your behalf concerning your personal property, real estate, business affairs and other interests. The powers continue until your death unless you revoke them in writing. The powers continue if you become disabled, incapacitated or incompetent. You have the right to revoke or change this General Durable Power of Attorney at any time during your life. Any revocation or change must be in writing.

I, _____ , of _____ , _____ am the Principal and create this General Durable Power of Attorney to enable the person named below to act as my Agent and attorney-in-fact. My Agent shall have the power to act in my name on all matters and at all times, either before or after my disability or incompetency.

1.   **Partner.** I am in a committed lifetime relationship with my partner, _____. My partner is to be treated in the same way as a "spouse" would be treated in financial, property and estate planning situations, including the Ohio Descent and Distribution Statute, RC 2105.06 (A).

2.   **Next-of-Kin.** Whenever a requirement exists that gives privileges and rights concerning my health care, in any aspect, to "next-of-kin," I direct that my partner, _____, be considered my "next-of-kin." It is my express desire that my partner be accorded the same privileges as immediate family member for the purpose of hospital visits, including but not limited to intensive care units, special care units, intermediate care units, general admission units, post operative units, emergency room, psychiatric care units and any other hospital area accessible to immediate family members or for notification purposes and sharing of pertinent information.

3.   **Designation of Agent.** I designate and appoint my partner, _____ , as my Agent and attorney-in-fact (Agent) and authorize **him/her** to act in my name and on my behalf for all purposes.

If my partner cannot or will not serve as my Agent, I name _____, to serve as my Alternate Agent and attorney-in-fact.

4. **Effective Date.** This General Durable Power of Attorney and the powers conferred shall be effective on the date I execute this document. This Power of Attorney shall continue in force until I change or revoke it in writing.

5. **Disability or Disappearance of Principal.** This General Durable Power of Attorney and the powers conferred shall not be affected by my disability, incapacity or incompetency. The powers conferred shall also be unaffected by any uncertainty concerning whether I am alive or dead.

All acts performed by my Agent under this General Durable Power of Attorney shall benefit and bind my heirs, devisees, personal representative and me.

6. **Nomination of Guardian of Person and Estate.** If I become disabled, incompetent or incapacitated and am unable to manage my affairs, I nominate my partner, _____, as the Guardian of my person and estate. I also nominate this person to serve as guardian of my person and estate if there is uncertainty concerning whether I am dead or alive.

I nominate my partner,_____, because **she** is best suited to carry out my wishes, desires and intentions concerning my person and property. **She** has my best interests at heart. I ask the Probate Court to honor my nominee and I ask that my nominee serve without bond.

If the Probate Court refuses to name my designated nominee, I demand that any person selected by the Probate Court be required to post bond in an amount equal to my gross estate. I make this demand to ensure that my person and property are adequately protected.

I also demand that there be no limitations on _____ access to me. I want her to visit me, participate in my life in every way, without any restrictions. I expect her to be treated with the same respect I am entitled to receive.

7. **Powers of Agent.** My Agent shall have the full power and authority to do and perform every act to the same extent as I could if personally present or present and under no disability. My Agent shall have all the powers, rights, discretions, elections and authority conferred by statute, common law or rule of court or government agency that are reasonably necessary to act on my behalf. In addition to these general powers, the Agent shall have the following specific powers:

A. **Financial Transactions.** The power to request, ask, demand, sue for, recover, sell, collect, forgive, receive and hold all financial transactions, whether personal or business, and in any form. This includes electronic and ACH transactions. This power shall include transactions involving my personal property or real property, wherever located, whether tangible or intangible.

My Agent shall have the power to handle all financial transactions that I now own or may accumulate in the future. This includes any property, tangible or intangible, in which I now have or may accrue an interest. This includes legal and equitable rights, remedies and procedures. My Agent shall also have the power to initiate any action necessary to collect money or property owed to my by anyone. My Agent shall have the power to make, execute and deliver, for my benefit and on my behalf, all endorsements, acceptances, releases, receipts or other similar documents.

My agent shall have the authority to access and transact business on through my online banking account. I authorize my bank to assist my agent in accessing my online account.

B. **Tax Returns.** The power to prepare, sign and file joint or separate income tax returns or other tax documents for any year, past, present or future. This includes tax returns on the federal, state and local levels. My Agent is authorized to consent to any gift and to utilize any gift-splitting provision or tax election. My Agent is authorized to prepare, sign and file any claim for refund of any tax.

My Agent has the power and authority to do anything necessary in connection with executing and filing tax returns and cashing any refund checks. My Agent is my designated attorney-in-fact for dealings with the United States Internal Revenue Service and any state or local government tax authority. This power includes anything involving gift, estate, income, inheritance or other tax and any audit or investigation by a tax authority.

This General Durable Power of Attorney includes the power to do all acts authorized by a properly executed I.R.S. Form 2848, entitled, "Power of Attorney and Declaration of Representative," granting the broadest powers provided to my Agent.

C. **Manage Affairs.** The power to conduct, engage in and transact any lawful matter of any nature on my behalf or in my name. The power to maintain, improve, invest, manage, insure, lease, encumber or deal with my real, personal, tangible or intangible property or any interest in them. This includes any interest I have now or acquire later. My Agent has the authority to determine the terms and conditions. This includes renewing my license plates and license stickers with the Ohio Bureau of Motor Vehicles and any other bureau of motor vehicles or vehicles titled outside Ohio.

D. **Property.** My Agent shall have the power and authority to act in my best interests and on my behalf as I would if able. This includes the right to enter into contracts for the sale of my property, whether real, personal, tangible or intangible. My Agent also has the authority to renounce or disclaim any testamentary or nontestamentary transfer intended for me if, in my Agent's discretion, such a transfer would be detrimental to me. This includes, but is not limited to, preparing or revoking a Transfer on Death deed if it is in my best interest to do so.

E. **Signature Authority.** My Agent shall have the power to make, receive, sign, endorse, acknowledge, deliver and possess insurance policies, title documents, stocks, bonds, negotiable instruments, proxies, warrants, retirement accounts, IRAs and other financial obligations. My Agent shall have the authority to execute instruments in writing of any kind or nature as necessary to exercise the rights and powers granted.

F. **Securities.** The power to sell shares of stocks, bonds and other securities that now belong to me or that I later acquire. This includes any securities issued by any entity, public or private. My Agent shall also have the power to make, execute and deliver any assignment(s) of any such securities.

G. **Business.** My Agent shall have the power to conduct or participate in any business of any nature for and in my name. This includes execution of partnership agreements and any amendments, incorporation documents, reorganization, merger or consolidation documents. My Agent shall have the power to elect or employ officers, directors and Agents for those businesses. My Agent may also sell any business interest or stock in such a business and exercise voting rights concerning stock either in person or by proxy and exercise stock options. My Agent may sell, liquidate or dissolve any business in which I am or may become involved if it is in my best interests.

H. **Safe Deposit Box.** The power to enter, surrender or relinquish any safe deposit box that I rent and remove any or all of the contents. No institution in which my safe-deposit box is located shall incur any liability to my estate or me for permitting my Agent to exercise these powers.

I. **Gifts.** The power to make outright gifts of cash or property to adults or minors in amounts not to exceed that established by the Internal Revenue Service for individual annual gifts in any calendar year. Any gifts to minors shall be in custodial form under the applicable Gifts to Minors Act.

My Agent shall have the power and authority to make gifts or transfer any form of property, real or personal, tangible or intangible, and in any amount to my partner personally or for either my partner's or my disability, long term care and estate planning.

J. **Conveyance Powers.** My Agent shall have the power to convey or assign cash or other property that I possess to the trustee or trustees of any revocable trust that I have created. My

Agent shall have the authority to revoke any trust that I have created if the revocation is in my best interests.

My Agent shall have the power to purchase United States Government Bonds (Flower Bonds) that may be used to pay any death taxes from my estate.

K. **Appoint Agents/Attorney in Fact.** My Agent shall have the power, subject to the provisions of Section 1 to appoint a substitute or alternate Agent and attorney-in-fact. This person shall have all the powers and authority of my Agent.

L. **HIPAA Authorization.** My Agent shall have the authority under the Health Information Portability and Accessibility Act of 1996 (HIPAA) to access all of my medical records and information concerning treatments, procedures, plans, etc. This includes the right to disclose information to other people and to discuss my care, prognosis and diagnosis with all health care personnel charged with my care.

I explicitly authorize any medical or health care provider to release information requested by my Agent and consider this person authorized to receive such information under the provisions of HIPAA and the accompanying federal regulations (45 C.F.R. §§160-164). It is intended to comply with all specific requirements of those regulations (45 C.F.R. §164.508(c)), and with the relevant privacy provisions of Ohio law.

My Agent has the authority to admit or discharge me from any hospital, nursing home, residential care, assisted living or similar facility. My Agent also has the authority to act as my "patient advocate" and hire and fire medical, social service and other support personnel. My Agent is primarily responsible for my medical and health care if I become disabled, incapacitated or incompetent, even if my Agent is not named my Guardian by the Probate Court. I have also executed a Living Will and Health Care Power of Attorney expressing my wishes.

M. **Pets.** My Agent shall have the power to care for any pets I may have. This includes providing veterinary care, day care, hiring pet sitters and obtaining similar help. My Agent has the authority and sole discretion to use my assets to care for my pets.

8. **Limitation of Agent's Powers.** I limit the powers and authority of my Agent and attorney-in-fact as follows: My Agent shall have no rights or powers concerning any act, power, duty, right or obligation relating to any person, matter, transaction or property held or possessed by me as trustee, custodian, personal representative or other fiduciary capacity.

9. **Ratification.** I ratify, acknowledge and declare valid all acts performed by my Agent and attorney-in-fact on my behalf as of the effective date of this General Durable Power of Attorney.

10. **Revocation and Termination.** I reserve the right to revoke, change or terminate this General Durable Power of Attorney at any time in writing. Such action will not affect any person, entity or institution that relied on the power conveyed in this document. Only a notice in writing executed by me and delivered to such person or entity or institution may revoke this power.

This General Durable Power of Attorney shall not be revoked or otherwise become ineffective by the mere passage of time. It shall remain in full force and effect until I revoke, change or terminate it in writing.

I revoke all General Durable Powers of Attorney that I have executed in the past. The same shall have no further force or effect. I do not intend this General Durable Power of Attorney to affect, modify or terminate any special, restricted or limited power or powers of attorney granted by me in connection with any banking, borrowing or commercial transaction.

11. **Construction.** This General Durable Power of Attorney is executed and delivered OHIO. And, OHIO law governs this document's validity and the construction of its provisions. This instrument is to be construed and interpreted as a General Durable Power of Attorney. The enumeration of specific powers is not intended to limit or restrict the general powers granted to the Agent in this instrument.

12. **Reliance.** Third parties may rely upon my Agent's representations concerning all matters related to any power granted in this instrument. No person who acts in reliance on my Agent's representations shall incur any liability to my estate or me by permitting the Agent to exercise any power. Third parties may rely on a photocopy of this executed General Durable Power of Attorney to the same extent as if the copy were the original instrument. This document consists of 5 pages.

IN WITNESS WHEREOF, I executed this General Durable Power of Attorney on _____ , 20_____ .

_____
Principal

State of _____
County of _____

_____ , the Principal, executed this General Durable Power of Attorney on _____ , 20_____ .

_____
Notary

ESTATE PLANNING FORM 12

NOTICE OF REVOCATION OF
POWER OF ATTORNEY

I, _____, of _____, City of

_____, County of _____, State of

_____, hereby give notice that I have revoked, and do hereby revoke,

the power of attorney dated _____, given to

_____ (name of attorney in fact), empowering said

_____, to act as my true and lawful attorney in fact, and I declare

that all power and authority granted under said power of attorney is hereby revoked and

withdrawn.

DATED: _____   _____

Signature of Principal

WITNESSES:

_____ Residing at _____

_____ Residing at _____

State of _____

County of _____

On this _____ day of _____, 20____, _____ personally

appeared before me and executed this document in my presence.

_____

Notary Public

ESTATE PLANNING FORM 13

DOMESTIC PARTNER AGREEMENT

_____, of _____, make the following Agreement:

A. INTRODUCTION

1. We enter into this contract to set forth our rights and responsibilities to each other. We establish that we are in a Domestic Partnership.

2. We intend to abide by the provisions of this Agreement in the spirit of love, joy, cooperation and good faith. Our mutual promises are sufficient consideration for this contract.

B. PROPERTY, INCOME & DEBTS

3. We agree that all property owned by either of us, as of the date of this agreement, shall be considered to be and shall remain, our individual separate property.

    Neither of us shall have any claim to the separate property of the other without a written agreement providing otherwise.

    We agree to list any property that we consider to be our separate property and incorporate it into this Agreement.

4. Our individual income, earned while we are living together and during this relationship shall belong to both of us in equal shares.

    All property that we accumulate during our relationship shall be jointly owned.

5. We agree to maintain joint bank accounts. This includes checking and savings accounts. In the event we decide to obtain a joint credit card account we agree to be jointly liable for the credit card balance.

6. Neither of us shall be responsible or liable for any credit card debt incurred by one of us on our individual credit card accounts.

7. Neither of us shall be liable or responsible for debts incurred by either of us as an individual.

8. We agree to be jointly responsible for all joint debts and expenses.

9. We agree to equally divide all household and living expenses. This includes, but is not limited to: groceries, utilities, rent and daily household expenses.

10. We own our real property jointly. All ownership in jointly held real property shall be reflected in the property title.

11. Any property received by one of us through gift or inheritance remains the separate property of the recipient. The other party has no claim on that separate property unless provided for in a written instrument.

12. Neither of us has any rights to, nor any financial interest in, any separate real estate owned entirely or partially by the other person. This includes any real property accumulated before or during our relationship.

C. SEPARATION or TERMINATION of RELATIONSHIP

13. We agree that either of us can terminate this Agreement by giving the other a one-week written notice of that intent.

14. If we separate and/or terminate this Domestic Partnership, we agree to divide all such accumulated property, in whatever form, equally between us.

15. If we dissolve our Domestic Partnership, we agree that all jointly held property shall be divided equally between us, unless we provide otherwise in a written document.

16. If either of us considers leaving the relationship we agree to a minimum of three joint counseling sessions with a professional counselor or therapist.

17. If we terminate our relationship we agree to and equal division of all property accumulated during our relationship.

18. Neither of us shall have any claim against the other for support, property or financial assistance.

19. We agree to resolve any dispute arising from this Agreement through mediation.

20. The mediator shall be an objective third party who is mutually agreed upon. The mediator's role shall be to help us dissolve our relationship and resolve any differences concerning a division of jointly held property or other issues in a mature and unemotional manner. We agree to enter into mediation in good faith.

21. If our attempt at good-faith mediation is unsuccessful to resolve all issues in dispute, either of us may seek to resolve the issues through arbitration through the following protocol:

   a. Deliver a written demand for arbitration to the other person and name one arbitrator. Delivery shall be by certified mail or another means from which delivery can be verified;

   b. The other party shall respond with the name of a second arbitrator within five days from receipt of the notice;

   c. The two named arbitrators shall select and name a third arbitrator;

   d. The arbitration meeting will take place within seven days following the selection of the third arbitrator, or such other time as the parties may agree, but no later than 30 days after the initial notice;

   e. Each party is entitled to retain legal counsel at her own expense;

   f. Each party may present witnesses and evidence at the arbitration hearing;

   g. The arbitrators shall issue their decision within five days after the hearing. Their decision shall set forth their findings and conclusion and shall be in writing. The decision shall be binding upon each of us. We agree that we shall not seek relief from the arbitration decision in court.

h. If the person to whom an arbitration demand is made fails to respond within five days, the other party may give an additional five days written notice of her intent to proceed. If there is still no response, the person initiating the arbitration may proceed with the arbitration before an arbitrator she has designated. Any award shall have the same force and effect as if all three arbitrators had settled it.

D. COMPLETE AGREEMENT

22. This Agreement represents our complete understanding concerning our Domestic Partnership. It replaces all other written or oral Agreements between us. Any amendments to this Agreement shall be in writing and signed by both.

E. CONSULTATION WITH ATTORNEY

23. We acknowledge that we have had the opportunity to consult with an attorney to review this document. We acknowledge that we are individually is responsible for consulting an attorney. The failure or refusal of either or both of us to do so shall not be construed to mean this Domestic Partnership Agreement was not entered into willingly, freely and voluntarily by either of us.

F. SEVERABILITY CLAUSE

24. We agree that if a court finds any portion of this contract to be illegal or unenforceable, the remainder of the contract shall remain in full force and effect.

Signed _____, 2011 at _____.

_____   _____
_____   _____

State of _____
County of _____

_____ personally appeared before me and executed this Domestic Partnership Agreement before me this _____, 2011.

_____
Notary Public

ESTATE PLANNING FORM 14

CHILDREN ADOPTION GUARDIANSHIP CLAUSE

Section 6. Children, Adoption and Guardianship

6.01   Guardianship. I am pregnant and I name my partner, _____, as the guardian of my children and their estate.

6.02   Bridge Guardian. I realize there may be a delay in appointing my partner, _____, as guardian of my children after my death. Therefore, I want my children to remain with her until the court appoints her as the guardian.

6.03   If _____ is not named guardian of my children's person, I name her as the guardian of my children's estate.

6.04   At the time I execute this Will, there remains a question about second parent adoption. It is my intention and desire that my partner, _____, adopt my children. We shall parent any children we have together. I recognize her as the children's co-parent. The fact that I am the biological parent does not detract from the parent-child relationship she develops with the children.

ESTATE PLANNING FORM 15

DOMESTIC PARTNERSHIP AGREEMENT WITH CHILDREN

DOMESTIC PARTNERSHIP AGREEMENT

THIS AGREEMENT is between _____, residing at _____ and _____ residing at _____.

We intend to establish a domestic partnership and raise children together, and desire to set forth our agreements and expectations regarding financial, property and other rights and obligations arising out of our relationship.

We execute this Agreement and revoke all other written agreements we executed. This Domestic Partnership Agreement is the only one that exists between us.

In consideration of our mutual promises and agreements included in this document, we agree as follows:

1. Separate Property of Each Party

The parties wish to identify what will remain the separate property of each party during the domestic partnership, and to determine their rights in the event of a separation or dissolution of their domestic partnership, as hereinafter discussed.

The following shall constitute and remain the "separate property" of the respective parties: (a) property, whether real or personal, and whether vested, contingent or inchoate, belonging to or acquired by a party prior to the contemplated domestic partnership of the parties, including without limitation the property listed on Schedules A-1 and A-2; (b) all property acquired by a party at any time by bequest, devise, inheritance, distribution from a trust, or by gift; (c) salary, wages and other compensation for personal services; (d) retirement and pension benefits; (e) compensation for personal injuries; (f) proceeds of insurance policies received from any sources; (g) the increase in value of such property, whether or not such increase in value is due in whole or in part to the contributions or efforts of the other party; (h) rents, issues, profits, dividends, interest or other income derived from other distributions upon such property; (i) the proceeds of the sale of such property; (j) property acquired in exchange for such property or acquired with the proceeds of the sale of such property; (k) any other property identified or defined as separate property elsewhere in this Agreement; and (l) any assets or property acquired at any time by either party in their singular name, or jointly with another person. It is the agreement of the parties that unless property is denoted in this Agreement as joint property, it shall be considered separate property. Except as otherwise expressly provided in this Agreement, or by way of an addendum to this Agreement, each party shall be responsible for his/her own debts, unless a debt was undertaken in a joint manner, as evidenced by the documents creating such debt. Each party hereby indemnifies and holds harmless the other for any debt incurred by the party that is not a joint debt.

Except as otherwise expressly provided in this Agreement, each party shall keep and retain sole ownership, enjoyment, control and power of disposal of his/her separate property of every kind and nature, now owned or hereafter acquired by such party, free and clear of any interest, rights or claims of the other party by reason of the domestic partnership or otherwise. These rights include the right to dispose of his/her separate property by gift, sale, testamentary transfer or in any other manner, and to encumber, pledge or hypothecate such property.

Each party covenants and agrees not to make any claim or demand on the separate property of the other party or on the heirs, legal representatives, executors or administrators of the other party with respect to the separate property of the other party, except as otherwise may be expressly provided in this Agreement. If the parties commingled their separate property to acquire new property, the interests of the parties in this new property shall be separate property interests in proportion to their original contributions to the acquisition of such property.

Except as otherwise expressly provided in this Agreement, the separate property now or hereafter owned by one party can become joint or the property of the other party only by a written instrument reclassifying the property for purposes of this Agreement executed by the party whose separate property is thereby reclassified. No acts, conduct or statements by either party shall change the status of separate property, other than an instrument executed by the party whose separate property is thereby reclassified.

No contribution by either party to the care, maintenance, improvement, custody or repair of the separate property of the other party, whether such contributions are in the form of money, property or personal services rendered, shall in any way after or convert any of such separate property, or any increase in the value thereof, to the status of joint property. Any contributions by either party to the care, maintenance, improvement, custody or repair of the separate property of the other party shall become part of the separate property of the other party and the contributing party shall not have any claim for reimbursement. No use by either party of earnings or other separate property for joint or household expenses shall be construed to imply joint ownership of such assets.

Each party agrees, upon request, to cooperate with the other in connection with procuring loans secured by the other party's separate property, including the execution of instruments waiving all rights with respect to the other's separate property. The party owning the separate property shall indemnify and hold the party requested to execute such instruments harmless from and against any liability with respect thereto. Any proceeds derived from loans secured by a party's separate property shall be said party's separate property.

2. Joint Property

The parties recognize that they may from time to time acquire property in their joint names. This may include, for example, sums deposited into bank accounts in their joint names and stock and bond portfolios, certificates of deposit and money market funds in their joint names.

Title to any and all savings accounts, certificates of deposit, money market certificates, cash reserve accounts, money management accounts, stocks, bonds, savings plans, securities or any other funds or assets of the same or a similar nature (other than joint checking accounts) acquired jointly by both of the parties during the domestic partnership shall be placed in the names of both parties hereto in such manner that such assets may not be withdrawn or disposed of without the signatures of both parties thereto.

3. Gifts

All gifts given to the parties jointly shall be the joint property of the parties. Any gifts given from one party to the other prior to or during the domestic partnership shall be considered the separate property of the recipient of the gift, unless the party making the gift specifies that the property is to be the joint property of the parties. Such specification shall be in writing and attached to this Domestic Partnership Agreement as an Attachment.

4. General Living Expenses

The day-to-day living expenses of the parties, such as normal expenses for food, clothing and entertainment shall be paid by the parties in such proportions as they from time to time may agree upon in light of the then available resources of each party.

5. Joint Checking Account

The parties shall establish a joint checking account from which either party may withdraw funds for the payment of household and other joint living expenses, including living expenses of the child(ren). The parties shall contribute funds to this checking account as they from time to time may agree in light of the available resources and income of each party. The funds in this checking account, and property purchased using these funds, shall be the joint property of the parties. This checking account is for the convenience of the parties, and the amounts deposited in the account are not intended to reflect the actual cost of living of either or both of the parties.

6. The Parties' Residence

_____ and _____ are the owners of a house known as _____ (primary residence). Said primary residence is encumbered by a mortgage and the principal balance presently outstanding is approximately $_____.

It is the intention of the parties to reside in said primary residence with their children.

The expenses of ownership of the primary residence, including without limitation utilities, homeowners' insurance, real estate taxes, maintenance and ordinary repairs, shall be paid by the parties in such proportions as they from time to time may agree upon in light of the then available resources of each party.

If, during the domestic partnership, the primary residence is sold and another residence is purchased in its place, the substitute residence shall be treated in the same manner under this Agreement as the primary residence for which it was substituted, unless the parties otherwise agree in a written instrument amending this Agreement.

The furniture, furnishings and other household effects in the primary residence shall be the joint property of the parties, with the exception of items which were the pre-domestic partnership separate property of either party and art, antiques or collectibles acquired as separate property of either party.

7. Other Real Estate

The parties from time to time may own real property other than the primary residence. If a party acquires such property in his/her sole name, it shall be said party's separate property for purposes of this Agreement. If the parties acquire such property as tenants in common, the interests of each party shall be separate property interests in the proportions set forth in the deed. If the parties acquire such property as joint tenants with rights of survivorship, it shall be joint property. The rights of the parties with respect to such property shall be governed by this Agreement unless they agree to some other treatment of such property in a written instrument amending this Agreement.

8. Pensions

Any pension plans of either party, heretofore or hereafter created, shall be and shall remain separate property of such party, free from any claim of the other party, notwithstanding the domestic partnership of the parties. Any pension plans that are the separate property of a party shall not be subject to equitable distribution and shall not be considered assets to which the other party would be entitled to share in, unless, in the event of death, the other party is designated on the pension plan documents as a beneficiary.

As used herein, "pension plan" shall mean any kind of pension plan, 401(k) plan, retirement plan, profit sharing plan, employee benefit plan or any other form of deferred compensation to which a party may be entitled because of his/her employment or work. References to a party's pension plan shall be deemed to include all monies held in such party's pension plan or thereafter added to or accumulated in that pension plan, and any increments, accretions or increases in the value of such pension plan, and any other rights such party has to the pension plan or such monies.

9. Children

It is the intention of the parties to have or adopt one or more children during the domestic partnership. It is the intention of the parties that during their domestic partnership, when one partner has a child, that partner will consent to the other partner's undertaking of any and all steps to adopt that child.

It is the intention of each party to create an irrevocable life insurance trust that will be funded by their separate funds, and that will provide for the maintenance of the surviving partner, if the domestic partnership is still in effect at the time the other partner dies. Regardless of the status of the domestic partnership, the irrevocable life insurance trust will provide for the maintenance, health, education and welfare of the parties' child(ren). The parties agree that each will continue to fund their own irrevocable life insurance trust until such time the life insurance policy has been paid in full or the youngest child reaches the age of twenty-five. The parties hereby agree that all indicia of life insurance shall be set forth in Schedule C, attached hereto.

10. Termination of the Domestic Partnership

The parties recognize that it is in their best interests to set forth their agreement as to their respective rights in the event of a termination of their domestic partnership by separation or dissolution of their domestic partnership.

The parties agree that the value of the primary residence and/or any other property that is owned jointly or by another entity whereby both are beneficiaries or own an equitable interest, shall be determined by obtaining a current appraisal from the lending institution that possesses a mortgage on the property. If either party feels the lending institution's appraisal is inaccurate, then a second appraisal will be obtained at the cost of the party seeking another appraisal. Both appraisals will be averaged and that average shall be the price the parties will use to determine the fair market value of the property.

The parties intend to agree upon which party will be able to remain in the primary residence, depending upon a variety of factors, the most important factor being the best interest of their child(ren). To exercise the option to purchase the primary residence one party (the Proposed Buyer) must give the other party (the Proposed Seller) written notice of her election to purchase the Proposed Seller's interest within 90 days after termination of the domestic partnership. Termination of the domestic partnership shall be considered as written notice defined herein. If the parties cannot agree upon which party will remain in the primary residence, the primary residence will be placed with a real estate broker at listing price of the fair market value as determined by the method set forth above. If practicable, the closing of title shall take place on a date not more than 60 days after the fair market value of the primary residence is determined. At the closing of title, the Proposed Buyer shall pay the amount due to the Proposed Seller and the Proposed Seller shall deliver good and clear title, free from encumbrances and any documents that may be necessary or appropriate to transfer all of his/her right, title and interest in the primary residence to the Proposed Buyer.

If either party elects to purchase the interest of the other party in the primary residence, the party who so elects shall also simultaneously purchase the interest of the other party in the jointly owned furniture, furnishings and other household effects of the residence for the fair market value of such interest.

If neither party exercises the aforesaid options, the primary residence shall be promptly listed for sale with a broker mutually agreeable to the parties. The parties shall jointly agree to the listing price. If the parties cannot agree, then the average of the appraisals discussed earlier in this section shall be used to determine the listing price.

If the primary residence does not sell at the listing price within a reasonable period of time, said price shall be reduced until the residence is sold. A reasonable period of time is agreed upon to be six to eight months. The parties agree that the reduction in price will begin at five percent of the listing price. The reduction will continue in increments of five percent until the primary residence is sold.

The net proceeds from the sale of the primary residence, after deducting for all related expenses in connection with the sale, shall be divided equally between the parties. That party shall pay any liens and encumbrances levied against the primary residence as the result of a debt owed by either party with his/her own separate assets prior to the passing of title to the Proposed Buyer.

In the event of the termination of the domestic partnership, the parties shall have joint legal custody of any minor children of the parties. It is the expectation of the parties, however, that the children will reside predominantly with their respective birth or legal parent, [however, the other party shall have frequent and meaningful contact/parenting time with the child(ren).]

Each party agrees to pay reasonable amounts, in light of his/her available income and resources, for the support of any minor children of the parties, at a minimum, in an amount that is set forth in the current child support guidelines of the state in which the parties reside. The parties agree to consult and negotiate in good faith regarding the children's education, visitation, payment of medical expenses and other issues that may arise regarding the children in the event of the termination of the domestic partnership.

In the event of the termination of the domestic partnership any joint property acquired by the parties during the domestic partnership shall be divided equally between the parties, notwithstanding the percentage contribution each party may have made to acquire of create such property.

The parties recognize that some items of joint property, such as tangible personal property, cannot be readily divided into shares. If the parties cannot agree on the division of any such items or the fair compensation that one party should pay to the other for his/her share of such items, such items shall be sold so that the proceeds of sale may be divided equally.

Each party hereby irrevocably waives, releases and relinquishes any and all claims or rights that he/she now or hereafter might otherwise have to or against the separate property now owned or hereafter acquired by the other party. This includes, without limitation, laws relating to equitable distribution, marital property, community property, curtesy, dower or any other interest or right of distribution of property by reason of domestic partnership, cohabitation, union or marriage. Each party recognizes that this waiver includes rights he/she might otherwise have or acquire in the future under the laws of the state in which the parties resided at the time the domestic partnership terminated.

As used herein, the term "termination of the domestic partnership" shall mean either party sending the other party written notice of their intent to terminate the domestic partnership. Notice shall be sent by first class mail, certified mail or any other form of mailing by which confirmation of delivery can be ascertained. Notice shall be sent to the party's current residence where that person normally receives mail or to the party's last known address.

11. Death of the Parties
The parties recognize that it is in their best interests to set forth their Agreement as to their respective rights upon the death of either party during the domestic partnership.

All jointly owned property shall pass in accordance with the laws of the state in which the property is located. Title to property held jointly with rights of survivorship will pass to the survivor in accordance with state law.

Each party retains sole control over his/her separate property. Each party shall have the right to dispose of that separate property either by will or inter vivos or in accordance with the rules of intestate succession of the state in which the decedent was domiciled.

Nothing in this Agreement shall restrict the right of either party to bequeath or give property to the other party. If either party should provide that the other party shall receive property, as a bequest or gift under his/her last will and testament or otherwise, including without limitation life insurance proceeds, pension or profit sharing plan benefits and assets held as joint tenants with rights of survivorship, such other party shall have the right to receive such property. The parties agree, however, that no promises of any kind have been made by either of them to the other with respect to any such bequest or gift.

The obligations set forth in this Article 11 shall terminate and cease to be binding in the event of the termination of the domestic partnership by separation or dissolution of their domestic partnership or annulment, except separate property shall always remain separate property.

If, upon the death of either party, an action for separation or dissolution of their domestic partnership or annulment has been commenced but a judgment has not been entered, any rights of the surviving party to share in the estate of the deceased party shall be extinguished and the surviving party shall be entitled to receive from the decedent's estate only what the surviving party would have been entitled to pursuant to the Agreement had a judgment of separation or dissolution of their domestic partnership been entered.

12. Full Disclosure

A copy of the parties' current net worth statement is attached hereto as Schedule B. The parties affirm that the contents of the net worth statement are accurate and true.

Each party has made independent inquiry, to his/her own satisfaction, into the complete financial circumstances of the other, and acknowledges that he/she is fully informed of the income, assets and financial prospects of the other.

[Neither of the parties has been previously married. Neither of the parties has living children.]

13. Legal Representation

The parties acknowledge that they have retained and have been represented by separate and independent legal counsel of their own choosing in connection with the negotiation of this Agreement. _____ consulted with Attorney _____. _____ consulted with Attorney _____. Each has been separately and independently advised regarding this Agreement including the rights waived or otherwise released herein.

14. Notices

Any notice, demand or other communication required or permitted under this Agreement shall be in writing and shall be delivered by hand or by Federal Express courier or by certified or registered mail, return receipt requested, to a party at his/her address stipulated above or at such other address as the party may designate.

15. General Provisions

This Agreement is entire and complete and embodies all understandings and agreements between the parties. All prior understandings, agreements, conversations, communications, representations, correspondence and other writings are merged into this instrument, which alone sets forth the understanding and agreement of the parties.

Each party acknowledges that all of the matters embodied in this Agreement, including all terms, covenants, conditions, waivers, releases and other provisions contained herein, are fully understood by each; that this Agreement is fair, just and reasonable; that each party is entering into this Agreement freely, voluntarily and after due consideration of the consequences of doing so; and that this Agreement is valid and binding upon each party.

This Agreement and each provision thereof shall not be amended, modified, discharge, waived or terminated except by a writing executed by the party sought to be bound. Failure of a party to insist upon strict performance of any provision of this Agreement shall not be construed as a waiver of any subsequent default of the same or similar nature, nor shall it affect the parties' rights to require strict performance of any other portion of this Agreement. Any waiver by either party of any provision of this Agreement, or of any right or option hereunder shall not be deemed a continuing waiver and shall not prevent such party from thereafter insisting upon the strict performance or enforcement of such provision, right or option.

The parties agree that each of them, upon request of the other party or the legal representatives of the other party, shall execute and deliver such other and further instruments as may be necessary or appropriate to effectuate the purposes and intent of this Agreement. Each party, upon request of the other, shall execute and deliver a confirmation that this Agreement remains in full force and effect.

This Agreement and all rights and obligations of the parties hereunder shall be governed by and construed in accordance with the laws of the State of _____. The laws of the State in which the parties reside with their child(ren) shall govern irrespective of whether either or both of the parties heretofore or hereafter reside or are domiciled in any other jurisdiction and irrespective of whether any property is located in any other jurisdiction. If any provision of this Agreement should be held to be invalid or unenforceable under the laws of any State, county or other jurisdiction in which enforcement is sought, the remainder of this Agreement shall continue in full force and effect.

This Agreement shall be binding upon and shall inure to the benefit of the parties hereto and their respective heirs, executors, administrators, successors and assigns.

IN WITNESS WHEREOF, the parties execute this Agreement on the date first written above, of his/her own free will and attests that neither is under the influence of any alcohol, drug or other substance that would affect the party's decision-making capability. Each party attests that he/she is competent to enter into this Agreement.

_____   _____
Signature   Signature

State of _____
County of _____

_____, the Principal, personally appeared before me and executed and acknowledged this Domestic Partnership Agreement before me this _____ day of _____, 20____.

                                           _____
                                           Notary Public

State of _____
County of _____

_____, the Principal, personally appeared before me and executed and acknowledged this Domestic Partnership Agreement before me this _____ day of _____, 20____.

                                           _____
                                           Notary Public

ESTATE PLANNING FORM 16

SIMPLE DOMESTIC PARTNER AGREEMENT
MAINTAINING SEPARATE PROPERTY

_____ and _____, make the following agreement:

1. We enter into this contract to set forth our rights and responsibilities to each other. Our mutual promises are sufficient consideration for this contract.

2. We intend to abide by the provisions of this agreement in the spirit of love, joy, cooperation and good faith.

3. We agree that all property owned by either of us, as of the date of this agreement, shall be considered to be and shall remain, the separate property of each. Neither of us will have any claim to the separate property of the other absent a written agreement transferring ownership. We attached a list of our major items of separate property and the list is incorporated into this agreement.

4. Our individual income and any property accumulated from that income shall remain the separate property of the person earning the income. Neither of us shall have any claim to this separate property.

5. Each of us is maintaining separate bank accounts. This includes, checking, savings and credit card accounts. We may decide to change that in the future.

6. Neither of us shall be liable or responsible for the individual debts incurred by the other in her own name.

7. We agree to be jointly responsible for all debts we enter into together.

8. We agree to equally divide all household and living expenses. This includes, but is not limited to: groceries, utilities, rent and daily household expenses.

9. We agree that there may be a need to maintain a joint bank account (checking or savings) for a specific purpose. In that event, we agree to contribute an equal amount to the bank account. Neither party will withdraw funds from that account without the permission and consent of the other.

10. We also agree that we may, at some time, agree to own property jointly. Any jointly held property ownership shall be reflected either in writing or on the title to said property. In the event we dissolve our domestic partnership, we provide that any jointly held property will be divided into equal shares, unless we provide otherwise in a written document.

11. Any property received by one of us through gift or inheritance remains the separate property of the recipient. The other party has no claim on that separate property unless provided for in a written instrument.

12. Neither of us has any rights to, nor any financial interest in, any real estate owned entirely or partially by the other person. This includes any real property accumulated before or during our relationship.

13. We agree that either party can terminate this contract by giving the other party a one-week written notice of that intent. If either of us seriously considers leaving the relationship we both agree to, at least, three counseling sessions with a professional counselor or therapist.

14. In the event that this relationship is terminated we agree to divide all jointly held property equally. Neither of us shall have any claim against the other for support, property or financial assistance.

15. We agree to resolve any dispute arising from this agreement through mediation. The mediator shall be an objective third party who is mutually agreed upon. The mediator's role shall be to help us dissolve our relationship and resolve any differences concerning a division of jointly held property or other issues in a mature and unemotional manner. We agree to enter into mediation in good faith.

16. In the event that our attempt at good-faith mediation is unsuccessful to resolve all issues in dispute, either party may seek to resolve the issues through arbitration through the use of the following protocol:

   a. Deliver a written demand for arbitration to the other person and name one arbitrator. Delivery shall be by certified mail or another means from which delivery can be verified;

   b. The other party shall respond with the name of a second arbitrator within five days from receipt of the notice;

   c. The two named arbitrators shall select and name a third arbitrator;

   d. The arbitration meeting will take place within seven days following the selection of the third arbitrator, or such other time as the parties may agree, but no later than 30 days after the initial notice;

   e. Each party is entitled to retain legal counsel at her own expense;

   f. Each party may present witnesses and evidence at the arbitration hearing;

   g. The arbitrators shall issue their decision within five days after the hearing. Their decision shall set forth their findings and conclusion and shall be in writing. The decision shall be binding upon each of us. We agree that we shall not seek relief from the arbitration decision in court.

   h. If the person to whom an arbitration demand is made fails to respond within five days, the other party may give an additional five days written notice of her intent to proceed. If there is still no response, the person initiating the arbitration may proceed with the arbitration before an arbitrator she has designated. Any award shall have the same force and effect as if all three arbitrators had settled it.

17. This agreement represents our complete understanding concerning our domestic partnership. It replaces any earlier agreements, written or oral, that we made. We agree that this document can only be amended in writing and must be signed by both of us.

18. We agree that, if a court finds any portion of this contract to be illegal or otherwise unenforceable, the remainder of the contract shall remain in full force and effect.

Signed on _____, 20___ at _____, Ohio.

_____   _____

State of _____
County of _____

_____   and   _____,   personally
appeared before me and executed and acknowledged this Domestic Partnership Agreement before
me on _____, 20____.

                                        _____
                                          Notary Public

ESTATE PLANNING FORM 17

DOMESTIC PARTNER AGREEMENT
SHARING MOST PROPERTY

_____, residing at _____, make the following agreement:

1. We enter into this contract to set forth our rights and responsibilities to each other.

2. We intend to abide by the provisions of this agreement in the spirit of love, joy, cooperation and good faith. Our mutual promises are sufficient consideration for this contract.

3. We agree that all property owned by either of us, as of the date of this agreement, shall be considered to be and shall remain, the separate property of each. Neither of us will have any claim to the separate property of the other absent a written agreement transferring ownership. We will list any major items of separate property in an attached statement that is incorporated into this agreement.

4. Our individual income, earned while we are living together and during this relationship shall belong to both of us in equal shares. Likewise, all property accumulated from that income shall belong to both of us in equal shares. In the event we separate and/or terminate this domestic partnership we agree to divide all such accumulated property, in whatever form, equally between us.

5. We agree to maintain joint bank accounts. This includes checking and savings accounts. In the event we decide to obtain a joint credit card account we agree to be jointly liable for the credit card balance.

6. Neither of us shall be responsible or liable for any credit card debt incurred by one of us on our individual credit card accounts.

7. Neither of us shall be liable or responsible for the debts incurred by either of us as an individual.

8. We agree to be jointly responsible for all joint debts and expenses.

9. We agree to equally divide all household and living expenses. This includes, but is not limited to: groceries, utilities, rent and daily household expenses.

10. We own our real property jointly. Any jointly held real property ownership shall be reflected either in writing or on the title to said property. In the event we dissolve our domestic partnership, we provide that any jointly held property shall be divided into equal shares, unless we provide otherwise in a written document.

11. Any property received by one of us through gift or inheritance remains the separate property of the recipient. The other party has no claim on that separate property unless provided for in a written instrument.

12. Neither of us has any rights to, nor any financial interest in, any separate real estate owned entirely or partially by the other person. This includes any real property accumulated before or during our relationship.

13. We agree that either party can terminate this contract by giving the other party a one-week written notice of that intent. If either of us seriously considers leaving the relationship we both agree to a minimum of three joint counseling sessions with a professional counselor or therapist.

14. In the event that this relationship is terminated we agree to divide all jointly held property equally. Neither of us shall have any claim against the other for support, property or financial assistance.

15. We agree to resolve any dispute arising from this agreement through mediation. The mediator shall be an objective third party who is mutually agreed upon. The mediator's role shall be to help us dissolve our relationship and resolve any differences concerning a division of jointly held property or other issues in a mature and unemotional manner. We agree to enter into mediation in good faith.

16. In the event that our attempt at good-faith mediation is unsuccessful to resolve all issues in dispute, either party may seek to resolve the issues through arbitration through the use of the following protocol:

    a. Deliver a written demand for arbitration to the other person and name one arbitrator. Delivery shall be by certified mail or another means from which delivery can be verified;

    b. The other party shall respond with the name of a second arbitrator within five days from receipt of the notice;

    c. The two named arbitrators shall select and name a third arbitrator;

    d. The arbitration meeting will take place within seven days following the selection of the third arbitrator, or such other time as the parties may agree, but no later than 30 days after the initial notice;

    e. Each party is entitled to retain legal counsel at her own expense;

    f. Each party may present witnesses and evidence at the arbitration hearing;

    g. The arbitrators shall issue their decision within five days after the hearing. Their decision shall set forth their findings and conclusion and shall be in writing. The decision shall be binding upon each of us. We agree that we shall not seek relief from the arbitration decision in court.

    h. If the person to whom an arbitration demand is made fails to respond within five days, the other party may give an additional five days written notice of her intent to proceed. If there is still no response, the person initiating the arbitration may proceed with the arbitration before an arbitrator she has designated. Any award shall have the same force and effect as if all three arbitrators had settled it.

17. This agreement represents our complete understanding concerning our domestic partnership. It replaces all other agreements between us either written or oral. We agree to only amend this agreement in writing and both of us will sign any amendment.

18. We acknowledge that we have had the opportunity to consult with an attorney to review this document. We also acknowledge that we, individually, is responsible for consulting with an attorney. The failure or refusal of either or both of us to do so shall not be construed to mean this Domestic Partnership Agreement was not entered into willingly, freely and voluntarily by either of us.

19. We agree that if a court finds any portion of this contract to be illegal or unenforceable, the remainder of the contract shall remain in full force and effect.

Signed _____, 20____ at _____, Ohio.

_____   _____

State of Ohio
County of _____

_____, personally appeared before me and executed this Domestic Partnership Agreement before me this _____, 20____.

_____
Notary Public

Exhibit A:
    Separate Property of _____

Exhibit B.
    Separate Property of _____

Exhibit C.
    Jointly Held Property of _____ **and** _____

ESTATE PLANNING FORM 18

TERMINATION OF DOMESTIC PARTNERSHIP

1. _____ and _____, who have been domestic partners living together at (specify address, type of premises, apartment or house), agree to separate and go their own way. At this time neither party has the intention of resuming their former domestic partnership arrangement.

2. It is also agreed that the each party shall retain complete and total control over his/her separate property, including any furnishings or furniture, the each brought into the relationship. A list of each party's separate property is attached hereto as Exhibit A.

3. It is further agreed that the items listed in Exhibit B were purchased and are owned jointly by the parties. The parties divided these items in a fair and equitable manner. Each party is entitled to complete and total control over the items listed under their respective names in Exhibit B.

4. The parties agree to dispose of any and all joint debts and other joint obligations in the following manner: [specify each creditor, amount owed, who will pay obligation, indemnification clause].

5. The parties also agree that [both of them are leaving the shared premises] or [that _____ is leaving the shared premises and _____ will remain in the shared premises. The one staying shall assume all responsibility for said premises from this date forward, except for any common debts incurred by the parties during their relationship. _____ will take whatever action is required to [remove _____'s name from the lease] or [refinance the mortgage].

6. The party who is leaving agrees not to reenter the premises without the remaining party's permission, nor will he/she remove any items from the premises without the other party's knowledge.

7. [Specify how jointly owned real estate is to be valued, listed and sold].

8. Neither party shall have any claim against the other party's business interests, pension or retirement funds, insurance proceeds, rights of inheritance or any other property not specifically described in this Agreement.

9. Neither party shall have a claim to compensation from the other for services rendered during the time they lived together, for financial support of any kind or for any other property, assets or money not described in this Agreement.

10. The parties agree to resolve any dispute arising from this agreement through mediation. The mediator shall be an objective third party who is mutually agreed upon. The mediator's role shall be to help the parties dissolve their relationship and resolve any differences concerning a division of jointly held property or other issues in a mature and unemotional manner. The parties agree to enter into mediation in good faith. [Parties agree to engage attorneys practicing collaborative law in order to resolve the issues involved in the termination of their relationship. Both parties understand that the collaborative process is engaged in with the specific intent to avoid litigation.]

11. In the event that the parties' attempt at good-faith mediation is unsuccessful to resolve all issues in dispute, either party may seek to resolve the issues through arbitration through the use of the following protocol:

    a. Deliver a written demand for arbitration to the other person and name one arbitrator; The other party shall respond with the name of a second arbitrator within five days from receipt of the notice;

    b. The two named arbitrators shall select and name a third arbitrator;

    c. The arbitration meeting will take place within seven days following the selection of the third arbitrator;

    d. Each party is entitled to retain legal counsel at his/her own expense;

    e. Each party may present witnesses and evidence at the arbitration hearing;

    f. The arbitrators shall issue their decision within five days after the hearing. Their decision shall set forth their findings and conclusion and shall be in writing. The decision shall be binding upon each party. The parties agree that neither one shall seek relief from the arbitration decision in court.

    g. If the person to whom an arbitration demand is made fails to respond within five days, the other party may give an additional five days written notice of his/her intent to proceed. If there is still no response, the person initiating the arbitration may proceed with the arbitration before an arbitrator he/she has designated. Any award shall have the same force and effect as if all three arbitrators had settled it.

If the person to whom an arbitration demand is made fails to respond within five days, the other party may give an additional five days written notice of his/her intent to proceed. If there is still no response, the person initiating the arbitration may proceed with the arbitration before an arbitrator he/she has designated. Any award shall have the same force and effect as if all three arbitrators had settled it.

12. Each party states that he/she entered into this Agreement freely, voluntarily, without fraud, duress, threats or coercion.

    The parties, by signing below, indicate their intention to participate in this Agreement and the provisions set forth.

_____   _____
           Signature   Signature

State of _____

County of _____

(Principals' names)_____ and _____, the Principals, personally appeared before me and executed and acknowledged this Termination of Domestic Partnership/Living Together Arrangement before me this ___ day of _____, 20__.

_____
                                    Notary Public

ESTATE PLANNING FORM 19

AUTHORIZATION FOR MEDICAL TREATMENT
FOR MINOR CHILD

We, _____ and _____, are the parents of _____, born December 6, 2010. We share joint custody of our child, _____.

Each of us is legally responsible for the care, custody and control of our minor child.

Each of us consents to any X-ray, examination, anesthetic, medical or surgical diagnosis or treatment and hospital care to be rendered to our child under the supervision and advice of a physician or other medical care provider licensed to practice medicine in any state in the United States.

We also consent to any X-ray, examination, dental or surgical diagnosis or treatment and hospital care to be rendered to our minor child by a dentist licensed to practice dentistry in any state in the United States.

This authority is valid until _____ turns 18.

Executed on _____, 20___ at _____, _____.

_____
Parent's Signature

_____
Parent's Signature

State of _____
County of _____

On _____, 2011 _____ and _____, personally appeared before me and executed this document.

_____
Notary Public

A COPY OF THIS DOCUMENT SHALL BE AS VALID AS THE ORIGINAL

ESTATE PLANNING FORM 20

AGREEMENT TO SHARE EXPENSES and PROPERTY

We, _____ and _____, are in a committed, intimate relationship. We intend this Agreement to reflect our commitment to jointly share all expenses and property that we acquire during our relationship.

Because federal and state law does not recognize our relationship, we enter into this Agreement to establish our joint responsibility.

We intend to be jointly responsible for all expenses incurred in our relationship. We jointly own the furniture, appliances and household goods in our home.

At present, we are renting an apartment. We do not own any real estate.

Our checking and savings accounts are held jointly, with right of survivorship. We contribute equal amounts to those accounts.

We make all purchases of furniture, appliances, household goods and similar items together. Each of us contributes equally to the cost of those purchases.

Everything we own has been purchased together with the intent that we both hold title to all those possessions.

_____   _____

_____   _____

_____ and _____, personally appeared before me on _____, 2010 and executed this Agreement.

_____
Notary

ESTATE PLANNING FORM 21

SHARED CUSTODY AGREEMENT

We, _____and _____ enter into this Shared Custody Agreement. We accept our mutual promises contained in this Agreement as sufficient consideration.

A. INTRODUCTION

1. We agree to share all legal parenting rights, responsibilities and obligations toward our children. At present, we have a child, _____, born _____. This Shared Custody Agreement shall apply specifically to _____, and to any other children we may have in the future.

2. We enter into this Shared Custody Agreement to ensure that _____ and any children born to us in the future receive the full benefit of two parents. We agree that it is in _____'s best interest to be raised by both of us and have the benefit of two loving parents.

3. We intend to update this Agreement as we have other children. However, if we do not execute an updated Agreement, we intend that this document cover our joint and individual responsibilities to any children we are parenting.

4. _____ requires a stable source of financial, academic, medical and emotional support. We agree to jointly provide for our children. This shall include current and future financial and emotional support and rights to inheritance.

B. INCORPORATE INTO BINDING COURT ORDER

5. We agree and guarantee that we are _____'s natural and legal parents. We ask any Court of competent jurisdiction to recognize, accept, adopt and enforce this Joint Custody Agreement and incorporate it into a binding court order.

[6. We intend this Shared Custody Agreement to meet the requirements established by the Ohio Supreme Court in *In re Mullen*, 2011-Ohio-3361 (July 12, 2011). We intend that both of us are to be considered our child's legal parents.] **[The Ohio Supreme Court referred to "legal parents" in its decision. It may be further proof of the parties' intent to use the phrase.]**

C. MUTUAL RESPONSIBILITIES AND OBLIGATIONS

In recognition and consideration of our mutual responsibilities and obligations to our children, we agree to share legal parenting as follows:

7. We made a joint decision to have children. We based our decision on our commitment to each other and to _____. We made a decision to jointly parent our children. We agree that both of us are _____'s primary parents and caregivers. We intend to co-parent _____.

8. We agree to share joint custody and legal parenting of _____ and any other children born in the future.

9. We acknowledge that _____ is _____'s biological mother. She understands that she has specific, constitutionally guaranteed parental rights. She willingly and voluntarily waives those rights in favor of jointly parenting _____ with _____. She acknowledges that _____ is also _____'s mother and agrees to protect those rights against all challenges. _____ agrees not to challenge _____'s legal parental status.

10. _____ agrees and acknowledges that _____ is _____'s legal parent.

D. SECOND PARENT ADOPTION

11. At the time this Agreement is signed, the status of second-parent adoption in Ohio is unclear. If second-parent adoption becomes available to us, we intend that _____ initiate adoption proceedings so she will be legally recognized as _____'s mother. This does not mean that _____ intends to relinquish her parental rights. Rather, we intend that both of us be recognized as _____'s legal parents. We believe this is in our child's best interests.

12. As parents, it is our responsibility and obligation to our child to do what is best for him. Through this Agreement _____ consents to _____ adopting _____. We shall be equally responsible for any expenses involved with the adoption.

13. Until we can finalize a second-parent adoption to establish _____ as _____'s mother, _____ intends that he be considered her heir-at-law and next-of-kin as Ohio law defines those terms.

E. SUPPORT OBLIGATION

14. _____ understands that she has no legal obligation to care for or support _____. She accepts this obligation willingly and with out reservation. She intends to support her child, _____, and any children born to her and _____ in the future.

15. We agree to jointly make all major decisions concerning our child.

16. We are equally responsible for all of _____'s expenses. We are equally responsible for his financial, emotional and spiritual well-being.

17. We agree to leave at least one-half of our individual estate to our children. If either of us creates a trust for the children, we agree to name the other parent as the trustee.

18. We agree to name the other as the children's guardian in our respective Wills. We agree to work together to name an alternate guardian for our children.

F. SEPARATION OR TERMINATION OF RELATIONSHIP

19. We entered into a Domestic Partnership Agreement. We incorporate the terms of that Agreement here.

20. We agree to abide by the terms of this Shared Custody Agreement.

21. If we terminate our relationship, we intend this Agreement to guide a Court in determining our respective rights. If we terminate our relationship, we intend to jointly parent _____. We agree that the local Juvenile Court shall have jurisdiction over any disputes arising during _____'s minority regarding custody, support or visitation.

22. We intend that this Agreement be recognized and enforced in court. Recent Ohio Supreme Court decisions have recognized the enforceability of Shared Custody Agreements.

23. We agree to do everything possible to create a legal relationship between _____ and _____. This will be done for purposes of custody, visitation, support, inheritance, health care insurance and guardianship.

G. POST RELATIONSHIP CUSTODY/SUPPORT/VISITATION PROVISIONS

24. We acknowledge and agree that, while we now live together as a family, there may come a time when we no longer do so. In that event, we agree that we will continue to provide for our children as follows:

   a. We will have joint custody of the children. Both of us will take whatever action is necessary to obtain a shared custody agreement from the court having jurisdiction over these matters.
   b. The children will spend approximately one-half of the time with each parent. Each parent shall share equally in the responsibility for the care of the children during school vacations or illness either by personally caring for the children or arranging for proper care.
   c. Each of us shall pay one-half of the normal daily living expenses and costs of the children while they live together; or the entire cost of daily living expenses when the children are with each one, should they stop living together.
   d. We agree that each of us shall claim the children as a dependent for tax purposes in alternate years. _____ shall claim the children during even numbered tax years and _____ during odd numbered tax years.
   e. Each parent shall maintain the children as a beneficiary of a life insurance policy in the minimum amount of $50,000 until all the children are over 18 and have graduated from high school.
   f. We agree that we will jointly make all major decisions regarding the physical location, support, education, medical care and religious training of the children.
   g. We agree that each of us will make a good faith effort to remain in the school district in where the children are attending school until the youngest child completes high school. We agree that neither one of us will may move out of the school district without the written consent of the other. Neither one of us shall not withhold such consent without legitimate justification. We make this agreement because we want to limit the disruption to our children as much as possible.

    h. We agree that should a significant discrepancy occur in our respective net monthly income, following a separation, we will negotiate child support payments consistent with the child support schedule then in effect in our State of domicile.

    i. We agree that, if one of us is no longer able to care and provide for the children because of death or legal disability, it will be in the best interests of the children to remain with the other parent. Neither one of us will allow the children to be adopted by any other per child so long as we both are living.

H. RESOLUTION OF DISPUTES

25. We agree to resolve any dispute involving this Agreement through mediation.

26. The mediator shall be a mutually agreed upon objective third party. Northcoast Conflict Solutions is an option.

27. The mediator's role shall be to help us resolve any disputes, dissolve our relationship and/or resolve any differences concerning the children. The parties agree to enter mediation in good faith.

28. We recognize that mediation may not be successful. Therefore, we also agree to consider using collaborative law to resolve any disputes that remain following mediation. We understand that in collaborative law the lawyers we choose to represent us will not represent us in court. Our goal is to resolve any disputes in a reachable manner without resorting to expensive litigation. We agree that litigation will hurt our children and will not be in their best interests.

29. If we are unsuccessful in resolving our disputes through the collaborative process or mediation, either of us may seek to initiate arbitration. We agree to use of the following protocol:

    a. Deliver a written demand for arbitration to the other person and name one arbitrator;

    b. The other party shall respond with the name of a second arbitrator within five days from receipt of the notice;

    c. The two named arbitrators shall select and name a third arbitrator;

    d. The arbitration meeting will take place within seven days following the selection of the third arbitrator;

    e. Each party is entitled to retain legal counsel at his/her own expense;

    f. Each party may present witnesses and evidence at the arbitration hearing;

    g. The arbitrators shall issue their decision within five days after the hearing. Their decision shall set forth their findings and conclusion and shall be in writing. The decision shall be binding upon each of us. We agree that neither party shall seek relief from the arbitration decision in court.

    h. If the person to whom an arbitration demand is made fails to respond within five days, the other party may give an additional five days written notice of her intent to proceed. If there is still no response, the person initiating the arbitration may proceed with the arbitration before an arbitrator he/she has designated. Any award shall have the same force and effect as if all three arbitrators had settled it.

    i.

I. LEGAL ISSUES

30.   We understand the legal questions raised by the issues involved in this Agreement may not yet be settled under Ohio law. Even though certain clauses in this Agreement may be

unenforceable in court, we choose to enter into this Agreement to clarify our intent to jointly provide and nurture our children, even when we are no longer living together in a single family residence.

31.   Specifically, we recognize that current Ohio law may not obligate _____ to financially support the children. We both agree that we are legally and morally bound to support our minor children until they turn 18. We willingly and voluntarily accept this responsibility even though there is no law that requires us to do so.

32.   Through this Agreement we intend to create legally enforceable rights for either of us to collect child support on behalf of our children, including the right to request that support be extended beyond minority consistent with the child support laws of the State of domicile.

33.   _____ agrees to do everything legally possible to create a legal relationship between the children and the non-legally recognized parent, _____. This will be done for purposes of custody, visitation, support, inheritance, health care insurance and guardianship of our minor children.

34.   _____ agrees to take no action, in or out of court, to avoid her obligations and responsibilities to our children.

J. ENFORCEMENT IN COURT

35. We intend this Agreement to guide any Court, should one become involved, in determining the best interests of the children. We agree that the Court shall have jurisdiction over any disputes arising during our children's minority regarding custody, support or visitation.

36.   We agree to participate in Court-ordered mediation concerning issues of custody or visitation and to be bound by court orders regarding the children.

37. Specifically, _____ agrees to be bound by a court order compelling her to pay support for the children or to have contact with the children on a set schedule.

38. _____, the biological parent, agrees to be bound by any court order granting visitation and/or joint custody to _____.

39. We agree to put aside any personal differences we may have with each other, in the event we separate or terminate our relationship, in order to do what is in the best interests 38. We agree that neither of us will raise legal arguments intended to interfere with the ongoing relationship between the other parent and the children. We also agree that we will not allow our lawyers to raise arguments contrary to the terms of this Agreement.

40. We agree that neither of us will contest or object to the Court's jurisdiction over any dispute involving the children, including custody, support, care or visitation.

41. We entered into this Agreement with the express purpose of doing what is best for our children. Neither one of us will take any action that interferes with our individual relationship with our children. The fact that both of us are benefitting from this Agreement is sufficient consideration to ensure its validity.

42. We each fully understand and accept the terms of this Agreement. We understand this Agreement is enforceable in court.

K. LIQUIDATED DAMAGES

43. We understand that when two people end their personal relationship, and children are involved, that either party can make bad decisions. If either of us successfully contests the Court's jurisdiction over any issue involving the custody, care, support or visitation of the children, that party shall be liable for liquidated damages in the amount of $25,000 for each year that this Agreement was in effect. The contesting party shall also be responsible for paying all costs and attorney fees incurred by the defending party.

L. CONTRACTUAL/LEGAL OBLIGATIONS

44. We agree that we are contractually bound by the terms of this Agreement even if either of us has specific, enumerated parental rights under the United States Constitution, Ohio's Constitution and/or Ohio and federal law.

45. We agree that the Uniform Child Custody Jurisdiction Enforcement Act (UCCJEA) and the Parental Kidnapping Protection Act (PKPA) apply to this Agreement.

M. ENTIRE AGREEMENT

46. This is the entire Agreement. We have not made any promises, understandings, agreements or representations that are not reflected in this Agreement.

47. Each of us signs this Agreement voluntarily and without any duress of any kind.

N. CONSULATION WITH ATTORNEY

48. We each had the opportunity to consult with an attorney before signing this Agreement.

We signed this Agreement on _____, 2011 in _____, Ohio.

_____   _____

State of _____
County of _____

_____ and _____, personally appeared before me and signed this Shared Custody Agreement on _____, 2011.

_____
Notary Public

ESTATE PLANNING FORM 22

ALTERNATIVE SHARED CUSTODY AGREEMENT

SHARED CUSTODY AGREEMENT

This Shared Parenting Agreement is between _____ and
_____. We accept our mutual promises in this Agreement as
sufficient consideration.

We agree to share all parenting rights, responsibilities and obligations toward our
children. At present, we have a child, _____, born on _____. This
Shared Parenting Agreement shall apply specifically to _____, and to any other
children we may have in the future.

We enter into this Shared Parenting Agreement to guarantee that our children receive the
full benefit of two parents. We agree that it is in our children's best interest to be raised by both
of us.

Our children require stable sources of financial, academic, medical and emotional
support. We agree to jointly provide for our children. This shall include current and future
financial and emotional support and rights to inheritance.

We also agree and guarantee that we are the natural and legal parents or our children. We
ask any Court of competent jurisdiction to recognize and adopt this Agreement as a binding court
order and accept and enforce this Agreement.

In recognition and consideration of our mutual responsibilities and obligations to our
children, we agree to share parenting as follows:

1. We entered into a joint decision to have children. The decision is based on our commitment to
jointly parent our children. We agree that both of us are the primary parents and caregivers to our
children. We intend to raise our children together.

2. We agree to share joint custody of our children.

3. _____ is the biological mother and the residential parent.

4. We intend both _____ and _____ to be considered legal parents.

5. We agree to jointly make all major decisions regarding the physical location, support,
education, medical care and religious training of our child.

6. Each of us will pay the entire cost of daily living expenses when _____ is with
us. We agree to child support payments that are consistent with Ohio law. We understand that
_____ is not legally obligated to pay child support and _____
voluntarily accepts this obligation _____ understands she has no legally
enforceable right to force _____ to pay child support. As the biological mother,
_____, voluntarily agrees to share parenting with _____. She has
done so since _____'s birth. It is her intention to continue to do so.

7. We agree that if either of us is no longer able to care and provide for _____
because of death or legal disability, it is in his best interests to remain with the other parent.
8. We agree that neither of us will allow _____ to be adopted by any other child so
long as both of us are living.

9. We agree to abide by the terms of this Shared Parenting Agreement. We intend this Agreement to guide the Court in determining what is in our child's best interests. We agree that the Court shall have jurisdiction over any disputes arising during _____'s minority regarding custody, support or visitation.

10. We intend that this Agreement be recognized and enforced in court. Recent This is in Ohio Supreme Court decisions have recognized the enforceability of Shared Parenting Agreements.

11. We agree to do everything possible to create a legal relationship between the _____ and _____. This will be done for purposes of custody, visitation, support, inheritance, health care insurance and guardianship.

12. We agree that the Uniform Child Custody Jurisdiction Enforcement Act (UCCJEA) and the Parental Kidnapping Protection Act (PKPA) to this Agreement.

13. This is the entire Agreement. There are no promises, understandings, agreements or representations between us that are not reflected in this Agreement.

14. Each of us signs this Agreement voluntarily and without any duress of any kind.
We also had the opportunity to consult with an attorney before signing this Agreement. We each fully understand the terms of this Agreement.

We signed this Agreement on _____, 2009 in _____, Ohio.

_____   _____

State of _____
County of _____

_____ and _____, personally appeared

before me and signed this Shared Custody Agreement on _____,
_____.

_____
Notary Public

ESTATE PLANNING FORM 23

PROBATE SURVIVOR AFFIDAVIT

STATE OF _____

                        SS.   AFFIDAVIT OF SURVIVOR

COUNTY OF _____

      [Surviving J&S owner's name as appears on existing deed], being first duly sworn according to law, deposes and states as follows:

1. That [Decedent's name as appears on existing deed] and [Surviving J&S owner's name as appears on existing J&S deed] are the owners of real property under a duly recorded Survivorship Deed;

2. That affiant is the joint owner of said property and the survivor of [Decedent's name as appears on existing J&S deed];

3. That the original Survivorship Deed was recorded in the records of the Cuyahoga County Recorder at Vol. _____, Page _____ on _____, 20___.

4. That the full description of the real property is as follows: (Insert legal description here)

Permanent Parcel No. ___ - ___ - ___
Property Address:

5. That [Decedent's name as appears on existing deed] died on _____, 20___ at _____, _____, and a death certificate has been issued, a certified copy of which is attached; and

6. That by virtue of the death of the party listed in Item 5 above, [Surviving J&S owner's name as appears on existing J&S deed], whose tax mailing address will be _____, is the fee simple owner of the above-described property and requests that this fact be reflected on the land and tax records of _____ County, Ohio.

_____

[Surviving J&S owner's name as appears on existing deed]

SWORN TO BEFORE ME AND SUBSCRIBED IN MY PRESENCE _____, 20___.

_____
Notary Public

This instrument Prepared By:

ESTATE PLANNING FORM 24

ANTENUPTIAL AGREEMENT FOR TRANSGENDER SPOUSE

Attorneys Keith D. Elston and Ross T. Ewing of Lexington, Kentucky, supplied this form. It is included only as an example of an Antenuptial Agreement where one spouse is transgender. Keith and Ross believe it is most useful for younger parties, with few assets, and primarily concerned with divorce. This form does not include any provisions concerning retirement. Anyone considering using this form must review the law and forms of the state in which the parties live. This is a starting point.

Contact Keith or Ross with any questions.

Ross T. Ewing
859-514-3311
http://www.FamilyLawLexington.com
ross@familylawlexington.com

Keith D. Elston
859.225-2348
http://elstonlawoffice.com
elstonlaw@windstream.net

ANTENUPTIAL AGREEMENT

THIS ANTENUPTIAL AGREEMENT, made and entered into this 6th day of August, 20__, by and between _____, of _____, _____ County, Kentucky, party of the first part, and _____, of _____, _____ County, Kentucky, party of the second part,

WITNESSETH:

THAT WHEREAS, the parties hereto are desirous of jointly entering into the bonds of holy matrimony, each with the other; and

WHEREAS, the parties acknowledge that the party of the first part is a post-surgical female-to-male transgendered person who has completed his transition to the male gender, and has changed his gender markers on his birth certificate, which is of record with the _____ Department of Vital Statistics, thereby legally being recognized by the state of _____ as male for all purposes; and the parties waive any future claim they might raise as to the validity of their marriage, or of this Agreement, based on the First Party's gender identity; and

WHEREAS, in anticipation of their marriage, the parties desire to fix and determine the rights and claims that will accrue to each of them in the property and the estate of the other by reason of the marriage and to accept the provisions of this Agreement in full discharge and satisfaction of such rights; and

WHEREAS, each party has heretofore accumulated a separate estate and acquainted the other with the nature, extent, and full value thereof; and

WHEREAS, each party is further desirous of retaining his and her respective properties as separate and distinct estates, insofar as it may be feasible to do so, and of fully and finally settling all property rights as they now or shall hereafter exist, and having reached an understanding in these respects which they desire to reduce in writing; and

WHEREAS, each of the parties acknowledges that this Agreement is in and of itself an inducement for each of them to marry; and

WHEREAS, each party has agreed to accept the provisions of this Agreement in lieu of all marital rights in the property now owned or hereafter acquired by either of them or in their estates upon the death of either of them;

NOW, THEREFORE, in consideration of the mutual love and respect each party has for the other, and their desire for a happy and peaceful marriage based upon such love and respect, and in consideration of such marriage and the marriage ceremony itself, and in consideration of the mutual representations, promises, covenants, and agreements herein contained, and such other good and valuable consideration as hereinafter stated, it is mutually understood and agreed by and between the parties hereto, and to which they respectively bind themselves, their heirs, personal representatives, and assignees, as follows:

ARTICLE I. JOINT AND SEPARATE PROPERTY

1.1. <u>Title to Property Determines Its Character As Joint or Separate</u>. All property owned or acquired by any means after the marriage shall be either "Separate Property" or "Joint Property." The parties intend that they shall have the freedom to determine whether their real estate, intangible personal property, and, to the extent possible, tangible personal property shall be separate or joint by the manner in which title to the property is designated. Property the title to which is in the name of one of the parties shall be that party's separate property. Property the title to which is in the name of both parties shall be joint property.

1.2. <u>Separate Property</u>. All property owned by each party on the date of the marriage shall be deemed to be the owner's separate property and shall remain his or her separate property after the marriage unless converted to joint property pursuant to paragraph 1.6. Any appreciation of, improvements to, or income earned by separate property shall be separate property and belong to the owner of the property which produced it. Any purchase, exchange, or acquisition of other property from the proceeds or exchange of either party's separate property shall be deemed the separate property of that party who exchanges, sells, or otherwise converts his or her separate property. All income, produced by separate property, which is earned by the parties after the marriage shall be the separate property of the party who earned the income. Any gift, inheritance, bequest, or devise shall be the separate property of the party who received it.

1.3. <u>Mutual Release of Claims to Separate Property During the Marriage and in the Event of Divorce</u>. During the marriage, each party shall be free to deal with his or her separate property free of any claim by the other party. This shall include, but not by way of limitation, the right to sell, encumber, make lifetime gifts of, pass by inheritance, and give by Last Will and Testament all such separate property, free of any claim by the other party or his or her heirs, representatives, and assigns.

In the event the parties divorce, each party agrees that all separate property, as identified in Exhibit A, attached hereto, shall be deemed nonmarital property, as defined by KRS Chapter 403, and neither party shall assert any claim to the other's separate property. All such separate property shall be set aside to the owner thereof.

1.4. <u>Mutual Release of Claims to Separate Property in the Event of Death</u>. In the event one of the parties dies during the first five (5) years of the marriage, the survivor waives and releases all claims which he or she may have by reason of the marriage against the separate property of the deceased party, but not against the one-half interest of the deceased party in joint-held property. This waiver includes, but not by way of limitation, rights of dower, curtesy, homestead, inheritance, descent and distribution, the right to elect against the other party's Will, and all rights or claims as widow or widower, heir, distributee, survivor, or next of kin, subject to the provisions set forth in this Agreement, regardless of the financial condition of either party at the time of death. However, this provision is not intended to prevent either party from conferring on the other by gift, legacy, devise, or bequest, any of their separate property to the other. This provision shall be effective under the present or future laws of the Commonwealth of Kentucky or any other jurisdiction.

1.5. Gifts of Tangible Personalty; Identification of Separate Property Owned on the Date of the Marriage. All real or personal property given by first party to second party as gifts, before or during their marriage, including, but not limited to, such items as automobiles, cash, stocks, furs, jewelry, and clothes, shall be deemed and remain the separate property of second party.

The parties hereby identify certain items of valuable property owned on the date of the marriage, which property shall be treated as the separate property of the owner thereof, to-wit:

See Attached Exhibit A.

1.6. Joint Property. Any other provisions of this Agreement to the contrary notwithstanding, the parties may, during the marriage, acquire property in their joint names, with or without rights of survivorship. In such event, if the marriage is terminated, each party shall have an undivided one-half interest in jointly owned property held without right of survivorship. In the event the marriage is terminated by the death of one of the parties, the survivor shall be entitled to receive the entirety of any property owned jointly with the right of survivorship, free of any claim by the deceased party's estate or his or her heirs or beneficiaries under his or her Will. In the event the marriage is terminated by divorce, each party shall be deemed to own an undivided one-half interest in all property owned jointly with right of survivorship.

1.7. Separate Liabilities. Any liability attributable to either party's separate property, or otherwise being either party's separate liability, whether presently existing or hereafter accruing, shall be satisfied exclusively from and out of that party's separate property. Each party agrees to hold the other party harmless from any personal responsibility or obligation resulting from, or attributable to, the other party's separate property, or otherwise considered as the other party's separate liability. To the extent that joint assets are used to satisfy separate liabilities, any resulting separate net worth shall, to that extent, become joint property. In the event the parties hereto file a joint income tax return, first party agrees to hold second party harmless from and indemnify her from any and all liabilities of whatsoever kind or nature, if any, which arise from the filing of said joint income tax return or returns and which may or may not result from, or be attributable to, the separate property of first party. Second party shall have the right prior to signing any tax return or returns in any year or years to have the same examined by a certified public accountant or lawyer of her choice, provided, however, that the exercise of said right shall not delay the timely filing of said tax returns.

ARTICLE II. MAINTENANCE AND SUPPORT

2.1. Maintenance and Support During the Marriage. So long as the parties are married and cohabiting, the parties agree to establish a joint checking account and to deposit therein sufficient money to pay all of the reasonable household expenses of the parties, and the parties agree to be jointly responsible for all such household expenses. If Second party becomes unemployed, First party also agrees that while the parties are married and cohabiting he will provide second party with a reasonable allowance for her personal needs, with said allowance to be deposited into the joint checking account herein described.

2.2. Cap on Maintenance in the Event of Legal Separation or Divorce. In the event the parties legally separate or divorce, each hereby waives any right he or she may have to receive maintenance, support, or alimony payments from the other, regardless of the length of the marriage, except as provided herein.

In the event that one party is a stay-at-home parent, or has reduced his or her employment by 50% or more in order to parent a child or children at the time of divorce, that party would be entitled to a lump sum maintenance award of $50,000. The parties agree that said maintenance award shall not be modifiable and shall terminate upon the remarriage or cohabitation of the recipient, or upon the death of either party.

2.3. <u>Second Party's Employment</u>. Second party is presently employed as _____. First party acknowledges that he has no objection to second party's continued employment in _____, or any other location.   First party is presently employed as a _____.   Second party acknowledges that she has no objection to first party's continued employment in _____, or any other location.

2.4. <u>Life Insurance</u>. Neither party presently owns a life insurance policy. First party agrees that he will obtain a life insurance policy with a face value of at least $250,000.00, that he will name the second party as the beneficiary of said life insurance policy, and that he will continue said policy in force as long as he is eligible for the coverage provided thereunder. In the event first party retires or otherwise becomes ineligible for said insurance coverage, he agrees to bequeath to second party in his Last Will and Testament the sum of $250,000.00 cash, free and clear of any estate, inheritance, legacy, or similar tax.

2.5. <u>Additional Rights</u>. Nothing herein shall be construed to preclude either party hereto from conferring upon the other by Last Will and Testament such rights, claims, interests, and benefits as are otherwise relinquished by this Agreement. Any gift, legacy, bequest, or devise which either party may make to the other shall not be construed as a waiver of any term of this Agreement, which shall continue in any event unabated and in full force and effect.

ARTICLE III. MUTUAL DISCLOSURE; ADVICE OF COUNSEL

3.1. <u>Disclosure</u>. Each party has made to the other a full, candid, and truthful disclosure of his or her property interests, both real and personal, and the estimated value thereof.   The parties each acknowledge that they have been made aware of each party's separate property, as outlined in Exhibit A, attached hereto.

(a) *First Party's Disclosure*. First party acknowledges that:

(1) He is fully acquainted with the business and resources of second party;

(2) He understands that second party has separate property interests that she wishes to segregate and maintain as her separate property;

(3) Second party has answered all of the questions first party has asked about second party's income, assets, and property;

(4) First party has had the opportunity at all times to obtain and receive the advice of counsel of his own choosing;

(5) First party has carefully weighed all of the facts and circumstances, and desires to marry the second party regardless of any financial arrangements made for ~~her~~ his benefit;

(6) First party is entering into this Agreement freely, voluntarily, and with full knowledge of the effects and conditions herein.

(b) *Second Party's Disclosure.* Second party acknowledges that:

    (1) She is fully acquainted with the business and resources of first party;

    (2) She understands that first party has separate property interests that he wishes to segregate and maintain as his separate property;

    (3) First party has answered all of the questions second party has asked about first party's income, assets, and property;

    (4) Second party has had the opportunity at all times to obtain and receive the advice of counsel of her own choosing;

    (5) Second party has carefully weighed all of the facts and circumstances, and desires to marry the first party regardless of any financial arrangements made for her benefit;

    (6) Second party is entering into this Agreement freely, voluntarily, and with full knowledge of the effects and conditions herein.

3.2. Independent Counsel. Each of the parties to this Agreement acknowledges that he or she has had the opportunity to be or has been independently and professionally advised by legal counsel or by certified public accountants with regard to his or her rights, liabilities, and duties as potential marital partners in relation to his or her property and financial affairs. The First Party has been represented by the Hon. Keith Doniphan Elston of Lexington, Kentucky; the Second Party has been represented by the Hon. Ross T. Ewing, of Lexington, Kentucky. This Agreement has been freely and voluntarily entered into by each respective party without coercion, constraint, or intimidation on the part of the other. Each party acknowledges that he or she has a full understanding of the provisions of this Agreement generally, and that this Agreement substantially alters the marital and property rights, claims, or interests that he or she would have had but for the execution of this Agreement.

ARTICLE IV. MISCELLANEOUS

4.1. Execution of Supplemental Documents. Both parties agree that in the event any document, legal instrument, or other writing is necessary to effect the terms and provisions of this Agreement, each party will produce, execute, and/or sign such documents in order to effect the intent and purposes of this Agreement.

4.2. Consideration. It is expressly understood and agreed that the primary consideration for this Agreement is the contemplated marriage of the parties. If for any reason, including withdrawal of either party from the present intention of the parties to marry, the marriage is not formalized, this Agreement shall become null, void, and of no force or effect.

4.3. Effective Period. This Agreement shall become effective upon the date of the marriage of the parties. No amendment to or change in this Agreement shall be effective unless made by a separate written instrument executed by the parties hereto, with the same formalities as this Agreement.

4.4. Conflict of Laws. The parties intend for this Agreement to be fully enforceable and therefore stipulate that it shall be construed under the laws of the Commonwealth of Kentucky, except insofar as any law of the Commonwealth would invalidate the parties' marriage. In no event shall the residence of either party in a community property jurisdiction or the location of specific property within any such jurisdiction cause the total rights of either spouse in any property of the parties to exceed the provisions for such spouse as set forth herein.

4.5. <u>Successors</u>. This Agreement shall inure to the benefit of, and shall be binding upon, the heirs, executors, administrators, and assigns of each party hereunto.

4.6. <u>Severability</u>. It is expressly agreed that if any provision or any part or portion of this Agreement is deemed invalid, void, or unenforceable for whatever reason, such invalidity, voidness, or unenforceability shall in no way affect any other provision or any other part or portion contained in the remainder of this Agreement.

4.7. <u>Default</u>. The parties covenant and agree that, should either party default in or breach any of his or her respective obligations and duties as contained in this Agreement, then, and in that event, the defaulting or breaching party shall be responsible for and pay to the injured party, in addition to such other damages as any court may award, all of his or her attorneys' fees, court costs, and other related expenses, including, but not limited to, deposition costs, transportation, and lodging as expended or incurred by the injured party to enforce the provisions contained herein against the defaulting party.

4.8. <u>Nonwaiver of Breach; Oral Amendments Prohibited</u>. No failure by either party hereto to insist upon the strict performance of any term or condition of this Agreement or to exercise any right or remedy available on a breach thereof, and no acceptance of full or partial performance of an obligation hereunder during the continuance of any such breach shall constitute a waiver of any such breach or of any such term or condition. No term or condition of this Agreement required to be performed by either party hereto, and no breach thereof, shall be waived, altered, or modified, except by a written instrument executed by both parties hereto. No waiver of any breach shall affect or alter any term or condition of this Agreement and each such term or condition shall continue in full force and effect with respect to any other then existing or subsequent breach thereof.

4.9. <u>Acknowledgement of Impending Marriage and Waiver of Right to Challenge Agreement Based on Timing</u>. The parties hereby acknowledge that they have sought legal counsel with less than one month remaining before their marriage, and agree that they have been given sufficient time to consider this Agreement before signing it. Therefore, the parties agree to waive any right to challenge the Agreement on the basis of a lack of proper time to consider the Agreement.

IN WITNESS WHEREOF, the parties have hereunto affixed their signatures to quadruplicates hereof, each of which shall have the force and effect of an original this the day and year first above written.

_____	_____
HON. KEITH DONIPHAN ELSTON	First Party
Attorney for First Party	

_____	_____
HON. ROSS T. EWING	Second Party
Attorney for Second Party	

Commonwealth of Kentucky   )
)
County of Fayette   )

The foregoing instrument was acknowledged before me this _____ day of _____, 2011, by _____, First Party.

_____
Notary Public
My commission expires: _____

Commonwealth of Kentucky   )
)
County of Fayette   )

The foregoing instrument was acknowledged before me this ____ day of _____, 2011, by _____, Second Party.

                                   .   _____
                                              Notary Public,
                                              My commission expires: _____

Exhibit A

I.   Separate Property held by the First Party, _____:

ASSET	DESCRIPTION	EST. PRESENT MARKET VALUE OF PARTY'S SHARE
Asset	**Description**	$ ***,***
APPROXIMATE TOTAL CURRENT VALUE:		$ *,***,***

II.   Separate Property held by the Second Party, _____:

ASSET	DESCRIPTION	EST. PRESENT MARKET VALUE OF PARTY'S SHARE
Asset	**Description**	$ ***,***
APPROXIMATE TOTAL CURRENT VALUE:		$ ***,***

We, _____ and _____, have reviewed the separate property of each of us, above, and affirm that the separate property listed herein is a complete list of all separate properties that we each own at the date of execution of this Agreement.

_____   _____

FIRST PARTY   SECOND PARTY

ESTATE PLANNING FORM 25

INSTRUCTIONS FOR FUNDING THE LIVING TRUST

The Trust needs to be funded by your property. There is a pour-over provision in your Will. That takes care of any property that you did not put into the Trust before you die.

However, the advantage of a Living Trust is that it takes effect during your life. Your real estate, cars, other kinds of titled property, bank accounts, investments, etc. need to be retitled into the Trust.

The Trust owns the property. You no longer own anything in your own name. You are also the Trustee of the property so you continue to control everything.

For example, your car would be owned by the "_____
Living Trust." You'll go to the Bureau of Motor Vehicles and have the title changed. You'll need to notify your insurer that you have done so.

Before you record a new deed for the house, you need to contact your lender and have them agree to it. Changing the deed can trigger the due on sale clause in your mortgage—something you do not want to happen.

Do NOT rely on someone's verbal agreement; get it in writing. And, keep the written authorization in a safe place. Once you have that, a new deed can be prepared for you to file with the County Recorder.

You'll also need to name the Trust the beneficiary of any life insurance, mutual funds, IRAs, etc. that you now own. Anything that allows you to name a beneficiary will need to be changed. Of course, if you want someone to receive an asset, outside the Living Trust, you can keep that person as a beneficiary. If the Trust is not named, that asset passes to the beneficiary outside the Trust.

Transferring assets will take some time to accomplish. I will be happy to answer your questions on the process.

ESTATE PLANNING FORM 26

REVOCABLE TRUST AGREEMENT

THIS TRUST AGREEMENT entered into by _____, as TRUSTOR and _____, TRUSTEE.

WITNESS: I will hold and administer all assets transferred to this trust in accordance with the following terms and provisions.

ARTICLE I
BENEFICIARIES

1.1 The term "children" shall be understood to mean my children, whose names are _____ and _____.

ARTICLE II
RIGHTS DURING LIFETIME

2.1 During my life, all or such part of the net income and principal of the trust as I may direct shall be paid to me or to such person or persons as I may designate from time to time. Net income not so distributed shall be accumulated and added to the principal of the trust.

2.2 Should I become incapacitated, then the Trustee shall use or expend so much of the income and principal of the trust for my benefit, and for the benefit of my children as the Trustee may deem advisable from time to time for the health, maintenance, support and education, including vocational, college, graduate, and professional schooling of my children.

2.3 During my lifetime, the Trustee shall follow my written directions, if they are given, with regard to the management and control of the trust estate. If I give no instructions as to the management and control of the trust estate, the Trustee may act in accordance with the powers granted in Article VI.

2.4 When acting at the discretion, or with my consent, the Trustee shall be relieved from any liability arising out of such action except such liability as may arise from the Trustee's own gross negligence or intentional misconduct.

ARTICLE III
RIGHTS AFTER MY DEATH

3.1 After my death, all assets transferred to the Trustee by my personal representative shall beadded to the other property that was transferred to the trust during my lifetime.

3.2 The Trustee shall divide and partition the trust property into trusts of equal value, one trust for each of my children then living, and one trust for the issue, if any, taken collectively and on a per stirpes basis, of each child of mine who shall have died. Each such trust above provided for shall be designed by the name of the particular child of mine living at my death or who shall have died leaving issue surviving. Each of said trusts shall be held and administered for the benefit of the child whose name designates that particular trust and for the surviving issue of any deceased child all as specified in this Trust. Each of the trusts shall be held and administered by the Trustee as a separate and distinct trust.

3.3 The Trustee shall pay to or for the benefit of each living child whose name designates each particular trust, and for any child not living, unto the issue of such child so much of the income and principal of the particular trust as the Trustee deems necessary and appropriate to provide for such child's health, maintenance, support and education, including vocational, college, graduate, and professional schooling. Any income of any particular trust not distributed shall be added to the principal of the child's trust. Any distributions made to the issue of a deceased child whose name designates a particular trust need not be equal among such issue and shall not be charged against their respective share of the particular trust.

3.4 Upon a child attaining the age of _____ (___) years, _____ (___%) of his or her trust shall be distributed to such child outright and free of any further trust; and upon such child attaining the age of _____ (___) years, the entire balance of his or her trust shall be distributed to such child outright and free of any further trust. The trust for the issue of a deceased child shall terminate upon the youngest issue reaching age twenty-one (21) and shall be distributed outright and per stirpes among the deceased child's issue.

ALTERNATIVE ARTICLE III
RIGHTS AFTER MY DEATH

3.1 After my death, all assets transferred to the Trustee by my personal representative shall be added to the other property that was transferred to the trust during my lifetime.

3.2 Until the _____ (_____) birthday of the youngest of my children, the Trustee shall collect the income from the property comprising the trust estate, and shall pay or use all, part, or none of the net income and principal of the trust, without regard to equality of distribution, to or for the benefit of my children, to be used for the support, maintenance, health, and education of such children, or for their benefit in the event of illness, emergency, or extraordinary or unusual circumstances, as the Trustee, in its sole discretion, may deem necessary after taking into consideration any other funds readily available for such purposes. Any net income not currently distributed shall be annually added to the principal of the trust. Further, disbursements of income and principal shall not be taken into account in the final distribution of the trust estate.

3.3 After each of my children reaches the age of _____ (_____) years, the Trustee, in its sole discretion, may advance to such child an amount to enable this child to enter into a trade, business, or profession, or to buy a home, and (regardless of other provisions to the contrary) such amount shall be charged as an advancement without interest to this child upon the final distribution of the trust. The Trustee, however, shall not be liable if, for any reason, such advancement exceeds the child's share upon the final distribution of the trust.

3.4 Upon the youngest of my children attaining the age of _____ (_____) years, the trust shall terminate and the Trustee shall distribute the trust estate to, or for, the benefit of each of my children, in equal shares. In the event any of my children should die prior to receiving his or her complete distribution from the trust estate, then the share to which that deceased child would have been entitled had that child been living at the time of distribution, shall be distributed per stirpes to the issue of that deceased child. If the deceased child should have no issue surviving at the time of distribution from the trust estate, then that child's share shall be distributed equally by the Trustee to my then surviving children.

ARTICLE IV
RESTRICTION ON BENEFICIARIES' RIGHTS

4.1 No Trust beneficiary shall have the right or power to anticipate, by assignment or otherwise, any income or principal given to such beneficiary by this instrument or any portion thereof; nor in advance of actually receiving same shall have the right or power to sell, transfer, encumber, or in any way charge same, nor shall such income or principal or any portion of same be subject to any execution, levy, sale, garnishment, attachment, insolvency, bankruptcy, or other legal proceeding of any character, or in any manner or event be subject to the payment of such beneficiary's debts.

ARTICLE V
MAXIMUM DURATION OF TRUST

5.1 Notwithstanding anything to the contrary, the trusts under this instrument shall terminate not later than twenty-one years after the death of the last survivor of me and my issue living on the date of my death, at the end of which period the Trustee shall distribute each remaining portion of the trust property to the beneficiary or beneficiaries, at that time, of the current income thereof, and if there is more than one beneficiary, in the proportions in which they are beneficiaries.

ARTICLE VI
POWERS OF TRUSTEE

6.1 With reference to this trust estate, the Trustee shall have the following rights and powers without limitation and in addition to power conferred by law:

6.2 The Trustee may sell publicly or privately, for cash or on time, without an order of court, upon such terms and conditions as to it shall seem best, any property of the trust estates; and no person dealing with the Trustee shall have any obligation to look to the application of the purchase money.

6.3 The Trustee may invest and reinvest all or any part of the principal of the trust estates in any stocks, bonds, mortgages, shares or interests in common trust funds, or other securities or property, real, personal, or mixed, and of any kind or nature whatsoever, as it may deem advisable, and without diversification if it deems it advisable, irrespective of whether or not such securities or property are eligible for trust investment under state or any other law, and may change any investment received or made by the Trustee, and may hold cash if it deems it advisable.

6.4 The Trustee may exercise broad discretion as to diversification of trust property, and shall not be required to reduce any concentrated holdings merely because of such concentration, and shall have full discretion as to the percentage to be invested in fixed income securities, and is specifically relieved from any requirements, legal or otherwise, as to the percentage of the trust estate to be invested in fixed income securities, and may invest and retain invested any trust estate wholly in common stocks.

6.5 The Trustee shall have full power to sell, convey, lease or mortgage, repair and improve, and take any and all other steps with regard to any real estate that may at any time be a part of the principal of the trust estates; and any lease of such real property or contract with regard thereto made by the Trustee shall be binding for the full period of the lease or contract, though said period shall extend beyond the termination of the trust.

6.6 The Trustee shall have the power to vote shares of stock held in the trust estates at stockholders' meetings in person or by special, limited, or general proxy, with or without power of substitution, as to the Trustee shall seem best.

6.7 The Trustee shall have the power to participate in the liquidation, reorganization, consolidation, incorporation and reincorporation, or any other financial readjustment of any corporation or business in which the trust estates are or shall be financially interested.

6.8 The Trustee shall have full power to borrow money from any source, for any purpose connected with the protection, preservation, improvement, or development of the trust estate hereunder, whenever in its judgment it deems it advisable, and as security to mortgage or pledge any real estate or personal property forming a part of the trust estate upon such terms and conditions as it may deem advisable.

6.9 The Trustee shall have authority to hold any and all securities in bearer form, in its own name, or the name of some other person, partnership, or corporation, or in the name of a duly appointed nominee, with or without disclosing the fiduciary ownership thereof.

6.10 Whenever the Trustee is required by this Trust to divide the principal of a trust estate into parts or shares and to distribute or allot same, the Trustee is authorized to make such division in cash or in kind or both; and for the purpose of such division or allotment, the judgment of the Trustee concerning the propriety thereof and relative value of property so distributed or allotted shall be binding and conclusive with respect to all interested persons.

6.11 During the minority or incapacity of any beneficiary to whom income is directed to be paid, or for whose benefit income and principal may be expended, the Trustee may pay such income and principal in any one or more of the following ways: (1) directly to said beneficiary; (2) to the legal guardian or committee of said beneficiary; (3) to a relative of said beneficiary to be expended by such relative for the maintenance, health and education of said beneficiary; (4) by expending the same directly for the maintenance, health, and education of said beneficiary. The Trustee shall not be obliged to see to the application of the funds so paid, but the receipt of such person shall be full acquittance to the Trustee.

6.12 The Trustee may pay to the Personal Representative of my estate from the principal of the Trust, such sum or sums as the Personal Representative may certify to be due and payable as inheritance and estate taxes (including interest and penalties thereon, if any) due from or assessed against my estate. The certificate of the Personal Representative of my estate as to the amount owed shall be sufficient authority to the Trustee to pay the same and shall be binding and conclusive upon all persons.

6.13 In determining whether or not I am incapacitated, the Trustee may rely upon the findings of my personal physician, if any, and if none, the Trustee may rely upon the findings of the physician or physicians the Trustee may employ, and the Trustee shall not be liable to anyone for so acting.

6.14 To continue and operate any business owned by me at my death and to do any and all things deemed appropriate by the Trustee, including the power to incorporate the business and to put additional capital into the business, for such time as it shall deem advisable, without liability for loss resulting from the continuance or operation of the business except for its own negligence; and to close out, liquidate, or sell the business at such time and upon such terms as it shall deem proper.

6.15 In general, the Trustee shall have the same powers, authorities, and discretions in the management of the trust estate as I would have in the management and control of my own personal estate. The Trustee may continue to exercise any powers and discretions hereunder for a reasonable period after the termination of any trust estate or estates, but only for so long as no rule of law relating to perpetuities would be violated.

ARTICLE VII
PROVISION RELATING TO TRUSTEES

7.1 Upon the death, resignation or incapacity of the present Trustee, XYZ Bank and Trust Company, Madisonville, Kentucky, shall be the successor Trustee. In determining whether or not the present Trustee is incapacitated, the successor Trustee may rely upon the findings of such individual Trustee's personal physician, if any, and if none, the successor Trustee may rely upon the findings of the physician or physicians the successor Trustee may employ.

7.2 Any successor Trustee shall have all the title, powers, and discretion of the Trustee succeeded, without the necessity of any conveyance or transfer.

7.3 After the death of the Settlor and during the existence of the trust, a majority of the adult beneficiaries age twenty-one or older shall have the right to remove any acting Trustee and appoint a successor Trustee, provided, however, that such successor Trustee must be a trust company or bank organized under the laws of the United States or one of the states thereof possessing trust powers and having trust assets under administration of not less than $100,000,000. Such right of removal shall be continuing and shall be exercised by serving the acting Trustee with written notice of its removal, which notice shall specify the successor Trustee and certify its willingness to serve as such. Within sixty days thereafter, the Trustee so removed shall institute proceedings for the settlement of its accounts and deliver all assets then held to its successor, whereupon it shall have full acquittance for all assets so delivered (subject to judicial settlement of its account, if required) and shall have no further duties hereunder.

7.4 Each Trustee hereunder shall have the right to resign at any time by giving thirty days written notice to that effect to the current income beneficiary or beneficiaries of the trust. Thereafter, such beneficiary or beneficiaries shall have the right within such thirty-day period to appoint a successor Trustee and shall notify the Trustee of such appointment. Such successor Trustee must be a trust company or bank possessing the qualifications set out in this Trust. If the current income beneficiary or beneficiaries shall fail to designate a successor Trustee within the time specified, then the acting Trustee may petition a court of competent jurisdiction for the appointment of a successor and the judicial settlement of its accounts.

ARTICLE VIII
AUDIT

8.1 The Trustee shall be under no duty to examine, verify, question, or audit the books, records, or accounts or transactions of any Executor, Administrator, Personal Representative, or prior Trustee of mine; nor shall the Trustee have any responsibility for any act or omission of any such Executor, Administrator, Personal Representative, or prior Trustee.

ARTICLE IX
LAW APPLICABLE

9.1 _____ law shall regulate and control this Agreement.

ARTICLE X
RIGHT TO AMEND OR REVOKE

10.1 I reserve the right and power to alter, amend or revoke this Agreement, at any time and from time to time, either in whole or in part, without the consent of the Trustee or any beneficiary hereunder, by written notice to the Trustee to that effect, provided, however, that the duties, responsibilities, and compensation of the Trustee shall not be altered or modified without the Trustee's written consent.

ARTICLE XI
ACCEPTANCE OF TRUST

11.1 The Trustee accepts this trust.

IN WITNESS WHEREOF, the parties hereto have executed this instrument on this the _____, 20____.

SETTLOR AND TRUSTEE:

_____

SUCCESSOR AND TRUSTEE:

_____

Schedule A

ASSETS   DATE TRANSFERRED

Attach copy of the Domestic Partnership Agreement

ESTATE PLANNING FORM 27

REVOCABLE LIVING TRUST

_____, of _____ enters into THIS TRUST AGREEMENT as both Grantor and Trustee.

I have delivered or will deliver to the Trustee the property described in Schedule A. Upon receipt of this property, the Trustee agrees to hold it in trust and manage and dispose of it according to the provisions of this Trust Agreement.

I.   SUCCESSOR TRUSTEES

The term "Trustee" as used in this Trust means one or more Trustees as well as any Successor Trustee and Successor Co-Trustees.

A.   Successors; Death of Grantor
In the event of my death, resignation, removal, or incapacity, I name _____, to serve as Successor Trustee.

If _____ is unable or unwilling to serve or continue to serve as Trustee, I name _____, to serve as the Sole Successor Trustee.

B.   Delegation of Trustee's Duties
The Successor Trustee, _____, shall not delegate the Trustee's duties to anyone other than the alternate Successor Trustee, _____.

C.   Removal of Trustee by Grantor
I reserve the right to remove any Trustee, Trustees, or Successor Trustees.

D.   Responsibility of Trustee
A Successor Trustee shall become responsible for the Trust Estate only when the same has been received by it. No Successor Trustee shall be responsible for any act or omission of any other Trustee. No Successor Trustee shall be under a duty to take any proceedings against any other Trustee for an act or omission of any other Trustee.

In determining what assets constitute the Trust Estate, the Successor Trustee shall be responsible only for the making of reasonable inquiry from records of the prior Trustee.

E.   Annual Statements by Successor Trustee
The Successor Trustee agrees to furnish annual statements to the beneficiaries receiving distributions, showing all receipts and disbursements during the period covered, and to submit annually a statement of the assets of the Trust. Any additional reports or statements to be provided to the beneficiaries shall be in the sole discretion of the Trustee. I intend this provision to take precedence over any provision of law that may require that additional, more frequent, or more detailed reports or statements be provided to any person.

F.   Resignation of Trustee
I retain the right to appoint any Successor Trustee. Any Trustee shall have the right to resign. Upon my death or if I fail or am unable to name a Successor, the resigning Trustee shall select a Successor Trustee. The selection shall take place no later than 30 days after the resigning Trustee submits the resignation notification.

The Trustee shall, upon the effective date of the resignation, deliver to the Successor Trustee and each beneficiary of the Trust a statement of the last two years' receipts and disbursements, together with an inventory of the assets belonging to the Trust.

G.   Persons Prohibited from Serving as Trustee

Under no circumstances shall _____, be permitted to serve as a Successor Trustee.

I am restricting _____, from serving as Successor Trustee because _____.

II.   TRANSFER OF PROPERTY AND BENEFICIARIES

A.   Assets Transferred
I have transferred to the Trust the property described on the attached Schedule A that is made a part of this Trust. Later, other property, real or personal, may be transferred, during life or by Will, to the Trust by me or by someone acting on my behalf.

If additional property is transferred to the Trust, it should be listed on the attached Schedule A, which is for reference only. All property transferred to this Trust formally or informally, whether or not listed on the attached Schedules, shall also be part of the Trust.

All property transferred to the Trust formally or informally, together with the investments and reinvestments, constituting additions to the principal of the Trust, and any income derived from those assets is sometimes collectively designated the "Trust Estate". All property transferred to or deposited with the Trustee shall be held by it in trust for the stated uses and purposes.

The Trustor, or any person or persons may add additional property to the trust estate at any time by inter vivos or testamentary transfer. Such additions and title to any such property may be, but need not be, evidenced by amendment to this agreement or by schedule, deed, assignment, or other writings transferring property to the Trustee. All such original and additional property is referred to here collectively as the trust estate and shall be held, managed and distributed as provided by the Trust's terms.

B.   Beneficiaries
In addition to me, the primary beneficiaries of this Trust, their birth dates and relationships to the Grantor are:

NAME	RELATIONSHIP	DATE OF BIRTH

III.   RIGHTS RESERVED BY GRANTOR (CREATOR)

I reserve the following rights during my lifetime:

A. The right to change, amend or alter any of the terms or provisions of this Trust Agreement at any time. All changes, amendments or alterations must be written and will not become effective until signed by the Trustee.

B. The right to terminate this Trust Agreement, in whole or in part, at any time. Any complete or partial termination shall become effective upon delivery of notice in writing to the Trustee.

C. The right to withdraw and return to me, all or any, part of the assets transferred to the Trust formally or informally, whether or not listed on the Schedules attached. The exercise of this right of withdrawal, in whole or in part, will become effective upon delivery of notice in writing to the Trustee.

IV.   INSURANCE PROVISIONS

A.   Policy Beneficiaries
I may make insurance policies payable to the Trust or the Trustee as primary or contingent beneficiary. I reserve the right to amend or terminate such beneficiary designations. A reference to a policy transferred or made payable to the Trust or the Trustee may be shown on Schedule "B" attached.

B.   Payment of Premiums
If I transfer any insurance policies to the Trust, the Trust shall be considered the policy owner. The Trustee shall ensure that all premiums or assessments are paid when due.

The owner of any policies that are not owned by the Trust shall pay all premiums or assessments on them, and the Trustee shall be under no obligation to see that the premiums or assessments are paid. The Trustee shall be under no obligation with respect to the policies, other than for their safekeeping, unless agreed otherwise.

Nothing contained in this Trust shall be interpreted as an obligation on the part of the owner or the Trustee to keep the policies in force.

C.   Ownership of Policies
The owner of the policies reserves all incidents of ownership in the insurance policies. It is my intention that the Trust be operative with respect to the proceeds of the policies which are payable to the Trustee at the time of the death of the insured.

D.   Pledging and Assigning Policies
If the policy owner requests, the Trustee will join with the policy owner in executing instruments assigning or pledging any subject insurance policies. Upon the execution of such instruments by the Trustee, all of the rights and interest of such Trustee, and this Trust, will be and remain subject to the rights and interest of such assignee or pledgee.

E.   Collecting Policy Proceeds
Upon my death, the Trustee shall collect the proceeds of the policies payable to this Trust or the Trustee. If necessary, the Trustee may institute legal proceedings to enforce the payment of the policies or do any other acts necessary to collect under the policies.

However, the Trustee shall not be required to maintain any litigation to enforce the payment of the policies until reasonably assured of reimbursement from the Trust against expenses and liabilities that may be associated with such litigation. The Trustee is authorized to compromise and adjust claims arising out of the insurance policies and the decision of the Trustee shall be binding and conclusive upon all interested persons and corporations.

**V.   DISTRIBUTION OF INCOME AND PRINCIPAL OF TRUST ESTATE
             DURING GRANTOR'S LIFETIME**

During my lifetime, the Trustee shall pay to _____, and me, or pay for our benefit, as much of the net income and principal from the trust as I shall request.

If I make no request, due to disability or otherwise, the Trustee may distribute to, or for the benefit of, my husband, me and our minor child, **REBECCA**, such amounts of income and principal as needed for our reasonable health, maintenance and support. If any net income remains at the end of each trust year, the Trustee shall add it to the principal of the trust.

A.   Distribution of Income
The Trustee may accumulate all of the income from the assets transferred to the Trust or distribute all or any portion of the income from the Trust to the Grantor. The Trustee may distribute income to third parties as determined by the Trustee or as directed by the Grantor.

B.   Distribution of Principal
Unless I am incapacitated, I may direct the Trustee to distribute any amount of principal to the me or a third party. This power can be exercised in such a manner that all of the assets may be taken from this Trust.

C.   Incapacity of Grantor
If I become incapacitated, the Successor Trustees described in this Trust shall become active in the order and capacity designated. The Successor Trustee may withdraw principal or income from the Trust for my benefit or for the benefit of those individuals who are dependent on me. Such withdrawals should be consistent with the value of the Trust and the mode of living to which my spouse, my dependents and I have been accustomed.

D.   Life Support Systems
If I am incapacitated or irreversibly comatose and am receiving life-prolonging medical treatment, the Successor Trustee shall consult with my health Care attorney-in-fact appointed r under the Health Care Power of Attorney to determine if such measures should be continued. "Life-prolonging treatment" as used here means "medication and artificially or technologically supplied respiration, nutrition, or hydration" that prolongs my life, as defined by Ohio law.

It is my desire that life-prolonging treatment not be continued for an unreasonable period when it is clear that my condition will not improve and the treatment merely prolongs my life without dignity. I executed a separate Health Care Power of Attorney and a Living Will regarding the my wishes concerning medical treatment under such circumstances.

The provisions of my Living Will and Health Care Power of Attorney shall supersede any conflicting Trust provision.

I authorize the Successor Trustees, under the Health Information Protection and Accountability Act (HIPAA), to discuss the my diagnosis, treatment plan and prognosis, with my health care providers. Such authorization is for the purpose of permitting the Successor Trustees to carry out their duties under this Trust.

VI.   DISTRIBUTION OF INCOME AND PRINCIPAL OF TRUST ESTATE SUBSEQUENT TO GRANTOR'S DEATH

A.   Upon my death, the Trustee shall pay all expenses and indebtedness of my estate, including the expenses of my last illness and funeral, unless other provisions have been made for their payment. Also, the Trustee shall pay any administrative expenses and any estate, inheritance or other taxes that are owed by my estate.

B. If _____, survive me, the trust shall continue and the Trustee shall manage and dispose of the Trust as follows:

1. The Trustee shall pay as much of the net income and principal as necessary to provide for the health, maintenance and support of my _____and the health, education, maintenance and support my minor children. If any net income remains at the end of the trust year, the Trustee shall add it to the principal of the trust.

2. Upon my _____ death, the Trustee shall pay all expenses and indebtedness of my estate, including the expenses of my last illness and funeral, unless other provisions have been made for their payment. Also, the Trustee shall pay any administrative expenses and any estate, inheritance or other taxes that are owed by my husband's estate.

C. After the death of both my _____ and me, the trust shall continue and the Trustee shall manage and dispose of the Trust as follows:

The Trustee shall pay as much of the net income and principal as necessary to provide for the health, education, maintenance and support of my minor children, _____.
If any net income remains at the end of the trust year, the Trustee shall add it to the principal of the trust.

This shall include distributing, for my children's benefit, and in the Trustee's sole discretion, so much of the net income for the following purposes:

(a) College or university education or other types of post-high school education;
(b) Assist in establishing, operating or maintaining a business or profession;
(c) Assist in the acquisition of a home;
(d) Assist in a financial emergency;
(e) For any other purpose that will, in the sole discretion of the Trustee, further my children's best interests.

Provided, however, that any such payments, other than payments for the education of any beneficiary, shall be deducted from such beneficiary's proportionate share, if any, of the Trust Estate.

If the Trustee is serving as a sole Trustee and is also a beneficiary or potential beneficiary of the Trust, the Trustee may distribute to, or for the benefit of, my spouse and children, only so much of the net income from the Trust as the Trustee deems necessary for the health, support, maintenance, and education of my spouse and children.

Trust income shall be distributed quarterly or more frequently in the sole discretion of the Trustee. Any net income not distributed at the Trust's year end shall be added to the principal of the Trust.

D. During my spouse's lifetime, if the income from the Trust, together with the receipts from other sources known to the Trustee, shall be insufficient for the health, support, maintenance, and education of my spouse and children, the Trustee is authorized to pay to the my spouse, or for his benefit, and for the benefit of my children, so much of the principal of the Trust as may be deemed necessary for such purposes.

E.   Distributions at Partner's/Spouse's Death
After the death of both my husband and me, the trust shall continue and the Trustee shall manage, administer and dispose of the Trust as follows:

1. The Trustee shall pay as much of the net income and principal as necessary to provide for the health, education, maintenance and support of my minor children, _____. If any net income remains at the end of the trust year, the Trustee shall add it to the principal of the trust.

2. Division Into Shares and Distribution
When my youngest surviving child turns 25 years of age, the Trustee shall divide the balance of the Trust equally between my children, _____, if both are living, or entirely to the survivor.

Each share shall be distributed to _____, if both are living, or entirely to the survivor.

In making the division of this Trust into separate shares for accounting purposes, the Trustee, in its sole discretion, is authorized to keep the Trust assets in one or more accounts without titling or retitling the Trust assets in separate accounts and to treat each share as having an undivided interest in the entire Trust.

3. Death of Child Before Age 25
If either of my children dies before turning 25, the surviving child shall receive all of the Trust Estate. If the surviving child is at least 25 years old, the Trustee shall terminate the Trust and distribute the assets to the surviving child.

4. Disaster Provision B: All Beneficiaries Dead
If all of my intended beneficiaries die before the distribution of all the assets, then the Trust shall terminate and the Trustee shall distribute 100% of the Trust Estate and all assets to my _____.

VII.   SIMULTANEOUS DEATH PROVISION

If my husband and I die under such circumstances that the order of death cannot be determined, then for the purposes of this Trust Agreement, my spouse shall be presumed to have predeceased me.

VIII.   ADMINISTRATIVE AND MISCELLANEOUS PROVISIONS

A.   Minors
If any of the beneficiaries are minors at the time of any distribution by the Trustee, the Trustee is authorized to pay or deliver the same, either directly to the minor or to either parent of the minor, as natural guardian, without the necessity of any judicial appointment. A receipt, in writing, by any such distributee, either guardian or minor, shall constitute a full and binding release of the Trustee.

B.   Rule Against Perpetuities
If any of the terms or provisions of this Trust continue beyond the period permitted by any applicable laws regulating restraints on alienation or prohibitions against perpetuities, or any similar laws, such offending provisions or terms to the extent of their continuance beyond the lawful period, shall be null and void. The remainder of the terms and provisions of the Trust shall

remain valid and binding. The undistributed portion of the Trust Estate held in violation of applicable laws shall immediately be distributed to the beneficiary of such portion.

C.   Spend-Thrift Provisions (Prohibition against Sale of Inheritance)
Neither the principal of any Trust or sub-trust created nor the resulting income, while in the hands of the Trustee, shall be subject to any voluntary or involuntary conveyance, transfer, or assignment, or be pledged as security for any debt of any beneficiary or other person, and shall not be subject to any claim of creditors of any such beneficiary or other person, through legal process or otherwise.

Any such attempted sale, anticipation, assignment or pledge of any of the funds or property held in any such Trust, or the income, by a beneficiary shall be null and void and shall not be recognized by the Trustee.

It is my intention to place the rights of any beneficiary under this Trust in a spendthrift trust and to place absolute title to the property held in trust and the income in the Trustee, with power and authority to pay out the same only as authorized hereby.

D.   Small Trust Termination
If the value of any Trust or any share of this Trust falls below the sum of $30,000, and if the beneficiary or beneficiaries entitled to receive the income have attained their majority, the Trustee may terminate the Trust or share of this Trust.

It is my intention that the Trustee not have the power to terminate the Trust or any share of this Trust, without court approval, on grounds of its value if the value of the Trust or share to be terminated is greater than $30,000.

In the event of termination under this provision, the Trustee will pay the beneficiary or beneficiaries the entire corpus of the Trust or share. In this event, any remainderman will not be considered as having a vested interest in the Trust Estate conveyed to the beneficiary or beneficiaries.

E.   Taxes

Upon my death and if I am the second to die, and if my estate shall be subject to Federal estate tax, the Trustee shall pay to the my Executor, from the Trust, an amount equal to the additional estate, inheritance, succession and other similar taxes, imposed by inclusion of the property in the Trust in the my gross estate for tax purposes. Provided, however, that no such tax shall be paid from assets not subject to the Federal estate tax.

F.   Miscellaneous

Words used in the singular or neuter form are to be construed in the plural, masculine or feminine where applicable. Section headings are for reference only.

G.   Applicable Law

Ohio law shall govern the validity of this Trust and the meaning and effect of its dispositive provisions. The law of the state in which the Trust is administered shall govern the administration of this Trust. Initially, the place of administration of this Trust is Ohio.

The place of administration of this Trust may be changed as follows:

(a) During my lifetime, so long as I am the Trustee, the place of administration shall be the state in which I maintain my primary residence unless I designate another location as the place of administration.

(b) A Successor Trustee may change the place of administration, as the Trustee deems appropriate.

IX.   TRUSTEE'S POWERS

The Trustee has the following powers, in addition to and not in limitation of its common law and statutory powers, all of which may be exercised without application to any court, for prior or subsequent approval.

A.   Maintaining and Selling Property

To retain all property in the form in which the Trustee received it without liability for any loss that may be incurred. To sell, at public or private sale, for cash or on credit, and upon such terms as it may deem proper, any property at any time held by it.

B.   Borrowing

To borrow money upon such terms and conditions as it may determine, from any person, firm or corporation, for the purpose of protecting, preserving or improving this Trust Estate; to execute promissory notes or other obligations for amounts so borrowed and to secure the payment of such amounts by mortgage or pledge of property in this Trust Estate.

C.   Lending

To make secured loans in such amounts, upon such terms, at such rates of interest, and to such persons, firms or corporations as the Trustee deems advisable.

D.   Real Property

To manage any real property held by it, in such manner as it determines. This power includes the authority to repair and improve such property; to mortgage or re-mortgage such property in such amount, on such conditions, and at such rates of interest as it deems advisable; to make, renew or modify leases on such property for such rentals, and on such terms and for such periods without reference to the term of any Trust created, to abandon such property; to adjust boundaries, to erect or demolish buildings; to convert for a different use; to dedicate for public use without compensation; to grant easements; to waive payment for property taken by right of eminent domain; to insure for any and all risks; to grant options; to partition; to enter into party wall contracts; and to insure or perfect title.

E.   Investments

To invest and reinvest all funds available for investment and reinvestment in any kind of property, real or personal, including by way of illustration: bonds, interest in common trust funds established by the Trustee or any successor, stocks of any class, mortgages, agreements of sale and other investments in property as the Trustee shall deem proper and for the best interest of the Trust Estate.

F.   Investment in Brokerage/Commodities

To buy, sell and trade in securities, commodities, futures, mutual funds, options and short sales on margin (securities), and for such purposes may maintain and operate a margin account with any broker and may pledge any securities held or purchased by it with such broker as security for loans or advances made to the Trustee. In connection with this, the Trustee is authorized to hold any securities in the name of a nominee or in other forms without disclosure of the Trust so that title to the property may pass by delivery.

G.   Manner of Holding Assets
To register any security or property in the name of a nominee, or in its own name, or to hold it unregistered, or in such form that title shall pass by delivery, but without increasing or decreasing its liability as Trustee.

H.   Voting
To vote, in person or by proxy, any equity interest held by this Trust; to participate in or consent to any voting trust, reorganization, dissolution, liquidation, merger or other action affecting any interest held by this Trust and to take any other action which it may deem advisable.

I.   Claim Handling
To pay, extend, renew, modify or compromise upon such terms as it may determine, and upon such evidence as it may deem sufficient, any obligation or claim, including taxes, either in favor of or against this Trust Estate.

J.   Bank Accounts
To establish such bank accounts, checking or savings, as the Trustee may deem proper, and to designate any person or persons to sign checks or make withdrawals from savings accounts.

K.   Dealing with Grantor's Estate
To purchase for the Trust Estate any securities or other property belonging to me estate, and to loan to the my estate Executor, whether the Trustee is at the same time Executor of my estate, out of either the principal or the accumulated income of the said Trust Estate, such amounts as the Trustee may deem necessary or advisable to protect and conserve the assets of my estate. The Trustee shall not be liable for the losses suffered by the Trust Estate as a result of its exercise of these powers.

L.   Payment of Trustee
To incur and pay from the Trust Estate and to charge against either income or principal all reasonable expenses in connection with the management of this Trust. A Corporate Trustee, if there is one, may be paid the fees normally charged by it whether or not there are individual Co-Trustees.

M.   Continuance of Business
To carry on, as long as, and in such manner as, it sees fit, any business enterprise in which I owned any interest during my lifetime.

This power includes the right to name or change officers, directors or employees; to expand, limit, alter, incorporate, merge, or reconstitute such business in any way it deems advisable; and to accept, in the absence of actual notice to the contrary, financial or other statements rendered by the managers of the business from time to time as to its conditions and operations.

The Trustee shall in no way be liable for any loss resulting from such retention or continuance or from the operation of such business or the acts of its officers and directors, except where such loss is the result of the Trustee's misconduct or gross negligence.

N.   **General Power**
To do all other acts which, in the Trustee's sole judgment, may be necessary or appropriate for the proper or advantageous management, investment or disposition of any property included in this Trust Estate.

IN WITNESS WHEREOF, _____, as Grantor and Trustee, has executed this instrument as of the day and year first above written.

_____ LIVING TRUST DATED _____, 20____.

WITNESSES: **GRANTOR and TRUSTEE:**

_____   _____

_____   _____

State of _____
County of _____

_____, personally came before me on _____, 20____ and executed this instrument.

                              _____
                                          Notary

_____**REVOCABLE LIVING TRUST**
SCHEDULE OF PROPERTY and DESCRIPTION

SCHEDULE "A"

Part I B Real Estate
The real estate described as follows:
(a)   A house at

Part II B Savings and Bank Accounts
(b)   An undivided one-half interest in various checking and savings accounts

Part III B Securities/Retirement
(c)   Retirement Plan
(d)   Mutual Funds
(e)   Stocks & Bonds

SCHEDULE "B"
Schedule of Insurance
Insured and Owner, _____

COMPANY NAME   **POLICY NUMBER**   **AMOUNT**

ESTATE PLANNING FORM 28

REVOCABLE LIVING TRUST

Contributed by:

Colleen Cleary Ortiz, Attorney at Law
1127 Palafox Street
Pensacola, Florida 32501-2607
850/466-3267

Partner 1
REVOCABLE LIVING TRUST

TABLE OF CONTENTS

Partner 1
REVOCABLE LIVING TRUST

This Declaration of Trust, made this __ day of __, 20__, between **Partner 1,** hereinafter referred to as Grantor, and **Partner 1,** referred to as Trustee, which trust shall also be known as the "Partner 1 Revocable Living Trust."

ARTICLE I
PROPERTY HELD IN TRUST
The Grantor has paid over, assigned, granted, conveyed, transferred and delivered, and by this Agreement pays over, assign, grant, convey, transfer and deliver to the Trustee the property described in Schedule A and incorporated in this document. Any other property that may be received or which has been received by the Trustee, as invested and reinvested (Trust Estate), shall be held, administered and distributed by the Trustee under the Trust provisions.

ARTICLE II
PROVISIONS DURING GRANTOR'S LIFETIME
The Trustee shall hold, manage, invest and reinvest the Trust Estate and shall collect the income
and dispose of the net income and principal as follows:

A. Distributions to Grantor. During the Grantor's lifetime, the Trustee shall have sole discretion
to pay to or apply for the Grantor's benefit such sums from the income and principal of the trust
estate as shall be necessary or advisable for the Grantor's health, maintenance and support in the
lifestyle to which the Grantor is accustomed. The Trustee shall take into consideration any other
income or resources of the Grantor known to the Trustee.

B. Grantor's Right of Withdrawal. The Grantor may at any time during the Grantor's lifetime and
from time to time, withdraw all or any part of the principal of this trust free of trust.

At the Grantor's request the Trustee shall convey and deliver to the Grantor, free of trust, any
property the Grantor desires to withdraw from the trust.

C. Grantor's Reservation of Right to Reside on Real Property. The Grantor reserves the right to
use, possess, occupy, and reside on any real property held in trust under to this agreement as the
Grantor's permanent residence during the Grantor's lifetime. The Grantor intends to retain an
interest and right in such real property in a manner that complies with [State] Statute Section
_____, and that shall constitute "equitable title to the real estate" as defined by state law.

Notwithstanding any provision of this trust agreement that is inconsistent with this paragraph of
Article II, the Grantor's interest in any real property in which the Grantor resides pursuant to the
terms of this agreement shall be deemed an interest in real property and not personalty and shall
be deemed the homestead of the Grantor.

ARTICLE III
GRANTOR'S RIGHT TO AMEND, CHANGE OR REVOKE THE TRUST
The Grantor may, by signed instruments delivered to the Trustee during the Grantor's life: (1)
withdraw property from this trust in any amount and at any time upon giving reasonable notice in
writing to the Trustee; (2) add other property to the trust; (3) change beneficiaries, their respective
shares and their plan of distribution; (4) amend this trust in any other respect; and (5) revoke this
trust in its entirety or any provision. However, the duties or responsibilities of the Trustee shall
not be enlarged without the Trustee's consent or without satisfactory adjustment of the Trustee's
compensation. The powers reserved to the Grantor under this paragraph are personal to the
Grantor and shall not be assignable or extend to any other person, including the personal
representative of Grantor's estate or any beneficiary named therein. Upon Grantor's death, this
instrument shall become irrevocable.

ARTICLE IV
**DISCRETIONARY PROVISIONS FOR TRUSTEE TO DEAL WITH GRANTOR'S
ESTATE; MAKE PAYMENTS OF DEBTS AND TAXES**
A. Payment of Debts and Taxes. After the Grantor's death, the successor Trustee, at the successor
Trustee's discretion, may (1) pay all or any part of the Grantor's legally enforceable claims,
funeral expenses, estate administration expenses, and any allowances by court order to those
dependent upon the Grantor, and (2) pay any estate, inheritance, succession, death or similar taxes
payable by reason of the Grantor's death, together with any interest thereon or any other additions
thereto, out of that portion of the trust property not qualifying for the marital or charitable
deductions. The preceding items shall be paid without reimbursement, recovery, or contribution

from any person. All such payments, except for interest, shall be charged generally against the principal of the Trust Estate includable in the Grantor's estate for Federal estate tax purposes and any interest so paid shall be charged generally against the income thereof.

B. Method of Payment. The Trustee may make such payments directly or may pay over the amounts thereof to the Personal Representatives of the Grantor's estate. Written statements by the Personal Representatives of such sums due and payable by the estate shall be sufficient evidence of their amount and propriety for the protection of the Trustee, and the Trustee shall be under no duty to see to the application of any such payments.

ARTICLE V
AFTER GRANTOR'S DEATH
Following the death of the Grantor, the Trustee shall divide the Trust Estate (which shall include any property which may be added from the Grantor's general estate) as follows:

A. Specific Distributions.

1. Separate Writing. The Grantor may leave a written statement or list disposing of certain items of tangible personal property not otherwise disposed of herein. Any such statement or list in existence at the time of the death of the Grantor shall be determinative with respect to distributions to be made therein. If no written statement or list is found and properly identified by the Trustee within thirty (30) days after the death of the Grantor, it shall be presumed that there is no such statement or list, and any subsequently discovered statement or list shall be ignored.

2. Personal Effects. The Trustee shall distribute all of the Grantor's remaining apparel, jewelry, books, pictures, automobiles, and all other objects of the Grantor's personal use, including any household furniture and furnishings which may be held in the Trust, together with any insurance thereon, to the Grantor's friend, **Partner 2**, if she survives the Grantor. If **Partner 2** does not survive the Grantor, then the Trustee shall distribute said personal property as directed in Article VI, below.

3. Delivery to Minor or Incapacitated Beneficiaries. If the Trustee is directed to distribute one or more items of personal property to a beneficiary who is under the age of twenty-one (21) or a beneficiary for whom a guardian of the person or property has been appointed, then the Trustee is authorized, in the Trustee's sole discretion, to distribute said personal property to the natural or court-appointed guardian of such beneficiary or to a custodian for said beneficiary under the Florida Uniform 'Transfers to Minors Act. In addition, if the Trustee is directed to distribute one or more items of personal property to a beneficiary who, though not formally adjudicated as incapacitated by a court of law, nevertheless is in the opinion of the Trustee incapable of owning and managing said assets in a responsible manner, then the Trustee shall retain possession of said personal property until the Trustee determines, in the Trustee's sole discretion, that the beneficiary is capable of owning and managing said assets in a responsible manner.

B. Residue. All the rest, residue, and remainder of the Trust Estate shall be distributed to the Grantor's friend, **Partner 2**, if she survives the Grantor. If **Partner 2** does not survive the Grantor, then the Trustee shall distribute the rest, residue, and remainder as directed in Article VI, below.

ARTICLE VI
AFTER GRANTOR'S DEATH IF NOT SURVIVED BY Partner 2
If **Partner 2** does not survive the Grantor, then the Successor Trustee shall distribute Grantor's

personal effects, and rest, residue and remainder of the Trust Estate as follows:

A. Home at _____: The Successor Trustee shall, at an appropriate time, sell the following parcel of real property:

LEGAL DESCRIPTION

otherwise known as the property located at _____.

The proceeds of the sale of this real property shall be segregated from other funds in this trust, and shall be used for the education of the Grantor's friend **Partner 2's** niece, **NIECE.** The Successor Trustee shall distribute any funds remaining from the sale of the home to **NIECE** on her twenty-fifth (25) birthday, so long as she has obtained a Bachelor's Degree. If she does not obtain a Bachelor's Degree, the Successor Trustee shall distribute any funds remaining from the sale of the home to **NIECE** on her thirtieth (30th) birthday.

B. Dollar Distributions: The Trustee shall distribute the sum of Fifty Thousand U.S. Dollars, ($50,000.00) to the Grantor's friend **Partner 2's** brother, **BROTHER** if he survives the Grantor, and if not, then this distribution shall lapse.

C. Fine Art: The Trustee shall retain a professional art broker, and all fine art remaining in the Trust Estate shall be sold at auction with the proceeds of such sale, after payment of any costs related to the sale, distributed to **CHARITY.**

D. Pets: Any and all animals owned by the Grantor shall be given to the Grantor's friend, **FRIEND.** A sum of Fifty Thousand U.S. Dollars, ($50,000.00), shall be distributed to **FRIEND**, for the care of Grantor's pets. Following the death of the last of the Grantor's surviving pets, if there are any funds remaining from the Fifty Thousand U.S. Dollars, ($50,000.00), such funds shall be distributed to the charitable foundation for rescued schnauzers, as described in **ARTICLE VII**, below.

E. Residue. All the rest, residue, and remainder of the Trust Estate, shall be used to establish a charitable foundation for rescued schnauzers, as described in **ARTICLE VII**, below. Any items of personal property not otherwise distributed as directed in this Revocable Living Trust, shall be sold at an estate sale, with the proceeds distributed the charitable foundation. If the Grantor, and **Partner 2** should die under such circumstances as would render it doubtful as to which of them died first, then it shall be conclusively presumed for the purposes of this Revocable Living Trust that the Grantor died first.

ARTICLE VII
CHARITABLE FOUNDATION FOR RESCUED SCHNAUZERS
Following the death of both the Grantor and **Partner 2,** the Successor Trustee, **FRIEND,** shall establish a charitable foundation, the purpose of which is to assist schnauzer rescue groups in the rehabilitation and re-homing of rescued schnauzers, including, but not limited to, the provision of grants for medical care needed by rescued schnauzers. This charitable foundation shall be administered by **FRIEND**, who will have complete authority and discretion to run the foundation for the purposes described herein. This foundation shall be organized exclusively for charitable purposes described above, including, the making of distributions to organizations that qualify as exempt organizations under section 501(c)(3) of the Internal Revenue Code, or the corresponding section of any future federal tax code. No part of the net earnings of the foundation shall inure to the benefit of, or be distributable to its members, trustees, officers, or other private persons,

except that the foundation shall be authorized and empowered to pay reasonable compensation for services rendered and to make payments and distributions in furtherance of its purposes. The foundation shall not carry on any activities not permitted to be carried on (a) by a corporation or foundation exempt from federal income tax under section 501(c)(3) of the Internal Revenue Code, or the corresponding section of any future federal tax code, or (b) by a foundation or corporation, contributions to which are deductible under section 170(c)(2) of the Internal Revenue Code, or the corresponding section of any future federal tax code. Upon the dissolution of the foundation, or in the event **FRIEND** is unable or unwilling to establish the foundation, the assets shall be distributed for one or more exempt purposes within the meaning of section 501(c)(3) of the Internal Revenue Code, or the corresponding section of any future federal tax code, to **CHARITY.,** for the purposes stated above. Any such assets not so disposed of shall be disposed of by a Court of Competent Jurisdiction located in _____ a County, _____, exclusively for such purposes or to such organization or organizations, as said Court shall determine, which are organized and operated exclusively for such purposes.

ARTICLE VIII
TRUSTEE
A. Appointment of Trustees. The Grantor, **Partner 1**, shall serve as the Trustee of the trust hereby created. Upon the resignation, death, or inability of the Grantor to manage the affairs of the Trust (as determined by two qualified physicians), then the Grantor's friend, **Partner 2**, shall serve as Successor Trustee hereunder. In the event of the resignation, death, or inability of **Partner 2** to manage the affairs of the Trust (as determined by two qualified physicians), then the Grantor's friend, **FRIEND**, shall serve as Successor Trustee hereunder.

B. Resignation: Any Trustee or Successor Trustee may resign by instrument in writing, with twenty (20) days advance notice.

C. Rights: Any Successor Trustee shall have all the rights, powers, duties, and discretion conferred or imposed on the original Trustee. No Trustee shall be liable for any act or omission unless the same be due to such Trustee's own default. In no event shall a corporate trustee be a corporation owned or controlled by any beneficiary hereof.

D. Responsibility: Upon accounting to the successor and delivery of the trust assets to the successor, any relieved Trustee shall be released and discharged from further responsibility hereunder. No successor Trustee shall be personally liable for any act or omission of any predecessor. Any such successor may accept without examination or review the account rendered and the property received, as a full and complete discharge to the predecessor Trustee, without incurring any liability or responsibility.

E. New Appointment: If all Trustees resign, die or become unable to manage the affairs of the Trust without having designated a successor Trustee to serve in their place, then a majority in interest of the beneficiaries of the Trust may designate and appoint some individual or bank or trust company, whether located in the State of Florida or elsewhere, to serve as Trustee under the Trust Agreement. If no such designation takes place, any beneficiary of the Trust may petition the Court of competent jurisdiction to appoint a successor Trustee under the Trust Agreement. The parent, guardian or conservator of a beneficiary under disability shall receive notice and have authority to act for such beneficiary under this section.

F. Trustee's Bond. No bond or surety shall be required of any Trustee serving under this Trust.

G. Trustee's Compensation. No compensation shall be paid for the services of the Grantor,

Partner 1 to the **Partner 1 REVOCABLE LIVING TRUST**. Any other Trustee, including professional fiduciary trustees, shall be entitled to fair and reasonable compensation, commensurate with prevailing rates for like trusts and instruments, from the Trust Estate for services rendered as Trustee.

H. Accountings by Trustee. The Trustee shall make annual statements showing the itemized receipts and disbursements of the income and principal of the trust, and otherwise reflecting the condition thereof, and shall furnish copies of such statements to the Grantor, while the Grantor is living, and after the Grantor has died, then to each adult income beneficiary and upon request to the parent or guardian of any minor beneficiary. Any person entitled to receive an accounting, or a person legally entitled to act for him, shall state, in writing, his objections to an accounting, and deliver the objections to the Trustee within six (6) months after receipt of a copy of the accounting. Failure to object in this manner shall constitute a waiver of objections.

I. Successor Trustee's Acceptance. Each successor Trustee shall accept the office in writing and shall be vested with the powers and duties of the trusteeship immediately upon delivery of the trust assets to the successor Trustee and written notice to one or more of the beneficiaries of the trust, without the necessity of any other act, conveyance or transfer.

J. Facility of Payment. If income or amounts of principal become payable to a minor or to a person under legal disability or to a person not adjudicated incompetent, but who by reason of illness or mental or physical disability, is in the opinion of the Trustee unable to properly manage his or her affairs, then such income or principal shall be paid or expended only in such of the following ways as the Trustee deems best: (a) To the beneficiary directly; (b) To the legally appointed guardian or conservator of the beneficiary; (c) To a custodian for the beneficiary under the Uniform Transfers to Minors Act; (d) By making payments directly to the entities assisting or providing for the support, maintenance, education, or other benefit of the beneficiary; (e) To an adult relative or friend in reimbursement for amounts properly advanced for the benefit of the beneficiary; or (f) To compensate the guardian of the person or the guardian of the property of any such minor or person under a legal disability.

K. Spendthrift Provision. The interests of beneficiaries in principal or income shall not be subject to the claims of any creditor, any spouse for alimony or support, or others, or to legal process and may not be voluntarily or involuntarily alienated or encumbered. This provision shall not limit the exercise of any power of appointment.

L. Rule Against Perpetuities. Unless sooner terminated in accordance with other provisions of this instrument, this Trust shall terminate no later than twenty-one (21) years after the death of the last survivor of the beneficiaries hereunder who are living at the date of creation of this trust agreement. Upon termination pursuant to this paragraph, the income and corpus of the Trust Estate shall be distributed free of trust to the then existing beneficiaries, each receiving the trust assets from which he or she derives their proportionate share, based upon the proportion each beneficiary is currently entitled to receive.

M. Common Funds. For convenience of administration or investment, the Trustee may hold the several trusts as a common fund dividing the income proportionately among them, assign undivided interests to the several trusts, and make joint investments of the funds belonging to them. The Trustee may consolidate any separate trust with any other trust with similar provisions for the same beneficiary or beneficiaries.

N. Standards Governing Discretionary Distributions by Trustee. In this instrument, the Trustee is authorized to make certain discretionary payments of income and/or principal to or for the benefit of designated persons. The Trustee may make these discretionary distributions whenever and in those amounts as in the discretion of the Trustee shall be necessary or appropriate for the health, support, education and maintenance of these persons at their accustomed standard of living. It is the Grantor's intention that the distributions shall not be limited to supplying necessities for these persons, but shall maintain them liberally according to their accustomed standard of living, account being taken of their possible desire for travel, owning a home and all other reasonable desires not clearly inconsistent with their accustomed standard of living. In addition, there may be paid to or for the benefit of these persons in order to permit them to enter into or continue in business or professional ventures that portion of income and/or principal as the Trustee, in the Trustee's discretion, may from time to time determine. However, the Trustee, based upon information reasonably available to the Trustee, shall make the distributions to any person for the purposes set forth above only to the extent the person's income, and funds available from others obligated to supply funds for such purposes, are insufficient in the Trustee's opinion for these purposes. The Trustee shall have no duty to try to equalize present or future distributions to, or among, any beneficiaries exactly; and the good faith decision of the Trustee with respect to any discretionary distributions of net income or principal shall fully protect the Trustee and shall be binding and conclusive upon all persons having an interest in any trust created hereunder.

O. Determinations Concerning Income and Principal. The Trustee may determine whether receipts are income or principal and whether disbursements are to be charged against income or principal, to the extent not established clearly by state law. Determinations made by the Trustee in good faith shall not require equitable adjustments.

P. Tax Elections and Allocations. The Trustee may make tax elections and allocations the Trustee considers appropriate. No tax elections or allocations made by the Trustee in good faith shall require equitable adjustments.

Q. Employment of Professional Advisors. The Trustee may employ such lawyers, accountants, and other advisers as the Trustee may deem useful and appropriate for the administration of the Trust. The Trustee may employ a professional investment adviser in managing the investments of the Trust (including any investment in mutual funds, investment trusts, or managed accounts), delegate to this adviser any discretionary investment authorities, and rely on the adviser's investment recommendations without liability to any beneficiary.

R. Decisions Concerning Division and Distribution of Assets. The Trustee shall equitably divide and distribute the Trust in kind, in money, or partly in each, taking into account the income tax basis of any asset. The decision of the Trustee in dividing any portion of the Trust between or among two or more beneficiaries shall be binding on all persons.

S. Distributions to Minors. The Trustee shall distribute any of the trust to a minor by distributing it to any appropriate person (who may be a Trustee) chosen by the Trustee, as custodian under any appropriate Uniform Transfers (or Gifts) to Minors Act, to be held for the maximum period of time allowed by law. The Trustee may also sell any asset that cannot legally be held under this custodianship and invest the sales proceeds in assets that can be held under this custodianship. Or, whenever pursuant to the provisions of this instrument, a distributive share of the trust property is payable to a beneficiary under the age of twenty-five (25) years, then title thereto shall pass to such beneficiary but the actual distribution shall be deferred until such beneficiary reaches the age of twenty-five (25) years. In the meantime, such share shall be held by such beneficiary's parent(s) or legal representative, with all the powers granted herein, who shall pay to or apply for the benefit of such beneficiary so much of the net income and principal thereof as the parent(s) or legal representative of such beneficiary shall determine for the health, education, support and maintenance of such beneficiary. When such beneficiary reaches the age of twenty-five (25) years, the parent(s) or legal representative shall deliver to him or her the then remaining principal of such share, together with any accumulations of income thereof. The parent(s) or legal representative may make payment of any income or principal directly to such beneficiary or may apply the same for his or her benefit, and the receipt from the recipient thereof, or evidence of the application of the income or principal for the benefit of such beneficiary, shall be a full and complete discharge and acquittance to the parent(s) or legal representative to the extent of such payment.

ARTICLE IX
TRUSTEE'S POWERS

The Trustee shall have all powers and protection granted by statute to trustees at the time of the application that are not in conflict with this Agreement. In addition, and not in limitation of any common law or statutory authority, and without application to any court, the Trustee shall have the powers and responsibilities described below, to be exercised in the Trustee's absolute discretion until distribution of the trusts created under this instrument, and shall observe the instructions hereafter given:

(a) Collect: To collect any income therefrom.

(b) Claims: To pay, compromise, adjust, settle, or release any claim or demands of the Trust Estate, or any Trust created hereunder, against others, or of others against the Trust Estate as the Trustee may deem advisable.

(c) Retention: To hold any property or securities originally received by the Trustee as part of the trust or to which the Trustee becomes entitled by virtue of incorporation, liquidation, reorganization, merger, consolidation or change of charter, or name, including any stock or interest in any family corporation, partnership, or enterprise, so long as the Trustee shall consider the retention in the best interests of the trust.

(d) Sell: To sell, transfer, exchange, convert, or otherwise dispose of, or grant options with respect to any security or property, real or personal, including homestead property, held as part of the Trust Estate, at public or private sale, with or without security, in such manner, at such time or times, for such purposes, for such prices, and upon such terms, credits, and conditions as the Trustee may deem advisable.

(e) Invest: To invest and reinvest all or any part of the Trust Estate and the proceeds of sale or disposition of any portion thereof, in such loans, bonds, stocks, mortgages, common trust funds, securities, or other property, real or personal, or to purchase options for such purposes, or to, exercise options, rights, or warrants to purchase securities or other property, as the Trustee may deem suitable.

(f) Liquidity: To render liquid the Trust Estate or any trust created hereunder, in whole or in part at any time or from time to time, and hold cash or readily marketable securities of little or no yield for such period as the Trustees may deem advisable.

(g) Lease: To lease Trust property for the terms within or beyond the period fixed by statutes for leases made by a Trustee and beyond the duration of the Trust Estate or any Trust created hereunder, for any purpose, including exploration for and removal of gas, oil, and other minerals; and to enter into community oil leases, pooling and unitization agreements.

(h) Securities: To buy, sell and trade in securities of any nature (including "short" sales) on margin, and for such purpose may maintain and operate margin accounts with brokers, and may pledge any securities held or purchased by it with such brokers as security for loans and advances made to the trustee.

(i) Vote: To vote in person at any meeting of stock or security holders, or any adjournment of such meetings, or to vote by special, general or limited proxy with respect to any such shares of stock or other securities held by the Trustees.

(j) Business Enterprise: To continue or dispose of any business enterprise without liability therefor, whether such enterprise be in the form of a sole proprietorship, partnership, corporation or otherwise, and to develop, add capital to, expand or alter the business of such enterprise, to liquidate, incorporate, reorganize, manage or consolidate the same, or change its charter or name; to enter into, continue or extend any voting trust for the duration of or beyond the term of the trust; to appoint directors and employ officers, managers, employees or agents (including any trustee or director, officers or employees thereof) and to compensate and offer stock options and other employee or fringe benefits to them, and in exercising the powers in relation to such business enterprise, to receive extra or extraordinary compensation therefor.

(k) Real Property: To possess, manage, sell, insure against loss by fire or other casualties, develop, subdivide, control, partition, mortgage, lease, or otherwise deal with any and all real property, including homestead property; to satisfy and discharge or extend the term of any mortgage thereon; to execute the necessary instruments and covenants to effectuate the foregoing powers, including the giving or granting of options in connection therewith; to make improvements, structural or otherwise, or abandon the same if deemed to be worthless or not of sufficient value to warrant keeping or protecting; to abstain from the payment of taxes, water rents, assessments, repairs, maintenance, or upkeep of the same; to permit to be lost by tax sale or other proceeding or to convey the same for a nominal consideration or without consideration; to set up appropriate reserves out of income for repairs, modernization, and upkeep of buildings, including reserves for depreciation and obsolescence, and to add such reserves to the principal, and, if the income from the property itself should not suffice for such purposes, if allowable in determining the federal estate tax payable from the Trust Estate, to advance any income of the Trust for the amortization of any mortgage on property held in the Trust.

(l) Distributions: To make distributions in cash or in kind, or partly in cash and partly in kind and to divide, partition, allocate, or distribute particular assets or undivided interests therein, without any obligation to make proportionate distributions or to distribute to all beneficiaries property having an equivalent income tax basis, and without regard to any provision of law expressing a preference for distribution in kind, and to value such property to the extent permitted by law, and to cause any share to be composed of cash, property, or undivided fractional shares in property different in kind from any other share.

(m) To Borrow: To borrow money from any source, excluding an individual Trustee, with any such indebtedness being repayable solely from the trust estate or a part of it, and to pledge or encumber the trust estate, or a part of it, for security for such loans.

(n) To Loan: To loan funds to the trust, it being understood that the Trustee shall be reimbursed for any funds so advanced and receive reasonable interest on any such loans made by the Trustee.

(o) Possession: To allow temporary possession of, and to make available, personal property for the personal use of any beneficiary hereof; if any item(s) of personal property are held in trust by the Trustees for the benefit of such beneficiary.

(p) Make Contracts and Execute Instruments: To make contracts and execute instruments as may be necessary in the exercise of the powers granted herein; and no party dealing with the Trustee need inquire as to the existence or proper exercise of any power of the Trustee, whether such power is granted directly or incorporated herein.

(q) To Hold Money: To hold money in the Trustee's custody while awaiting distribution or investment under the terms hereof, even though such money shall be commingled with other trust funds (in which case the Trustee shall keep a separate account of the same on the Trustee's books), and the Trustee shall not be required to pay interest thereon.

(r) To Employ Experts: To employ attorneys, accountants, investment managers, specialists and such other agents as the Trustee shall deem necessary or desirable. The Trustee shall have the authority to appoint an investment manager or managers to manage all or any part of the assets of the trust, and to delegate to said manager investment discretion. Such appointment shall include the power to acquire and dispose of such assets. The Trustee may charge the compensation of such attorneys, accountants, investment advisors, investment managers, specialists and other agents and any other expenses against the trust.

(s) Nominee: To hold property or securities in bearer form, in the name of the Trustee, or in the name of the Trustee's nominee, without disclosing any fiduciary relationship.

(t) To Protect Property: To keep any property constituting a part of said trust property insured against hazards; to pay all taxes and assessments, mortgages, or other liens now or hereafter resting on said property; and to create reserves for depreciation, depletion, or such other purposes as the Trustee deems necessary or desirable.

(u) Allocations: To determine, irrespective of statute or rule of law, what shall be fairly and equitably charged or credited to income and what to principal, notwithstanding any determination by the courts or by any custom or statute, and whether or not establish depreciation reserves. (v) To Litigate: To prosecute, defend, contest or otherwise litigate legal actions or other proceedings for the protection or benefit of a trust or the Trustee; to pay, compromise, release, adjust or submit to arbitration any debt, claim or controversy; and to insure the trust against any risk, and the Trustee against liability with respect to third persons.

(w) To Prepare Tax Returns and Make Elections: To prepare and file returns and arrange for payment with respect to all local, state, federal, and foreign taxes incident to this agreement; to prepare all necessary fiduciary income tax returns; to make all necessary and appropriate elections in connection therewith in its discretion.

(x) To Seek and Maintain Public Benefits for a Beneficiary: To take any and all steps necessary, in the Trustee's discretion, to obtain and maintain eligibility of any beneficiary under this trust for any and all public benefits and entitlement programs. Such programs include but are not limited to Social Security, Supplemental Security Income, Medicare, Medicaid, and In Home Support Services.

ARTICLE X
TERMINATION OF TRUST
In the event that the size of any trust estate created hereunder, or the share of any distributee or beneficiary, is of a size or reduced to the point that, in the opinion of the Trustee, retention

thereof will not further the purposes of the trust, the Trustee, in the Trustee's sole discretion, may make a complete distribution of the trust and entirely terminate the share or trust earlier than herein provided and the share so distributed or terminated shall be distributed to the beneficiaries of said trust estate according to their interest therein or to the distributee or beneficiary, as the case may be. It is recognized that a trust may include both income and remainder beneficiaries in which case the trust shall be distributed to the beneficiaries according to each such beneficiary's actuarially determined percentage share of the trust estate. This power is given to the Trustee to be exercised in the Trustee's sole and absolute discretion, without court approval.

ARTICLE XI
ADDITIONAL TRANSFERS TO TRUST

The Grantor or any other person shall have the right, from time to time, to grant, transfer, or convey, either by inter vivos transfer or by will, to the Trustee, such additional property as the Grantor, or such other person shall desire to become part of the trust herein created, and such additional property shall be allocated to the trust on the basis specified in the instrument by which such property is transferred, and shall thereafter be held, administered and distributed by the Trustee in accordance with the provisions of this trust agreement.

ARTICLE XII
_____ LAW CONTROLS

The validity, effect and interpretation of this trust instrument and of the property interests created shall be controlled by the laws of the State _____.

* * * * * * * * * *

IN WITNESS WHEREOF, the Grantor, individually and as Trustee, has set her hand and seal on _____ in the presence of the witnesses and notary listed below.

_____
Partner 1 - GRANTOR/TRUSTEE

The foregoing instrument, consisting of ____ pages was signed, sealed, published and declared by Partner 1, as Grantor/Trustee, in our presence, and we, at her request, and in her presence, and in the presence of each other, have hereunto subscribed our names as witnesses on _____.

WITNESSES:

_____   _____

STATE OF _____
COUNTY OF _____

I, Partner 1, declare to the officer taking my acknowledgment of this instrument, and to the subscribing witnesses, that I signed this Instrument as my Revocable Living Trust.

_____
Partner 1 - GRANTOR/TRUSTEE

We, [Witnesses] having been sworn by the officer signing below, declare to that officer on our oaths, that the Grantor/Trustee declared this instrument to be her Revocable Living Trust, we were present where it was signed, that it was signed in our presence, and that each of us signed this instrument as a witness, in the presence of the Grantor/Trustee, and of each other.

_____   _____
WITNESS   WITNESS

STATE OF _____
COUNTY OF _____

Acknowledged and subscribed before me by Partner 1, Grantor and Trustee, who has produced as identification, and sworn to and subscribed before me by the witnesses: _____, who is personally known to me, and _____, who is personally known to me, and subscribed by me in the presence of the Grantor and Trustee and the subscribing witnesses, all on _____.

                                    _____
                                    NOTARY PUBLIC - State of Florida

(SEAL) My Notary Expires:_____

SCHEDULE A
TO THE Partner 1
REVOCABLE LIVING TRUST

Personal Property:

All of the Grantor's vehicles, furniture, appliances, interest in any business owned, collectibles, art objects, books, records, jewelry, musical instruments, clothing, dogs, cats and other family pets, and all other items of a personal nature, including all after acquired property of a similar nature conveyed by separate Assignment.

Real Property:
Grantor's interest in the following parcel of real property:

LEGAL DESCRIPTION

otherwise known as the property located at _____.

Financial Assets:

ESTATE PLANNING FORM 29

ALTERNATE CLIENT CHECKLIST

Contributed by:

Anthony M. Brown
Albert W. Chianese and Associates
100 Merrick Rd., Ste. 103E
Rockville Center, NY 11570
brown@msclaw.net
519.599.2020, ext. 23

ESTATE PLANNING AND WILL CHECKLIST

Confidential Information Form of: _____

Date: _____

Personal Information

Address**:** _____
            _____
            _____

Date of Birth: _____   Home Phone: _____

Social Security Number: _____   Work Phone: _____
State of Legal Residence: _____   Fax: _____
Citizenship: _____   Email: _____
Marital Status: _____   Prior Marriages: _____

Name of Spouse or Domestic Partner (if any): _____

Dependents: Name Address, Age:

    1.
    2.

Immediate Family Members: Name, Address (**prepare and attach a family tree if necessary**)
    Parents:

    Children:

    Brothers & Sisters:

    Pets:

Present Will
(Please provide a copy of your present will.)

Date of Present Will:

Location:

Name of Executor & Trustees:

Changes Since Execution of Present Will:

Liabilities
Loans and Mortgages:

Alimony:

Other Debts:

Prior Taxable Gifts:

Will Provisions
(Please indicate your directions concerning your new will.)

Beneficiaries (names and addresses):
    1.
    2.
    3.

Alternate Beneficiaries:

Charitable Bequests:

Business Successors (if applicable):

Guardianships for Children (if applicable):

Executor(s):
    Alternate Executor(s):

Trusts (if applicable):

Disinheritances:

Special Burial Instructions (inform immediate family and executor):

Where Is Will Kept:

Special Will Provisions:

Other Documents and Information

Have you executed a health care proxy, advanced directive, designation of guardian, or power of attorney? (If so, please provide copies.)

Location of Important Records, Tax Returns, Real Estate Deeds:

Location of Safe Deposit Boxes (if any):

Property Interests

Business Interests:

Name and Address of Employer or Interest:

Type of Business and Position:

Partnership or Stock Holder Agreements:

Trust Interests:

Please list any interests you have in trusts, and any duties you have as a trustee.

Assets (please indicate if jointly owned)

For the purposes of this form, estimated dollar amount of your assets and liabilities are sufficient. Please provide a copy of your most recent statement for all bank accounts, as well as life insurance policies, 401(k)s, IRAs, etc.

Bank Accounts:

Stocks and Bonds:

Life Insurance Policies:

Real Estate, Coops, Condos:

Corporate or Partnership Interests:

Deferred Compensation, Retirement and Pension:

Tangible Personal Property (Cars, Artwork):

Other Assets:

Out of State Assets:

Assets Held by You but Owned by Others:

ESTATE PLANNING FORM 30

Contributed by:
Tamara Kolz Griffin
102 Lakeshore Dr.
Wayland, MA 01778
617.797.1892
attorneytkolz@gmail.com

ESTATE PLANNING
PERSONAL AND FINANCIAL QUESTIONNAIRE

If you and you partner will have different estate plans, then each must complete a separate questionnaire.

PERSONAL INFORMATION   DATE: _____

1. Marital Status						
☐ Married	☐ Single	☐ Widowed	☐ Divorced	☐ Separated	☐ Domestic Partnership	☐ Civil Union

2. Your Name (First, Middle, Last)	Soc. Sec. No.	Date of Birth
3. Partner's Name (First, Middle, Last)	Soc. Sec. No.	Date of Birth

4. Home Address (Number, Street)	City	State	Zip
5. Mailing Address If Different From Above (Number, Street)	City	State	Zip

6. Home Phone ( )	Your Work Phone ( )	Partner's Work Phone ( )
7. Your Cellular Phone ( )	Partner's Cellular Phone ( )	
8. Your Employer	Your Occupation	Your Email Address
9. Partner's Employer	Partner's Occupation	Partner's Email Address

Circle or fill in your answers	You	Your Partner
1. Are you a U.S. citizen?	Yes No	Yes No
2. Do you have a will or trust now?	Yes No	Yes No
3. Are you expecting to receive property or money from (circle all that apply): If so, approximately how much?	Gift Inheritance Lawsuit - Other $	Gift Inheritance Lawsuit - Other $
4. How many living children do you have?		
5. Are all your children legally yours (biologically or legally adopted)?	Yes No	Yes No
6. How many stepchildren do you have?		
7. In which state do you vote?		
8. Which state issued your driver's license ?		
9. In which state is your car registered?		
10. In which state(s) do you own real estate?		
11. Do you pay state income tax? If yes to which state?		
12. In which state do you plan to retire/live permanently?		
13. Have you ever lived in a Community Property State? (AZ,CA,ID,LA,NV,NM,TX,WA,WI & PR)	Yes No	Yes No
14. Do you have a pre-nuptial or post-nuptial agreement?	Yes No	Yes No
15. Do you have a divorce decree affecting your pension or other property rights?	Yes No	Yes No
16. Have you ever given more than $10,000 to a person in any one year?	Yes No	Yes No
If "yes' to questions 2, 14 or 15, please provide copies of these documents		

FINANCIAL INFORMATION

1. Do you own a home or any other real estate? Indicate which is your residence/homestead.

Description and Location	Titled in whose name (Indicate if Joint or Beneficiary and name)	Purchase Price	Market Value	Mortgage	Market Value – Mortgage Equity
				Total Net Value	

2. Do you own any other titled property such as a car, boat, etc.?

Description	Titled in whose name (Indicate if Joint or Beneficiary and name)	Market Value	Less Mortgage	Equity
			Total Net Value	

3. Do you have any checking accounts?

Name of Bank	Titled in whose name (Indicate if Joint or Beneficiary and name)	Approx. Balance
	Total Value	

4. Do you have any interest bearing accounts (savings, money market) and/or CD's?

Name of Bank	Titled in whose name (Indicate if Joint or Beneficiary and name)	Approx. Balance
	Total Value	

5. Do you own any stocks, bonds or mutual funds (including company stock) or have a stock portfolio with a money manger?

Number Shares	Name of Security or Location of Stock Portfolio/ Money Manager	Titled in Whose Name (Indicate if Joint or Beneficiary and name)	Purchase Price	Current Value
			Total Value	

6. Do you have any profit sharing, IRAs or pension plans?

Description/Location	Beneficiary	Current Value
	Total Value	

7. Do you have any life insurance policies and/or annuities?

Name of Company	Insured	Policy Owner	Named Beneficiaries (primary and contingent)	Cash Value and Type of Policy	Death Benefit
				Total Value	

8.   Does anyone owe you money?

Description	Approx. Value
Total Net Value	

9. Do you have any special items of value such as coin collections, antiques, jewelry, etc.?

Description	Approx. Value
Total Net Value	

10. What is the approximate total value of all your remaining personal property--whatever you own that has not been included above? (clothes, furniture, etc.) Just estimate $ _____

11. Do you have any debts other than mortgage(s) and loans listed above (credit cards, personal loans, etc.)?

Description	Amount Owned
Total Debt	

12. Total value of everything you (and your Partner) own (add totals of line 1 thru line 10 above) $ _____

13. Total amount you (and your Partner) owe (total of line 11 above) $_____

14. Subtract line 13 from line 12.   **TOTAL NET ESTATE VALUE**

15. Do you have a safe deposit box(es)?

Location	Titled in whose name

MANAGEMENT DECISIONS: YOUR ESTATE MANAGEMENT TEAM

1. Executor/Personal Representative: Manages the probate and settlement of your estate. Can be your Partner, adult children, trusted friends, and/or a professional or corporate fiduciary.

For You   **For Your Partner**

Name:_____   Name:_____

2. Successor Executor/Personal Representative: Back-up Manager-Steps in after your first Executor/personal representative dies/resigns; in the case of a living trust at your death or disability. Can be your adult children, trusted friends, and/or a professional or corporate fiduciary.

                           For You   **For Your Partner**

1st Successor: Name:_____   Name:_____

                      Address:_____   Address:_____

2nd Successor: Name:_____   Name:_____

                      Address:_____   Address:_____

3. Trustee: Manages the administration and investments in your trust. Should be someone with financial responsibility and experience. If you are creating a trust of which your Partner is to be both the beneficiary and trustee (e.g, a tax saving Credit Shelter Trust (B Trust) you **should** also name a co-trustee to make discretionary decisions.

                   For You   **For Your Partner**

Name:_____   Name:_____

4. Successor Trustee (or Co Trustee): Back-up Manager-Steps in after your first Trustee dies/resigns. Can be your adult children, trusted friends, and/or a professional/corporate fiduciary.

                           For You   **For Your Partner**

1st Successor: Name:_____   Name:_____

                      Address:_____   Address:_____

2nd Successor: Name:_____   Name:_____

                      Address:_____   Address:_____

You may provide that the Executor/Personal Representatives and/or Trustees be insured, or bonded, to protect the beneficiaries:
The Executor/Personal Representative should be bonded ☐ Yes ☐ No   The Trustee should be bonded ☐ Yes ☐ No

5.   Guardians For Minor Children: Responsible adult who will raise your children if something happens to you.

                           For You   **For Your Partner**

#1 Choice: Name:_____   Name:_____

                      Address:_____   Address:_____

#2 Choice: Name:_____   Name:_____

                      Address:_____   Address:_____

#3 Choice: Name:_____   Name:_____

                      Address:_____   Address:_____

BENEFICIARIES

1. Special Gifts To Organizations

Do you want to make a gift (cash or a specific item) to a charity, foundation, religious or fraternal organization?

Name of Organization	Description of Gift	Alternate Beneficiary

2. Special Gifts To Individuals

Do you want to give any specific items or cash gifts to a family member or other individual? (For example: ring to your daughter, art collection to a son or nephew, etc.)

Name of Person	Description of Gift or Amount	Alternate Beneficiary

3. Beneficiaries

Who do you want to receive the rest of your estate after these special gifts have been distributed? You can designate a dollar amount or percentage, however the percentages are easier, and must add to 100 per cent.

Name of Person/Organization	Amount/Percentage	Alternate Beneficiary

4. Inheriting Instructions

List your children

Name	Address	Age	T=This partnership P=Previous Partnership	Married/ Partnered? Y or N	Number of Grandchildren

5. Do you want your children to receive their inheritance in installments, at certain ages, or all at once? In what amounts and at what age(s)? Your children's inheritance can be held in trust and managed for them until they are at any age you chose (21, 25, 30, etc.) and used for their education and other needs until that time. This method waits until the children are mature enough to handle money.

_____

_____

_____

_____

6. If a child dies, do you want that child's share to go to that child's children, your grandchildren, (Per Stirpes) ☐ or do you want that child's share to be divided among *only* your other living children (Per Capita). ☐, nothing to a grandchild whose parent died.

                                                                              You   Your Partner

7. Do you want to ensure that your children from a previous marriage receive a share of your estate?   Yes ☐ No ☐ Yes ☐ No ☐

8. List Dependents Who Require Special Care

Do you want to provide for "basic" care or luxuries and other extras to supplement government benefits?   ☐ Yes   ☐ No

_____

_____

_____

_____

9. Alternative Beneficiaries
Who do you want to receive your estate if you (and your Partner) outlive the beneficiaries you've named above?

Name of Person/Organization	Amount/Percentage

10. Disinheriting
Are there any relatives that you specifically do not want to receive anything from your estate?

_____
_____
_____

SPECIAL INSTRUCTIONS FOR INCOMPETENCY

1. Keeping/Selling Assets
If necessary to pay for your care, do you want certain assets sold first? Are there potential buyers you want contacted?

_____
_____
_____

2. Medical Care
Do you want to be in ☐ (or avoid ☐) a certain hospital/nursing home? _____

	You	Your Partner
A Living Will makes your wishes known to family and doctors regarding life support and the following decisions in the event you become terminally ill or injured with no hope for recovery. Do you want a living will?	☐ Yes ☐ No	☐ Yes ☐ No

Please answer the following for your Living Will:

If you have a terminal condition, do you want:	You	Your Partner
Your life artificially prolonged by machine?	☐ Yes ☐ No	☐ Yes ☐ No
Nutrition and Hydration (Food and Water) by tube?	☐ Yes ☐ No	☐ Yes ☐ No
Blood Transfusions?	☐ Yes ☐ No	☐ Yes ☐ No
Organ Transplants?	☐ Yes ☐ No	☐ Yes ☐ No
Upon your death, do you wish to donate your organs?	☐ Yes ☐ No	☐ Yes ☐ No
For transplants	☐ Yes ☐ No	☐ Yes ☐ No
For science or medical research	☐ Yes ☐ No	☐ Yes ☐ No
Do you wish to die at home rather than in a hospital or nursing home?	☐ At home ☐ Hosp / Nur Home	☐ At home ☐ Hosp / Nur Home

A **_Durable Power of Attorney For Health Care_** gives broader protection. Do you want to appoint someone (Partner, child, friend) to make health care decisions for you when you are unable to, but not necessarily terminal? If so provide the following:

	For You	**For Your Partner**
1st Choice:	Name:_____	Name:_____
	Address:_____	Address:_____
	Telephone Number:_____	Telephone Number:_____
2nd Choice:	Name:_____	Name:_____
	Address:_____	Address:_____
	Telephone Number:_____	Telephone Number:_____

A ***Durable General Power of Attorney*** appoints an agent that can make any decision and do any act that you can, and it will continue to be in force even after you become incapacitated. It is a very powerful document and should only be granted with great care, and then only to a person that you have the utmost trust in. If you wish a Durable General Power of Attorney provide the following:

	For You	**For Your Partner**
1st Choice:	Name:_____	Name:_____
	Address:_____	Address:_____
2nd Choice:	Name:_____	Name:_____
	Address:_____	Address:_____

SPECIAL INSTRUCTIONS FOR FUNERAL/BURIAL

1. What type of service do you want, how elaborate, and where? Any special person to contact? Do you want cremation?

_____
_____
_____
_____

2. If you have a cemetery lot, where is it located?

        Cemetery Name   City   State

Appendix B

Resources

APPENDIX B-I

Requirements Related to CMS Patient Visitation Rights Conditions of Participation (CoPs)

Hospital Accreditation Program

RI.01.01.01

The hospital respects, protects, and promotes patient rights.

Elements of Performance for RI.01.01.01

1. The hospital has written policies on patient rights.
   Note: For hospitals that use Joint Commission accreditation for deemed status purposes: The hospital's written policies address procedures regarding patient visitation rights, including any clinically necessary or reasonable restrictions or limitations.

2. The hospital informs the patient of his or her rights. (See also RI.01.01.03, EPs 1-3)
   Note: For hospitals that use Joint Commission accreditation for deemed status purposes: The hospital informs the patient (or support person, where appropriate) of his or her visitation rights. Visitation rights include the right to receive the visitors designated by the patient, including, but not limited to, a spouse, a domestic partner (including a same-sex domestic partner), another family member, or a friend. Also included is the right to withdraw or deny such consent at any time.

4. The hospital treats the patient in a dignified and respectful manner that supports his or her dignity.

5. The hospital respects the patient's right to and need for effective communication. (See also RI.01.01.03, EP 1)

6. The hospital respects the patient's cultural and personal values, beliefs, and preferences.

7. The hospital respects the patient's right to privacy. (See also IM.02.01.01, EPs 1-5)
   Note: This element of performance (EP) addresses a patient's personal privacy. For EPs addressing the privacy of a patient's health information, please refer to Standard IM.02.01.01.

8. The hospital respects the patient's right to pain management. (See also HR.01.04.01, EP 4; PC.01.02.07, EP 1; MS.03.01.03, EP 2)

9. The hospital accommodates the patient's right to religious and other spiritual services.

10. The hospital allows the patient to access, request amendment to, and obtain information on disclosures of his or her health information, in accordance with law and regulation.

Hospital Accreditation Program

28. The hospital allows a family member, friend, or other individual to be present with the patient for emotional support during the course of stay. Note: The hospital allows for the presence of a support individual of the patient's choice, unless the individual's presence infringes on others' rights, safety, or is medically or therapeutically contraindicated. The individual may or may not be the patient's surrogate decision-maker or legally authorized representative. (For more information on surrogate or family involvement in patient care, treatment, and services, refer to RI.01.02.01, EPs 6-8.)

29. The hospital prohibits discrimination based on age, race, ethnicity, religion, culture, language, physical or mental disability, socioeconomic status, sex, sexual orientation, and gender identity or expression.

APPENDIX B-2

Sources of Authority to Amend Sex Designation on Birth Certificates

Alabama Alabama will issue a birth certificate reflecting the proper sex. Amended birth certificates will note that the sex designation has been changed.

Statute: Ala. Code § 22-9A-19(d) (2004).

Text: (d) Upon receipt of a certified copy of an order of a court of competent jurisdiction indicating that the sex of an individual born in this state has been changed by surgical procedure and that the name of the individual has been changed, the certificate of birth of the individual shall be amended as prescribed by rules to reflect the changes.

Alaska Alaska will issue a birth certificate reflecting the proper sex. Alaska has a general regulation providing for the change of information on birth certificates. As with changes of name, changes of sex will be recognized with a court order. Amended birth certificates will note that the sex designation has been changed.

Statute: Alaska Stat. § 18.50.290 (2005).
Administrative Code: Alaska Admin. Code, tit. 7 §§ 05.895, 05.900 (2005)

Arizona Arizona will issue a birth certificate reflecting the proper sex.

Statute: Ariz. Rev. Stat. § 36-337 (A)(3) (2006).

Text:

A. The state registrar shall amend the birth certificate for a person born in this state when the state registrar receives any of the following: . . .

3. For a person who has undergone a sex change operation or has a chromosomal count that establishes the sex of the person as different than in the registered birth certificate, both of the following:

(a) A written request for an amended birth certificate from the person or, if the person is a child, from the child's parent or legal guardian.

(b) A written statement by a physician that verifies the sex change operation or chromosomal count.

Arkansas: Arkansas will issue a birth certificate reflecting the proper sex.

Statute: Ark. Code Ann. § 20-18-307(d) (2005).

Text: (d) Upon receipt of a certified copy of an order of a court of competent jurisdiction indicating that the sex of an individual born in this state has been changed by surgical procedure and that such individual's name has been changed, the certificate of birth of such individual shall be amended accordingly.

California California will issue a birth certificate reflecting the proper sex.

327

Statute: Cal. Health & Safety Code § 103425 (2006).

Text: Whenever a person born in this state has undergone surgical treatment for the purpose of altering his or her sexual characteristics to those of the opposite sex, a new birth certificate may be prepared for the person reflecting the change of gender and any change of name accomplished by an order of a court of this state, another state, the District of Columbia, or any territory of the United States. A petition for the issuance of a new birth certificate in those cases shall be filed with the superior court of the county where the petitioner resides.

Colorado   Colorado will issue a birth certificate reflecting the proper sex.

Statute: Colo. Rev. Stat. § 25-2-115(4) (2006).

Text: (4) Upon receipt of a certified copy of an order of a court of competent jurisdiction indicating that the sex of an individual born in this state has been changed by surgical procedure and that such individual's name has been changed, the certificate of birth of such individual shall be amended as prescribed by regulation.

Connecticut   Connecticut will issue a birth certificate reflecting the proper sex.

Statute: Conn. Gen. Stat. § 19a-42 (2003).

(a) … Only the commissioner may amend birth certificates to reflect changes concerning parentage or gender change. Amendments related to parentage or gender change shall result in the creation of a replacement certificate that supersedes the original, and shall in no way reveal the original language changed by the amendment. …

See also Conn. Gen. Stat. § 19a-42b (specifying procedure for changing out-of-state birth certificates for Connecticut residents); Conn. Agencies Regs. § 19a-41-9(e) (procedure for changing Connecticut birth certificates).

Delaware   Delaware will issue a birth certificate reflecting the proper sex.

Statute: Del. Code Ann. Tit. 16 § 3131(a) (2006).
Administrative Code: 40 700 049. Regulations for Title 16, Chapter 31 Relating to Vital Statistics Regulation 10.9(d)

Text: (d) Upon receipt of a certified copy of an order of a court of competent jurisdiction indicating the sex of an individual born in Delaware has been changed by surgical procedure and whether such individual's name has been changed, the certificate of birth of such individual shall be amended by preparing a new certificate. The item numbers of the entries that were amended shall not, however, be identified on the new certificate or on any certified copies that may be issued of that certificate.

District of Columbia   DC will issue a birth certificate reflecting the proper sex.

Statute: D.C. Code Ann. § 7-217 (d) (2006).

Text: (d) Upon receipt of a certified copy of an order of the Court indicating that the sex of an individual born in the District has changed by surgical procedure and that such individual's name has been changed, the certificate of birth of such individual shall be amended as prescribed by regulation.

Florida   Florida will issue a birth certificate reflecting the proper sex.

Statute: Fla. Stat. Ann. § 382.016 (2006)
Administrative Code: Fla. Admin. Code Ann. r. 64V-1.003(1)(f) (2006)

Notes: Florida Office of Vital Statistics policy allows for the change of sex designation on birth certificates upon the provision of: a completed Application for Amended Birth Certificate and notarized Affidavit of Amendment to Certificate of Live Birth; a certified copy of a court order of name change; a sworn affidavit from the physician who performed sex reassignment surgery, containing the medical license number, stating that you have completed sex reassignment in accordance with appropriate medical procedures and that you are now considered to be a member of the reassigned gender; and the required fee.

Georgia   Georgia will issue a birth certificate reflecting the proper sex.

Statute: Ga. Code Ann. § 31-10-23(e) (2005).

Text: (e) Upon receipt of a certified copy of a court order indicating the sex of an individual born in this state has been changed by surgical procedure and that such individual's name has been changed, the certificate of birth of such individual shall be amended as prescribed by regulation.

Hawai'i   Hawai'i will issue a birth certificate reflecting the proper sex.

Statute: Haw. Rev. Stat. Ann. § 338-17.7(a)(4)(B) (2005).

Text: (a) The department of health shall establish, in the following circumstances, a new certificate of birth for a person born in this State who already has a birth certificate filed with the department and who is referred to below as the "birth registrant": …

(4) Upon receipt of an affidavit of a physician that the physician has examined the birth registrant and has determined the following: …

(B) The birth registrant has had a sex change operation and the sex designation on the birth registrant's birth certificate is no longer correct; provided that the director of health may further investigate and require additional information that the director deems necessary.

Idaho   Idaho **will not** issue a birth certificate reflecting the proper sex. Although Idaho generally permits amendment of birth records upon an appropriate evidentiary showing, the Idaho Office of Vital Statistics reports that Idaho does not currently amend birth records to reflect the correct sex of individuals who have changed their sex by surgical procedure.

Statute: Idaho Code § 39-250 (2005).
Administrative Code: Idaho Admin. Code § 16.02.08.201 (2006).

Illinois   Illinois will issue a birth certificate reflecting the proper sex. The Division of Vital Records' current policy requires that individuals seeking to change the sex designation on their birth certificate have undergone sex reassignment surgery with a surgeon licensed to practice in the United States. Its policy also requires "completion of the entire gender reassignment" before the birth certificate will be changed.

Statute: 410 Ill. Comp. Stat. 535/17(1)(d) (2006).

Text: (1) For a person born in this State, the State Registrar of Vital Records shall establish a new certificate of birth when he receives any of the following . . .

(d) An affidavit by a physician that he has performed an operation on a person, and that by reason of the operation the sex designation on such person's birth record should be changed. The State Registrar of Vital Records may make any investigation or require any further information he deems necessary.

Indiana   Indiana will issue a birth certificate reflecting the proper sex. Indiana has a general statute providing for the change of information on birth certificates. The Vital Statistics Division will issue an amended birth certificate upon showing of a court order.

Statute: Ind. Code Ann. § 16-37-2-10(b) (2006)

Iowa   Iowa will issue a birth certificate reflecting the proper sex.

Statute: Iowa Code Ann. § 144.23(3) (2004).

Text: The state registrar shall establish a new certificate of birth for a person born in this state, when the state registrar receives the following: . . .

3. A notarized affidavit by a licensed physician and surgeon or osteopathic physician and surgeon stating that by reason of surgery or other treatment by the licensee, the sex designation of the person has been changed. The state registrar may make a further investigation or require further information necessary to determine whether a sex change has occurred.

Kansas   Kansas will issue a birth certificate reflecting the proper sex. Amended certificates will be marked "Amended," though the amended sections will not be specified.

Administrative Code: K.A.R. § 28-17-20 (b)(1)(A)(i) (2006).

Text: (i) The items recording the registrant's sex may be amended if the amendment is substantiated with the applicant's affidavit that the sex was incorrectly recorded or with a medical certificate substantiating that a physiological or anatomical change occurred.

Kentucky   Kentucky will issue a birth certificate reflecting the proper sex.

Statute: Ky. Rev. Stat. Ann. § 213.121(5) (2005).

Text: (5) Upon receipt of a sworn statement by a licensed physician indicating that the gender of an individual born in the Commonwealth has been changed by surgical procedure and a certified copy of an order of a court of competent jurisdiction changing that individual's name, the certificate of birth of the individual shall be amended as prescribed by regulation to reflect the change.

Louisiana   Louisiana will issue a birth certificate reflecting the proper sex.

Statute: La. Rev. Stat. Ann. § 40:62 (2006).

Text: (A) Any person born in Louisiana who has sustained sex reassignment or corrective surgery which has changed the anatomical structure of the sex of the individual to that of a sex other than that which appears on the original birth certificate of the individual, may petition a court of competent jurisdiction as provided in this Section to obtain a new certificate of birth.

Maine   Maine will issue a birth certificate reflecting the proper sex. The Office of Vital Records will issue an amended birth certificate upon the order of the local probate court and the payment of a fee. Applicants must submit to the court an Application for Correction and a letter from the treating physician verifying that the surgery/treatment has been "completed." The Office of Vital Records may issue a new certificate with no indication of the changes made.

Statute: Me. Rev. Stat. Ann. tit 22, § 2705 (2005).

Text: 1. Amended certificate. A certificate that has been altered or amended after its filing must be marked "amended," and the date on which the certificate or record was amended and a summary description of the evidence submitted in support of the correction must be endorsed on the record or permanently attached to it. Any certified copies of certificates or records amended under this section must be marked "amended." Notwithstanding this subsection, administrative correction of clerical errors within one year after the date of filing does not cause the certificate or record to be considered altered or amended.

Maryland   Maryland will issue a birth certificate reflecting the proper sex. Unless the court order specifies otherwise, amended certificates will show any changes that have been made.

Statute: Md. Code Ann, [Health - Gen.] § 4-214(b)(5) (2006).

Text: (5) Upon receipt of a certified copy of an order of a court of competent jurisdiction indicating the sex of an individual born in this State has been changed by surgical procedure and whether such individual's name has been changed, the Secretary shall amend the certificate of birth of the individual as prescribed by regulation.

Massachusetts   Massachusetts will issue a birth certificate reflecting the proper sex.

Statute: Mass Gen. Laws Ann. ch. 46, § 13(e) (2006).

Text: (e) If a person has completed sex reassignment surgery, so-called, and has had his name legally changed by a court of competent jurisdiction, the birth record of said person shall be amended to reflect the newly acquired sex and name, provided that an affidavit is received by the town clerk, executed by the person to whom the record relates, and accompanied by a physician's notarized statement that the person named on the birth record has completed sex reassignment surgery, so-called, and is not of the sex recorded on said record. Said affidavit shall also be accompanied by a certified copy of the legal change of name aforementioned above.

Michigan   Michigan will issue a birth certificate reflecting the proper sex.

Statute: Mich. Comp. Laws Ann. § 333.2831(c) (2006).

Text: (c) A request that a new certificate be established to show a sex designation other than that designated at birth. The request shall be accompanied by an affidavit of a physician certifying that sex-reassignment surgery has been performed.

Minnesota   Minnesota will issue a birth certificate reflecting the proper sex. The Minnesota Office of the State Registrar requires a court order in order to amend the sex designation on birth certificates. The court order must specify whether the original certificate is to be amended or a new certificate is to be issued.

Statute: Minn. Stat. Ann. § 144.218 (2006)
Administrative Code: Minn. Rules 4601.1100 (2006)

Mississippi   Mississippi will issue a birth certificate reflecting the proper sex.

Statute: Miss. Code Ann. § 41-57-21 (2006).
Administrative Code: Code Miss. R. 12 000 052, Rules 31-32

Text: Where there has been a bona fide effort to register a birth and the certificate thereof on file with the office of vital records does not divulge all of the information required by said certificate, or such certificate contains an incorrect first name, middle name, or sex, then the state registrar of vital records may, in his discretion, correct such certificate upon affidavit of at least two (2) reputable persons having personal knowledge of the facts in relation thereto. All other alterations shall be made as provided in Section 41-57-23. Anyone giving false information in such affidavit shall be subject to the penalties of perjury.

Missouri   Missouri will issue a birth certificate reflecting the proper sex. Amended birth certificates will be marked "Amended."

Statute: Mo. Ann. Stat. § 193.215(9) (2006).

Text: 9. Upon receipt of a certified copy of an order of a court of competent jurisdiction indicating the sex of an individual born in this state has been changed by surgical procedure and that such individual's name has been changed, the certificate of birth of such individual shall be amended.

Montana   Montana will issue a birth certificate reflecting the proper sex. The court order must specify whether the original certificate is to be amended or a new certificate issued.

Statute: Mont. Code Ann. § 50-15-204 (2005)

Administrative Code: Admin. R. Mont. 37.8.106(6) (2005).

Text: (6) The sex of a registrant as cited on a certificate may be amended only if the department receives a certified copy of the order of a court of competent jurisdiction indicating that the sex of an individual born in Montana has been changed by surgical procedure. The order must contain sufficient information for the department to locate the record. If the registrant's name is also to be changed, the court order must indicate the full name of the registrant as it appears on the birth certificate and the full name to which it is to be altered. Any certified copy issued after the amendment must indicate it was altered.

Nebraska   Nebraska will issue a birth certificate reflecting the proper sex.

Statute: Neb. Rev. Stat. § 71-604.01 (2005).

Text: Upon receipt of a notarized affidavit from the physician that performed sex reassignment surgery on an individual born in this state and a certified copy of an order of a court of competent jurisdiction changing the name of such person, the Department of Health and Human Services Finance and Support shall prepare a new certificate of birth in the new name and sex of such person in substantially the same form as that used for other live births. The evidence from which the new certificate is prepared and the original certificate of birth shall be available for inspection only upon the order of a court of competent jurisdiction.

Nevada   Nevada will issue a birth certificate reflecting the proper sex.

Administrative Code: Nev. Admin. Code. Ch. 440, § 130 (2006).

Text: 1. The state registrar may prepare a new certificate of birth for a person having a sexual transformation only upon order of a court of competent jurisdiction. 2. The court order must specify those facts to be changed on the new certificate. All other items must remain as on the original certificate.

New Hampshire   New Hampshire will issue a birth certificate reflecting the proper sex. Obtaining an order from the local probate court requires submission of an application, payment of a fee, and an evidentiary hearing. Unless otherwise specified by the court order, the amended certificate will specify what changes have been made.

Administrative Code: N.H. Code Admin. R. He-P 7007.03(e) (2004).

Text: (e) Upon receipt of a court order advising that such individual born in the state of New Hampshire has had a sex change, a new birth record shall be prepared in accordance with He-P 7007.02 to reflect such change.

New Jersey   New Jersey will issue a birth certificate reflecting the proper sex.

Statute: N.J. Stat. Ann. § 26:8-40.12 (2006).

Text: The State registrar shall issue an amended certificate of birth to a person born in this State who undergoes sex reassignment surgery and requests an amended certificate of birth which shows the sex and name of the person as it has been changed.

New Mexico   New Mexico will issue a birth certificate reflecting the proper sex.

Statute: N.M. Stat. Ann. § 24-14-25(D) (2006).

Text: D. Upon receipt of a duly notarized statement from the person in charge of an institution or from the attending physician indicating that the sex of an individual born in this state has been changed by surgical procedure, together with a certified copy of an order changing the name of the person, the certificate of birth of the individual shall be amended as prescribed by regulation.

New York   The state of New York will issue a birth certificate reflecting the proper sex. The New York State Department of Health, Vital Records Division has a policy providing for the change of sex designation on birth certificates upon the receipt of a completed application; a letter from the surgeon specifying date, place, and type of sex reassignment surgery performed; an operative report from the sex reassignment surgery; and some additional medical documentation. More detailed information can be obtained from the Department of Health, Vital Records Division in Albany, NY.

Administrative Code: N.Y. Comp. Codes R. & Regs. Tit 10, § 35.2 (2005)

New York City (has separate vital records division from the state) New York City will issue a birth certificate reflecting the proper sex.

Administrative Code: 24 RCNY Hlth. Code § 207.05(a)(5) (2005).

Text: (a) A new birth certificate shall be filed when . . . (5) The name of the person has been changed pursuant to court order and proof satisfactory to the Department has been submitted that such person has undergone convertive surgery.

North Carolina   North Carolina will issue a birth certificate reflecting the proper sex

Statute: N.C. Gen. Stat. §§ 130A-118(b)(4), (e) (2005).

Text: (b) A new certificate of birth shall be made by the State Registrar when . . .

(4) A written request from an individual is received by the State Registrar to change the sex on that individual's birth record because of sex reassignment surgery, if the request is accompanied by a notarized statement from the physician who performed the sex reassignment surgery or from a physician licensed to practice medicine who has examined the individual and can certify that the person has undergone sex reassignment surgery.

North Dakota   North Dakota will issue a birth certificate reflecting the proper sex.

Statute: N.D. Cent. Code § 23-02.1-25 (2005)
Administrative Code: N.D. Admin. Code § 33-04-12-02 (2006).

Text: Amendments as a result of gender identity change.

1. Evidence and documents required. The birth certificate of a person born in this state who has undergone a sex conversion operation may be amended as follows:

a. Upon written request of the person who has undergone the operation; and

b. An affidavit by a physician that the physician has performed an operation on the person, and that by reason of the operation, the sex designation of such person's birth certificate should be changed; and

c. An order of a court of competent jurisdiction decreeing a legal change in name.

2. New certificate. Pursuant to such amendment, a new certificate of birth will be created by the state registrar showing original data as transcribed from the original certificate excepting those

items that have been amended. The new certificate will be clearly marked in the upper margin with the word "amended".

3. Sealing of original certificate. The original certificate shall be then placed in a special file and shall not be open to inspection except by order of a court of competent jurisdiction or by the state registrar for purpose of carrying out the provisions of North Dakota Century Code chapter 23-02.1 and properly administering the vital records registration program.

Ohio   Ohio **will not issue** a birth certificate reflecting the correct sex.

Statute: Ohio Rev. Code § 3705.15 (2006).

Controlling case law: In re Ladrach, 32 Ohio Misc. 2d 6, 513 N.E.2d 828 (Ohio Prob. Ct. 1987) interpreting Ohio's birth certificate statute to be only a correction statute that does not encompass correction of sex on birth certificates of individuals who have changed their sex by surgical procedure.

Oklahoma   Oklahoma will issue a birth certificate reflecting the proper sex. While not specifically provided for by statute or regulation, it is the policy of the Vital Records Bureau to issue new birth certificates for applicants who have undergone sex reassignment, pursuant to the generally applicable procedures.

Statute: 63 Okl. Stat. Ann. § 1-321 (2006).
Administrative Code: Okla. Admin. Code 310:105-3-3 (2006).

Oregon   Oregon will issue a birth certificate reflecting the proper sex.

Statute: Or. Rev. Stat. § 432.235(4) (2005).

Text: (4) Upon receipt of a certified copy of an order of a court of competent jurisdiction indicating that the sex of an individual born in this state has been changed by surgical procedure and whether such individual's name has been changed, the certificate of birth of such individual shall be amended as prescribed by rule of the state registrar.

Pennsylvania   Pennsylvania will issue a birth certificate reflecting the proper sex. Although not specifically mentioned in the statute, the Division of Vital Records will issue a revised birth certificate upon court order. If the applicant has only obtained a court order for name change, a statement from the treating surgeon is also necessary, stating that reassignment surgery has been performed.

Statute: 35 Penn. Stat. § 450.603 (2005).

Rhode Island   Rhode Island will issue a birth certificate reflecting the proper sex. For changes to the sex designation on birth certificates, the Office of Vital Records has a policy requiring a notarized statement from the hospital or clinic where surgery was performed, signed by the physician in charge of the surgery. The amended certificate will state only that the name has been amended; it will not show the former name.

Statute: R.I. Gen. Laws § 23-3-21 (2005).
Administrative Code: R.I. Code R. 14 170 001 §§ 35-37 (2004).

South Carolina   South Carolina will issue a birth certificate reflecting the proper sex. Although not explicitly addressed by statute or administrative code, South Carolina will issue an amendment as an attachment to the original birth certificate.

Statute: S.C. Code Ann. § 44-63-150 (2005).
Administrative Code: S.C. Code Ann. Regs. 61-19 (2006).

South Dakota   South Dakota will issue a birth certificate reflecting the proper sex. Although not specifically mentioned in the statute, the State Registrar does provides amended certificates to reflect sex reassignment. Although the Registrar will follow any specific instructions in a court order, their general policy is to issue a new certificate with no indication of amendment.

Administrative Code: S.D. Admin. R. 44:09:05:02 (2006).

Tennessee   Tennessee **will not** issue a birth certificate reflecting the proper sex. This is the only state that has a statute specifically forbidding the correction of sex designations on birth certificates for transgender people.

Statute: Tenn. Code Ann. § 68-3-203(d) (2006).

Text: The sex of an individual will not be changed on the original certificate of birth as a result of sex change surgery.

Texas   Before *Littleton v. Prange*, Texas issued new birth certificates. Anecdotal reports now indicate that **some officials refuse to correct the sex designation** on transgender people's birth certificates, although judges may order such a change.

Statue: Tex. Health & Safety Code Ann. § 192.011 (2006).

Controlling case law: *Littleton v. Prange*, 9 S.W.3d 223 (Tex. Civ. App., 1999) (holding that a postoperative male-to-female transsexual is male as a matter of law). Anecdotal reports indicate that some Texas officials do not permit postoperative transsexuals to correct the sex designation on their birth certificate.

Utah   Utah will issue a birth certificate reflecting the proper sex. Amended certificates will state that an amendment has been made. Older certificates may simply be amended directly on the face of the document, with all changes visible.

Statute: Utah Code Ann. § 26-2-11 (2004).

Text: § 26-2-11. Name or sex change -- Registration of court order and amendment of birth certificate

(1) When a person born in this state has a name change or sex change approved by an order of a Utah district court or a court of competent jurisdiction of another state or a province of Canada, a certified copy of the order may be filed with the state registrar with an application form provided by the registrar.
(2) (a) Upon receipt of the application, a certified copy of the order, and payment of the required fee, the state registrar shall review the application, and if complete, register it and note the fact of the amendment on the otherwise unaltered original certificate.

(b) The amendment shall be registered with and become a part of the original certificate and a certified copy shall be issued to the applicant without additional cost.

Vermont   Vermont will issue a birth certificate reflecting the proper sex. Vermont has a general statute providing for the change of information on birth certificates via court order. Unless specified by the court order, the amended certificate will show all changes that have been made.

Statute: 18 Vt. Stat. §§ 5075, 5076 (2005).

Virginia   Virginia will issue a birth certificate reflecting the proper sex. The Virginia Department of Health has indicated that it is not necessary to present a court order designating the new sex as long as the necessary medical documentation is provided.

Statute: Va. Code Ann. § 32.1-269(E) (2006).

Text: E. Upon receipt of a certified copy of an order of a court of competent jurisdiction indicating that the sex of an individual has been changed by medical procedure and upon request of such person, the State Registrar shall amend such person's certificate of birth to show the change of sex and, if a certified copy of a court order changing the person's name is submitted, to show a new name.

Administrative Code: 12 Va. Admin. Code § 5-550-320 (2006).

Text: 5-550-420 Change of Sex. Except as provided in subdivision 3 of 12 VAC 5-550-450 [concerning intersex conditions], upon presentation of acceptable evidence (preoperative diagnosis, postoperative diagnosis and description of procedure) and a notarized affidavit from the physician performing the surgery, a new certificate of birth may be prepared by the State Registrar for a person born in this Commonwealth whose sex has been changed by surgical gender reassignment procedure. A certified copy of the court order changing the name of the registrant as well as designating the sex of the registrant must be in the possession of the State Registrar together with a request that a new certificate be prepared.

Washington   The State of Washington will issue a birth certificate reflecting the proper sex. **Washington's statutes and administrative code are silent** about amending vital records. The Department of Health's policy is to issue an amended certificate upon submission of either a court order or a letter from the treating surgeon attesting to the change of sex.

West Virginia   West Virginia will issue a birth certificate reflecting the proper sex. The practice of the State Registrar is to issue an amended birth certificate upon submission of either a court order or a notarized statement from the treating physician that reassignment surgery has been completed.

Statute: W. Va. Code § 16-5-24 (2006).
Administrative Code: W. Va. Code St. R. § 64-32-6 (2006).

Wisconsin   Wisconsin will issue a birth certificate reflecting the proper sex. The court order must specify whether the original certificate is to be amended or a new certificate issued.

Statute: Wis. Stat. Ann. § 69.15 (2006).

Text: (1) BIRTH CERTIFICATE INFORMATION CHANGES. The state registrar may change information on a birth certificate registered in this state which was correct at the time the birth certificate was filed under a court or administrative order issued in this state, in another state or in Canada or under the valid order of a court of any federally recognized Indian tribe, band or nation if:

(a)   The order provides for an adoption, name change or name change with sex change or establishes paternity; and

(b)   A clerk of court or, for a paternity action, a clerk of court or county child support agency under s. 59.53 (5), sends the state registrar a certified report of an order of a court in this state on a form supplied by the state registrar or, in the case of any other order, the state registrar receives a certified copy of the order and the proper fee under s. 69.22.

Wyoming   Wyoming will issue a birth certificate reflecting the proper sex. Unless other specified by court order, the amended certificate will show all changes that have been made.

Statute: Wyo. Stat. Ann. § 35-1-424 (2005).
Administrative Code: WY Rules and Regulations HLTH VR Ch. 10 s 4(e)(iii) (2004).

Text: (iii) When the sex of an individual has been changed, a court order shall be required to amend the birth certificate.

APPENDIX B-3

U.S. Department of Justice
Civil Division, Appellate Staff
950 Pennsylvania Ave., NW, Rm 7261
Washington, DC 20530

Tel: (202) 353-8253
Fax: (202) 514-8151

February 24, 2010

VIA ELECTRONIC FILING

Margaret Carter
Clerk of the United States Court of Appeals
 for the First Circuit
John Joseph Moakley U.S. Courthouse
1 Courthouse Way, Suite 2500
Boston, MA 02210

>   Re: Massachusetts v. HHS et al., No. 10-2204
>   Hara et al. v. OPM et al., Nos. 10-2207, and 10-2214

Dear Ms. Carter:

Please see the attached letters relating to the above-captioned cases.

Respectfully submitted,

/s/ Benjamin S. Kingsley
Benjamin S. Kingsley
Attorney, Appellate Staff
Civil Division, Room 7261
United States Department of Justice
950 Pennsylvania Ave., NW
Washington, DC 20530-0001

Counsel for Respondents

CERTIFICATE OF SERVICE

I hereby certify that on February 24, 2011, I caused a copy of the foregoing to be filed

electronically with the Court using the Court's CM/ECF system, and also caused four paper

copies to be delivered to the Court by hand delivery within two business days. I also hereby

certify that the participants in the case will be served via the CM/ECF system.

/s/ Benjamin S. Kingsley
Benjamin S. Kingsley
Benjamin.S.Kingsley@usdoj.gov
Attorney, Appellate Staff
Civil Division, Room 7261
United States Department of Justice
950 Pennsylvania Ave., NW
Washington, DC 20530-0001

U. S. Department of Justice

Civil Division

Assistant Attorney General   *Washington. D.C. 20530*

February 24, 2011

VIA ECF

Margaret Carter
Clerk of the United States Court of Appeals
 for the First Circuit
John Joseph Moakley U.S. Courthouse
1 Courthouse Way, Suite 2500
Boston, MA 02210

       Re: Litigation Involving Section 3 of the Defense of Marriage Act, 1 U.S.C. § 7

Dear Ms. Carter:

       The President and Attorney General have recently made a determination regarding the constitutionality of Section 3 of the Defense of Marriage Act ("DOMA"), 1 U.S.C. § 7. Pursuant to the attached letter, the Attorney General and President have concluded: that heightened scrutiny is the appropriate standard of review for classifications based on sexual orientation; that, consistent with that standard, Section 3 of DOMA may not be constitutionally applied to same-sex couples whose marriages are legally recognized under state law; and that the Department will cease its defense of Section 3 in such cases.

       The following cases involving Section 3 of DOMA are pending in this jurisdiction:

Massachusetts v. HHS et al. (1st Cir. No. 10-2204)
Hara et al. v. OPM et al. (1st Cir. Nos. 10-2207 and 10-2214)

       Further, as the Attorney General explained in the attached letter, we hereby "notify the courts of our interest in providing Congress a full and fair opportunity to participate in the litigation in those cases." In addition, we "will remain parties to the case and continue to represent the interests of the United States throughout the litigation."

                                Respectfully submitted,

                                Tony West
                                Assistant Attorney General

Office of the Attorney General
Washington, D. C. 20530

February 23, 2011

The Honorable John A. Boehner
Speaker
U.S. House of Representatives
Washington, DC 20515

Re: <u>Defense of Marriage Act</u>

Dear Mr. Speaker:

After careful consideration, including review of a recommendation from me, the President of the United States has made the determination that Section 3 of the Defense of Marriage Act ("DOMA"), 1 U.S.C. § 7,[1] as applied to same-sex couples who are legally married under state law, violates the equal protection component of the Fifth Amendment. Pursuant to 28 U.S.C. § 530D, I am writing to advise you of the Executive Branch's determination and to inform you of the steps the Department will take in two pending DOMA cases to implement that determination.

While the Department has previously defended DOMA against legal challenges involving legally married same-sex couples, recent lawsuits that challenge the constitutionality of DOMA Section 3 have caused the President and the Department to conduct a new examination of the defense of this provision. In particular, in November 2011, plaintiffs filed two new lawsuits challenging the constitutionality of Section 3 of DOMA in jurisdictions without precedent on whether sexual-orientation classifications are subject to rational basis review or whether they must satisfy some form of heightened scrutiny. *Windsor v. United States*, No. 1:10-cv-8435 (S.D.N.Y.); *Pedersen v. OPM*, No. 3:10-cv-1750 (D. Conn.). Previously, the Administration has defended Section 3 in jurisdictions where circuit courts have already held that classifications

---

[1] DOMA Section 3 states: "In determining the meaning of any Act of Congress, or of any ruling, regulation, or interpretation of the various administrative bureaus and agencies of the United States, the word 'marriage' means only a legal union between one man and one woman as husband and wife, and the word 'spouse' refers only to a person of the opposite sex who is a husband or a wife."

based on sexual orientation are subject to rational basis review, and it has advanced arguments to defend DOMA Section 3 under the binding standard that has applied in those cases.[2]

These new lawsuits, by contrast, will require the Department to take an affirmative position on the level of scrutiny that should be applied to DOMA Section 3 in a circuit without binding precedent on the issue. As described more fully below, the President and I have concluded that classifications based on sexual orientation warrant heightened scrutiny and that, as applied to same-sex couples legally married under state law, Section 3 of DOMA is unconstitutional.

Standard of Review

The Supreme Court has yet to rule on the appropriate level of scrutiny for classifications based on sexual orientation. It has, however, rendered a number of decisions that set forth the criteria that should inform this and any other judgment as to whether heightened scrutiny applies: (1) whether the group in question has suffered a history of discrimination; (2) whether individuals "exhibit obvious, immutable, or distinguishing characteristics that define them as a discrete group"; (3) whether the group is a minority or is politically powerless; and (4) whether the characteristics distinguishing the group have little relation to legitimate policy objectives or to an individual's "ability to perform or contribute to society." *See Bowen v. Gilliard*, 483 U.S. 587, 602-03 (1987); *City of Cleburne v. Cleburne Living Ctr.*, 473 U.S. 432, 441-42 (1985).

Each of these factors counsels in favor of being suspicious of classifications based on sexual orientation. First and most importantly, there is, regrettably, a significant history of purposeful discrimination against gay and lesbian people, by governmental as well as private entities, based on prejudice and stereotypes that continue to have ramifications today. Indeed, until very recently, states have "demean[ed] the[] existence" of gays and lesbians "by making their private sexual conduct a crime." *Lawrence v. Texas*, 539 U.S. 558, 578 (2003).[3]

---

[2] *See, e.g., Dragovich v. U.S. Department of the Treasury*, 2011 WL 175502 (N.D. Cal. Jan. 18, 2011); *Gill v. Office of Personnel Management*, 699 F. Supp. 2d 374 (D. Mass. 2010); *Smelt v. County of Orange*, 374 F. Supp. 2d 861, 880 (C.D. Cal.,2005); *Wilson v. Ake*, 354 F.Supp.2d 1298, 1308 (M.D. Fla. 2005); *In re Kandu*, 315 B.R. 123, 145 (Bkrtcy. W.D. Wash. 2004); *In re Levenson*, 587 F.3d 925, 931 (9th Cir. E.D.R. Plan Administrative Ruling 2009).
[3] While significant, that history of discrimination is different in some respects from the discrimination that burdened African-Americans and women. *See Adarand Constructors, Inc. v. Pena*, 515 U.S. 200, 216 (1995) (classifications based on race "must be viewed in light of the historical fact that the central purpose of the Fourteenth Amendment was to eliminate racial discrimination emanating from official sources in the States," and "[t]his strong policy renders racial classifications 'constitutionally suspect.'"); *United States v. Virginia*, 518 U.S. 515, 531 (1996) (observing that "'our Nation has had a long and unfortunate history of sex discrimination'" and pointing out the denial of the right to vote to women until 1920). In the case of sexual orientation, some of the discrimination has been based on the incorrect belief that sexual orientation is a behavioral characteristic that can be changed or subject to moral approbation. *Cf. Cleburne*, 473 U.S. at 441 (heightened scrutiny may be warranted for characteristics "beyond the individual's control" and that "very likely reflect outmoded notions of the relative capabilities of" the group at issue); *Boy Scouts of America v. Dale*, 530 U.S. 640 (2000) (Stevens, J., dissenting) ("Unfavorable opinions about homosexuals 'have ancient roots.'" (quoting *Bowers*, 478 U.S. at 192)).

2

Second, while sexual orientation carries no visible badge, a growing scientific consensus accepts that sexual orientation is a characteristic that is immutable, *see* Richard A. Posner, Sex and Reason 101 (1992); it is undoubtedly unfair to require sexual orientation to be hidden from view to avoid discrimination, *see* Don't Ask, Don't Tell Repeal Act of 2010, Pub. L. No. 111-321, 124 Stat. 3515 (2010).

Third, the adoption of laws like those at issue in *Romer v. Evans,* 517 U.S. 620 (1996), and *Lawrence*, the longstanding ban on gays and lesbians in the military, and the absence of federal protection for employment discrimination on the basis of sexual orientation show the group to have limited political power and "ability to attract the [favorable] attention of the lawmakers." *Cleburne*, 473 U.S. at 445. And while the enactment of the Matthew Shepard Act and pending repeal of Don't Ask, Don't Tell indicate that the political process is not closed *entirely* to gay and lesbian people, that is not the standard by which the Court has judged "political powerlessness." Indeed, when the Court ruled that gender-based classifications were subject to heightened scrutiny, women already had won major political victories such as the Nineteenth Amendment (right to vote) and protection under Title VII (employment discrimination).

Finally, there is a growing acknowledgment that sexual orientation "bears no relation to ability to perform or contribute to society." *Frontiero v. Richardson*, 411 U.S. 677, 686 (1973) (plurality). Recent evolutions in legislation (including the pending repeal of Don't Ask, Don't Tell), in community practices and attitudes, in case law (including the Supreme Court's holdings in *Lawrence* and *Romer*), and in social science regarding sexual orientation all make clear that sexual orientation is not a characteristic that generally bears on legitimate policy objectives. *See, e.g.,* Statement by the President on the Don't Ask, Don't Tell Repeal Act of 2010 ("It is time to recognize that sacrifice, valor and integrity are no more defined by sexual orientation than they are by race or gender, religion or creed.")

To be sure, there is substantial circuit court authority applying rational basis review to sexual-orientation classifications. We have carefully examined each of those decisions. Many of them reason only that if consensual same-sex sodomy may be criminalized under *Bowers v. Hardwick*, then it follows that no heightened review is appropriate – a line of reasoning that does not survive the overruling of *Bowers* in *Lawrence v. Texas*, 538 U.S. 558 (2003).[4] Others rely on claims regarding "procreational responsibility" that the Department has disavowed already in litigation as unreasonable, or claims regarding the immutability of sexual orientation that we do not believe can be reconciled with more recent social science understandings.[5] And none

---

[4] *See Equality Foundation v. City of Cincinnati*, 54 F.3d 261, 266–67 & n. 2. (6th Cir. 1995); *Steffan v. Perry*, 41 F.3d 677, 685 (D.C. Cir. 1994); *Woodward v. United States*, 871 F.2d 1068, 1076 (Fed. Cir. 1989); *Ben-Shalom v. Marsh*, 881 F.2d 454, 464 (7th Cir. 1989); *Padula v. Webster*, 822 F.2d 97, 103 (D.C. Cir. 1987).

[5] *See, e.g., Lofton v. Secretary of the Dep't of Children & Family Servs.*, 358 F.3d 804, 818 (11th Cir. 2004) (discussing child-rearing rationale*); High Tech Gays v. Defense Indust. Sec. Clearance Office*, 895 F.2d 563, 571 (9th Cir. 1990) (discussing immutability). As noted, this Administration has already disavowed in litigation the

engages in an examination of all the factors that the Supreme Court has identified as relevant to a decision about the appropriate level of scrutiny. Finally, many of the more recent decisions have relied on the fact that the Supreme Court has not recognized that gays and lesbians constitute a suspect class or the fact that the Court has applied rational basis review in its most recent decisions addressing classifications based on sexual orientation, *Lawrence* and *Romer*.[6] But neither of those decisions reached, let alone resolved, the level of scrutiny issue because in both the Court concluded that the laws could not even survive the more deferential rational basis standard.

Application to Section 3 of DOMA

In reviewing a legislative classification under heightened scrutiny, the government must establish that the classification is "substantially related to an important government objective." *Clark v. Jeter*, 486 U.S. 456, 461 (1988). Under heightened scrutiny, "a tenable justification must describe actual state purposes, not rationalizations for actions in fact differently grounded." *United States v. Virginia*, 518 U.S. 515, 535-36 (1996). "The justification must be genuine, not hypothesized or invented post hoc in response to litigation." *Id.* at 533.

In other words, under heightened scrutiny, the United States cannot defend Section 3 by advancing hypothetical rationales, independent of the legislative record, as it has done in circuits where precedent mandates application of rational basis review. Instead, the United States can defend Section 3 only by invoking Congress' actual justifications for the law.

Moreover, the legislative record underlying DOMA's passage contains discussion and debate that undermines any defense under heightened scrutiny. The record contains numerous expressions reflecting moral disapproval of gays and lesbians and their intimate and family relationships – precisely the kind of stereotype-based thinking and animus the Equal Protection Clause is designed to guard against.[7] *See Cleburne*, 473 U.S. at 448 ("mere negative attitudes, or

---

argument that DOMA serves a governmental interest in "responsible procreation and child-rearing." H.R. Rep. No. 104-664, at 13. As the Department has explained in numerous filings, since the enactment of DOMA, many leading medical, psychological, and social welfare organizations have concluded, based on numerous studies, that children raised by gay and lesbian parents are as likely to be well-adjusted as children raised by heterosexual parents.
[6] *See Cook v. Gates*, 528 F.3d 42, 61 (1st Cir. 2008); *Citizens for Equal Prot. v. Bruning*, 455 F.3d 859, 866 (8th Cir. 2006); *Johnson v. Johnson*, 385 F.3d 503, 532 (5th Cir. 2004); *Veney v. Wyche*, 293 F.3d 726, 732 (4th Cir. 2002); *Equality Foundation of Greater Cincinnati, Inc. v. City of Cincinnati*, 128 F.3d 289, 292-94 (6th Cir. 1997).

[7] *See, e.g.*, H.R. Rep. at 15–16 (judgment [opposing same-sex marriage] entails both moral disapproval of homosexuality and a moral conviction that heterosexuality better comports with traditional (especially Judeo-Christian) morality"); *id.* at 16 (same-sex marriage "legitimates a public union, a legal status that most people . . . feel ought to be illegitimate" and "put[s] a stamp of approval . . . on a union that many people . . . think is immoral"); *id.* at 15 ("Civil laws that permit only heterosexual marriage reflect and honor a collective moral judgment about human sexuality"); *id.* (reasons behind heterosexual marriage—procreation and child-rearing—are "in accord with nature and hence have a moral component"); *id.* at 31 (favorably citing the holding in *Bowers* that an "anti-sodomy law served the rational purpose of expressing the presumed belief . . . that homosexual sodomy is immoral and unacceptable"); *id.* at 17 n.56 (favorably citing statement in dissenting opinion in *Romer* that "[t]his Court has no business . . . pronouncing that 'animosity' toward homosexuality is evil").

4

fear" are not permissible bases for discriminatory treatment); *see also Romer*, 517 U.S. at 635 (rejecting rationale that law was supported by "the liberties of landlords or employers who have personal or religious objections to homosexuality"); *Palmore v. Sidotti*, 466 U.S. 429, 433 (1984) ("Private biases may be outside the reach of the law, but the law cannot, directly or indirectly, give them effect.").

Application to Second Circuit Cases

After careful consideration, including a review of my recommendation, the President has concluded that given a number of factors, including a documented history of discrimination, classifications based on sexual orientation should be subject to a heightened standard of scrutiny. The President has also concluded that Section 3 of DOMA, as applied to legally married same-sex couples, fails to meet that standard and is therefore unconstitutional. Given that conclusion, the President has instructed the Department not to defend the statute in *Windsor* and *Pedersen*, now pending in the Southern District of New York and the District of Connecticut. I concur in this determination.

Notwithstanding this determination, the President has informed me that Section 3 will continue to be enforced by the Executive Branch. To that end, the President has instructed Executive agencies to continue to comply with Section 3 of DOMA, consistent with the Executive's obligation to take care that the laws be faithfully executed, unless and until Congress repeals Section 3 or the judicial branch renders a definitive verdict against the law's constitutionality. This course of action respects the actions of the prior Congress that enacted DOMA, and it recognizes the judiciary as the final arbiter of the constitutional claims raised.

As you know, the Department has a longstanding practice of defending the constitutionality of duly-enacted statutes if reasonable arguments can be made in their defense, a practice that accords the respect appropriately due to a coequal branch of government. However, the Department in the past has declined to defend statutes despite the availability of professionally responsible arguments, in part because the Department does not consider every plausible argument to be a "reasonable" one. "[D]ifferent cases can raise very different issues with respect to statutes of doubtful constitutional validity," and thus there are "a variety of factors that bear on whether the Department will defend the constitutionality of a statute." Letter to Hon. Orrin G. Hatch from Assistant Attorney General Andrew Fois at 7 (Mar. 22, 1996). This is the rare case where the proper course is to forgo the defense of this statute. Moreover, the Department has declined to defend a statute "in cases in which it is manifest that the President has concluded that the statute is unconstitutional," as is the case here. Seth P. Waxman, *Defending Congress*, 79 N.C. L.Rev. 1073, 1083 (2001).

In light of the foregoing, I will instruct the Department's lawyers to immediately inform the district courts in *Windsor* and *Pedersen* of the Executive Branch's view that heightened scrutiny is the appropriate standard of review and that, consistent with that standard, Section 3 of

Case: 10-2204   Document: 00116175339   Page: 9   Date Filed: 02/24/2011   Entry ID: 5528735

DOMA may not be constitutionally applied to same-sex couples whose marriages are legally recognized under state law. If asked by the district courts in the Second Circuit for the position of the United States in the event those courts determine that the applicable standard is rational basis, the Department will state that, consistent with the position it has taken in prior cases, a reasonable argument for Section 3's constitutionality may be proffered under that permissive standard. Our attorneys will also notify the courts of our interest in providing Congress a full and fair opportunity to participate in the litigation in those cases. We will remain parties to the case and continue to represent the interests of the United States throughout the litigation.

Furthermore, pursuant to the President's instructions, and upon further notification to Congress, I will instruct Department attorneys to advise courts in other pending DOMA litigation of the President's and my conclusions that a heightened standard should apply, that Section 3 is unconstitutional under that standard and that the Department will cease defense of Section 3.

A motion to dismiss in the *Windsor* and *Pedersen* cases would be due on March 11, 2011. Please do not hesitate to contact us if you have any questions.

Sincerely yours,

Eric H. Holder, Jr.
Attorney General

APPENDIX B-4

DEPARTMENT OF HEALTH & HUMAN SERVICES
Centers for Medicare & Medicaid Services
7500 Security Boulevard, Mail Stop S2-26-12
Baltimore, Maryland 21244-1850

Center for Medicaid, CHIP and Survey & Certification

SMDL # 11-006

June 10, 2011

**RE: Same Sex Partners and Medicaid Liens,
Transfers of Assets, and Estate Recovery**

Dear State Medicaid Director:

The purpose of this letter is to ensure that States are informed of the existing options and flexibilities regarding the application of Medicaid liens, transfer of assets, and estate recovery. Specifically, this letter is intended to advise States of existing choices and options regarding spousal and domestic partner protections related to liens, transfer of assets, and estate recovery.

Liens:
Section 1917(a) of the Social Security Act (the Act) allows, but does not require, States to impose liens on the property of a Medicaid beneficiary under certain circumstances.

More specifically, liens are permitted in two instances prior to a beneficiary's death:
1) when there has been a court judgment that benefits were incorrectly paid; or
2) when the lien is imposed against the real property of an individual
   a. who is an inpatient in a nursing facility, intermediate care facility for the mentally retarded, or other medical institution, if the individual is required to spend for medical care all but a minimal amount of his or her income, and
   b. with whom the State determines that the individual cannot reasonably be expected to be discharged from the institution and return home.

State plans must specify the medical assistance services that are subject to recovery.

Section 1917(a)(2) of the Act provides important beneficiary protections from liens. Liens may not be imposed in instances where certain people are lawfully residing in the home. These individuals include:
1) a spouse (as defined in the Defense of Marriage Act of 1996 [DOMA] Pub. L. No. 104-199),
2) a child under age 21,
3) children who are blind or totally/permanently disabled, and
4) siblings residing in the beneficiary's home who have an equity interest in such home and were residing in the home for at least 1 year immediately before the date the individual was admitted to the medical institution.

Page 2 – State Medicaid Director

The Federal beneficiary protections listed above represent the minimum level of protection, in other words, the "floor" for protection from imposition of liens, that must be implemented by the State. States have considerable flexibility to determine the "ceiling" for such protection and to develop their own rules regarding when they will impose/pursue liens, as long as the Federal beneficiary protections noted above are fully implemented. A State can have a policy or rule not to pursue liens when the same-sex spouse or domestic partner of the Medicaid beneficiary continues to lawfully reside in the home.

States choosing not to pursue liens when the same-sex spouse or domestic partner beneficiary continues to lawfully reside in the home would exercise their existing discretion in determining the scope or circumstances, either prior to, or when pursuing liens. States are encouraged to incorporate their criteria for determining when to impose a lien in the Medicaid State plan.

Transfers of Assets:
States are required to have provisions regarding transfers of assets for less than fair market value under sections 1902(a)(18) and 1917(c) of the Act. A State Medicaid plan must provide that, if an institutionalized individual or the spouse of an individual transfers assets for less than fair market value after the "look-back" date defined in the statute, the State will calculate and impose a period of ineligibility. Medicaid payment is not available for the long-term care services the individual receives during the period of ineligibility, although the individual remains eligible for Medicaid coverage of non-long term care State plan services.

While periods of ineligibility are generally required, the Act establishes certain exceptions to the provisions regarding transfers of assets to prevent hardship, allowing individuals who have transferred assets to receive long-term care services without the imposition of any penalty period in certain circumstances. The statute specifically exempts transfers of any type of asset to a spouse or to another person for the sole benefit of the spouse under section 1917(c)(2)(B)(i) of the Act, and also exempts the transfer of a home to a spouse under section 1917(c)(2)(A)(i) of the Act. The exemptions for transferring assets to a spouse cannot be directly applied to same-sex spouses or partners as a result of DOMA.

However, under section 1917(c)(2)(D) of the Act, a transfer of assets penalty period will not be applied if the State determines, under procedures established by the State, that denial of eligibility would create an undue hardship. The Deficit Reduction Act of 2005 (DRA, Pub. L. No. 109-171) provided that, in applying this provision, States should determine that an undue hardship exists when application of the transfer of assets penalty and denial of eligibility for Medicaid payment for long-term care would deprive the individual of medical care such that the individual's health or life would be endangered, or the individual would be deprived of food, clothing, shelter, or other necessities of life.

The Centers for Medicare & Medicaid Services has provided guidance on undue hardship determinations in the State Medicaid Manual and in a State Medicaid Director letter (SMD #06-018, dated July 27, 2006) emphasizing that States have considerable flexibility in determining whether undue hardship exists, and the circumstances under which they will not impose transfer of assets penalties. Because of the flexibility afforded to States in determining undue hardship, we believe that States may adopt criteria, or even presumptions, that recognize

Page 3 – State Medicaid Director

that imposing transfer of assets penalties on the basis of the transfer of ownership interests in a shared home to a same-sex spouse or domestic partner would constitute an undue hardship.

Estate Recovery:
Sections 1902(a)(18) and 1917(b)(1) of the Act require States to pursue estate recovery when a Medicaid beneficiary received medical assistance under the State plan: 1) in cases where a lien has been imposed under the State's lien authority, and 2) for recipients age 55 and over, who received nursing facility services, home and community-based services, or related hospital and prescription drug services. States may optionally seek recovery to pay for costs of other approved State plan services provided to those 55 and over, except Medicare cost sharing paid on behalf of Medicare Savings Program beneficiaries on or after January 1, 2010, as provided in Section 115 of the Medicare Improvements for Patients and Providers Act of 2008 (MIPPA), Pub. L. 110-275).

Per section 1917(b)(2) of the Act, Medicaid estate recovery may be made only when there is no surviving spouse (subject to the provisions in DOMA) and when there is no surviving child under age 21, or blind or disabled child of any age. When estate recovery occurs pursuant to a lien, protections are afforded for siblings still lawfully residing in the home, as well as for sons or daughters who provided care to the parents and who continue to lawfully reside in the home.

In addition, States are required by section 1917(b)(3) of the Act to have procedures to waive estate recovery where it would create an undue hardship for the deceased Medicaid recipient's heirs. States have flexibility to design reasonable criteria for determining what constitutes an undue hardship and who may be afforded protection from estate recovery in such instances. At the State's discretion, this may include establishing reasonable protections applicable to the same-sex spouse or domestic partner of a deceased Medicaid recipient. The State plan need only specify the criteria for waiver of estate recovery claims due to undue hardship.

We hope this guidance regarding existing options for liens, transfer of assets, and estate recovery provides useful clarification regarding State plan flexibilities available to all Medicaid recipients, regardless of sexual orientation. If you have any questions regarding the guidance pertaining to liens and estate recovery, please contact Nancy Dieter, Technical Director, Division of Integrated Health Systems at 410-786-7219, or by email at nancy.dieter@cms.hhs.gov. Questions pertaining to transfers of assets may be referred to Roy Trudel, Technical Director, Division of Eligibility, Enrollment and Outreach at 410-786-3417, or by email at roy.trudel@cms.hhs.gov.

Sincerely,

/s/

Cindy Mann
Director

Page 4 – State Medicaid Director

cc:

CMS Regional Administrators

CMS Associate Regional Administrators
Division of Medicaid and Children's Health

Matt Salo
President
National Association of Medicaid Directors

Alan R. Weil, J.D., M.P.P.
Executive Director
National Academy for State Health Policy

Director of Health Legislation
National Governors Association

Christine Evans, M.P.H.
Director, Government Relations
Association of State and Territorial Health Officials

Rick Fenton
Acting Director
Health Services Division
American Public Human Services Association

Joy Wilson
Director, Health Committee
National Conference of State Legislatures

Debra Miller
Director for Health Policy
Council of State Governments

APPENDIX B-5

DEPARTMENT OF HEALTH AND HUMAN SERVICES

Centers for Medicare & Medicaid Services

42 CFR Parts 482 and 485

[CMS-3228-F]

RIN 0938-AQ06

Medicare and Medicaid Programs: Changes to the Hospital and Critical Access Hospital Conditions of Participation to Ensure Visitation Rights for All Patients

AGENCY: Centers for Medicare & Medicaid Services (CMS), HHS.

ACTION: Final rule.

SUMMARY: This final rule will revise the Medicare conditions of participation for hospitals and critical access hospitals (CAHs) to provide visitation rights to Medicare and Medicaid patients. Specifically, Medicare- and Medicaid-participating hospitals and CAHs will be required to have written policies and procedures regarding the visitation rights of patients, including those setting forth any clinically necessary or reasonable restriction or limitation that the hospital or CAH may need to place on such rights as well as the reasons for the clinical restriction or limitation.

EFFECTIVE DATE: These regulations are effective on **[OFR-- insert date 60 days after date of publication in the Federal Register]**.

CMS-3228-F   2

FOR FURTHER INFORMATION CONTACT:

Scott Cooper, (410) 786-9465.

Danielle Shearer, (410) 786-6617.

Jeannie Miller, (410) 786-3164.

SUPPLEMENTARY INFORMATION:

I. Background

On April 15, 2010, the President issued a Presidential
Memorandum on Hospital Visitation to the Secretary of Health
and Human Services. The memorandum may be viewed on the Web
at: http://www.whitehouse.gov/the-press-office/presidential-
memorandum-hospital-visitation. As part of the directives of
the memorandum, the Department, through the Office of the
Secretary, tasked CMS with developing proposed requirements
for hospitals (including Critical Access Hospitals (CAHs)),
that would address the right of a patient to choose who may
and may not visit him or her. In the memorandum, the
President pointed out the plight of individuals who are denied
the comfort of a loved one, whether a family member or a close
friend, at their side during a time of pain or anxiety after
they are admitted to a hospital. The memorandum indicated
that these individuals are often denied this most basic of
human needs simply because the loved ones who provide them
comfort and support do not fit into a traditional concept of
"family."

Section 1861(e)(1) through (9) of the Social
Security Act -- (1) defines the term "hospital"; (2) lists the
statutory requirements that a hospital must meet to be
eligible for Medicare participation; and (3) specifies that a
hospital must also meet other requirements as the Secretary
finds necessary in the interest of the health and safety of
individuals who are furnished services in the facility. Under
this authority, the Secretary has established in the
regulations at 42 CFR part 482 the requirements that a
hospital must meet in order to participate in the Medicare
program. This authority extends as well to the separate
requirements that a CAH must also meet to participate in the
Medicare program, established in the regulations at 42 CFR
part 485. Additionally, section 1820 of the Act sets forth
the conditions for designating certain hospitals as CAHs.
Section 1905(a) of the Act provides that Medicaid payments may
be applied to hospital services. Regulations at
42 CFR 440.10(a)(3)(iii) require hospitals to meet the
Medicare CoPs to receive payment under States' Medicaid
programs.

While the existing hospital conditions of participation
(CoPs) in our regulations at 42 CFR part 482 do not address
patient visitation rights specifically, there is a specific
CoP regarding the overall rights of hospital patients

CMS-3228-F   4

contained in §482.13. We note that the existing CoPs for CAHs

in our regulations do not address patient rights in any form.

The hospital CoP for patient rights at §482.13 specifically

requires hospitals to -- (1) inform each patient or, when

appropriate, the patient's representative (as allowed under

State law) of the patient's rights; (2) ensure the patient's

right to participate in the development and implementation of

the plan of care; (3) ensure the patient's (or his or her

representative's) right to make informed decisions about care;

(4) ensure the patient's right to formulate advance directives

and have hospital staff comply with these directives (in

accordance with the provisions at 42 CFR §489.102); (5) ensure

the patient's right to have a family member or representative

of his or her choice and his or her own physician notified

promptly of admission to the hospital; (6) inform each patient

whom to contact at the hospital to file a grievance; and

(7) ensure that the hospital's grievance process has a

mechanism for timely referral of patient concerns regarding

quality of care or premature discharge to the appropriate

Utilization and Quality Control Quality Improvement

Organization (QIO). (Additional information regarding the

Medicare beneficiary patient's right to file a grievance or a

complaint with a QIO may be found at the HHS Centers for

Medicare & Medicaid Services website:

http://www.cms.gov/QualityImprovementOrgs/). The hospital

patient rights CoP also guarantees a patient's right to

privacy; care in a safe setting; freedom from all forms of

harassment and abuse; and confidentiality of patient records.

In addition, this CoP contains detailed standards on the use

of restraint and seclusion in the hospital, including

provisions regarding the training of staff on appropriate

restraint and seclusion of patients as well as a requirement

for the hospital to report any and all deaths associated with

the use of restraint or seclusion.

As the President noted in his memorandum to the

Secretary, many States have already taken steps to ensure that

a patient has the right to determine who may and may not visit

him or her, regardless of whether the visitor is legally

related to the patient. In addressing the President's request

to ensure patient visitation rights, we focused on developing

requirements to ensure that hospitals and CAHs protect and

promote patient visitation rights in a manner consistent with

that in which hospitals are currently required to protect and

promote all patient rights under the current CoPs. Therefore,

we proposed a visitation rights requirement for hospitals and

CAHs as a CoP in the Medicare and Medicaid programs. In

addition to addressing the President's directives regarding

patient rights, we are also ensuring that all hospitals and

CMS-3228-F   6

CAHs fully inform patients (or their representatives) of this
right, and that all patients are guaranteed full participation
in designating who may and who may not visit them. Therefore,
we solicited public comment on how to best implement this
requirement. In the proposed rule we noted that, at a
minimum, the requirement should exclude a hospital or CAH from
requiring documentation when the patient has the capacity to
speak or otherwise communicate for himself or herself; where
patient representation automatically follows from a legal
relationship recognized under State law (for example, a
marriage, a civil union, a domestic partnership, or a
parent-child relationship); or where requiring documentation
would discriminate on an impermissible basis.

In the April 15, 2010 Presidential Memorandum, the
President also emphasized the consequences that restricted or
limited visitation has for patients. Specifically, when a
patient does not have the right to designate who may visit him
or her simply because there is not a legal relationship
between the patient and the visitor, physicians, nurses, and
other staff caring for the patient often miss an opportunity
to gain valuable patient information from those who may know
the patient best with respect to the patient's medical
history, conditions, medications, and allergies, particularly
if the patient has difficulties recalling or articulating, or

is totally unable to recall or articulate, this vital personal
information. Many times, these individuals who may know the
patient best act as an intermediary for the patient, helping
to communicate the patient's needs to hospital staff. We
agree that restricted or limited hospital and CAH visitation
can effectively eliminate these advocates for many patients,
potentially to the detriment of the patient's health and
safety.

An article published in 2004 in the *Journal of the
American Medical Association* (Berwick, D.M. and Kotagal, M.:
"Restricted visiting hours in ICUs: time to change."
JAMA. 2004; Vol. 292, pp. 736-737) discusses the health and
safety benefits of open visitation for patients, families, and
intensive care unit (ICU) staff and debunks some of the myths
surrounding the issue (physiologic stress for the patient;
barriers to provision of care; exhaustion of family and
friends) through a review of the literature and through the
authors' own experiences working with hospitals that were
attempting a systematic approach to liberalizing ICU
visitation as part of a collaborative with the Institute for
Healthcare Improvement. The authors of the article ultimately
concluded that "available evidence indicates that hazards and
problems regarding open visitation are generally overstated
and manageable," and that such visitation policies "do not

harm patients but rather may help them by providing a support

system and shaping a more familiar environment" as they

"engender trust in families, creating a better working

relationship between hospital staff and family members."

II.   Provisions of the Proposed Rule and Response to Comments

We published a proposed rule in the **Federal Register** on

May 26, 2010 (75 FR 29479). In that rule, we proposed to

revise the Medicare hospital and CAH CoPs to provide

visitation rights to Medicare and Medicaid patients.

We provided a 60-day public comment period in which we

received approximately 7600 timely comments from individuals,

advocacy organizations, legal firms, and health care

facilities. Of the approximately 7600 timely comments, more

than 6300 were versions of a form letter that all expressed

the same sentiment of strong support for the proposed

regulation. The remaining comments, with very few exceptions,

also expressed strong support for the concept and overall

goals of the proposed regulation. Summaries of the public

comments are set forth below.

Hospital Visitation Rights

We proposed a visitation rights requirement for hospitals

as a new standard within the patient rights CoP at §482.13.

In that provision, we specified that hospitals would be

required to have written policies and procedures regarding the

visitation rights of patients, including those setting forth
any clinically necessary or reasonable restriction or
limitation that the hospital may need to place on such rights
as well as the reasons for the clinical restriction or
limitation. As part of these requirements, the hospital must
inform each patient, or his or her representative where
appropriate, of the patient's visitation rights, including any
clinical restriction or limitation on those rights, when the
patient, or his or her representative where appropriate, is
informed of the other rights specified in §482.13. We also
proposed that, as part of his or her visitation rights, each
patient (or representative where appropriate) must be informed
of his or her right, subject to his or her consent, to receive
the visitors whom he or she designates, whether a spouse, a
domestic partner (including a same-sex domestic partner),
another family member, or a friend, and of the right to
withdraw or deny such consent at any time. We solicited
public comment on the style and form that patient notices or
disclosures would need to follow so that patients would be
best informed of these rights.

We also proposed that hospitals would not be permitted to
restrict, limit, or otherwise deny visitation privileges on
the basis of race, color, national origin, religion, sex,
gender identity, sexual orientation, or disability. In

addition, we proposed to require hospitals to ensure that all visitors designated by the patient (or representative where appropriate) enjoy visitation privileges that are no more restrictive than those that immediate family members would enjoy.

Visitation Rights with Respect to CAHs

We proposed to apply the same visitation requirements to CAHs by revising the CoPs for CAHs. Because the CoPs for CAHs do not contain patient rights provisions, we proposed to add a new standard on patient visitation rights at §485.635(f) within the existing CoP on provision of services.

Comment: The vast majority of commenters expressed support for the proposed regulation. Of those commenters who submitted positive comments, many also included a rationale for their positive support. Many commenters noted the harm in keeping loved ones apart, and expressed support for the rule based on the need for compassionate treatment of all patients and loved ones. One commenter indicated it is shameful and embarrassing to ask for "special" treatment to visit a sick loved one, when it is not the hospital's decision to make in the first place. Another commenter felt there was "no excuse" for hospitals to make such visitation decisions. One commenter stated that affording the right of an individual to choose their visitors or seek comfort is a crucial step

towards challenging discrimination and improving health
outcomes. A few commenters supported the proposed regulation
based on the doctrine of the separation of Church (in the form
of the personal religious beliefs of hospital staff) and State
(in the form of official hospital policies and procedures).
Other commenters supported the proposed regulation, citing the
benefits that they personally experienced when their loved one
was ill and they were granted access, even without having an
advance directive naming them as the patient's representative.
Still others described scenarios where an individual was
permitted to visit a patient only because the individual lied
about his or her relationship to the patient (such as claiming
to be a biological relation).

Many commenters supported the rule because they believed
that denying access to hospitalized loved ones is cruel and
inhumane; some commenters even described such a denial as a
form of punishment. The commenters expressed the sentiment
that visitation is a moral issue and a basic human right, and
that regardless of sexual identity or recognized marital
status, one person being permitted to visit and care for
another should not require a law.

Other commenters noted that some current visitation
policies in facilities are discriminatory, unjust, and deny
basic equal rights to some patients. Several commenters noted

that facilities should be focused on providing medical
treatment in keeping with the tenets of the Hippocratic oath,
rather than dictating what constitutes an appropriate visitor.
Commenters agreed that equal visitation rights are critical to
the safety, welfare and equal treatment of persons who may
unexpectedly find themselves under the care of a hospital or
CAH.

Response: We thank the commenters for their support, and
agree that all patients must be ensured the right to choose
their own visitors. We agree that all Medicare- and Medicaid-
participating hospitals and CAHs must have written policies
and procedures regarding the visitation rights of patients,
including those setting forth any clinically necessary or
reasonable restriction or limitation that the hospital or CAH
may need to place on such rights as well as the reasons for
the clinical restriction or limitation.

Comment: A few commenters approved of the proposed
regulation, and suggested that fines, civil penalties, and/or
jail time should be imposed upon hospitals and individuals
that deny loved ones access to patients on an impermissible
basis. Others suggested that a list of non-compliant
facilities should be made available to the public.

Response: As a CoP for hospitals and CAHs, noncompliance
with this provision could result in the provider's termination

from the Medicare program. Medicare is the single largest
health care payer in the country; therefore, being terminated
from participation in the Medicare program, and therefore
unable to receive Medicare payments, is a very serious
consequence that all participating hospitals endeavor to
avoid. Hospitals and CAHs that have been terminated from
Medicare participation may also not receive Medicaid payments.
Therefore, we believe that hospitals and CAHs already have a
very strong incentive, absent fines and other consequences, to
comply with this requirement. In addition, CMS does not have
the legal authority to impose other types of sanctions for
non-compliant hospitals or CAHs outside of the existing
scheme. Because, at this time, no quality measures have been
developed relating to compliance with this requirement, CMS is
not in a position to publicly report this data. However,
should a quality measure be developed in the future, this
information could be included on the Hospital Compare website
(http://www.hospitalcompare.hhs.gov/).

Comment: Many commenters were confused by the use of the
term "representative" in this section. Commenters were
unclear about whether the patient's representative for
visitation purposes needed to be the patient's legal
representative for decision-making purposes.

Response: We agree that using the term "representative"

CMS-3228-F   14

in this rule is confusing and may be misleading. For purposes
of exercising visitation rights, we do not believe that the
individual exercising the patient's visitation rights needs to
be the same individual who is legally responsible for making
medical decisions on the patient's behalf, though it is
certainly possible for both roles to be filled by the same
individual. To avoid potential confusion, we have replaced
the word "representative" with the term "support person." The
term "support person" will, we believe, allow for a broader
interpretation of the requirement and increase flexibility for
patients and providers alike. A support person could be a
family member, friend, or other individual who is there to
support the patient during the course of the stay. This
concept is currently expressed in standard RI.01.01.01 of The
Joint Commission guidelines for hospitals, and we believe that
it appropriately reflects our broad interpretation of the
individual who may exercise a patient's visitation rights on
his or her behalf.

Comment: Commenters were uniformly supportive of the
requirement for hospitals and CAHs to have written policies
and procedures on visitation. Commenters were also strongly
supportive of a clear, formalized, written notice process for
informing the patient and, as appropriate, would-be visitors
and/or family and friends, of the patient's visitation rights.

Some commenters recommended specific times as to when notice should be given, such as upon admission, as early as possible in the admissions process, and/or whenever copies of the visitation policy are requested. Other commenters suggested that the notice of visitation rights be limited to a single page. Several other commenters requested that the notice also be provided orally and in an accessible manner in accordance with Title VI of the 1964 Civil Rights Act, in order to ensure the communication of the content in an appropriate manner. Still other commenters suggested that the notice of visitation rights should be posted in public spaces and in the patient's room.

Response: We thank the commenters for their support of the need to notify patients or their support person about their rights. We agree that hospitals and CAHs should be required to notify patients or their support person , in writing, of the patient's rights, including their right to receive visitors of their choosing. In accordance with the current requirements at §482.13(a), Notice of rights, hospitals must inform patients or their support person , where appropriate, of the patient's rights in that hospital before care is furnished to a patient whenever possible. This requirement for providing the notice of patient rights, now including the right to designate and receive visitors, before

CMS-3228-F 16

care is initiated meets the concerns of some commenters

regarding the timing of the notice. Therefore, we are

retaining the current requirements of §482.13(a) related to

the timing of the notice of rights, and are finalizing the

requirements of §482.13(h)(1) and (2) specifically related to

the written notice of visitation rights. Likewise, we are

modifying the requirement of proposed §485.635(f)(1) to

require CAHs to notify patients of their visitation rights in

advance of furnishing patient care whenever possible.

While we are finalizing the written notice of visitation

rights requirement under the authority of sections 1861(e)(9)

and 1820 of the Act, we agree with commenters that there are

other legal requirements, most notably those under Title VI of

the Civil Rights Act of 1964, that are related to this

provision. Our requirement is compatible with recent guidance

on Title VI of the Civil Rights Act of 1964. The Department

of Health and Human Services' (HHS) guidance related to Title

VI of the Civil Rights Act of 1964, "Guidance to Federal

Assistance Recipients Regarding Title VI Prohibition Against

National Origin Discrimination Affecting Limited English

Proficient Persons" (August 8, 2003, 68 FR 47311) applies to

those entities that receive federal financial assistance from

HHS, including Medicare- and Medicaid-participating hospitals

and CAHs. This guidance may assist hospitals and CAHs in

ensuring that patient rights information is provided in a
language and manner the patient understands.

Providing each patient or support person with the written
notice of visitation rights before the start of care
sufficiently achieves the goal of informing patients;
therefore, we are not requiring such notice to be posted
within the facility. This rule does not prohibit hospitals
and CAHs from posting information about their visitation
policies of their own volition. Furthermore, we are not
requiring facilities to provide the notice of rights in any
particular format or to individuals other than the patient or
support person. Facilities are already providing a notice of
rights to patients in accordance with the requirements of the
current rule and contemporary standards of practice. In order
to facilitate prompt compliance and minimize the burden upon
facilities, it is essential to allow them the flexibility to
adapt their current notice procedures and documents to include
this new notice of visitation rights requirement and to
continue the strong focus on patients, rather than the many
visitors who may pass through a facility in any given day.

Comment: In addition to notifying patients of their
visitation rights, some commenters suggested that the notice
should include information about any restrictions on those
visitation rights, including common examples of situations

when visitation may be restricted, and any specific
restrictions applicable to the patient. Additionally, the
following items were proposed as elements of the disclosure
notice:

o Recitation of the specific language from the
regulation (that "hospitals cannot restrict, limit, or
otherwise deny visitation privileges on the basis of race,
color, national origin, religion, sex, gender identity,
sexual orientation, or disability");

o Accompanying notice related to a patient's right to
complete an advance directive or other designation of a health
care agent to represent the patient;

o Accompanying notice about the grievance process that a
patient (or a visitor) may follow to appeal a denial of
visitation; and

o Contact information for a dedicated hospital staff
person who can resolve visitation conflicts.

Response: We agree that the notice of visitation rights
should include information related to reasonable, clinically
necessary restrictions or limitations on those rights.
Therefore, we are finalizing §482.13(h)(1) and §485.635(f)(1),
which require hospitals and CAHs to "inform each patient (or
support person, where appropriate) of his or her visitation
rights, including any clinical restriction or limitation on

such rights." In order to improve compliance with this requirement and minimize the burden on providers, it is necessary to allow hospitals and CAHs flexibility in meeting this requirement. These facilities can consider the usefulness of providing examples, developing medical condition-specific notices tailored to the common needs of different patient populations, and/or reciting the text of this rule as they develop their visitation rights notice.

We also agree that hospitals should notify patients of their advance directive rights and their right to access the hospital's grievance system, and information on how to do so. This information is currently required to be provided to patients or their support person in accordance with §482.13(a) and (b).

Comment: Several commenters suggested that CMS identify (and create, where necessary) best practices for training staff and administrators on cultural competency and the benefits of open visitation policies. Several commenters suggested that hospitals should be required to train their staff in discrimination prevention and cultural competency, to better assure that the rights of patients are promoted and protected.

Response: We thank the commenters for their suggestions. However, we believe that it is outside the scope of this rule

CMS-3228-F   **20**

for CMS to identify or create best practices for training
various healthcare facility staff on cultural competency and
the benefits of open visitation policies. We believe that the
establishment of these rules will lead hospitals and CAHs to
actively seek out and implement best practices and other
recommendations for training staff on these issues in order to
fully comply with the CoPs and continue participation in the
Medicare and Medicaid programs. We encourage hospitals to
address issues of cultural competencies specific to the needs
of their unique patient populations as part of their quality
assessment and performance improvement programs. In the
future, CMS may use subregulatory guidance and technical
assistance programs (such as Medicare Learning Network at
http://www.cms.gov/MLNGenInfo/) to make known best practice
information that is developed by other entities and
organizations.

Comment: Several commenters suggested that complaints
regarding the patient's visitation rights should be subject to
a grievance process, and that the right to file a grievance
should be readily available to the patient as well as any
would-be visitor.

Response: If a patient believes that his or her
visitation rights have been violated, the patient or his or
her representative may file a grievance with the hospital

using the hospital's internal grievance resolution process.

We note that CAHs are not currently required to have an

internal complaint process; nonetheless, they may have such a

process in place for quality improvement, State licensure,

accreditation, or other reasons. If the patient believes that

the quality of their care was negatively impacted by a

violation of his or her rights, the patient may also file a

complaint with the State survey agency responsible for

oversight of the facility, or the body responsible for

accrediting the facility (if applicable). In the case of

Medicare beneficiaries, complaints may also be filed with the

QIO in that State. These external complaint processes are

available to both hospital and CAH patients. We believe that

these current complaint resolution mechanisms offer the

necessary protections for patients who believe that their

rights have been violated. Likewise, if a visitor believes

that a hospital or CAH is not complying with the requirements

of this rule, the visitor may file a complaint with the State

survey agency responsible for oversight of the facility, as

well as the body responsible for accrediting the facility (if

applicable).

Comment: A few commenters requested examples of how the

new regulation will be implemented in facilities.

CMS-3228-F

22

Response: This final rule requires hospitals and CAHs to notify a patient or support person of his or her visitation rights, and sets forth the need for all hospitals and CAHs to establish non-discriminatory visitation policies that treat all visitors equally, consistent with the designations of patients or support persons. This applies to all patients, regardless of their payment source. These are broad expectations and rights that afford facilities the flexibility to revise current practices and procedures as necessary to meet these expectations. As such, we are not in a position to provide specific examples of how the regulation will be implemented in any facility because we do not know the particular circumstances of each facility, their current policies and practices, their particular patient populations, etc.

Comment: Several commenters suggested additional protected categories that should be added so that hospitals and CAHs are explicitly prohibited in regulation from discriminating against additional specified populations. Commenters stated that the protected categories in the proposed rule should be expanded to also include: marital status, family composition, age, primary language and immigration status. In addition, commenters suggested that the proposed rule make explicit that institutional or

individual conscience cannot be used to deny a visitor access
to the patient.

Response: As revised, we believe that this rule makes
clear that hospitals must establish and implement visitation
policies that grant full and equal visitation access to all
individuals designated by the patient or support person,
consistent with patient preferences. Patients (or their
support persons) may designate anyone as an approved visitor,
and a hospital or CAH may not discriminate against any
approved visitors(and may impose only reasonable, clinically
necessary restrictions or limitations on visitation). We
believe that this regulatory policy is responsive to the
concerns of commenters while still adhering to the specific
instructions of the President's April 15, 2010 memorandum to
the Secretary. Therefore, we are not expanding the list of
explicitly protected classes at this time.

Comment: Several commenters stated that they feared
crossing state lines because not all States recognize the
legal status of relationships in the same way. Without such
consistent recognition of legal status, an individual may be
recognized as the default decision making authority by one
State, but may not be recognized as such by another State. A
few commenters also stated that, while traveling, it could be
difficult to obtain the documentation required to verify the

legal status of a relationship, particularly in emergency

situations. Commenters noted that, even if documentation of a

legal relationship as recognized in a certain State was

available while traveling and medical attention was needed,

people may not seek treatment because they fear that their

legal relationship documentation may not be recognized by the

State in which they are traveling.

Response: We understand the concerns of commenters in

this area. These concerns highlight the need for individuals

to establish an advance directive as described in 42 CFR Part

489. As a legal document expressing the patient's preferences

in one or more areas related to medical treatment, an advance

directive can designate the individual who is permitted to

represent the patient, should the patient become

incapacitated. Although section 1866(f)(1) of the Act defers

to State law (whether statutory or established by the courts)

to govern the establishment and recognition of advance

directives, we believe that this type of document continues to

be a generally viable option for patients seeking to document,

in writing, their representative and/or support person

designation and treatment preferences. Consistent with

provisions concerning the establishment and recognition of

advance directives, all States continue to have the right to

determine the legal relationships that will be recognized by

State law and practice, to the extent that they do so in
accordance with constitutional principles. We do not have the
authority in this rule to compel one State to recognize a
legal relationship that is established in another State. That
said, we remind hospitals and CAHs that this rule does require
full and equal visitation for all visitors who are designated
by the patient or support person, consistent with the
patient's preferences. It is our understanding that, even
where one State does not recognize a legal relationship
recognized by another State, the law of that State generally
does not prohibit a private actor in that State - such as a
hospital or CAH - from recognizing that legal relationship.
Thus, there generally appear to be no barriers to such a
hospital or CAH recognizing a legal relationship recognized by
another State, even if its own State does not recognize that
legal relationship.

Comment: A few commenters expressed concern that the
validity of an adoption in one State may not be recognized by
another State in cases where a minor is the patient.
Commenters feared being required to verify proof of parenthood
at the height of a medical emergency if located in a different
state than where adoption occurred. Concern about the minor
patient's representative having the right to make decisions
about medical care "as allowed under State law" was also noted

by few commenters. Commenters felt that, as the language in the regulation stands, it may allow hospitals to deny the ability of adoptive parents to act as a minor patient's representative, even though the adoptive relationship is recognized under the laws of a different State. Other commenters expressed concern about the ability of non-biological parents to make decisions for their child in the absence of a legal adoption. Commenters expressed these same concerns with respect to the ability to visit a minor child.

Response: A legal adoption in one State is generally recognized as a legal parent-child relationship in another State, along with all of the default decision-making authorities that such a legal relationship confers upon a legal parent. This legal relationship continues to exist even if that parent and minor crosses State lines into another State in which that parent would have been prohibited from adopting that child. As a legal parent and representative of the minor child, the legal parent is, in accordance with the requirements of this final rule, able to designate those individuals who are permitted to visit the child. Thus, this rule ensures the representative's ability to ensure visitation access for other individuals.

Under this rule, issues of non-biological and non-adoptive parents acting as the minor child's decision maker are governed by State law. While we do not have the authority

in this final rule to compel a State to generally recognize

such parents as legal parents, we note that some States in

fact recognize "de facto" or "functional" or "equitable"

parenthood, i.e., recognize non-biological and non-adoptive

parents as legal parents. Nothing in this rule prohibits a

hospital or CAH from recognizing non-biological and non-

adoptive parents as legal parents for purposes of the

visitation policies set forth in this rule.

Comment: Several commenters stated that they supported

the proposed visitation regulation because it is critical for

patients to be able to choose their own visitors, particularly

for those patients who belong to blended families. Commenters

described "families of choice" - strong relationships with

friends and other people who support the patient and who can

be contacted during times of need. Accordingly, commenters

stated that, when a patient is incapacitated, the patient's

representative (which we now refer to as a support person)

should not be chosen solely based on an individual's legal

relationship with the patient. Commenters noted the lack of

protection for "families of choice," which do not necessarily

fit a traditional definition of a family, one based on

bloodlines, marriage, or adoption, make it difficult for

visitors to gain access to sick loved ones. Commenters noted that these representatives and sources of support should enjoy full visitation rights as any biological family member of the patient would.

Response: We appreciate the support of commenters, as it confirms our understanding that this visitation rights rule will help ensure that patients have access to their chosen loved ones while the patient is being cared for in a hospital or CAH. We also agree that oral designation of a support person, regardless of a particular relationship's legal status, should be sufficient for establishing the individual who may exercise the patient's visitation rights on his or her behalf, should the patient be unable to do so. In the absence of a verbal support person designation, hospitals and CAHs would look to their established policies and procedures for establishing a support person for the purpose of exercising a patient's visitation rights. As discussed later in this section, there are numerous sources of information and documentation that may be appropriate to establish the appropriateness of an individual to exercise an incapacitated patient's visitation rights on his or her behalf. We note that this section does not apply to designation of an individual as the patient's representative for purposes of medical decision making, as this designation may be governed by State law and regulation.

Comment: Many commenters submitted personal anecdotes
related to their hospital and CAH visitation experiences.
Some stated that they were denied information about or access
to a sick loved one while in the hospital. In contrast, some
commenters requested examples of situations where patient
visitation rights have been violated. Other commenters noted
that if they were to be hospitalized in the future, they would
like for their spouse or domestic partner to be able to make
medical decisions on their behalf. Several commenters stated
that they had prepared advance directive documentation in the
event something should warrant a hospital visit for themselves
and/or a spouse or domestic partner, while others expressed
concern about advance directives, stating that they cannot
rely on those directives being honored in all health care
settings, institutions, or States uniformly, based on their
marital/ relationship status. Still other commenters appeared
to believe that this final rule removes the need for advance
directives to designate healthcare decision makers.

Response: We appreciate all of the experiences and
concerns shared by the commenters, and we encourage those
commenters who sought examples of patient visitation rights
being denied to refer to the many detailed personal examples
that were submitted to us (see http://www.regulations.gov. In
the "key word or I.D." entry field, enter the docket ID

(CMS-2010-0207). Then, select "public submissions" from the drop-down menu under "select document type"). Numerous comments reaffirmed our understanding of the current practice in some medical institutions that denies patients access to their loved ones in times of need. The commenters also confirmed our understanding of the public's deeply-held desire to be with loved ones in such medical institutions, which further validates the need for this final rule. We also appreciate the comments related to advance directives, and encourage individuals to establish written advance directives that document the selection of a designated patient representative, support person, and/or the patient's choices about specific medical conditions and treatments. We believe that such documentation will help ensure that the patient's wishes are honored. We acknowledge that the Act defers to State law to govern advance directive issues, and that such deference may be a source of concern to commenters. However these advance directive issues are beyond the purview of this rule.

Comment: We received numerous comments affirming our general position that, when a patient can speak for himself or herself, a hospital or CAH does not need to require written documentation of a patient representative. That is, the commenters supported our contention that oral designation of

"representative" status is sufficient. Comments also
suggested that no proof should be required in cases where the
patient provides oral confirmation that he or she would like
to receive any particular visitor. Furthermore, the
commenters advocated against a formal documentation process,
whereby the hospital would be asked to obtain a list of
permitted and non-permitted visitors from each patient. They
stated that, as a practical matter, it would be simpler for
the hospital to recognize as welcome or not any particular
potential visitor, per the patient's wishes, when that patient
make his or her wishes known.

     Response: We agree that an oral designation of a support
person (formerly known as a "representative") is sufficient
for establishing the individual who may exercise the patient's
visitation rights on his or her behalf, should the patient be
unable to do so. We also agree that the patient's or support
person's oral consent to admit a visitor or to deny a visitor
is sufficient evidence of their wishes, and that further proof
of those wishes should not be required. However, hospitals
and CAHs are permitted to record such information in the
patient's record for future reference, if they so choose.

     Comment: Some commenters submitted comments related to
the rare cases in which hospitals may need to require written
documentation of patient representation. Of these, some

commenters suggested that documentation should be required

only in cases where more than one person claims to be the

patient's spouse, domestic partner or surrogate. Others

suggested that proof should be required only if the patient is

incapacitated. Other commenters suggested dropping "proof"

requirements altogether in an emergency situation and/or if

the patient is unconscious or otherwise incapacitated. A few

commenters stated that the visitor should not have to leave

the bedside of the patient to obtain proper documentation,

while others stated that proof should not be required of same-

sex couples where it is not required of similarly-situated

different-sex couples. Other comments to this effect went

further, suggesting that hospitals requiring documentation

from a same-sex couple but not a different-sex couple in the

same situation would be engaging in discrimination on an

impermissible basis (i.e. on the basis of sexual orientation).

Response: We agree with those commenters who stated that

a hospital or CAH must apply its documentation policy equally

for all patients and support persons. In accordance with the

comments submitted with respect to this rule, we believe that

documentation to establish support person status for the

purpose of exercising a patient's visitation rights should be

required only in the event that the patient is incapacitated

and two or more individuals claim to be the patient's support person. Since the visitation rights provision is new, we do

not believe that States have established separate laws and

regulations that would require documentation to establish an

individual as the support person in other circumstances.

While we acknowledge the desire of the individuals who claim

to be the patient's support person to remain at the patient's

bedside, we recognize that this is not possible in every

situation. In these situations, such individuals may need to

leave the area in order to obtain written documentation of the

patient's wishes. Individuals may wish to maintain such

documentation on their person and/or maintain such

documentation in an electronic database, such as an advance

directive registry, that grants access to health care

facilities in order to avoid leaving the patient's bedside to

obtain proof of support person status.

Comment: A few comments spoke to matters beyond a

support person's ability to visit and designate other

visitors, suggesting that, where the patient is unable to

communicate and decisions related to providing or withdrawing

medical care are necessary, documentation should be required,

unless the patient designated the representative for health

care decision making before being unable to communicate.

Response: We agree that situations related to medical

decision making are governed by State law, whether established

CMS-3228-F   34

under legislative or judicial authority. We note that issues
of surrogate medical decision making fall outside the scope of
this rule on visitation policies. Hospitals and CAHs must
always comply with their State laws and regulations, and we
remind facilities that their policies and procedures related
to requiring documentation of support person status must be
applied in a non-discriminatory manner.

Comment: Comments were received regarding what forms of
proof might suffice to establish the appropriateness of a
visitor where the patient is incapacitated or otherwise unable
to designate visitors, and a representative in accordance with
State law or a patient-designated support person is not
available to exercise the patient's rights on his or her
behalf. Comments also suggested that these forms of "proof"
could also be used to help establish a support person's status
as such.

The following forms of "proof" were suggested:

• An advance directive naming the individual as a support
person, approved visitor or designated decision maker
(regardless of the State in which the directive is
established);

• Shared residence;

• Shared ownership of a property or business;

• Financial interdependence;

- Marital/Relationship status;

- Existence of a legal relationship recognized in another jurisdiction, even if not recognized in another jurisdiction, including: parent-child, civil union, marriage, domestic partnership;

- Acknowledgment of a committed relationship (e.g. an affidavit); and

- Written documentation of the patient's chosen individual(s) even if it is not a legally recognized advance directive.

Response: We agree that any of these forms of proof could be sufficient for hospitals and CAHs to establish the appropriateness of a visitor when a patient is incapacitated and no representative or support person is available to exercise a patient's visitation rights on his or her behalf. We also agree that these forms of proof may be helpful for establishing support person status for the purpose of exercising the patient's visitation rights when the patient is incapacitated. In order to obtain this information, hospitals and CAHs may choose to examine licenses, State identification cards, bank statements, deeds, lease agreements, etc. These lists of proof and documentation are not intended to be exhaustive of all potential sources of information regarding patient visitation or support person preferences. Our overall

expectation is that hospitals and CAHs will use this
information to guide the establishment of flexible policies
and procedures that balance the dual needs of ensuring patient
safety and ensuring patient access to loved ones.

Comment: A few commenters suggested that the final rule
should ensure that patients have the right to exclude certain
visitors to assure their well-being, and that the patient's
support person should have the highest level of authority to
do so.

Response: We agree that the patient's right to choose
visitors also includes the right to deny visitors. We
included this concept at proposed §482.13(h)(2) and
§485.635(f)(2), stating, "Inform each patient (or
representative, where appropriate) of his or her visitation
rights … and his or her right to withdraw or deny such consent
at any time." We continue to believe that this is an
appropriate provision and are finalizing it as such.
Patients, or their support person acting on their behalf, have
the right to deny visitors.

Comment: Some commenters suggested that the regulation
should include an explicit requirement granting the patient's
support person direct access to the patient. One commenter
suggested that health care proxies or powers of attorney that
are legally recognized in one State also be recognized by

hospitals and CAHs in other States for the purpose of
establishing visitation rights.

Response: We agree that the patient's representative
and/or support person, as the individual responsible for
exercising the patient's rights on the patient's behalf when
the patient is incapacitated or otherwise unable to do so
directly, should be granted direct access to the patient.
This basic concept is embodied throughout the current hospital
regulations, including through the requirement at §482.13(a)
and (b) that the patient or patient's representative must be
informed of the patient's rights and how to exercise those
rights. We also agree that using the information provided in
an advance directive or other written document, whether it is
or is not legally recognized by the State, may be useful for
hospitals and CAHs when trying to determine appropriate
visitors when a patient is unable to communicate his or her
own wishes and a legal representative as established
consistent with State law or a support person is not available
to exercise the patient's visitation rights on his or her
behalf.

Comment: A number of commenters expressed the concern
that the regulation's reference to State law, as it pertains
to the hospital's recognition of a patient's representative,
could be interpreted as inappropriately limiting the

designation of a representative, and suggested that we remove "as allowed under State law" from the regulation.

Response: As previously discussed, we agree that using the term "representative," with its implicit links to state law, is too narrow for this regulation. Therefore, we have replaced the term "representative" with the term "support person," which is intended to broadly describe the family member, friend, or other individual who supports the patient during his or her hospital or CAH stay and may exercise the patient's visitation rights on his or her behalf. Issues of legal representation and health care decision making are beyond the purview of this final rule. We remind all hospitals and CAHs that these issues are generally addressed in State law (including case law). All Medicare-participating providers, including hospitals and CAHs, are required to remain in full compliance with the laws and regulations of their State, in addition to these Federal requirements.

Comment: A few commenters noted that they were denied access to visit a loved one by the patient's representative, although they believed that such a denial was not in the best interest of the patient. The commenters cited their ability to provide pertinent medical information about the patient as a primary reason for allowing them access to the patient despite the decision of the patient's representative. A few comments also noted the impact of the well-recognized legal concept of "substituted judgment" as requiring patients' families and representatives to make medical decisions based on the patient's values and interests and not their own.

Response: As the individual responsible for making decisions on the patient's behalf, the patient representative has the authority to exercise a patient's right to designate and deny visitors just as the patient would if he or she were capable of doing so. The designation of and exercise of authority by the patient's representative is governed by State law, including statutory and case law. Many State courts have addressed the concept of substituted judgment, whereby the patient representative is expected to make medical decisions based on the patient's values and interests, rather than the representative's own values and interests. State courts have also developed a body of closely related law around the matter of a representative acting in the patient's best interest. Such case law regarding substituted judgment and best interest may be a resource for hospitals and CAHs as they establish policies and procedures intended to address these difficult situations. Hospitals and CAHs may also choose to utilize their own social work and pastoral counseling resources to resolve such conflicts to assure the patient's well-being.

Comment: Some commenters suggested that we replace the term "immediate family," as proposed at §482.13(h)(4) and §485.635(f)(4), with a broader requirement that does not distinguish among different types of relationships. Some commenters asserted that the regulation, as proposed, would be difficult to define, measure, and enforce. Furthermore, some commenters stated that the regulation, as proposed, created the appearance of a hierarchy of family relationship status that could put other chosen family members and loved ones at risk of unequal treatment.

Response: We agree that the proposed language may have been difficult to define, measure, and enforce, and that amending the requirement would further clarify our intent to assure equal visitation privileges for all visitors in accordance with the patient's preferences. Therefore, we have amended the requirements at §482.13(h)(4) and §485.635(f)(4) to state, "Ensure that all visitors enjoy full and equal visitation privileges consistent with patient preferences." This revised requirement is patient-centered and will, we believe, ensure that all visitors are treated in a fair and equal manner by a hospital or CAH.

Comment: Many commenters suggested that we broaden the context in which the word "family" is used. Commenters presented a variety of options, citing sources such as the

Joint Commission, the Office of Personnel Management for the
United States government, and current practices in New York
State. All of these commenters suggested a broad concept of
family, including any individual who plays a significant role
in the patient's life, such as spouses, domestic partners,
significant others (whether different-sex or same-sex), and
other individuals not legally related to the patient.
Commenters also provided a list of specific types of family
relationships, and described the challenges that can be faced
with respect to each.

Response: We believe that both the preamble to the
proposed rule and the language of the proposed requirements
broaden the definition of "family" in the context of hospital
and CAH visitation rights of patients. The language of the
proposed rule (see 75 FR 36612) provides examples of visitors
very similar to those given by the commenters ("a spouse, a
domestic partner (including a same-sex domestic partner),
another family member, or a friend"). Most importantly, the
proposed requirements go beyond these examples by specifying
that the patient has the right to designate all visitors,
regardless of type of relationship, and, while patient-
designated visitors may obviously include those mentioned, the
requirements do not place limits on who may be designated as a
visitor by the patient. This final rule maintains the

policies articulated in the proposed rule in this regard.

Comment: Commenters from the provider community
expressed broad support for the rule's recognition of the need
for clinically necessary or reasonable restrictions or
limitations on visitation. In addition to supporting the
overall concept of "necessary restrictions," some commenters
stated that restrictions must be enforced uniformly and
restrictions must be clearly communicated, along with their
medical basis, to would-be visitors and/or the patient. These
commenters stressed that such additional measures would reduce
the opportunity for discrimination and increase understanding.
These comments reflect the concerns of some commenters that an
allowance for "reasonable" restrictions would be too broad.
There were concerns among some of the commenters that a
hospital or CAH might apply this exception capriciously and
without adequate clinical justification, and that such a broad
exception might also allow for restrictions rooted in
discriminatory attitudes toward lesbian, gay, bisexual, and
transgender people or their families.

Several commenters asked for clarification on the
language in the proposed regulation that would allow for a
hospital or CAH to place limitations or restrictions on a
patient's visitation rights when it determined that it was
clinically reasonable or necessary to do so. A commenter

requested that one of the examples of a clinically reasonable restriction on visitation, which was used in the preamble ("when the patient is undergoing care interventions"), be stricken entirely from this rule. This commenter was concerned that a hospital or CAH might apply this example too broadly when restricting visitation for a patient, and that the reasons for applying it might be more logistical than clinical (e.g., it may be used by overworked staff to justify a restriction or limitation).

The commenters provided numerous examples of legitimate reasons for restricting or limiting visitors, including:

o Any court order limiting or restraining contact;

o Behavior presenting a direct risk or threat to the patient, hospital staff, or others in the immediate environment;

o Behavior disruptive of the functioning of the patient care unit;

o Reasonable limitations on the number of visitors at any one time;

o Patient's risk of infection by the visitor;

o Visitor's risk of infection by the patient;

o Extraordinary protections because of a pandemic or infectious disease outbreak;

o Substance abuse treatment protocols requiring restricted visitation;

o Patient's need for privacy or rest;

o Need for privacy or rest by another individual in the patient's shared room.

Response: We appreciate the support of commenters for this provision of the proposed rule, and agree that this list, though not exhaustive, is an appropriate way to begin considering clinically appropriate restrictions on visitation privileges.

In his April 15, 2010 memorandum on hospital visitation rights, the President directed the Secretary to initiate appropriate rulemaking that "should take into account the need for hospitals to restrict visitation in medically appropriate circumstances as well as the clinical decisions that medical professionals make about a patient's care or treatment." In crafting the language of the requirements, we took this Presidential directive into account, and thoroughly weighed the rights of a patient to receive visitors of his or her choosing against the obligation and duty of a hospital or CAH to provide the best possible care to all of its patients. We firmly believe that the requirements must allow hospitals and CAHs some flexibility regarding patient visitation so that healthcare professionals may exercise their best clinical judgment when determining when visitation is, and is not,

appropriate. We believe that the best clinical judgment takes

into account all aspects of patient health and safety,

including any negative impact that patients, visitors, and

staff may have on other patients in the hospital or CAH.

In the preamble to the proposed rule, we provided three

broad examples of clinically reasonable areas where hospitals

and CAHs might impose restrictions or limitations on visitors:

when the patient is undergoing care interventions; when there

may be infection control issues; and when visitation may

interfere with the care of other patients. There are other,

similarly obvious areas where restriction or limitation of

visitation would also be appropriate, and which commenters

also pointed out: existing court orders restricting contact of

which the hospital or CAH is aware; disruptive, threatening,

or violent behavior of any kind; patient need for rest or

privacy; limitations on the number of visitors during a

specific period of time; minimum age requirements for child

visitors; and inpatient substance abuse treatment programs

that have protocols limiting visitation. While all of these

instances can be discussed individually, it may be more useful

to group all of these examples, plus those examples that we

mentioned in the preamble, under an even broader category of

clinically appropriate and reasonable restriction or

limitation on visitation: when visitation would interfere

with the care of the patient and/or the care of other

patients. Whether the reason for limiting or restricting

visitation is infection control, disruptive behavior of

visitors, or patient or roommate need for rest or privacy, all

of these reasons may be considered as clinically reasonable

and necessary when viewed in light of a hospital's or CAH's

overarching goal of advancing the care, safety, and well-being

of all of its patients. As we discussed in the preamble, we

believe that current clinical thinking, along with some

evidence in this area, supports the role of visitation in

advancing the care, safety, and well-being of patients.

However, we must caution commenters that visitation is but one

aspect of patient care. Hospitals and CAHs must balance *all*

aspects of care for *all* patients. Through the hospital and

CAH CoPs, CMS expects all hospitals and CAHs to provide care

to patients in a safe manner that follows nationally

recognized guidelines and standards. As part of this

expectation, CMS recognizes that hospitals and CAHs must be

allowed some degree of flexibility when developing policies

and procedures for patient care and safety, and in order to

comply with the CoPs. We remind hospitals and CAHs that, when

establishing and implementing visitation policies and

procedures, the burden of proof is upon the hospital or CAH to demonstrate that the visitation restriction is necessary to provide safe care.

As it is written, the requirement does allow a hospital or CAH a degree of flexibility when developing and imposing policies that may limit or restrict visitation. However, the rule does require that a hospital or CAH must contain these policies in written form, including the reasons for such restrictions, and must inform a patient (or his or her support person) of its policies regarding clinical limitations or restrictions on visitation rights.

However, while we agree that a hospital or CAH must communicate its policy on limited or restricted visitation to patients when apprising them of their rights (and the requirement is written as such), we do not believe that a hospital or CAH must delineate each of the clinical reasons that may warrant imposition of this policy because it may be impossible to anticipate every instance that may give rise to such a situation. We do believe that hospitals and CAHs should clearly communicate how such policies are aimed at protecting the health and safety of all patients. Additionally, in situations where it may be necessary for patient visitation to be limited or restricted, hospitals and CAHs have a duty to the patient to clearly explain the reasons for such restrictions or limitations.

Further, we disagree that the example given in the
preamble of a clinically reasonable or necessary restriction
or limitation on visitation ("when the patient is undergoing
care interventions") should be stricken from the rule
entirely. This language was not included in the proposed
requirements nor is it being finalized here; it was used
merely as an example. However, we are aware that in some
hospitals and CAHs throughout the nation, there still exists
an unwritten policy of "clearing the room" of all visitors
when a patient is undergoing an intervention. It should be
noted here that there are often valid reasons for doing this.
For instance, many patients prefer privacy during this time;
many visitors are not prepared to witness the physical aspects
of some patient care interventions and procedures; the
physical limitations of the patient's room can make the
intervention difficult to perform with visitors in the room;
and, when performing interventions or procedures that require
aseptic technique, additional persons or visitors in the room
may compromise the healthcare professional's ability to
control for infection. CMS believes that it is in the
patient's best interest to allow those healthcare
professionals responsible for the care of the patient to make
these clinical decisions regarding restricting or limiting

visitation when the patient is undergoing a procedure or intervention.

However, we must emphasize here that we strongly encourage hospitals and CAHs to be aware of, and sensitive to, the needs of any patient who may request that at least one visitor be allowed to stay in the room to provide support and comfort when undergoing a procedure, and to make a best effort at accommodating such requests if the clinical situation allows for it. Despite the hospital culture of "clearing the room" for patient care interventions that may still exist in some hospitals and CAHs, we believe that many more hospitals and CAHs are making a best effort at recognizing and honoring the need of many patients to have a loved one close by while undergoing a potentially frightening and painful procedure. In this regard, we respectfully disagree with the comment stating that staff may justify such restrictions or limitations for logistical, rather than clinical, reasons. This comment voices a concern that "overworked staff" would apply restrictions or limitations for logistical reasons and implies that logistical reasons are more conveniences for the staff than they are clinical reasons for the patient. In the hospital setting, the logistical and the clinical are often one and the same, and the logistics of the situation must sometimes be taken into account by healthcare professionals in order to ensure the best clinical outcomes for patients. Of the examples given above for restricting or limiting visitation during a care intervention, it can be argued that all are both clinical and logistical in nature, with each impacting the other. Again, CMS believes that, in the interests of patient safety, such decisions are best left to the healthcare professionals responsible for the care of the patient, and should not be dictated through overly prescriptive regulations.

Comment: Several commenters stated that written documentation of patient representation in the form of legally valid advance directives, such as durable powers of attorney and healthcare proxies, (as opposed to oral designation of the support person by the patient) should be required only in the very rarest of cases - such as when more than one person claims to be a patient's spouse, domestic partner, or surrogate. In all other cases, oral confirmation of an individual acting as the support person should suffice. Commenters suggested that a hospital or CAH may not require documentation in a discriminatory manner.

Response: In the preamble, we specifically asked for comments on how to best identify those rare cases where hospitals and CAHs should be permitted to ask for written documentation to establish the support person as such in order

to allow the support person the right to designate visitors if
the patient is unable to do so. We appreciate the comments
offered on this issue. We agree that this practice would most
clearly be justified in those rare cases where the hospital or
CAH faces a dispute among two or more persons claiming to be
the patient's support person, and the patient is
incapacitated.

Comment: One provider urged CMS to be cautious about
fashioning "overly prescriptive" policies in the interpretive
guidelines.

Response: We appreciate the commenter's warning, and
agree that being overly prescriptive may stifle the
flexibility that we intend hospitals and CAHs to exercise when
establishing and implementing full and equal visitation for
all visitors in accordance with patient preferences. We note
that the Interpretive Guidelines for the CoPs, which will be
updated to reflect these new requirements, fall outside of the
scope of this rulemaking process and are not addressed here.

Comment: A very small number of commenters suggested
that CMS should not adopt this proposed rule, believing that
there does not exist a pressing need for it to exist, and that
adding the additional patient rights information to the
existing notice of patient rights disclosure would serve only

to increase hospital costs, lengthen the admission process, and further overwhelm patients.

Response: While we recognize the commenters' concern regarding the large amount of information that is provided to patients and the time that it takes to do so, we continue to believe that it is better to apprise patients and their support person of the patient's rights, and to ensure this practice through the requirements of the conditions of participation. We also continue to believe that this regulation will address a very real problem that negatively impacts patient outcomes and that runs contrary to our goal of safe and effective care for every patient, every time. Furthermore, we continue to believe that the flexible structure of these requirements minimizes the cost impact of this final rule.

Comment: Several commenters made ambiguous statements that did not speak to either support for or disagreement with the proposed rule.

Response: While we believe that statements such as "Please come into the new millennium" may be in support of the proposed regulation, encouraging CMS to adopt regulations that address changing social norms and contemporary situations, we were unable to classify these comments as such due to their ambiguous nature. Nonetheless, we thank the commenters for

expressing their thoughts on this proposed regulation and will
make all efforts to assure that the final regulation is fair
and balanced to protect patient rights, as well as patient
health and safety.

Comment: Several commenters in favor of the regulation
proposed that all hospitals, whether they are receiving
federal funding from CMS or not, respect this directive and
its intention.

Response: While we agree that the intent and spirit of
this regulation should be honored by all hospitals and CAHs,
even those that do not receive Medicare or Medicaid funds, we
do not have the authority to enforce these requirements upon
non-Medicare or Medicaid hospitals and CAHs. CMS's authority
to enforce this and other CMS regulations stems from the
agreement that hospitals and CAHs enter into with CMS whereby
those hospitals and CAHs agree to abide by Medicare's
regulations in exchange for their ability to participate in
the Medicare and Medicaid programs, see and treat Medicare and
Medicaid patients, and be paid by Medicare or Medicaid for the
care and services furnished to those Medicare and Medicaid
patients. Absent that voluntary agreement, CMS lacks
authority to enforce its rules upon non-participating
providers and suppliers.

Comment: Several commenters suggested that the requirements of this rule should apply to hospices, nursing homes, ambulatory surgical centers (ASCs), and intermediate care facilities for the mentally disabled (ICF/MRs). Commenters noted that the need for and the benefits that flow from visitation are just as important – and sometimes even more so – for patients in hospices and nursing homes than for those in hospitals. Many commenters asserted that the standards and rules for all facilities should be consistent.

Response: While we agree that the benefits of visitation go beyond hospital and CAH patients, and we appreciate the suggestions that this rule should apply to other types of Medicare and Medicaid providers, such revisions would fall outside the scope of this rule. We note that the current regulations for hospices (§418.52, §418.100, and §418.110 in particular) and nursing homes (§483.10(j)) already require generous visitation privileges for all patients, and that these generous allowances minimize the need for new regulations at this time. We also believe that the short-term nature of ASC services, which must be less than 24 hours in duration, and the fact surgery centers generally require each patient to be accompanied by a responsible adult for discharge purposes, naturally minimize the need for open visitation regulations in ASCs. However, we will continue to consider

modifying the requirements for these provider types in the
future to ensure consistent requirements and patient rights
across providers.

Each of these providers is required by regulation to have
an internal system to handle patient grievances. If patients
of these providers believe that their rights have been
violated, they may file a complaint using their provider's
internal grievance system. All patients may also file a
complaint with the state survey agency and/or the agency that
accredits the provider (if applicable). Furthermore, Medicare
beneficiaries may file quality of care complaints with the QIO
in that state. We believe that these robust complaint options
help assure that patient complaints are documented,
investigated, and resolved in an appropriate manner.

Informed Decisions

The President's Memorandum also directed the Secretary to
ensure that patients' representatives have the right to make
informed decisions regarding patients' care.

The hospital CoPs at 42 CFR 482.13(b)(2) state: "The
patient or his or her representative (as allowed under State
law) has the right to make informed decisions regarding his or
her care. The patient's rights include being informed of his
or her health status, being involved in care planning and
treatment, and being able to request or refuse treatment.

This right must not be construed as a mechanism to demand the provision of treatment or services deemed medically unnecessary or inappropriate."

We believe that the ability of a patient to designate a support person who can act on behalf of the patient is critical to the assurance of the patient's health and safety. Regardless of whether a patient is incapacitated, the designation of a support person, who is likely to be especially familiar with the patient, including his or her medical history, conditions, medications, and allergies, can serve as an invaluable asset to the patient and caregivers during the development and revision of the course of treatment and associated decision making.

In the proposed rule, we explained that the requirement at §482.13(b)(2) was intended to ensure the patient's right to designate a representative for health care decision-making purposes. We solicited public comment on whether, as a health and safety measure, this requirement effectively addresses any inappropriate barriers to a patient's ability to designate a representative for visitation purposes, and consistently ensures the right to designate a representative (for all purposes) for all patients in all Medicare- and Medicaid-participating hospitals.

Comment: Several commenters noted suggestions to ensure
that all patients are able to designate a decision-maker, have
that designation respected, and receive meaningful
representation by that individual regardless of whether the
State in which the patient is hospitalized recognizes a formal
legal relationship between the two persons. This would
include hospitals' obligations to provide patients with
designation forms. In urgent situations, commenters suggested
that patients have the right to orally designate a
representative for decision-making purposes. One commenter
suggested that CMS should create a model advance directive
rule that States could use to revise their current legislation
and regulations related to advance directives.

Response: We thank commenters for their suggestions
regarding the designation of a representative by a patient.
With respect to designations in advance directives,
§1866(f)(1) of the Act defers to State law (whether statutory
or established by the courts) to govern the establishment and
recognition of advance directives (which can be used by the
patient to designate a representative). Thus, we do not have
the authority in this rule to change this aspect of advance
directives policy. We believe, however, that an advance
directive remains a viable and important option for those
seeking to document treatment preferences, informed decision-

making regarding care, designation of a representative, and

designation of a support person (who may be the

representative). And we encourage hospitals to consider

advance directives established in other States as a viable

source of information about patient preferences, including

visitation preferences. It is not within the scope of this

regulation to draft sample legislation that could guide State

laws and regulations on advance directives.

Comment: Commenters expressed various concerns related

to the current requirements for the establishment and

implementation of advance directives, State requirements for

designating a patient's representative for decision-making

purposes, methods for producing a copy of an existing advance

directive in a time of need (including the hospital's role in

obtaining a copy), and the practicalities involved with

establishing advance directives. These commenters highlighted

the complexities of establishing, accessing, and implementing

advance directives in a variety of circumstances, and focused

particular attention on the role of advance directives in

establishing patient "representative" status.

Response: We appreciate the comments received in regard

to advance directive issues. We refer readers to the

statutory language at §1866(f)(3) of the Act, which defines an

advance directive as "a written instruction, such as a living

will or durable power of attorney for health care, recognized
under State law (whether statutory or as recognized by the
courts of the State) and relating to the provision of such
care when the individual is incapacitated." All CMS
regulations related to advance directives, including those
advance directives that designate a patient's representative
for health care decision making, are based on this statute
which, in turn, defers to State laws in all forms to govern
the establishment and implementation of such documents. As
such, CMS does not have the legal authority to broadly
preempt, through regulation or other administrative action,
those State laws that relate to advance directives.

In regard to current CMS regulations related to advance
directives, we note that the provider agreement regulations at
§489.102, referenced by §482.13, specify very limited
instances in which services or procedures specified in a
State-recognized advance health care directive may be refused.
Section 489.102(c)(2) is limited to refusals to provide
services or procedures called for in an advance health care
directive, as described in §489.102(a)(1)(ii)(C), which refers
specifically to "the range of medical conditions or procedures
affected by the conscience objection." We believe that this
narrow window allowing for certain objections to the content
of an advance directive would not allow a health care provider

to refuse to honor those portions of a State-recognized

advance directive that designate an individual as the

patient's representative, support person, or health care

decision-maker, since such designation is not a medical

condition or procedure.

Comment: Some commenters noted a variety of barriers

that inhibit the establishment of an advance directive. Such

barriers include the cost associated with obtaining legal

counsel to help establish an advance directive that is legal

in the patient's State, a lack of knowledge about the need for

and benefits of an advance directive, an overall cultural

apathy towards advance care planning as indicated by the low

percentage of the population that has an advance directive,

and the disadvantages faced by non-English-proficient

individuals.

Response: In the proposed rule, we solicited comment on

whether the current requirement (at §482.13(b)(2), which is

intended to ensure a patient's right to designate a

representative to make informed decisions about his or her

care) effectively addresses any inappropriate barriers to a

patient's ability to designate a representative, and whether

it consistently ensures the right to designate a

representative for all patients in all Medicare- and

Medicaid-participating hospitals. We also stated our

intention to consider public comments received in response to this request as we consider any revision to the current regulation that would eliminate any inappropriate restriction or limitation on a patient's ability to designate a representative that may be permitted under the existing regulation.

In light of our direct solicitation of comments on this issue, we greatly appreciate the comments offered here regarding various barriers that a patient may experience when attempting to designate a representative for health care decision-making purposes. We will give due consideration to these comments when we contemplate future rulemaking in this area of the CoPs.

Comment: Commenters observed that in addition to establishing an advance directive, patients, representatives, and support persons must also be able to produce the document in a time of urgent need. These commenters also observed that being able to do so may be challenging and inconvenient for people, given the nature of urgent medical situations.

Response: Urgent situations are, by nature, unplanned. As such, patients, representatives, and support persons may not have ready access to the necessary medical documentation at the time that the urgent situation occurs. In addition to keeping such documentation in a readily accessible physical location, we are aware of the existence of advance directive registries that store advance directives and other legal documents in an electronic format that can be retrieved by individuals and health care facilities alike. Such document storage and access facilities may be an appropriate source of the proper documentation in urgent situations.

III. Collection of Information Requirements

Under the Paperwork Reduction Act of 1995, we are required to provide 30-day notice in the **Federal Register** and solicit public comment before a collection of information requirement is submitted to the Office of Management and Budget (OMB) for review and approval. In order to fairly evaluate whether an information collection should be approved by OMB, section 3506(c)(2)(A) of the Paperwork Reduction Act of 1995 requires that we solicit comment on the following issues:

● The need for the information collection and its usefulness in carrying out the proper functions of our agency.

● The accuracy of our estimate of the information collection burden.

● The quality, utility, and clarity of the information to be collected.

- Recommendations to minimize the information collection burden on the affected public, including automated collection techniques.

We solicited public comment on each of these issues for the following sections of this document that contain information collection requirements (ICRs):

A. ICRs Regarding Condition of Participation: Patient's rights (§482.13)

Section §482.13(h) requires a hospital to have written policies and procedures regarding the visitation rights of patients, including any clinically necessary or reasonable restriction or limitation that the hospital may need to place on such rights and the reasons for the clinical restriction or limitation. Specifically, the written policies and procedures must contain the information listed in §482.13(h)(1) through (h)(4). The burden associated with this requirement is the time and effort necessary for a hospital to develop written policies and procedures with respect to visitation rights of patients and to distribute that information to the patients.

We believe that most hospitals already have established policies and procedures regarding visitation rights of patients. Therefore, we are adding only a minimal amount of additional burden hours to comply with this requirement.

CMS-3228-F   64

Additionally, we believe that most hospitals include the
visitation policies and procedures as part of their standard
notice of patient rights. The burden associated with the
notice of patient rights is currently approved under OMB
control number 0938-0328. We will be submitting a revision of
the currently approved information collection request to
account for the following burden.

We estimate that 4,860 hospitals must comply with the
aforementioned information collection requirements. We
further estimate that it will take each hospital 0.25 hours to
comply with the requirement in proposed §482.13(h). The total
estimated annual burden associated with this requirement is
1,215 hours at a cost of $71,746.

B. ICRs Regarding Condition of Participation: Provision of
services (§485.635)

Section 485.635(f) requires a CAH to have written
policies and procedures regarding the visitation rights of
patients, including any clinically necessary or reasonable
restriction or limitation that the CAH may need to place on
such rights and the reasons for the clinical restriction or
limitation. Specifically, the written policies and procedures
must contain the information listed in §485.635(f)(1) through
(f)(4). The burden associated with this requirement is the
time and effort necessary for a CAH to develop written

policies and procedures with respect to visitation rights of patients and to distribute the information to the patients.

We believe that most CAHs already have established policies and procedures regarding visitation rights of patients. These policies and procedures are most likely included as part of a CAH's patient care policies as required for CAHs under §485.635. Therefore, we are adding a minimal amount of additional burden hours to comply with this requirement. We will be submitting a revision of the ICR currently approved under OMB control number 0938-1043 to account for the burden associated with the requirements in §485.635.

We estimate that 1,314 CAHs must comply with the aforementioned information collection requirements. We further estimate that it will take each CAH 0.25 hours to comply with the requirement at §482.13(h). The total estimated annual burden associated with this requirement is 329 hours at a cost of $19,398.

Table 1: Annual Recordkeeping and Reporting Requirements

Regulation Section(s)	OMB Control No.	Respondents	Responses	Burden per Response (hours)	Total Annual Burden (hours)	Hourly Labor Cost of Reporting ($)	Total Labor Cost of Reporting ($)	Total Capital/Maintenance Costs ($)	Total Cost ($)
§482.13	0938-0328	4,860	4,860	.25	1,215	59.05	71,746	0	71,746
§485.635	0938-1034	1,314	1,314	.25	329	58.96	19,398	0	19,398
Total		6,174	6,174		1,544				91,144

IV. Regulatory Impact Statement

CMS-3228-F 66

We have examined the impact of this proposed rule as required by Executive Order 12866 on Regulatory Planning and Review (September 30, 1993), the Regulatory Flexibility Act (RFA) (September 19, 1980, Pub. L. 96-354), section 1102(b) of the Social Security Act, section 202 of the Unfunded Mandates Reform Act of 1995 (March 22, 1995; Pub. L. 104-4), Executive Order 13132 on Federalism (August 4, 1999) and the Congressional Review Act (5 U.S.C. 804(2)).

Executive Order 12866 directs agencies to assess all costs and benefits of available regulatory alternatives and, if regulation is necessary, to select regulatory approaches that maximize net benefits (including potential economic, environmental, public health and safety effects, distributive impacts, and equity). A regulatory impact analysis (RIA) must be prepared for major rules with economically significant effects ($100 million or more in any 1 year). This rule does not reach the $100 million economic threshold and therefore is not considered a major rule under the Congressional Review Act.

We believe that the benefits of this rule will amply justify its relatively minimal costs. Executive Order 12866 explicitly requires agencies to consider non-quantifiable benefits, including "distributive impacts" and "equity," and the benefits of the final rule, in these terms, will be

significant. In the words of Executive Order 12866, these
benefits are "difficult to quantify, but nevertheless
essential to consider."

More specifically, the benefits of this rule include:
(1) ensuring the protection of a patient's ability to
designate who may and may not visit the patient;
(2) broadening patient participation in the care received (a
benefit that would have, among other things, significant
emotional benefits for many patients); and
(3) creating a more patient-designated support system, with
potentially large improvements in hospital and CAH experiences
and health outcomes for patients.

The cost of implementing these changes will largely be
limited to the one-time cost related to the revisions of
hospital and CAH policies and procedures as they relate to the
requirements for patient visitation rights. There will also
be the one-time cost of producing a printed page detailing the
patient visitation rights that will be provided to patients
upon admission. We have estimated the total cost of revising
the policies and procedures related to patient visitation
rights as well as the total cost of producing a printed page
detailing these rights that will be provided to hospital and
CAH patients upon admission. No burden is being assessed on
the communication of these revisions to hospital and CAH staff

or on the distribution of the visitation rights to patients

that will be required by this rule, as these practices are

usual and customary business practices.

CMS data, as of March 31, 2010, indicated that there were

4,860 hospitals and 1,314 CAHs (for a total of 6,174) in the

United States. We prepared the cost estimates for hospitals

and CAHs together since both types of providers will be

required to perform the same functions. Regarding the costs

of revising hospital and CAH policies and procedures as

related to the proposed patient visitation rights

requirements, this function will be performed by the hospital

or CAH administrator at an hourly salary (including a 35

percent benefits) of $59.05 (based on wage estimates for a

Medical and Health Services Manager in the May 2009 National,

State, Metropolitan, and Nonmetropolitan Area Occupational

Employment and Wage Estimates report from the Bureau of Labor

Statistics)) and that this function will require approximately

15 minutes of an administrator's time to accomplish.

Therefore, the total one-time cost for all hospitals and CAHs

would be $59.05 x .25 hours x 6,174 total hospitals/CAHs =

$91,144.

The most recent CMS figures from 2008 also indicate that

there were 37,529,270 total hospital (and CAH) patient

admissions in that year. Using that as an estimate, we then

calculated the total cost for hospitals and CAHs to produce a

one-page printed disclosure form detailing the patient

visitation rights that would be provided to all patients upon

admission. We estimated the cost of production to be 2 cents

per page. Therefore, the total estimated cost for all

hospitals and CAHs to produce this one-page printed patient

visitation rights disclosure form and provide it to all

patients upon admission (based on the most recent hospital

admission figures) will be 37,529,270 total hospital patient

admissions x $0.02 = $750,585 for the first year. We will

anticipate that this form would be incorporated into hospital

and CAH admission materials for subsequent years; therefore,

we have no way to estimate the future costs to provide this

form, but expect the costs to be minimal once all hospitals

and CAHs have incorporated this disclosure of patient

visitation rights. In conclusion, the total first-year cost

for all hospitals and CAHs to meet the requirements of the

patient visitation rights will be $841,729. We believe that

the annual benefits of the rule, though not susceptible to

quantification, far exceed that amount.

The RFA requires agencies to analyze options for

regulatory relief of small businesses. For purposes of the

RFA, small entities include small businesses, nonprofit

organizations, and small governmental jurisdictions. Most

hospitals and most other providers and suppliers are small

entities, either by nonprofit status or by having revenues of

$7.0 million to $34.5 million in any 1 year. Individuals and

States are not included in the definition of a small entity.

We are not preparing an analysis for the RFA because the

Secretary has determined that this rule will not have a

significant economic impact on a substantial number of small

entities.

In addition, section 1102(b) of the Act requires us to

prepare a regulatory impact analysis if a rule may have a

significant impact on the operations of a substantial number

of small rural hospitals. This analysis must conform to the

provisions of section 604 of the RFA. For purposes of section

1102(b) of the Act, we define a small rural hospital as a

hospital that is located outside of a Metropolitan Statistical

Area for Medicare payment regulations and has fewer than 100

beds. We are not preparing an analysis for section 1102(b) of

the Act because the Secretary has determined that this rule

will not have a significant impact on the operations of a

substantial number of small rural hospitals.

Section 202 of the Unfunded Mandates Reform Act of 1995

also requires that agencies assess anticipated costs and

benefits before issuing any rule whose mandates require

spending in any 1 year of $100 million in 1995 dollars,

updated annually for inflation. In 2010, that threshold is
approximately $135 million. This rule will have no
consequential effect on State, local, or tribal governments in
the aggregate or on the private sector.

Executive Order 13132 establishes certain requirements
that an agency must meet when it promulgates a rule that
imposes substantial direct requirement costs on State and
local governments, preempts State law, or otherwise has
Federalism implications. Because this regulation will not
impose any substantial costs on State or local governments,
the requirements of Executive Order 13132 are not applicable.

In accordance with the provisions of Executive Order
12866, this regulation was reviewed by the Office of
Management and Budget.

CMS-3228-F   72

List of Subjects

42 CFR Part 482

Grant programs—Health, Hospitals, Medicaid, Medicare,
Reporting and Recordkeeping requirements

42 CFR Part 485

Grant programs—Health, Health facilities, Medicaid,
Medicare, Reporting and Recordkeeping requirements.

.

For the reasons set forth in the preamble, the Centers for Medicare & Medicaid Services amends 42 CFR chapter IV as set forth below:

PART 482—CONDITIONS OF PARTICIPATION FOR HOSPITALS

1. The authority citation for Part 482 continues to read as follows:

Authority: Secs. 1102 and 1871 of the Social Security Act (42 U.S.C. 1302 and 1395(hh)).

2. Section 482.13 is amended by adding a new paragraph (h) to read as follows:

§482.13 Condition of participation: Patient's rights.

* * * * *

(h) <u>Standard: Patient visitation rights</u>. A hospital must have written policies and procedures regarding the visitation rights of patients, including those setting forth any clinically necessary or reasonable restriction or limitation that the hospital may need to place on such rights and the reasons for the clinical restriction or limitation. A hospital must meet the following requirements:

(1) Inform each patient (or support person, where appropriate) of his or her visitation rights, including any clinical restriction or limitation on such rights, when he or she is informed of his or her other rights under this section.

(2)   Inform each patient (or support person, where appropriate) of the right, subject to his or her consent, to receive the visitors whom he or she designates, including, but not limited to, a spouse, a domestic partner (including a same-sex domestic partner), another family member, or a friend, and his or her right to withdraw or deny such consent at any time.

(3)   Not restrict, limit, or otherwise deny visitation privileges on the basis of race, color, national origin, religion, sex, gender identity, sexual orientation, or disability.

(4)   Ensure that all visitors enjoy full and equal visitation privileges consistent with patient preferences.

PART 485—CONDITIONS OF PARTICIPATION: SPECIALIZED PROVIDERS

3.   The authority citation for Part 485 continues to read as follows:

Authority: Secs. 1102 and 1871 of the Social Security Act (42 U.S.C. 1302 and 1395(hh)).

4.   Section 485.635 is amended by adding a new paragraph (f) to read as follows:

§485.635 Condition of participation: Provision of services.

*   *   *   *   *

(f) Standard: Patient visitation rights. A CAH must
have written policies and procedures regarding the visitation
rights of patients, including those setting forth any
clinically necessary or reasonable restriction or limitation
that the CAH may need to place on such rights and the reasons
for the clinical restriction or limitation. A CAH must meet
the following requirements:

(1) Inform each patient (or support person, where
appropriate) of his or her visitation rights, including any
clinical restriction or limitation on such rights, in advance
of furnishing patient care whenever possible.

(2) Inform each patient (or support person, where
appropriate) of the right, subject to his or her consent, to
receive the visitors whom he or she designates, including, but
not limited to, a spouse, a domestic partner (including a
same-sex domestic partner), another family member, or a
friend, and his or her right to withdraw or deny such consent
at any time.

(3) Not restrict, limit, or otherwise deny visitation
privileges on the basis of race, color, national origin,
religion, sex, gender identity, sexual orientation, or
disability.

CMS-3228-F 76

(4) Ensure that all visitors enjoy full and equal visitation privileges consistent with patient preferences.

CMS-3228-F

(Catalog of Federal Domestic Assistance Program No. 93.773,
Medicare--Hospital Insurance; and Program No. 93.774,
Medicare--Supplementary Medical Insurance Program). (Catalog
of Federal Domestic Assistance Program No. 93.778, Medical
Assistance Program).

Dated: October 21, 2010

_____

Donald M. Berwick,

Administrator,

Centers for Medicare & Medicaid

Services.

Approved: November 15, 2010

_____

Kathleen Sebelius,

Secretary.

BILLING CODE 4120-01-P

CMS-3228-F   78

[FR Doc. 2010-29194 Filed 11/17/2010 at 11:15 am; Publication

Date: 11/19/2010]

APPENDIX B-6

FEDERAL REGISTER

Vol. 76   Monday,

No. 15   January 24, 2011

Part IV

Department of Housing and Urban Development

24 CFR Parts 5, 200, 203, et al.
Equal Access to Housing in HUD Programs—Regardless of Sexual Orientation or Gender Identity; Proposed Rule

DEPARTMENT OF HOUSING AND URBAN DEVELOPMENT

24 CFR Parts 5, 200, 203, 236, 570, 574, and 982

[Docket No. FR 5359–P–01]

RIN 2501–AD49

Equal Access to Housing in HUD Programs—Regardless of Sexual Orientation or Gender Identity

AGENCY: Office of the Secretary, HUD.

ACTION: Proposed rule.

SUMMARY: As the Nation's housing agency, HUD administers programs designed to meet the goal of ensuring decent housing and suitable living environment for all. In pursuit of this goal, it is HUD's responsibility to ensure that all who are otherwise eligible to participate in HUD's programs have equal access to these programs and have the opportunity to compete fairly for HUD funds without being subject to arbitrary exclusion.

There is evidence, however, that lesbian, gay, bisexual, and transgender (LGBT) individuals and families are being arbitrarily excluded from some housing opportunities in the private sector. Through this proposed rule, HUD strives to ensure that its core programs are open to all eligible individuals and families regardless of sexual orientation or gender identity.

DATES: *Comment Due Date:* March 25, 2011.

ADDRESSES: Interested persons are invited to submit comments regarding this proposed rule to the Regulations Division, Office of General Counsel, Department of Housing and Urban Development, 451 7th Street, SW., Room 10276, Washington, DC 20410–0500. There are two methods for submitting public comments. All submissions and other communications must refer to the above docket number and title.

1. *Electronic Submission of Comments.* Interested persons may submit comments electronically through the Federal eRulemaking Portal at *http://www.regulations.gov.* HUD strongly encourages commenters to submit comments electronically. Electronic submission of comments allows the commenter maximum time to prepare and submit a comment, ensures timely receipt by HUD, and enables HUD to make them immediately available to the public. Comments submitted electronically through the *http://www.regulations.gov* Web site can be viewed by other commenters and interested members of the public.

Commenters should follow the instructions provided on that site to submit comments electronically.

2. *Submission of Comments by Mail.* Comments may be submitted by mail to the Regulations Division, Office of General Counsel, Department of Housing and Urban Development, 451 7th Street, SW., Room 10276, Washington, DC 20410–0500.

Note: To receive consideration as public comments, comments must be submitted through one of the two methods specified above. Again, all submissions must refer to the docket number and title of the rule.

No Facsimile Comments. Facsimile (FAX) comments are not acceptable.

Public Inspection of Public Comments. All properly submitted comments and communications submitted to HUD will be available for public inspection and copying between 8 a.m. and 5 p.m. weekdays at the above address. Due to security measures at the HUD Headquarters building, an appointment to review the public comments must be scheduled in advance by calling the Regulations Division at 202–708–3055 (this is not a toll-free number). Individuals with speech or hearing impairments may access this number via TTY by calling the Federal Information Relay Service at 800–877–8339. Copies of all comments submitted are available for inspection and downloading at *http:// www.regulations.gov.*

FOR FURTHER INFORMATION CONTACT: Kenneth J. Carroll, Director, Fair Housing Assistance Program Division, Office of Fair Housing and Equal Opportunity, Department of Housing and Urban Development, 451 7th Street, SW., Room 5206, Washington, DC 20410–8000; telephone number 202–708–2333 (this is not a toll-free number). Persons with hearing or speech challenges may access this number through TTY by calling the toll-free Federal Information Relay Service at 800–877–8339.

SUPPLEMENTARY INFORMATION:

I. Background

Like all Federal agencies, HUD is charged with ensuring equal access to Federal programs that it administers. HUD also has a unique charge, as the Nation's housing agency, to promote the Federal goal of providing decent housing and a suitable living environment for all.[1] Accordingly, HUD has a responsibility to ensure equal access to its core rental assistance and homeownership programs for all eligible

[1] This goal is rooted in section 2 of the Housing Act of 1949, 42 U.S.C. 1441.

individuals and families. HUD fulfills this responsibility by taking such actions as necessary so that all who are otherwise eligible to participate in HUD programs will not be excluded based on criteria that are irrelevant to the purpose of HUD's programs, such as sexual orientation or gender identity.

There is evidence suggesting that LGBT individuals and families do not have equal access to housing. For example, a 2007 study of housing discrimination based on sexual orientation conducted by Michigan fair housing centers found disparate treatment in 32 out of 120 fair housing tests it conducted. Testers posing as gay or lesbian home seekers received unfavorable treatment on issues such as whether housing was available, the amount of rent, application fees, and levels of encouragement as compared to testers posing as heterosexual home seekers. The gay and lesbian testers also were subjected to offensive comments. *See* Michigan Fair Housing Center's Report on "Sexual Orientation and Housing Discrimination in Michigan" January 2007 at *http:// www.fhcmichigan.org/images/ Arcus_web1.pdf.*

A recent survey of more than 6,000 transgender persons conducted by the National Center for Transgender Equality and the National Gay and Lesbian Task Force (Task Force) indicated significant levels of housing instability for transgender people. Twenty-six percent of respondents reported having to find different places to sleep for short periods of time due to bias. Eleven percent of respondents reported having been evicted due to bias, and 19 percent reported becoming homeless due to bias. *See* November 2009, "Preliminary Findings, National Transgender Discrimination Survey," at *http://www.thetaskforce.org/ reports_and_research/ trans_survey_preliminary_findings.*

In light of the increasing awareness of housing discrimination against LGBT persons, a growing number of States, counties, and cities are enacting laws that prohibit discrimination in housing on the basis of sexual orientation or gender identity. Twenty States, the District of Columbia, and over 200 localities have enacted such laws.[2] The legislative records of some of these enactments are a source of further evidence of housing discrimination

[2] *See, e.g.,* Laws Prohibiting Discrimination Based on Sexual Orientation and Gender Identity (Institute of Real Estate Management (IREM) Legislative Staff July 2007, which is available at *http://www.irem.org/pdfs/publicpolicy/Anti- discrimination.pdf); see also http://www.hrc.org/ issues/5499.htm.*

Federal Register / Vol. 76, No. 15 / Monday, January 24, 2011 / Proposed Rules   **4195**

based on sexual orientation or gender identity. For example, in a State legislative hearing on a proposed amendment to the North Dakota fair housing law that would add sexual orientation to the list of protected characteristics, a woman recounted how she and her partner were evicted once the landlord learned her partner was not a man. *See* "Gay-rights Advocates Press for Change in N.D. Law," February 4, 2009, Bismarck Tribune, at *http:// www.bismarcktribune.com/news/state- and-regional/article_fb795f86-fc42- 5184-b6d6-ad424e3243ce.html.*

The U.S. Congress has acted to protect the rights of LGBT individuals to be free from bias-motivated crime. In October 2009, Federal legislation was enacted adding certain crimes motivated by a victim's actual or perceived sexual orientation or gender identity to the list of hate crimes covered by existing Federal law. *See* Matthew Shepard and James Byrd, Jr. Hate Crimes Prevention Act, Division E of the National Defense Authorization Act for Fiscal Year 2010 (Pub. L. 111–84, approved October 28, 2009). In support of this enactment, Congress found that violence motivated by the actual or perceived sexual orientation or gender identity of the victim "poses a serious national problem" because, among other things, it "devastates not just the actual victim and the family and friends of the victim, but frequently savages the community sharing the traits that caused the victim to be selected." (*See* Pub. L. 111–84, Division E, Sec. 4702(1), (5).)

In considering the mounting evidence of violence and discrimination against LGBT persons, the Department is concerned that its own programs may not be fully open to LGBT individuals and families. Accordingly, consistent with steps being taken at all levels of government to protect LGBT persons from discrimination, HUD is initiating this rulemaking in an effort to ensure that its rental housing and homeownership programs remain open to all eligible persons regardless of sexual orientation or gender identity.

II. This Proposed Rule

A. Defining Sexual Orientation and Gender Identity

The proposed rule would amend 24 CFR 5.100, which contains definitions generally applicable to HUD programs, to include definitions of "sexual orientation" and "gender identity." Section 5.100 would define "sexual orientation" as "homosexuality, heterosexuality, or bisexuality." This is the definition that the Office of Personnel Management (OPM) uses in

the context of the Federal workforce in its publication "Addressing Sexual Orientation in Federal Civilian Employment: A Guide to Employee Rights." (*See http://www.opm.gov/er/ address.pdf* at page 4.) The rule would define "gender identity," consistent with the definition of "gender identity" in the Matthew Shepard and James Byrd, Jr. Hate Crimes Prevention Act, Public Law 111–84, Division E, Section 4707(c)(4) (18 U.S.C. 249(c)(4)), as "actual or perceived gender-related characteristics."

B. Prohibiting Inquiries Regarding Sexual Orientation or Gender Identity

To further ensure equal access to HUD's housing and housing-related service programs without regard to sexual orientation or gender identity, HUD is proposing to prohibit inquiries regarding sexual orientation or gender identity. This prohibition would preclude owners and operators of HUD-assisted housing or housing whose financing is insured by HUD from inquiring about the sexual orientation or gender identity of an applicant for, or occupant of, the dwelling, whether renter- or owner-occupied. While the rule prohibits inquiries regarding sexual orientation or gender identity, nothing in the rule prohibits any individual from voluntarily self-identifying his or her sexual orientation or gender identity. Additionally, this rule is not intended to prohibit otherwise lawful inquiries of an applicant or occupant's sex where the housing provided or to be provided to the individual involves the sharing of sleeping areas or bathrooms. Through this rulemaking, HUD is proposing to institute this policy in its rental assistance and homeownership programs, which include HUD's Federal Housing Administration (FHA) mortgage insurance programs, community development programs, and public and assisted housing programs.[3] This prohibition on inquiries regarding sexual orientation or gender identity would be provided in a new paragraph (a)(2) added to 24 CFR 5.105. Section 5.105 of HUD's regulations is entitled "Other Federal Requirements." The proposed rule would divide the existing paragraph (a) into two new subparagraphs. The text in the current paragraph (a) would become subparagraph (a)(1), but retain the heading and content as currently found in § 5.105(a). A new subparagraph (a)(2) would be added, entitled "Prohibition on inquiries regarding sexual

---

[3] Institution of this policy in HUD's Native American programs will be undertaken by separate rulemaking.

orientation or gender identity." The regulations for the HUD programs to which the prohibition on such inquiries apply already include cross-reference to § 5.105, and with the amendment to this section, the cross-reference would now include the prohibition in § 5.105(a).

This policy prohibiting inquiries regarding sexual orientation or gender identity is undertaken pursuant to HUD's general rulemaking authority granted by section 7(d) of the Department of Housing and Urban Development Act (42 U.S.C. 3535(d)) and HUD's specific rulemaking authority to establish eligibility criteria for participation in HUD programs granted by the statutes that establish the various HUD programs.

C. Prohibiting Sexual Orientation and Gender Identity as Grounds for Decisionmaking in Federal Housing Administration (FHA) Programs

Section 203.33(b) of HUD's FHA regulations (24 CFR 203.33(b)) provides that a mortgagee's determination of the adequacy of a single-family mortgagor's income "shall be made in a uniform manner without regard to" specified prohibited grounds. The proposed rule would add actual or perceived sexual orientation and gender identity to the prohibited grounds enumerated in 24 CFR 203.33(b) to ensure FHA-insured lenders do not deny or otherwise alter the terms of mortgages on the basis of criteria that are irrelevant to the purpose of obtaining FHA-mortgage insurance.

D. Eligible Families in HUD Programs

For the following HUD regulations specified below, this proposed rule clarifies that all otherwise eligible families, regardless of marital status, sexual orientation, or gender identity, have the opportunity to participate in HUD programs. The majority of HUD's rental housing and homeownership programs already interpret "family" broadly. Family includes a single person and families with or without children, just to cite two examples. This proposed rule clarifies that families who are otherwise eligible for HUD programs may not be excluded because one or more members of the family may be an LGBT individual or have an LGBT relationship or be perceived to be such an individual or in such relationship.

This section lists the HUD programs for which this proposed rule clarifies and confirms the broad meaning of family.

1. *Section 8 Tenant-Based Assistance (Housing Choice Voucher Program) and Public Housing Programs (24 CFR part 5 and 24 CFR part 982).* The proposed rule would amend the regulations in 24

CFR 5.403, which contains the definitions applicable to HUD's Housing Choice Voucher (HCV) and public housing programs. The term "family," provided in part 5 for these HUD programs, is based on section 3 of the U.S. Housing Act of 1937 (42 U.S. 1437a) (1937 Act). Section 3(b)(3)(B) of the 1937 Act provides as follows:

Families.—The term "families" includes families with children and, in the cases of elderly families, near-elderly families, and disabled families, means families whose heads (or their spouses), or whose sole members, are elderly, near-elderly, or persons with disabilities, respectively. The term includes, in the cases of elderly families, near-elderly families, and disabled families, 2 or more elderly persons, near-elderly persons, or persons with disabilities living together, and 1 or more such persons living with 1 or more persons determined under the public housing agency plan to be essential to their care or well-being.

Section 3(b)(3)(A) of the 1937 Act provides that the term "single person" includes a family that consists of a single person. (*See* Section 3(b)(3)(C) of the 1937 Act.) Section 3(b)(3)(C) provides that the temporary absence of a child from a home due to placement in foster care shall not be considered in determining family composition and family size, meaning that a child, although absent from the home, is still considered a family member. Sections 3(b)(3)(D), (E), (F), and (G) also specify the meaning of the following terms: elderly person, person with disabilities, displaced person, and near-elderly person. All of these statutory terms are currently captured in the term "family" in § 5.403.

These statutory terms result in an expansive view of what can constitute a family, and the 1937 Act provides examples of what the term "families" includes but does not limit the composition of families to the statutory examples. Consistent with the broad meaning given to the term family by the 1937 Act, this proposed rule, clarifies that a family, however composed, is a family regardless of marital status, sexual orientation, or gender. The term "family" in § 5.403 is similar in substance to the term "family composition" in § 982.201, but HUD finds that the statutory terms are more coherently reflected in § 982.201. Therefore, in addressing the term "family" in § 5.403, HUD has structured the organization of this term as found in § 982.201.

This proposed rule also would amend the terms "disabled family," "elderly family," and "near-elderly family" in § 5.403. Each of these terms is stated as a family whose head, spouse, or sole

member is, respectively, for each of these terms, a person with disabilities, a person at least 62 years of age, or a person who is at least 50 years of age but below the age of 62. To each of these terms, the proposed rule adds the term "co-head."

"Co-head" is a term that has long been used in supplementary documents to HUD's rental assistance programs. Form HUD–50058 pertaining to the Multifamily Tenant Characteristics System (MTCS) and its accompanying Instruction Booklet use the term "co-head" and provides that "co-head" is an individual in the household who is equally responsible for the lease with the head of household. HUD's Web page devoted to frequently asked questions about general income and rent determination for HUD's rental housing programs provides in the answer to question 38 an example of co-head as follows: "An example of this [co-head] would be an unmarried couple or two persons living together and listed as head and co-head on the lease agreement." (*See http://www.hud.gov/ offices/pih/programs/ph/rhiip/ faq_gird.cfm*).

The inclusion in the proposed amendment to § 5.403 of "co-head," again a familiar term to housing providers of HUD assistance, would not change the meaning of the statutory term "heads" of household, which is not currently defined in statute or regulation. The inclusion would merely codify HUD's existing interpretation of "heads," which, as noted above, recognizes that some families living in HUD-assisted rental housing have more than one family head. Nor would including the term "co-head" in "disabled family," "elderly family," and "near-elderly family" alter or expand the meaning of "spouse." Consistent with longstanding HUD interpretation, a head and co-head of the family may be a married couple, an unmarried couple, or two adults living together who are listed as head and co-head on the lease agreement.

The proposed rule would add "family," as provided in 24 CFR 5.403, to the list of general definitions in § 5.100, and clarify that the term is applicable to all HUD programs unless otherwise provided in the regulations for a specific HUD program.

The proposed rule also would add to 24 CFR 982.4 and § 982.201 a cross-reference to the term "family" in 24 CFR 5.403.

2. *Federal Housing Administration (FHA) Programs (24 CFR Parts 200, 203, 236, and 291).* Basic definitions that are generally applicable to all FHA multifamily programs are found in 24

CFR 200.3. This regulatory section would be amended to cross-reference to "family" in 24 CFR 5.403.

In addition to the proposed amendment to 24 CFR 200.3, HUD proposes to amend 24 CFR 236.1. Section 236.1(a) contains the savings clause of applicable regulations for the mortgages insured under the Rental and Cooperative Housing for Lower Income Families Program, for which new mortgages have not been insured since 1983. Although no new mortgages are insured under this program, authority remains to refinance mortgages insured under section 236 of the National Housing Act (NHA) or to finance, pursuant to section 236(j)(3) of the NHA, the purchase by a cooperative or nonprofit corporation or association of a project assisted under section 236. The proposed amendment would provide that the term "family" in 24 CFR 200.3(a) applies to any refinancing of a mortgage insured under section 236 of the NHA, or to financing, pursuant to section 236(j)(3) of the NHA, of the purchase, by a cooperative or nonprofit corporation or association, of a project assisted under section 236.

3. *Community Development Block Grants (CDBG) Programs (24 CFR Part 570).* Section 570.3 of the CDBG regulations (24 CFR part 570, subpart A) provides basic definitions that are applicable to all CDBG programs. The proposed rule would amend 24 CFR 570.3 to cross-reference to the term "family" in 24 CFR 5.403. The proposed rule would revise the term "household" in § 570.3, another term used in CDBG programs, to ensure there is no exclusion of an eligible household on the basis of sexual orientation or gender identity. The revisions to "household" would also remove some redundancy in terminology. The current term "household" provides that occupants of a household may be a single family or one person living alone, but the term "family," as discussed earlier in this preamble, includes a single person. Accordingly, the revisions to "household" are designed to eliminate any conflict between the terms "household" and "family."

4. *Housing Opportunities for Persons With AIDS (HOPWA) (24 CFR Part 574).* The proposed rule would amend 24 CFR 574.3 to cross-reference to "family" in 24 CFR 5.403, and to remove obsolete language that states that for a person to be eligible to live with another person, the other person must be determined to be important to the person's care or well-being.

E. HUD Programs for Which Eligible Family Does Not Require Amendment

The proposed rule does not revise the term "family" in the regulations for the Home Investment Partnership Program, which are codified at 24 CFR part 92. "Family" in § 92.2 already cross-references to the term family in § 5.403. The proposed rule would not amend the part 891 definitions of "household" (§ 891.105), "elderly person" (§ 891.205), or "disabled household" (§ 891.305) governing programs that provide Supportive Housing for the Elderly and Persons with Disabilities. These programs already provide meanings for the term family.

Additionally, the rule does not propose to amend the term "family" in the Project-Based Voucher (PBV) Program regulations, codified at 24 CFR part 983. The PBV regulations, in § 983.4, already cross-reference to the definitions in 24 CFR part 5, subpart D, which includes the § 5.403.

F. Changes to HUD Forms

This rule, as proposed, does not impose any new information collection requirements on participants in the covered HUD programs. Rather than requiring collection of information, the rule prohibits inquiries regarding sexual orientation or gender identity of any individual or family receiving housing assistance or benefitting from mortgage insurance under the covered HUD programs. At the final rule stage, if HUD identifies any forms for which the regulatory citation to the term "family" must be included as a result of promulgation of this rule, HUD will work with the Office of Management and Budget (OMB) to include such term. As noted earlier in this preamble, such inquiry is irrelevant to an individual's or family's eligibility to participate in a HUD-covered program.

III. Solicitation of Comments

The Department welcomes comment on the amendments proposed in this rule, including identification of any program area which may have been inadvertently overlooked and should reference "family" in 24 CFR 5.403. The Department also welcomes any information regarding exclusion or discrimination on the basis of sexual orientation or gender identity in HUD programs. Such information will help the Department in its effort to craft regulations that will effectively ensure access to HUD programs by all eligible persons regardless of sexual orientation or gender identity.

IV. Findings and Certifications

Executive Order 12866, Regulatory Planning and Review

OMB reviewed this proposed rule under Executive Order 12866 (entitled "Regulatory Planning and Review"). A determination was made that this proposed rule is a "significant regulatory action," as defined in section 3(f) of the Order (although not economically significant, as provided in section 3(f)(1) of the Order). The docket file is available for public inspection in the Regulations Division, Office of General Counsel, Department of Housing and Urban Development, 451 7th Street, SW., Room 10276, Washington, DC 20410–0500. Due to security measures at the HUD Headquarters building, please schedule an appointment to review the docket file by calling the Regulations Division at 202–402–3055 (this is not a toll-free number). Individuals with speech or hearing impairments may access this number via TTY by calling the Federal Information Relay Service at 800–877–8339.

Regulatory Flexibility Act

The Regulatory Flexibility Act (RFA) (5 U.S.C. 601 *et seq.*) generally requires an agency to conduct a regulatory flexibility analysis of any rule subject to notice and comment rulemaking requirements, unless the agency certifies that the rule will not have a significant economic impact on a substantial number of small entities. This proposed rule would not impose any new costs, or modify existing costs, applicable to HUD grantees. Rather, the purpose of the proposed rule is to ensure open access to HUD's core programs, regardless of sexual orientation or gender identity. In this rule, HUD affirms the broad meaning of "family" that is already provided for in HUD programs by statute. The only clarification that HUD makes is that a family is a family as currently provided in statute and regulation, regardless of marital status, sexual orientation, or gender identity. Accordingly, the undersigned certifies that this rule will not have a significant economic impact on a substantial number of small entities.

Notwithstanding HUD's determination that this rule will not have a significant effect on a substantial number of small entities, HUD specifically invites comments regarding any less burdensome alternatives to this rule that will meet HUD's objectives as described in the preamble to this rule.

Environmental Impact

This proposed rule sets forth nondiscrimination standards. Accordingly, under 24 CFR 50.19(c)(3), this rule is categorically excluded from environmental review under the National Environmental Policy Act of 1969 (42 U.S.C. 4321).

Executive Order 13132, Federalism

Executive Order 13132 (entitled "Federalism") prohibits an agency from publishing any rule that has federalism implications if the rule either: (i) Imposes substantial direct compliance costs on State and local governments and is not required by statute, or (ii) preempts State law, unless the agency meets the consultation and funding requirements of section 6 of the Executive Order. This proposed rule would not have federalism implications and would not impose substantial direct compliance costs on State and local governments or preempt State law within the meaning of the Executive Order.

Unfunded Mandates Reform Act

Title II of the Unfunded Mandates Reform Act of 1995 (2 U.S.C. 1531–1538) (UMRA) establishes requirements for Federal agencies to assess the effects of their regulatory actions on State, local, and Tribal governments, and on the private sector. This proposed rule would not impose any Federal mandates on any State, local, or Tribal governments, or on the private sector, within the meaning of the UMRA.

List of Subjects

24 CFR Part 5

Administrative practice and procedure, Aged, Claims, Drug abuse, Drug traffic control, Grant programs—housing and community development, Grant programs—Indians, Individuals with disabilities, Loan programs—housing and community development, Low and moderate income housing, Mortgage insurance, Pets, Public housing, Rent subsidies, Reporting and recordkeeping requirements.

24 CFR Part 200

Administrative practice and procedure, Claims, Equal employment opportunity, Fair housing, Home improvement, Housing standards, Lead poisoning, Loan programs—housing and community development, Mortgage insurance, Organization and functions (Government agencies), Penalties, Reporting and recordkeeping.

4198   Federal Register / Vol. 76, No. 15 / Monday, January 24, 2011 / Proposed Rules

24 CFR Part 203

Hawaiian Natives, Home improvement, Indians—lands, Loan programs—housing and community development, Mortgage insurance, Reporting and recordkeeping requirements, Solar energy.

24 CFR Part 236

Grant programs—housing and community development, Low- and moderate-income housing, Mortgage insurance, Rent subsidies, Reporting and recordkeeping requirements.

24 CFR Part 570

Administrative practice and procedure, American Samoa, Community development block grants, Grant programs—education, Grant programs—housing and community development, Guam, Indians, Loan programs—housing and community development, Low and moderate income housing, Northern Mariana Islands, Pacific Islands Trust Territory, Puerto Rico, Reporting and recordkeeping requirements, Student aid, Virgin Islands.

24 CFR Part 574

Community facilities, Grant programs—health programs, Grant programs—housing and community development, Grant programs—social programs, HIV/AIDS, Low and moderate income housing, Reporting and recordkeeping requirements.

24 CFR Part 982

Grant programs—housing and community development, Grant programs—Indians, Indians, Public housing, Rent subsidies, Reporting and recordkeeping requirements.

Accordingly, for the reasons stated above, HUD proposes to amend 24 CFR parts 5, 200, 203, 236, 570, 574, and 982 as follows:

PART 5—GENERAL HUD PROGRAM REQUIREMENTS; WAIVERS

1. The authority citation for 24 CFR part 5 continues to read as follows:

Authority: 42 U.S.C. 3535(d), unless otherwise noted.

2. The heading of subpart A is revised to read as follows:

Subpart A—Generally Applicable Definitions and Requirements; Waivers

3. In § 5.100, definitions for "family," "gender identity," and "sexual orientation" are added to read as follows:

§ 5.100   Definitions.

*   *   *   *   *

Family has the meaning provided this term in § 5.403, and applies to all HUD programs unless otherwise provided in the regulations for a specific HUD program.

*   *   *   *   *

Gender identity means actual or perceived gender-related characteristics.

*   *   *   *   *

Sexual orientation means homosexuality, heterosexuality, or bisexuality.

*   *   *   *   *

4. In § 5.105, the introductory text is revised, paragraph (a) is redesignated as paragraph (a)(1), and a new paragraph (a)(2) is added to read as follows:

§ 5.105   Other Federal requirements.

The requirements set forth in this section apply to all HUD programs, except as may be otherwise noted in the respective program regulations in title 24 of the CFR, or unless inconsistent with statutes authorizing certain HUD programs:

(a)(1) *Nondiscrimination and equal opportunity.* * * *

(2) *Prohibition on inquiries regarding sexual orientation or gender identity.* No owner or administrator of HUD-assisted or HUD-insured housing, approved lender in an FHA mortgage insurance program, nor any (or any other) recipient or subrecipient of HUD funds may inquire about the sexual orientation, or gender identity of an applicant for, or occupant of, a HUD-assisted dwelling or a dwelling whose financing is insured by HUD, whether renter- or owner-occupied. This prohibition on inquiries regarding sexual orientation or gender identity does not prohibit any individual from voluntarily self-identifying his or her sexual orientation or gender identity. This prohibition on inquiries regarding sexual orientation or gender identity does not prohibit lawful inquiries of an applicant or occupant's sex where the housing provided or to be provided to the individual involves the sharing of sleeping areas or bathrooms.

*   *   *   *   *

Subpart D—Definitions for Section 8 and Public Housing Assistance Under the United States Housing Act of 1937

5. In § 5.403, the definitions of "Disabled family," "Elderly family," "family," and "Near-elderly family" are revised to read as follows:

§ 5.403   Definitions.

*   *   *   *   *

Disabled family means a family whose head (including co-head), spouse, or sole member is a person with a disability. It may include two or more persons with disabilities living together, or one or more persons with disabilities living with one or more live-in aides.

*   *   *   *   *

Elderly family means a family whose head (including co-head), spouse, or sole member is a person who is at least 62 years of age. It may include two or more persons who are at least 62 years of age living together, or one or more persons who are at least 62 years of age living with one or more live-in aides.

Family includes but is not limited to, regardless of marital status, actual or perceived sexual orientation, or gender identity, the following:

(1) A single person, who may be an elderly person, displaced person, disabled person, near-elderly person, or any other single person; or

(2) A group of persons residing together, and such group includes, but is not limited to:

(i) A family with or without children (a child who is temporarily away from the home because of placement in foster care is considered a member of the family);

(ii) An elderly family;

(iii) A near-elderly family;

(iv) A disabled family;

(v) A displaced family; and

(vi) The remaining member of a tenant family.

*   *   *   *   *

Near-elderly family means a family whose head (including co-head), spouse, or sole member is a person who is at least 50 years of age but below the age of 62; or two or more persons, who are at least 50 years of age but below the age of 62, living together; or one or more persons who are at least 50 years of age but below the age of 62, living with one or more live-in aides.

*   *   *   *   *

PART 200—INTRODUCTION TO FHA PROGRAMS

6. The authority citation for 24 CFR part 200 continues to read as follows:

Authority: 12 U.S.C. 1702–1715z–21; 42 U.S.C. 3535(d).

7. Section 200.3(a) is revised to read as follows:

§ 200.3   Definitions.

(a) The definitions "Department," "Elderly person," "Family," "HUD," and "Secretary," as used in this subpart A, shall have the meanings given these definitions in 24 CFR part 5.

*   *   *   *   *

8. Section 200.300 is revised to read as follows:

Federal Register / Vol. 76, No. 15 / Monday, January 24, 2011 / Proposed Rules   **4199**

§ 200.300 Nondiscrimination and fair housing policy.

Federal Housing Administration programs shall be administered in accordance with:

(a) The nondiscrimination and fair housing requirements set forth in 24 CFR part 5, including the prohibition on inquiries regarding sexual orientation or gender identity set forth in 24 CFR 5.105(a)(2); and

(b) The affirmative fair housing marketing requirements in 24 CFR part 200, subpart M and 24 CFR part 108.

PART 203—SINGLE FAMILY MORTGAGE INSURANCE

9. The authority citation for 24 CFR part 203 continues to read as follows:

Authority: 12 U.S.C. 1709, 1710, 1715b, 1715z–16, and 1715u; 42 U.S.C. 3535(d).

10. In § 203.33, paragraph (b) is revised to read as follows:

§ 203.33 Relationship of income to mortgage payments.

*   *   *   *   *

(b) Determinations of adequacy of mortgagor income under this section shall be made in a uniform manner without regard to race, color, religion, sex, national origin, familial status, handicap, marital status, actual or perceived sexual orientation, gender identity, source of income of the mortgagor, or location of the property.

PART 236—MORTGAGE INSURANCE AND INTEREST REDUCTION PAYMENT FOR RENTAL PROJECTS

11. The authority citation for 24 CFR part 236 continues to read as follows:

Authority: 12 U.S.C. 1715b and 1715z–1; 42 U.S.C. 3535(d).

12. Section 236.1 is amended to add a sentence at the end of paragraph (a) to read as follows:

§ 236.1 Applicability, cross-reference, and savings clause.

(a) *Applicability.* * * * The definition of family in 24 CFR 200.3(a) applies to any refinancing of a mortgage insured

under section 236, or to financing pursuant to section 236(j)(3) of the purchase, by a cooperative or nonprofit corporation or association of a project assisted under section 236.

*   *   *   *   *

PART 570—COMMUNITY DEVELOPMENT BLOCK GRANTS

13. The authority citation for 24 CFR part 570 continues to read as follows:

Authority: 42 U.S.C. 3535(d), and 5301–5320.

Subpart A—General Provisions

14. In § 570.3, the definitions of "family" and "household" are revised to read as follows:

§ 570.3 Definitions.

*   *   *   *   *

Family refers to the definition of "family" set out in 24 CFR 5.403.

Household means all persons occupying a housing unit. The occupants may be a family, as defined in 24 CFR 5.403, two or more families living together, or any other group of related or unrelated persons who share living arrangements, regardless of marital status, actual or perceived sexual orientation, or gender identity.

*   *   *   *   *

PART 574—HOUSING OPPORTUNITIES FOR PERSONS WITH AIDS

15. The authority citation for 24 CFR part 574 continues to read as follows:

Authority: 42 U.S.C. 3535(d) and 12901–12912.

16. In § 574.3, the definition of "family" is revised to read as follows:

§ 574.3 Definitions.

*   *   *   *   *

Family is defined as set forth in 24 CFR 5.403 and includes one or more eligible persons living with another person or persons, regardless of marital status, or actual or perceived sexual orientation or gender identity, and the surviving member or members of any

family described in this definition who were living in a unit assisted under the HOPWA program with the person with AIDS at the time of his or her death.

*   *   *   *   *

PART 982—SECTION 8 TENANT-BASED ASSISTANCE: HOUSING CHOICE VOUCHER PROGRAM

17. The authority citation for 24 CFR part 982 continues to read as follows:

Authority: 42 U.S.C. 1437f and 3535(d).

18. In § 982.4, paragraphs (a)(1) is revised, paragraph (a)(2) is removed, paragraph (a)(3) is redesignated as new paragraph (a)(2), and the definition of "family" in paragraph (b) is revised to read as follows:

§ 982.4 Definitions.

(a) *Definitions found elsewhere.* (1) *General definitions.* The following terms are defined in part 5, subpart A of this title: 1937 Act, covered person, drug, drug-related criminal activity, Federally assisted housing, guest, household, HUD, MSA, other person under the tenant's control, public housing, Section 8, and violent criminal activity.

*   *   *   *   *

(b) * * *

Family. A person or group of persons, as determined by the PHA consistent with 24 CFR 5.403, approved to reside in a unit with assistance under the program. *See* discussion of family composition at § 982.201(c).

*   *   *   *   *

19. In § 982.201, paragraph (c) is revised to read as follows:

§ 982.201 Eligibility and targeting.

*   *   *   *   *

(c) *Family composition. See* definition of "family" in 24 CFR 5.403.

*   *   *   *   *

Dated: December 1, 2010.

Shaun Donovan,

Secretary.

[FR Doc. 2011–1346 Filed 1–21–11; 8:45 am]

BILLING CODE 4210–67–P

APPENDIX B-7

R³ Report Requirement, Rationale, Reference

A complimentary publication of The Joint Commission   Issue 1, February 9, 2011

Published for Joint Commission accredited organizations and interested health care professionals, *R³ Report* provides the rationale and references that The Joint Commission employs in the development of new requirements. While the standards manuals also provide a rationale, the rationale provided in *R³ Report* goes into more depth. The references provide the evidence that supports the requirement. *R³ Report* may be reproduced only in its entirety and credited to The Joint Commission. To receive by e-mail, visit www.jointcommission.org.

Patient-centered communication standards for hospitals

Requirements

The full text of the patient-centered communication standards is provided in the Joint Commission monograph, *Advancing Effective Communication, Cultural Competence, and Patient- and Family-Centered Care: A Roadmap for Hospitals*. The *Roadmap for Hospitals* provides recommendations to help hospitals address unique patient needs and meet and exceed compliance with the new patient-centered communication standards and other related Joint Commission requirements. The *Roadmap for Hospitals* is available to download for free from http://www.jointcommission.org/Advancing_Effective_Communication/. Selected patient-centered communication standards and elements of performance (EPs) are provided below.

PC.02.01.21: The hospital effectively communicates with patients when providing care, treatment, and services.

EP 1   The hospital identifies the patient's oral and written communication needs, including the patient's preferred language for discussing health care. (Also see RC.02.01.01 EP 1)
Note: *Examples of communication needs include the need for personal devices such as hearing aids or glasses, language interpreters, communication boards, and translated or plain language materials.*

EP 2   The hospital communicates with the patient during the provision of care, treatment, and services in a manner that meets the patient's oral and written communication needs. (Also see RI.01.01.03 EPs 1-3)

> **Tell us what you think about *R³ Report***
>
> The Joint Commission is interested in your thoughts about the new *R³ Report* quarterly e-newsletter. Please take a few minutes to complete a short on-line survey. The survey will be open through **March 30, 2011**. The goal of this survey is to evaluate the effectiveness of this new publication in providing the rationale for The Joint Commission requirement addressed in this issue.

RC.02.01.01: The medical record contains information that reflects the patient's care, treatment, and services.
EP 28   The medical record contains the patient's race and ethnicity.

RI.01.01.01: The hospital respects, protects, and promotes patient rights.
EP 28   The hospital allows a family member, friend, or other individual to be present with the patient for emotional support during the course of stay.
Note: *The hospital allows for the presence of a support individual of the patient's choice, unless the individual's presence infringes on others' rights, safety, or is medically or therapeutically contraindicated. The individual may or may not be the patient's surrogate decision-maker or legally authorized representative. (For more information on surrogate or family involvement in patient care, treatment and services, refer to RI.01.02.01 EPs 6-8.)*

EP 29   The hospital prohibits discrimination based on age, race, ethnicity, religion, culture, language, physical or mental disability, socioeconomic status, sex, sexual orientation, and gender identity or expression.

Joint Commission surveyors began evaluating compliance with the patient-centered communication standards on January 1, 2011; however, findings will not affect the accreditation decision until January 1, 2012 at the earliest.* The information collected by Joint Commission surveyors and staff during this implementation pilot phase will be used to address common implementation questions and concerns.

Rationale

* Due to recent changes to the Centers for Medicare & Medicaid Services Conditions of Participation regarding equal visitation rights for all patients, standard RI.01.01.01 EPs 28 and 29 are scheduled for an earlier implementation date, July 1, 2011.

www.jointcommission.org

In January 2010, The Joint Commission released a set of new and revised standards for patient-centered communication as part of an initiative to advance effective communication, cultural competence, and patient- and family-centered care. These standards are designed to improve the safety and quality of care for all patients and to inspire hospitals to adopt practices promoting better communication and patient engagement. A growing body of research documents that a variety of patient populations experience less safe or lower quality of care or poorer health outcomes associated with their race, ethnicity, language, disability, or sexual orientation. Among other factors, these studies document that these disparities in health care can be caused by cultural or language barriers that impair communication with caregivers, impeded access to care, or fear of discrimination.[1,2,3,4] Hospitals that do not adequately address cultural, communication, mobility, and other patient needs will continue to put themselves and their patients at risk for negative consequences. The Joint Commission has made several efforts to better understand individual patients' needs and to provide guidance for organizations working to address those needs. The Joint Commission first focused on studying language, culture and health literacy issues, but later expanded its scope of work to include the broader issues of effective communication, cultural competence, and patient and family-centered care. No longer considered to be simply a patient's right, effective communication is now accepted as an essential component of quality care and patient safety.[5,6] Additional studies show that incorporating the concepts of cultural competence and patient- and family-centeredness into the care process can increase patient satisfaction and adherence with treatment.[7,8]

Reference
Effective Communication (PC.02.01.21 EPs 1 and 2)
Identifying the patient's oral and written communication needs is an essential step in determining how to facilitate the exchange of information with the patient during the care process. Patients may have hearing or visual needs, speak or read in a primary language other than English, experience difficulty understanding health information, or may be unable to speak fully or well due to their medical condition or treatment. Additionally, some communication needs may change during the course of care. Once the patient's communication needs are identified, the hospital can determine the best way to promote two-way communication between the patient and his or her providers in a manner that meets the patient's needs. Research shows that patients with communication problems are at an increased risk of experiencing preventable adverse events,[6] and that patients with limited English proficiency are more likely to experience adverse events than English speaking patients.[5,9] In addition, Title VI of the Civil Rights Act of 1964 prohibits discrimination based on "national origin," which includes language. Federal policies state that "reasonable steps" need to be taken to ensure that limited English proficient patients have "meaningful access" to any program or activity provided by hospitals that receive federal funding.[10,11] The Americans with Disabilities Act of 1990 and Section 504 of the Rehabilitation Act of 1973 prohibit discrimination based on disability and require hospitals to provide auxiliary aids and services to effectively communicate with patients who are deaf or hard of hearing.[12,13]

Collecting Race and Ethnicity Data (RC.02.01.01 EP 28)
The collection of patient-level demographic data on race and ethnicity provides hospitals with information on the potential cultural needs of each patient, as well as an opportunity to monitor and analyze health disparities at the population level.[14] Although the Joint Commission standards do not specify how to categorize data when collecting race and ethnicity data, many state reporting entities and payors do specify these requirements. Numerous research studies and reports have shown that racial and ethnic minorities are in poorer health, experience more significant problems accessing care, are more likely to be uninsured, and often receive lower quality health care than other Americans.[1,2,15] Collecting race and ethnicity information for each patient also provides the hospital an opportunity to: better plan for needed services; identify members of a target population to whom elements of an intervention would apply; understand potential patterns in access and outcomes for different segments of the patient population; and increase patient and provider understanding.[16,17]

Access to a Support Individual (RI.01.01.01 EP 28)

Access to a family member, friend, or other trusted individual provides a patient with emotional support, comfort, and alleviates fear during the course of the hospital stay. Some hospitals have implemented unrestricted or flexible visitation hours as part of patient- and family-centered care initiatives. Results indicate that increased visitation hours provide a better understanding of the patient and the patient's problems, better communication, and increased patient satisfaction.[18,19] An increased family presence may also provide some sensory organization to an environment that may be overwhelming to patients. Unrestricted visiting hours can enhance the family's role as a patient support system and allow them to assist with care planning, clarify information and reinforce patient education.[20,21] While the concept of access to a support individual highlighted in RI.01.01.01, EP 28 is not intended to dictate hospital visitation policy, it is intended to raise awareness of the need for visitation policies that are inclusive of those who the patient identifies as important. The Joint Commission has expanded its definition of *family* to include individuals who may not be legally related to the patient, which could incorporate someone who serves as the patient's support person.

Non-Discrimination in Care (RI.01.01.01 EP 29)

Research has shown that perceived discrimination was negatively correlated with health status for African Americans and whites, and individuals who reported discrimination were less likely to receive preventive services.[22,23] In addition, studies of lesbian and bisexual women indicated that disclosing sexual orientation to their physicians would negatively affect their health care,[24] and women who received care from providers who were knowledgeable and sensitive to lesbian issues were significantly more likely to have received a Pap test.[25] There are several federal laws and regulations that protect patients from various forms of discrimination. Title VI of the Civil Rights Act of 1964 prohibits discrimination based on "national origin,"[10] and the Americans with Disabilities Act of 1990 and Section 504 of the Rehabilitation Act of 1973 prohibit discrimination based on physical disability.[12] However, although these laws and regulations include some anti-discrimination protections, state laws vary and not all potential forms of discrimination are covered. The requirement in RI.01.01.01, EP 29 underscores the importance of providing equitable care to all patients and applies to hospitals nationwide.

Expert panel input

A multidisciplinary Expert Advisory Panel, representing a broad range of stakeholders, provided guidance regarding the principles, measures, structures and processes that serve as the foundation for the patient-centered communication standards. The panel included consumers, clinicians, researchers, purchasers, administrators, educators, quality improvement organization representatives, and others.

Level of evidence

Although The Joint Commission has gathered information from peer-reviewed literature and law and regulation for this requirement, there is no grading of the level of evidence to report.

Selected Bibliography

1. Smedley B.D., Stith A.Y., Nelson A.R.: *Unequal Treatment: Confronting Racial and Ethnic Disparities in Health Care.* Washington, D.C.: National Academy Press, 2002.
2. Agency for Healthcare Research and Quality: *National Healthcare Disparities Report, 2006.* Rockville, Md.: U.S. Department of Health and Human Services, Agency for Healthcare Research and Quality, 2006. Available at http://www.ahrq.gov/qual/nhdr06/nhdr06.htm. (Accessed January 14, 2011.)
3. Office of the Surgeon General: *The 2005 Surgeon General's Call to Action to Improve the Health and Wellness of Persons with Disabilities: What It Means to You.* Rockville, Md.: U.S. Department of Health and Human Services, Office of the Surgeon General, 2005. Available at http://www.surgeongeneral.gov/library/disabilities/calltoaction/whatitmeanstoyou.pdf. (Accessed January 14, 2011.)
4. Delpercio A.: Healthcare Equality Index 2010. Washington, D.C.: Human Rights Campaign Foundation and Gay and Lesbian Medical Association, 2010. Available at http://www.hrc.org/documents/HRC-Healthcare-Equality-Index-2010.pdf. (Accessed January 14, 2011.)
5. Divi C., Koss R.G., Schmaltz S.P., Loeb J.M.: Language proficiency and adverse events in U.S. hospitals: A pilot study. *International Journal for Quality in Health Care* 19(2):60-67, April 2007.
6. Bartlett G., Blais R., Tamblyn R., Clermont R.J., MacGibbon B.: Impact of patient communication problems on the risk of preventable adverse events in acute care settings. *Canadian Medical Association Journal* 178(12):1555-1562, June 3, 2008.
7. Wolf D.M., Lehman L., Quinlin R., Zullo T., Hoffman L.: Effect of patient-centered care on patient satisfaction and quality of care. *Journal of Nursing Care Quality* 23(4):316-321, October-December 2008.

8.   La Roche M.J., Koinis-Mitchell D., Gualdron L.: A culturally competent asthma management intervention: a randomized controlled pilot study. *Annals of Allergy, Asthma and Immunology* 96(1):80-85, January 2006.

9.   Cohen A.L., Rivara F., Marcuse E.K., McPhillips H., Davis R.: Are language barriers associated with serious medical events in hospitalized pediatric patients? *Pediatrics* 116(3):575-9, September 2005.

10. 42 U.S.C. § 2000d; *See also* 45 C.F.R. § 80 App. A.

11. Office for Civil Rights: *Guidance to Federal Financial Assistance Recipients Regarding Title VI Prohibition against National Origin Discrimination Affecting Limited English Proficient Persons.* Washington, D.C.: U.S. Department of Health and Human Services, Office for Civil Rights, 2003. Available at http://www.hhs.gov/ocr/civilrights/resources/specialtopics/lep/policyguidancedocument.html. (Accessed January 14, 2011.)

12. *Rehabilitation Act of 1973,* 29 U.S.C. § 794.

13. Office for Civil Rights: *Fact Sheet: Your Rights under Section 504 and the Americans with Disabilities Act.* Washington, D.C.: U.S. Department of Health and Human Services, Office for Civil Rights, 2006. Available at: http://www.hhs.gov/ocr/civilrights/resources/factsheets/504ada.pdf. (Accessed January 14, 2011.)

14. Siegel B., Bretsch J., Sears V., Regenstein M., Wilson M.: Assumed equity: early observations from the first hospital disparities collaborative. *Journal for Healthcare Quality* 29(5):11-5, September-October 2007.

15. Bradley E.H., Herrin J., Wang Y., et al.: Racial and ethnic differences in time to acute reperfusion therapy for patients hospitalized with myocardial infarction. *Journal of the American Medical Association* 292(13):1563-1572, October 6, 2004.

16. Ulmer C., McFadden B., Nerenz D.R., eds.: *Race, Ethnicity, and Language Data: Standardization for Health Care Quality Improvement.* Washington, D.C.: The National Academies Press; 2009.

17. Hasnain-Wynia R., Baker D.W.: Obtaining data on patient race, ethnicity, and primary language in health care organizations: current challenges and proposed solutions. *Health Services Research* 41(4 Pt 1):1501-18, August 2006.

18. Institute for Healthcare Improvement: *A Challenge Accepted: Open Visiting in the ICU at Geisinger.* Boston, Mass.: IHI. Available at http://www.ihi.org/IHI/Topics/CriticalCare/IntensiveCare/ImprovementStories/AChallengeAcceptedOpenVisitingintheICUatGeisinger.htm. (Accessed January 14, 2011.)

19. Agency for Healthcare Research and Quality: *Innovation Profile: Cardiac Unit Features Acuity-Adjustable Rooms and Other Patient-Centered Programs, Leading to Well-Above Average Outcomes and Patient Satisfaction.* Rockville, Md.: AHRQ, 2010. Available at http://www.innovations.ahrq.gov/content.aspx?id=2273. (Accessed January 14, 2011.)

20. Marfell J.A., Garcia J.S.: Contracted visiting hours in the coronary care unit. A patient-centered quality improvement project. *Nursing Clinics of North America* 30(1):87-96, March 1995.

21. Schulte D.A., Burrell L.O., Gueldner S.H., et al.: Pilot study of the relationship between heart rate and ectopy and unrestricted vs restricted visiting hours in the coronary care unit. *American Journal of Critical Care* 2(2):134-136, March 1993.

22. Hausmann L.R., Jeong K., Bost J.E., Ibrahim S.A.: Perceived discrimination in health care and health status in a racially diverse sample. *Medical Care* 46(9):905-914, September 2008.

23. Trivedi A.N., Ayanian J.Z.: Perceived discrimination and use of preventive health services. *Journal of General Internal Medicine* 21(6):553-8, June 2006.

24. Smith E.M., Johnson S.R., Guenther S.M.: Health care attitudes and experiences during gynecologic care among lesbians and bisexuals. *American Journal of Public Health* 75(9):1085-1087, September 1985.

25. Rankow E.J., Tessaro I.: Cervical cancer risk and Papanicolaou screening in a sample of lesbian and bisexual women. *Journal of Family Practice* 47(2):139-143, August 1998.

APPENDIX B-8

The Joint Commission

Requirements Related to CMS Patient Visitation Rights
Conditions of Participation (CoPs)
Critical Access Hospital Accreditation Program

RI.01.01.01

The critical access hospital respects, protects, and promotes patient rights.

Elements of Performance for RI.01.01.01

1. The critical access hospital has written policies on patient rights.
   Note: The critical access hospital's written policies address procedures regarding patient visitation rights, including any clinically necessary or reasonable restrictions or limitations.

2. The critical access hospital informs the patient of his or her rights. (See also RI.01.01.03, EPs 1-3)
   Note: The critical access hospital informs the patient (or support person, where appropriate) of his or her visitation rights. Visitation rights include the right to receive the visitors designated by the patient, including, but not limited to, a spouse, a domestic partner (including a same-sex domestic partner), another family member, or a friend. Also included is the right to withdraw or deny such consent at any time.

4. The critical access hospital treats the patient in a dignified and respectful manner that supports his or her dignity.

5. The critical access hospital respects the patient's right to and need for effective communication. (See also RI.01.01.03, EP 1)

6. The critical access hospital respects the patient's cultural and personal values, beliefs, and preferences.

7. The critical access hospital respects the patient's right to privacy. (See also IM.02.01.01, EPs 1-5)
   Note: This element of performance (EP) addresses a patient's personal privacy. For EPs addressing the privacy of a patient's health information, please refer to Standard IM.02.01.01.

8. The critical access hospital respects the patient's right to pain management. (See also HR.01.04.01, EP 4; PC.01.02.07, EP 1; MS.03.01.03, EP 2)

9. The critical access hospital accommodates the patient's right to religious and other spiritual services.

10. The critical access hospital allows the patient to access, request amendment to, and obtain information on disclosures of his or her health information, in accordance with law and regulation.

28. The critical access hospital allows a family member, friend, or other individual to be present with the patient for emotional support during the course of stay.
Note: The critical access hospital allows for the presence of a support individual of the patient's choice, unless the individual's presence infringes on others' rights, safety, or is medically or therapeutically contraindicated. The individual may or may not be the patient's surrogate decision-maker or legally authorized representative. (For more information on surrogate or family involvement in patient care, treatment, and services, refer to RI.01.02.01 EPs 6-8.)

29. The critical access hospital prohibits discrimination based on age, race, ethnicity, religion, culture, language, physical or mental disability, socioeconomic status, sex, sexual orientation, and gender identity or expression.

APPENDIX B-9

LGBT RESOURCES

Lambda Legal Defense and Education Fund
www.lambdalegal.org

National Office: 120 Wall St., Ste. 1500, New York, New York 10005-3904
212.809.8585

National Center for Lesbian Rights
www.nclrights.org

870 Market St., Ste. 570, San Francisco, CA 94102
415.392.6257

National Lesbian and Gay Bar Association
www.nlgla.org

1301 K St., NW, Ste 1100, East Tower, Washington, D.C. 20005-3823
202.637.7661
info@lgbtbar.org

Immigration Equality
www.immigrationequality.org

40 Exchange Place, Ste. 1705, New York, NY 10005
212.714.2904

Transgender Law and Policy Institute
www.transgenderlaw.org

Transgender Law Center
www.transgenderlawcenter.org

870 Market St., Ste. 400, San Francisco, CA 94102
415.865.0176
info@transgenderlawcenter.org

Gay and Lesbian Advocates and Defenders (GLAD)
www.glad.org

30 Winter St., Ste 800, Boston, MA 02108
614.426.1350
gladlaw@glad.org

Human Rights Campaign
 www.hrc.org

 1640 Rhode Island Ave., NW, Washington, D.C. 20036-3278
 202.628.4160

ACLU National Lesbian and Gay Rights Project
 www.aclu.org/lgbt-rights

Gay & Lesbian Alliance Against Defamation (GLAAD)
 www.glaad.org

National Gay and Lesbian Task Force
 www.thetaskforce.org

Gay, Lesbian and Straight Education Network (GLSEN)
 www.glsen.org

Parents and Friends of Lesbians and Gays (PFLAG)
 www.pflag.org

Gay and Lesbian Medical Association
 www.glma.org

Joint Commission on Accreditation of Healthcare Organizations (JCAHO)
 www.jointcommission.org

 Complaints: complaint@jointcommission.org
 Hotline: 800.994.6610

 This organization evaluates and accredits hospitals nationwide. It provides the
 essential seal of approval that reflects the hospitals high performance standards.
 JCAHO has a system for reviewing complaints against an accredited health care
 facility. They will investigate the situation and recommend changes to prevent
 future repetition. Complaints can be mailed, emailed or faxed. Submit a 1-2 page
 summary describing the situation encountered and state your concerns. Identify
 the healthcare organization by name, address and try to identify the personnel
 with whom you dealt.

Association of Gay and Lesbian Psychiatrists
 www.aglp.org

Family Equality Council
www.familyequality.org

Senior Action in a Gay Environment (SAGE)
www.sage.org

Old Lesbians Organizing for Change (OLOC)
www.oloc.org

Gay, Lesbian International Therapist Referral Network (GLITSE)
www.glitse.com

Help Us Adopt
www.helpusadopt.org

APPENDIX B-10

SOME LEGAL BENEFITS OF MARRIAGE

During Lifetime:

1. Make unlimited gifts to spouses without gift tax;
2. Add spouse to real estate without incurring gift taxes or conveyance fees;
3. Share in spouse's COBRA and net benefits;
4. Be beneficiary of spouse on most employer provided life insurance policies;
5. Receive benefits under spouse's disability insurance policy;
6. Be considered first for appointment as spouse's guardian or conservator;
7. Make joint tax free gifts up to $22,000 per year to anyone;
8. Divorce automatically revokes any referring to the spouse;
9. Divorce automatically removes the spouse as beneficiary on retirement plans;
10. Divorce automatically removes the spouse as nominee for guardian, conservator, or executor.

Benefits at Death:

1. Receive payments from the spouse's pension plan;
2. Automatically roll over IRA proceeds to survivor without adverse tax consequences;
3. Claim Worker's Compensation survivor benefits;
4. Claim unlimited marital deduction for tax purposes;
5. On death all assets transfer to surviving spouse tax free;
6. Ability to take advantage of both spouse's lifetime tax exclusion;
7. Claim spouse's body/remains on death;
8. Claim survivor benefits under Social Security;
9. Claim homestead exemption on home;
10. Intestate rights;
11. Spousal right to elect against the will of decedent spouse;
12. Statutory spousal share if decedent spouse attempts disinheritance;
13. Presumption of joint ownership of personal property;
14. Presumption of equal ownership of jointly held property;
15. Obtain bereavement leave;
16. Priority for appointment as executor of intestate estate.

APPENDIX B-11

What a Trust Can Do

➢ Avoids probate

➢ Administer personal/financial affairs during lifetime

➢ Name Trustee/Successors for the Trust

➢ Private transfer of assets

➢ Provide for minor children and to a later age (25, 30)

➢ Include provisions for future changes in tax policy to benefit survivors

➢ Pay for child's education, health, medical care

➢ Protects assets from creditors

➢ Create spendthrift trust to control beneficiaries bad behavior

➢ Minimize post-death disputes by beneficiaries over inheritance/money

➢ Can address sale/liquidation of business

➢ Tax planning available via generation-skipping tax, reducing other taxes (gift, income and estate)

➢ Revocable Living Trusts can be modified during the Testator's lifetime

➢ Beneficiaries can be changed

➢ Trust terms can be amended

➢ Revocable Living Trusts allow flexible planning

You still need a Will. The two documents are not mutually exclusive.

Index